TAKING SIDES

Clashing Views in

Childhood and Society

NINTH EDITION

Selected, Edited, and with Introductions by

Robert L. DelCampo
New Mexico State University

Diana S. DelCampo
New Mexico State University

Kourtney T. Vaillancourt
New Mexico State University

TAKING SIDES: CLASHING VIEWS IN CHILDHOOD AND SOCIETY, NINTH EDITION

Published by McGraw-Hill, a business unit of The McGraw-Hill Companies, Inc., 1221 Avenue of the Americas, New York, NY 10020. Copyright © 2012 by The McGraw-Hill Companies, Inc. All rights reserved. Previous editions © 2010, 2008, and 2006. Printed in the United States of America. No part of this publication may be reproduced or distributed in any form or by any means, or stored in a database or retrieval system, without the prior written consent of The McGraw-Hill Companies, Inc., including, but not limited to, in any network or other electronic storage or transmission, or broadcast for distance learning.

Some ancillaries, including electronic and print components, may not be available to customers outside the United States.

Taking Sides® is a registered trademark of the McGraw-Hill Companies, Inc.
Taking Sides is published by the **Contemporary Learning Series** group within the McGraw-Hill Higher Education division.

1 2 3 4 5 6 7 8 9 0 DOC/DOC 0 9 8 7 6 5 4 3 2 1

MHID: 0-07-805021-9
ISBN: 978-0-07-805021-3
ISSN: 1094-7558

Managing Editor: *Larry Loeppke*
Senior Developmental Editor: *Jill Meloy*
Permissions Coordinator: *DeAnna Dausener*
Senior Marketing Communications Specialist: *Mary Klein*
Marketing Specialist: *Alice Link*
Project Manager: *Erin Melloy*
Design Coordinator: *Brenda A. Rolwes*
Cover Graphics: *Rick D. Noel*
Buyer: *Nicole Baumgartner*
Media Project Manager: *Sridevi Palani*

Compositor: MPS Limited, a Macmillan Company
Cover Image: © Comstock/Jupiter Images RF

Editors/Academic Advisory Board

Members of the Academic Advisory Board are instrumental in the final selection of articles for each edition of TAKING SIDES. Their review of articles for content, level, and appropriateness provides critical direction to the editors and staff. We think that you will find their careful consideration well reflected in this volume.

TAKING SIDES: Clashing Views in CHILDHOOD AND SOCIETY
Ninth Edition

EDITORS

Robert L. DelCampo
New Mexico State University

Diana S. DelCampo
New Mexico State University

Kourtney T. Vaillancourt
New Mexico State University

ACADEMIC ADVISORY BOARD MEMBERS

Preface

Children are society's most valuable resource, and however clichéd that idea may be, there can be no doubt about the urgency of the issues confronting children today and the people who care for them and care about them. Each day we are bombarded with media reports on issues affecting children—complex issues related to child care, schooling, violence, morality, gangs, divorce; the list goes on. In this book we look at 17 of those controversial issues and ask you to think about them, perhaps for the first time, perhaps in ways you may not have previously considered.

For the student who likes to memorize facts and learn *the* right answer, the controversies in this book could be most unsettling! However, a good education should include the nurturing of your ability to think critically and to be an active learner. This book endeavors to put you on the path toward further developing these skills. As you read each side of an issue and grapple with the points made by the authors, you will be moved to consider the merits of each position. In the process, you may adopt the point of view of one side or the other, or formulate an opinion completely your own on the issue. And when you attend class, you will be exposed to your classmates' and instructor's ideas on the issue as well. This may further challenge you to reconsider and defend your position, which is the essence of critical thinking and a primary purpose of this book.

Plan of the book   *Taking Sides: Clashing Views in Childhood and Society,* ninth edition, is designed to be used for courses in child development, human development, or parenting. The issues can be studied consecutively or in any order, as each is designed to be independent of the other. We have included 17 issues encompassing 34 selections from a wide variety of sources and authors. Each unit of the book deals with one of four developmental phases of childhood: infancy, early childhood, middle childhood, and adolescence. Within each unit are issues related to aspects of child development at that stage. Each issue has an *introduction,* which provides some background about the controversy, briefly describes the authors, and gives a brief summary of the positions reflected in the issue. Each issue concludes with critical thinking and reflection questions and some points to consider about whether there is a common ground to the debates and offers a bibliography of related readings, should you want to explore the topic further.

A listing of all the *contributors* to this volume is included at the back of the book to give you additional information on the scholars, practitioners, educators, policymakers, and social critics whose views are debated here.

Changes to this edition   The ninth edition of *Taking Sides: Clashing Views in Childhood and Society* includes some important changes from the eighth edition. No new issues have been added, but three previous issues have new selections. As a result, there are four new readings. In addition, editorial notes with updates and new developments have been added to the existing selections.

Issue 6, "Are Fathers Really Necessary?" has one new selection. Issue 7, "Does Divorce Create Long-Term Negative Effects for Children?" has two new readings. And, Issue 16, "Is Abstinence-Only Sex Education the Best Way to Teach About Sex?" has one new selection.

In addition to changes in topics and selections, each issue has been updated to include learning objectives, critical thinking and reflection questions, discussion(s) about common ground, and Internet references that can be useful for finding additional information about a topic.

A word to the instructor   An *Instructor's Resource Guide with Test Questions* (both multiple-choice and essay) is available through the publisher for the instructor using this volume of *Taking Sides*. A general guidebook, *Using Taking Sides in the Classroom,* which discusses methods and techniques for integrating the pro–con approach into any classroom setting, is also available. An online version of *Using Taking Sides in the Classroom* and a correspondence service for Taking Sides adopters can be found at http://www.mhcls.com/usingts.

Taking Sides: Clashing Views in Childhood and Society is only one title in the Taking Sides series. If you are interested in seeing the table of contents for any of the other titles, please visit the Taking Sides Web site at http://www.mhcls .com/takingsides/.

Acknowledgments   We would like to thank Christina Gutierrez for assisting with the ninth edition of the book.

We also want to extend warm thanks to Jill Meloy, Senior Developmental Editor, McGraw-Hill Contemporary Learning Series.

We look forward to receiving feedback and comments on this ninth edition of *Taking Sides: Clashing Views in Childhood and Society* from both faculty and students who experience the book. We can be reached via the Internet (ddelcamp@nmsu.edu, rdelcamp@nmsu.edu, or kvaillan@nmsu.edu), or you can write to us in care of the Taking Sides series at McGraw-Hill Contemporary Learning Series.

Robert L. DelCampo
New Mexico State University

Diana S. DelCampo
New Mexico State University

Kourtney T. Vaillancourt
New Mexico State University

Contents In Brief

Contents

UNIT 1   INFANCY   1

Issue 1.   Is Institutional Child Care Beneficial to Children?   2

YES: Greg Parks, from "The High/Scope Perry Preschool Project," *Juvenile Justice Bulletin* (October 2000)   *5*

NO: T. Berry Brazelton and Stanley I. Greenspan, from *The Irreducible Needs of Children: What Every Child Must Have to Grow, Learn, and Flourish* (Perseus, 2000)   *14*

Greg Parks, an intern program specialist at the Office of Juvenile Justice and Delinquency Prevention, details the results of the Perry Preschool Project. Parks contends that evaluations of the program show significant benefits in adulthood for the children who attended the preschool. Pediatrician T. Berry Brazelton and Stanley I. Greenspan, clinical professor of psychiatry and pediatrics at George Washington University Medical School, question the practice by many families of placing their children into the institutional settings of child-care centers.

Issue 2.   Does Maternal Employment Have Negative Effects on Children's Development?   26

YES: Wen-Jui Han, Jane Waldfogel, and Jeanne Brooks-Gunn, from "The Effects of Early Maternal Employment on Later Cognitive and Behavioral Outcomes," *Journal of Marriage and Family* (February 2001)   *29*

NO: Thomas M. Vander Ven, Francis T. Cullen, Mark A. Carrozza, and John Paul Wright, from "Home Alone: The Impact of Maternal Employment on Delinquency," *Social Problems* (May 2001)   *42*

University professors and researchers Wen-Jui Han, Jane Waldfogel, and Jeanne Brooks-Gunn from Columbia University conclude that maternal employment in the first year of a child's life has a significant negative effect on verbal ability at age 3 or 4 and lowered math achievement when children were 7 to 8. When ethnicity was controlled for, these negative effects were found for white children, but not for African-American children. University professors and researchers Thomas M. Vander Ven, Francis T. Cullen, Mark A. Carrozza, and John Paul Wright found that mother's employment in the first year of the baby's life had no effect on child delinquency when the child got older.

Columbia University researcher Elizabeth Thompson Gershoff analyzed results from 88 studies and concluded that corporal punishment negatively affected children's behavior. Among the 10 negative outcomes were increased child aggression, decreased quality of the parent-child relationship, and increased risk of abusing a child or spouse in adulthood. Diana Baumrind and Philip Cowan, researchers from the University of California–Berkeley, and Robert Larzelere, from the Nebraska Medical Center, refuted Gershoff's findings by questioning her definition of corporal punishment and analysis techniques of the 88 studies. They feel mild spankings, when appropriately administered, are useful in shaping children's behavior.

Natasha Cabrera, associate professor of human development, Jacqueline Shannon, assistant professor of early childhood education, and Catherine Tamis-LeMonda, professor of applied psychology, found that young children who experience positive father interaction have increased intellectual, social, emotional, and language development. Peggy Drexler, assistant professor of psychology in psychiatry, and special features editor, and Linden Gross assert that women are capable of raising children without a father figure in the home. Their book is based on Drexler's research that compared boys from female-headed households with boys from traditional mom-and-dad families.

Elizabeth Marquardt, author and director of the Center for Marriage and Families, states that divorce is a tragedy, which has negative lifelong effects on children. She specifically argues against the data collection method that Constance Ahrons used in her current study. Constance Ahrons, author, therapist, and co-chair of the Council on Contemporary Families, believes that the idea that children of divorce end up troubled and unable to form adult attachments is a myth. Her research found that children of divorce were strong, wise, and had close family relationships.

L. Rowell Huesmann, Jessica Moise-Titus, Cheryl-Lynn Podolski, and Leonard Eron, from the Research Center for Group Dynamics, Institute for Social Research at the University of Michigan, found that both males and females are more likely to develop violent behavior in adulthood as a result of watching violent TV shows in early childhood. Jib Fowles, a professor of communication at the University of Houston, asserts that television violence has increased steadily, but the violent crime rate has in fact decreased.

UNIT 3   MIDDLE CHILDHOOD   195

Wade F. Horn, who heads the Marriage Initiative for President George W. Bush, asserts that marriage can remedy the ills of society, including family poverty and poor living standards for children. Stephanie Coontz, author and family advocate, and Nancy Folbre, professor of economics at the University of Massachusetts, contend that improving the living standards of children is a complicated issue, which needs to be approached from many different angles in order to make improvements.

Rob Reich, assistant professor of political science, at Stanford University, states that children who are homeschooled are limited by their teachers, who are usually their parents. Thomas Washburne, director of the National Center for Home Education, disagrees with Reich and believes his opposition to homeschooling denies parents their unalienable right to educate their children as they choose.

The Henry J. Kaiser Family Foundation, a private nonprofit foundation focusing on major health care issues facing the nation, cites research studies that show that the more children watch television, the more likely they will be overweight. They also contend that the rise in childhood obesity can be traced to the increased use of media. The Center for Science in the Public Interest, a consumer advocacy organization on nutrition and health, views the high-calorie, nonnutritious foods found in school vending machines as the culprit in the rise in childhood obesity rates.

Jill Wu, a former graduate student at the University of Colorado, shares her experiences in helping students develop literacy skills in their native languages first, as a more effective means of transferring those skills to learning English. Christine Rossell, a professor of political science at Boston University, suggests that English immersion programs tend to be a more effective for students learning English because they actually learn in the second language (i.e., English).

The National Adoption Information Clearinghouse (NAIC) presents facts regarding gay and lesbian adoptive parents. The NAIC gives current information on the background and laws regarding homosexual parenting, and confronts the issues and concerns many people have regarding homosexual adoption, including the idea that children are molested by homosexual parents. Dr. Paul Cameron, of the Family Research Institute, presents his case against allowing homosexuals to become parents— foster parents in particular. He mainly discusses case study information regarding the proclivity for homosexual parents to molest foster children.

Cynthia Dailard, a senior public policy associate for the Alan Guttmacher Institute, suggests that the HPV vaccine be administered to females as a school entry requirement. She believes the vaccine is safe and effective and therefore should be universally administered to young girls. The best way to ensure the vaccine is available to these girls is by enacting state laws or policies requiring children to be vaccinated before school or day care enrollment. Roni Rabin, a columnist for *The New York Times*, objects to making the HPV vaccine mandatory for girls. She agrees that the vaccine is a significant development for the health and safety of our children. However, she does not believe every girl should be required to be vaccinated because the vaccine is costly and HRV can be managed through current, less costly procedures such as Pap smears.

Christina Salmivalli and Ari Kaukiainen, both professors of psychology at the University of Turku, argue that on the whole male teens are more relationally and physically aggressive than female teens. However, there is a small subset of girls who when in a group are more aggressive than males. Melanie Zimmer-Gembeck, Tasha Geiger, and Nicki Crick, researchers at Griffith University, University of Rochester, and the University of Minnesota, argue that once they attain the age of 10 years, girls are actually more relationally aggressive than boys.

Robert Rector, who is a research fellow for the Heritage Foundation, and Melissa Pardue and Shannan Martin, policy analysts for the Heritage Foundation, argue that comprehensive sex education approaches are misleading because they do little to promote abstinence. Under the auspices of the Heritage Foundation, a conservative organization based in Washington, D.C., they present the results of a poll they conducted that sought to measure parental support for ideas taught in "abstinence-only" and "comprehensive sex education" programs. Debra Hauser, vice president of Advocates for Youth, argues that the assertions made by proponents of *abstinence-only sex education* are unfounded. In reviewing the efficacy of abstinence-only programs, she found that although these programs may show changes in attitudes about abstinence, they also discourage safe sexual practices and actually increase the risks of premarital pregnancy and the spread of sexually transmitted infections.

Michele Fleming and Debra Rickwood, professors at the University of Canberra in Australia, contend that parents need to be vigilant about their teens surfing the Web, but that it is generally a safe place and that the prevalence of cyber predators is overstated. Chang-Hoan Cho, assistant professor at the University of Florida, and Hongsik John Cheon, assistant professor at Frostburg State University, believe that the Web can be a dangerous place for teens to explore. They conducted a study that found that children are exposed to more negative Internet content than parents expect. Factors that reduced children's exposure to negative Internet content included parental interaction and family cohesion.

Topic Guide

This topic guide suggests how the selections in this book relate to the subjects covered in your course. You may want to use the topics listed on these pages to search the Web more easily. On the following pages, a number of Web sites have been gathered specifically for this book. They are arranged to reflect the issues of this Taking Sides reader. You can link to these sites by going to www.mhhe.com/cls.

All issues and their articles that relate to each topic are listed below the bold-faced term.

Abuse

5. Is Spanking Detrimental to Children?

Adolescents

15. Are Male Teens More Aggressive Than Female Teens?
16. Is Abstinence-Only Sex Education the Best Way to Teach About Sex?
17. Is the Internet a Safe Place for Teens to Explore?

Adoption

4. Do Federal Laws Make Transracial Adoptions More Commonplace?
13. Is Gay Adoption and Foster Parenting Healthy for Children?

Aggression

8. Is Viewing Television Violence Harmful for Children?
15. Are Male Teens More Aggressive Than Female Teens?

Behavior

5. Is Spanking Detrimental to Children?
15. Are Male Teens More Aggressive Than Female Teens?

Child Care

1. Is Institutional Child Care Beneficial to Children?
2. Does Maternal Employment Have Negative Effects on Children's Development?

Child Development

1. Is Institutional Child Care Beneficial to Children?

Cloning

2. Does Maternal Employment Have Negative Effects on Children's Development?

3. Should Scientists Be Allowed to Clone Children?

Communication

12. Do Bilingual Education Programs Help Non-English-Speaking Children Succeed?

Computers

17. Is the Internet a Safe Place for Teens to Explore?

Culture

12. Do Bilingual Education Programs Help Non-English-Speaking Children Succeed?

Cyber-bullying

17. Is the Internet a Safe Place for Teens to Explore?

Development, Social

1. Is Institutional Child Care Beneficial to Children?
2. Does Maternal Employment Have Negative Effects on Children's Development?
6. Are Fathers Really Necessary?
10. Do Children Who Are Homeschooled Have a Limited View of Society?

Discipline

5. Is Spanking Detrimental to Children?

(Continued)

Media

8. Is Viewing Television Violence Harmful for Children?
11. Is Television Viewing Responsible for the Rise in Childhood Obesity?
17. Is the Internet a Safe Place for Teens to Explore?

Middle Childhood

9. Does Marriage Improve Living Standards for Children?
10. Do Children Who Are Homeschooled Have a Limited View of Society?
11. Is Television Viewing Responsible for the Rise in Childhood Obesity?
12. Do Bilingual Education Programs Help Non-English-Speaking Children Succeed?
13. Is Gay Adoption and Foster Parenting Healthy for Children?
14. Should the HPV Vaccination Be Mandatory for Girls in Later Childhood?

Motherhood

2. Does Maternal Employment Have Negative Effects on Children's Development?

Parenting

1. Is Institutional Child Care Beneficial to Children?
2. Does Maternal Employment Have Negative Effects on Children's Development?
5. Is Spanking Detrimental to Children?
6. Are Fathers Really Necessary?
7. Does Divorce Create Long-Term Negative Effects for Children?
10. Do Children Who Are Homeschooled Have a Limited View of Society?
11. Is Television Viewing Responsible for the Rise in Childhood Obesity?
13. Is Gay Adoption and Foster Parenting Healthy for Children?
16. Is Abstinence-Only Sex Education the Best Way to Teach About Sex?
17. Is the Internet a Safe Place for Teens to Explore?

Punishment

5. Is Spanking Detrimental to Children?

Relationships

2. Does Maternal Employment Have Negative Effects on Children's Development?

9. Does Marriage Improve Living Standards for Children?

Schools

1. Is Institutional Child Care Beneficial to Children?
10. Do Children Who Are Homeschooled Have a Limited View of Society?

School Curriculum

10. Do Children Who Are Homeschooled Have a Limited View of Society?
12. Do Bilingual Education Programs Help Non-English-Speaking Children Succeed?
16. Is Abstinence-Only Sex Education the Best Way to Teach About Sex?

School Reform

12. Do Bilingual Education Programs Help Non-English-Speaking Children Succeed?
16. Is Abstinence-Only Sex Education the Best Way to Teach About Sex?

Sex Education

16. Is Abstinence-Only Sex Education the Best Way to Teach About Sex?

Social Change

3. Should Scientists Be Allowed to Clone Children?
4. Do Federal Laws Make Transracial Adoptions More Commonplace?
9. Does Marriage Improve Living Standards for Children?
13. Is Gay Adoption and Foster Parenting Healthy for Children?
16. Is Abstinence-Only Sex Education the Best Way to Teach About Sex?

Social Media

17. Is the Internet a Safe Place for Teens to Explore?

Teaching

10. Do Children Who Are Homeschooled Have a Limited View of Society?

Television

8. Is Viewing Television Violence Harmful for Children?

(Continued)

Correlation Guide

The *Taking Sides* series presents current issues in a debate-style format designed to stimulate student interest and develop critical thinking skills. Each issue is thoughtfully framed with an issue summary, an issue introduction, learning outcomes, and critical-thinking questions. The pro and con essays—selected for their liveliness and substance—represent the arguments of leading scholars and commentators in their fields.

Taking Sides: Clashing Views in Childhood and Society, 9/e is an easy-to-use reader that presents issues on important topics such as *homeschooling, bilingual education programs, transracial adoptions,* and *male aggression.* For more information on *Taking Sides* and other *McGraw-Hill Contemporary Learning Series* titles, visit http://www.mhhe.com/cls.

This convenient guide matches the issues in **Taking Sides: Childhood and Society, 9/e** with the corresponding chapters in two of our best-selling McGraw-Hill Psychology textbooks by Papalia/Feldman and Santrock.

Taking Sides: Childhood and Society, 9/e	A Child's World: Infancy Through Adolescence, 12/e by Papalia/Feldman	Children, 12/e by Santrock
Issue 1: Is Institutional Child Care Beneficial to Children?	**Chapter 6:** Physical Development and Health During the First Three Years **Chapter 7:** Cognitive Development During the First Three Years **Chapter 8:** Psychosocial Development During the First Three Years	**Chapter 5:** Physical Development in Infancy **Chapter 7:** Socioemotional Development in Infancy
Issue 2: Does Maternal Employment Have Negative Effects on Children's Development?	**Chapter 6:** Physical Development and Health During the First Three Years **Chapter 7:** Cognitive Development During the First Three Years **Chapter 8:** Psychosocial Development During the First Three Years	**Chapter 7:** Socioemotional Development in Infancy
Issue 3: Should Scientists Be Allowed to Clone Children?	**Chapter 1:** Studying a Child's World **Chapter 2:** A Child's World: How We Discover It	**Chapter 2:** Biological Beginnings
Issue 4: Do Federal Laws Make Transracial Adoptions More Commonplace?		
Issue 5: Is Spanking Detrimental to Children?	**Chapter 10:** Cognitive Development in Early Childhood **Chapter 11:** Psychosocial Development in Early Childhood	**Chapter 9:** Cognitive Development in Early Childhood

(Continued)

Taking Sides: Childhood and Society, 9/e	*A Child's World: Infancy Through Adolescence,* 12/e by Papalia/ Feldman	*Children,* 12/e by Santrock
Issue 6: Are Fathers Really Necessary?	**Chapter 5:** Birth and the Newborn Baby **Chapter 8:** Psychosocial Development During the First Three Years **Chapter 11:** Psychosocial Development in Early Childhood **Chapter 14:** Psychosocial Development in Middle Childhood **Chapter 17:** Psychosocial Development in Adolescence	**Chapter 10:** Socioemotional Development in Early Childhood
Issue 7: Does Divorce Create Long-Term Negative Effects for Children?	**Chapter 7:** Cognitive Development During the First Three Years **Chapter 8:** Psychosocial Development During the First Three Years **Chapter 10:** Cognitive Development in Early Childhood **Chapter 11:** Psychosocial Development in Early Childhood **Chapter 13:** Cognitive Development in Middle Childhood **Chapter 14:** Psychosocial Development in Middle Childhood **Chapter 16:** Cognitive Development in Adolescence **Chapter 17:** Psychosocial Development in Adolescence	**Chapter 6:** Cognitive Development in Infancy **Chapter 8:** Physical Development in Early Childhood **Chapter 10:** Socioemotional Development in Early Childhood **Chapter 11:** Physical Development in Middle and Late Childhood **Chapter 13:** Socioemotional Development in Middle and Late Childhood
Issue 8: Is Viewing Television Violence Harmful for Children?	**Chapter 8:** Psychosocial Development During the First Three Years **Chapter 11:** Psychosocial Development in Early Childhood **Chapter 14:** Psychosocial Development in Middle Childhood **Chapter 17:** Psychosocial Development in Adolescence	**Chapter 8:** Physical Development in Early Childhood **Chapter 10:** Socioemotional Development in Early Childhood **Chapter 16:** Socioemotional Development in Adolescence
Issue 9: Does Marriage Improve Living Standards for Children?	**Chapter 8:** Psychosocial Development During the First Three Years **Chapter 11:** Psychosocial Development in Early Childhood **Chapter 14:** Psychosocial Development in Middle Childhood **Chapter 17:** Psychosocial Development in Adolescence	**Chapter 10:** Socioemotional Development in Early Childhood **Chapter 13:** Socioemotional Development in Middle and Late Childhood **Chapter 16:** Socioemotional Development in Adolescence
Issue 10: Do Children Who Are Homeschooled Have a Limited View of Society?	**Chapter 8:** Psychosocial Development During the First Three Years **Chapter 11:** Psychosocial Development in Early Childhood **Chapter 14:** Psychosocial Development in Middle Childhood **Chapter 17:** Psychosocial Development in Adolescence	**Chapter 7:** Socioemotional Development in Infancy **Chapter 13:** Socioemotional Development in Middle and Late Childhood **Chapter 16:** Socioemotional Development in Adolescence

Taking Sides: Childhood and Society, 9/e	*A Child's World: Infancy Through Adolescence*, 12/e by Papalia/Feldman	*Children*, 12/e by Santrock
Issue 11: Is Television Viewing Responsible for the Rise in Childhood Obesity?	**Chapter 6:** Physical Development and Health During the First Three Years **Chapter 9:** Physical Development and Health in Early Childhood **Chapter 12:** Physical Development and Health in Middle Childhood **Chapter 15:** Physical Development and Health in Adolescence	**Chapter 8:** Physical Development in Early Childhood **Chapter 11:** Physical Development in Middle and Late Childhood **Chapter 14:** Physical Development in Adolescence
Issue 12: Do Bilingual Education Programs Help Non-English-Speaking Children Succeed?	**Chapter 7:** Cognitive Development During the First Three Years **Chapter 10:** Cognitive Development in Early Childhood **Chapter 13:** Cognitive Development in Middle Childhood **Chapter 16:** Cognitive Development in Adolescence	**Chapter 9:** Cognitive Development in Early Childhood **Chapter 12:** Cognitive Development in Middle and Late Childhood **Chapter 15:** Cognitive Development in Adolescence
Issue 13: Is Gay Adoption and Foster Parenting Healthy for Children?	**Chapter 8:** Psychosocial Development During the First Three Years **Chapter 11:** Psychosocial Development in Early Childhood **Chapter 14:** Psychosocial Development in Middle Childhood **Chapter 17:** Psychosocial Development in Adolescence	**Chapter 7:** Socioemotional Development in Infancy **Chapter 10:** Socioemotional Development in Early Childhood **Chapter 13:** Socioemotional Development in Middle and Late Childhood **Chapter 16:** Socioemotional Development in Adolescence
Issue 14: Should the HPV Vaccination Be Mandatory for Girls in Later Childhood?	**Chapter 12:** Physical Development and Health in Middle Childhood **Chapter 15:** Physical Development and Health in Adolescence	**Chapter 11:** Physical Development in Middle and Late Childhood
Issue 15: Are Male Teens More Aggressive Than Female Teens?	**Chapter 17:** Psychosocial Development in Adolescence	**Chapter 16:** Socioemotional Development in Adolescence
Issue 16: Is Abstinence-Only Sex Education the Best Way to Teach About Sex?	**Chapter 15:** Physical Development and Health in Adolescence **Chapter 16:** Cognitive Development in Adolescence **Chapter 17:** Psychosocial Development in Adolescence	**Chapter 14:** Physical Development in Adolescence **Chapter 15:** Cognitive Development in Adolescence **Chapter 16:** Socioemotional Development in Adolescence
Issue 17: Is the Internet a Safe Place for Teens to Explore?	**Chapter 17:** Psychosocial Development in Adolescence	**Chapter 16:** Socioemotional Development in Adolescence

Introduction

Children in Society

Robert L. DelCampo
Diana S. DelCampo
Kourtney T. Vaillancourt

Childhood can be a wondrous time when days are filled with play and new discoveries, nights provide rest and security, and dedicated, loving parents nurture their children and meet their needs. Some children do indeed experience the full joy of childhood; however, regretfully, there are other, more sobering scenarios: There are children who do not have nurturing adults to guide them, who go to bed hungry, and some who do not even have homes. Most typically, childhood experiences fall between these two extremes. So there is a wide variety of experiences that can impact the developing child, and larger social forces are at work as well. Ask yourself as you debate the issues in this book the extent to which society must collectively address and resolve them. This is a vital function of society because children are society's future.

To understand and appreciate children in contemporary society, it may be useful to briefly review how society's views of children have changed over time. Most child development texts review the history of adult perceptions of children in western European society. Would it surprise you to know that in ancient times children were sometimes killed as religious sacrifices and buried in the walls of buildings? People believed that this practice would strengthen a building's structure. Up until the fourth century, parents were legally allowed to kill their newborns if the children were not in good health at birth. They were also permitted to do away with a child if they already had too many children, if the child was female, or if the child was illegitimate. In 374 A.D., the Romans outlawed infanticide, hoping that this would end the killing. Since parents could no longer legally kill their children, unwanted infants began to be abandoned. This practice endured for more than 1000 years. It was not until the 1600s that child abandonment was outlawed throughout most of Europe.

During the seventeenth century, foundling homes were established to provide for the needs of unwanted children. During this period, children were considered to be miniature adults. They were dressed like adults and were expected to act as adults would act. By contemporary standards, parents took a rather casual attitude toward their children. This was probably due to the high child mortality rate at the time. Since parents thought it likely that their children would die in infancy or childhood, they did not get as emotionally close to their young children as parents typically do today. It was not until the end of the century that society began to look upon children as different from adults.

Early in the 1700s European societal attitudes about children underwent further change. Children were no longer considered to be miniature adults, and literature written specifically for children began to emerge. By the end of the century, children who went to school were grouped by age, reflecting an awareness of stages of growth. The eighteenth century also marked the rise of the systematic study of children, which centered around the moral development of children and child-rearing problems.

It was not until the beginning of the twentieth century that three distinct age groupings emerged in the study of human development: infancy through age four or five; childhood to late puberty or early adulthood; and adulthood. This time period also marked the beginnings of the distinct field of child study. Early child study emphasized descriptive accounts of individual children and was mainly concerned with aspects of physical growth. As the century progressed, the term *child study* was changed to *research in child development.* Mothering became an important concept in the study of early child development, and the psychological aspects of development began to be examined more rigorously. Today, in the twenty-first century, research in child development focuses on issues related to family systems and the larger social issues that affect child development.

Nature-Nurture Controversy

There are many things that impact individuals as they progress through the human life cycle. People, places, events, illnesses, education, success, failure—have you ever thought about the number of experiences each of us encounters in our lives? If one were to place all of the variables that influence human development into two general categories, those categories would be heredity and environment. As you may know, your genetic blueprint was determined at the moment of conception with chromosomes contributed by your father and mother. In a sense, for many of us, environment is also determined at the moment of conception. A good portion of the major elements of what makes up one's environment is often determined before a person is born. The society in which one will live, one's cultural and ethnic heritage, and one's family and subsequent socioeconomic status, for example, are usually predetermined for a child.

For this edition of *Taking Sides: Clashing Views in Childhood and Society,* we have selected articles that look at children in general and how they affect or are affected by the issues raised, rather than give you, the reader, clinical case examples of issues related to a certain child or children. For the purposes of this book, we make three assumptions: (1) When we discuss a child's environment, we are usually describing elements of the society in which a child is growing, developing, and otherwise being socialized; (2) all child development occurs within this social context; and (3) children cannot help but affect and be affected by the societal forces that surround them. In most university classes, students derive a certain sense of security in receiving definitions of terms that are used frequently in a given class. We offer the following one for *society,* which we have adapted from Richard J. Gelles's 1995 textbook *Contemporary Families:*

> Society is a collection of people who interact within socially structured relationships. The only way that societies can survive their original

members is by replacing them. These "replacements" are the children about whom the issues in this book are concerned.

Determining an appropriate group of societal issues and fitting them into the confines of only one work on children and society is a challenging task. Consider, for example, the diversity of contemporary society. We live in a sea of divergent and unique subcultures and ethnicities. Categorizing and describing the myriad values, customs, and belief systems of these groups could fill many volumes. In America and Canada, for example, there are many ethnic subgroups of citizens who are considered to be of Anglo descent, such as English, Irish, Italian, Polish, German, Greek, Russian, and Scottish. There are people of native descent, who are affiliated with scores of different tribes and subtribes. Some Canadian and American citizens trace their heritages to a variety of Asian countries, including China, Japan, Vietnam, Cambodia, Thailand, and the Philippines. Among blacks, there are those who trace their roots to the Caribbean region and those who identify with different regions of Africa.

In light of the foregoing, it may be reasoned that there are really no "typical" children in society! Although there are strong arguments supporting similarities within each of these general groups, there is a wide array of sub-groupings and differences in customs and beliefs. As a consequence, when reading a book such as this one, it is important to be mindful of the extent to which differences might exist for those who may be of another race, ethnicity, religion, or socioeconomic status than the target group of children about which a selection focuses. It would also be prudent to consider geographic locale—rural, urban, northeastern, southwestern—when considering the relevance of a given argument to a specific subgroup of children.

Children in Contemporary Society

It is worth understanding children's points of view as they are molded by society. It can be astonishing to take a step back and observe children as they undergo the socialization process in contemporary society. They come into the world totally helpless, unable to feed, care for, or protect themselves. As they grow and develop, children undertake the process of acquiring a sense of identity and learning the rules of the society in which they live. This process of socialization is fostered by many of the subsystems of society that provide prescriptions for behavior in particular areas of life. These subsystems include the family, the peer group, the school system, religion, and the media.

One important consideration is that up to about age five, children are oblivious to most racial, ethnic, religious, or socioeconomic differences. Typically, children can only realize differences in external appearance. One implication of this fact is that children can be much more amenable to learning and embracing a variety of cultural behaviors, attitudes, and even languages when they are young. Only as children move into middle childhood do they begin to recognize and understand other, more subtle differences. It is important to note that although young children may be oblivious to these differences, they are nonetheless impacted by them in the way they are socialized by their parents, families, and the significant others in their lives. This is done through family rituals, traditions, and outings; religious ceremonies; types of food prepared in the home; location where children live; and things that are found in the home, such as books, magazines, music, and so on.

Societal influences on children do not stop within the family system. As children grow, other institutions in society, such as schools, the economy, politics, and religion, expand their life experiences. Controversy arises as to how children react to these experiences. Consider, for example, what happens to children when both parents are employed outside the home. There are factions in our society who adamantly ascribe many of the problems associated with children to the fact that many parents are overly involved with work at the expense of time with their children. They contend that one parent (usually the mother) should stay home with the children, especially when they are young. Children who care for themselves after school and the quality of after-school child care are also hotly contested, related issues.

Few readers of this book will be unfamiliar with the attacks on the mass media for its portrayal of violence in movies, television programming, and video games targeted at children. Again, researchers, clinicians, teachers, policymakers, and others fall on both sides of what should be done to address this.

As children move toward adolescence and become more independent, concerns regarding identity, values, morals, and sexual behavior become issues of controversy. Homosexuality, for example, which often is first evidenced by a person in adolescence, is considered by many to be a learned and abhorrent form of sexual expression. Others believe that there are people who are predisposed to homosexuality for reasons that are as yet unclear.

Events in contemporary society have a direct or indirect impact on children, despite attempts to protect them. Violence, inflation, war, poverty, AIDS, racism, and new technology are just a few of the phenomena that shape the society in which our children are socialized.

Researching Children

In finding answers to controversial topics, policymakers and the public alike often look to research literature for clues. The typical college student might think of researching a topic as going to the library or logging onto the Internet and looking up information on a subject, reading that information, formulating a conclusion or opinion about the topic, and writing a paper that conveys the student's findings. This is not the type of research about which we are referring! The type of research that we refer to here is called empirical research. This means that there is some question or group of interrelated questions to be answered about a topic. Data are then collected relative to the topic, and these typically shed light on how one goes about answering the question.

Data collection in research on children is undertaken from a variety of approaches. It could entail things like observing children at play in preschool or interacting with their parents at home. This is called observing children in a natural setting. With this method, observers must code behavior in the same way each and every time it is seen. Most of the information we have today on physical growth and developmental stages was acquired through observation by child development pioneers such as Arnold Gessell and Louise Bates Ames. You can imagine how time consuming this form of study must be.

Another type of data collection is called an experiment. Experimental researchers systematically control how certain things happen in a situation and then observe the results. In this type of research, an experimental group and a control group are chosen. Both groups are examined to determine that they are the same before the experiment begins. The experimental group then receives some kind of treatment, while the control group receives no treatment. Then tests are conducted to see what kind of change, if any, has occurred between the two groups.

Interviewing children with a structured set of questions or giving children a structured questionnaire on a given research topic are other ways of collecting data. Projective techniques, where children might reveal their first thoughts about a picture or word, is also a form of the interview method.

The study of children can be organized in a variety of ways. One is by stages. The parts of this book (infancy, early childhood, middle childhood, and adolescence) are one type of stage organization. Another way to organize research endeavors is by topics. Topics are usually organized within the context of social, emotional, intellectual, physical, creative, and even spiritual aspects of development.

The time frames used to gather data on children also vary. In longitudinal data collection, information is collected from the same subjects over a long period of time. For example, one could examine the effects of preschool education on performance in elementary school by following and testing the same children during the preschool years and all the way through the elementary years. Because this type of research can take years to complete, a shorter method, cross-sectional research, could be used. In the previous example, one group of preschoolers would be compared with a similar group of elementary school children in order to answer the research question.

There are ethical considerations in studying children that some other disciplines may not face. Children should never be manipulated or put in danger in designing an experiment to answer research questions. Similarly, experiments that would not be in a child's best interests should not be conducted. Studies of abuse and neglect, for example, rely on retrospective techniques in which children who have already been abused report what has previously happened to them. No ethical researcher would ever put children at risk in order to observe the effects of abuse on children. Because of these ethical constraints, it can be frustrating for a researcher to fully answer questions raised in a research project. Additionally, it may take years to demonstrate the effectiveness of intervention for a particular social problem. Consequently, research on children and resultant intervention initiatives rarely offer "quick fixes" to the problems of children and society.

Future Directions

The study of children in society can begin to offer solutions to many of the more pressing societal problems. Quality child care, parenting skills, education, stress reduction, affordable housing, job training, and humane political policies are a few ideas for solutions to some of the controversies that will be raised in this book.

The imbalance between work and family in the United States has created problems in the economy as well as in the family system. Workers are expected to produce quality goods and services, but they receive little social support in raising their families. Employers must acknowledge the strain that workers feel as they are pulled between work and family responsibilities. Health insurance, family-friendly work policies, flexible work schedules, parental and dependent care leave, exercise facilities, quality child care and sick child care, on-site or nearby one-stop service centers with post offices, grocery stores, and dry cleaners would be ways of providing support for families in the workplace.

Schools contribute to the problems of child-care arrangements by keeping to an antiquated schedule that was first developed to meet the needs of the farm family. Years ago, schools were let out in the early afternoon and all summer so that children could help with the crops, livestock, and other farm-related chores before sunset. However, ours has been a predominantly industrial society for a large part of the twentieth century and into the twenty-first century. As a result, a different type of schedule is required. Many concerned families advocate activities for children after school and schools that are open all year long to match the schedules of workers. The economy has changed and families have changed; why have educational institutions remained static?

The majority of children somehow manage to grow and develop successfully in a variety of family forms, but the stressors on all families are constantly increasing, which may, in turn, decrease the likelihood of continued success. Parents worry that the cost of a college education will be more than they can afford; parents worry about their children and AIDS, violence, and drugs; parents are concerned that in adulthood their children will not be able to live as well as they have lived. Families need emotional support, and parents need opportunities to learn stress management and parenting skills.

Society can promote the optimal growth and development of its children by taking responsibility for them. There is an old saying, "It takes a village to raise a child." Our society can raise its children by establishing policies in schools, workplaces, and other institutions that reflect the importance of nurturing children.

Internet References . . .

Families and Work Institute

This Web site provides resources from the Families and Work Institute, which conducts policy research on issues related to the changing workforce and operates a national clearinghouse on work and family life.

http://www.familiesandwork.org

Human Cloning Foundation

The Human Cloning Foundation is one of the strongest proponents of human cloning. This Web site includes information on essays, books, reviews, and personalities advocating human cloning.

http://www.humancloning.org

The National Parent Information Network (NPIN)

The National Parent Information Network contains resources related to many of the controversial issues faced by parents raising children in contemporary society. In addition to articles and resources, discussion groups are available.

http://npin.org

Zero to Three: National Center for Infants, Toddlers, and Families

Zero to Three: National Center for Infants, Toddlers, and Families is a national organization dedicated solely to infants, toddlers, and their families. It is headed by recognized experts in the field and provides technical assistance to communities, states, and the U.S. federal government. The site provides information that the organization gathers and disseminates through its publications.

http://www.zerotothree.org

The Future of Children

The Future of Children is a publication of the Woodrow Wilson School of Public and International Affairs at Princeton University and The Brookings Institution. The Future of Children Web site provides research and analysis that promotes effective policies and programs for children.

http://www.futureofchildren.org

American Academy of Pediatrics (AAP)

The American Academy of Pediatrics (AAP) and its member pediatricians dedicate their efforts and resources to the health, safety, and well-being of infants, children, adolescents, and young adults.

http://www.aap.org

Infancy

*I*nfancy and toddlerhood encompass the time period from birth to age two or three. During this time, the most dramatic growth of a child's life takes place. Traditionally, much of the literature on infancy has dealt with the physical aspects of development; more recently, however, researchers, practitioners, and policymakers have begun to be concerned with the interaction of brain development on later learning and the social and emotional aspects of the infant's development. The issues examined in this section focus on how the family and social institutions influence children's development from the time they are born.

- Is Institutional Child Care Beneficial to Children?
- Does Maternal Employment Have Negative Effects on Children's Development?
- Should Scientists Be Allowed to Clone Children?
- Do Federal Laws Make Transracial Adoptions More Commonplace?

ISSUE 1

Is Institutional Child Care Beneficial to Children?

YES: Greg Parks, from "The High/Scope Perry Preschool Project," *Juvenile Justice Bulletin* (October 2000)

NO: T. Berry Brazelton and Stanley I. Greenspan, from *The Irreducible Needs of Children: What Every Child Must Have to Grow, Learn, and Flourish* (Perseus, 2000)

Learning Outcomes

After reading this issue, you should be able to:

- Summarize the dilemmas faced by families when deciding who will care for their children.
- Explain the impact that institutional childcare can have on children.
- Discuss risk factors for delinquency and some of the prevention models that have been developed.
- Discuss recommendations for providing quality childcare in institutional settings.

ISSUE SUMMARY

YES: Greg Parks, an intern program specialist at the Office of Juvenile Justice and Delinquency Prevention, details the results of the Perry Preschool Project. Parks contends that evaluations of the program show significant benefits in adulthood for the children who attended the preschool.

NO: Pediatrician T. Berry Brazelton and Stanley I. Greenspan, clinical professor of psychiatry and pediatrics at George Washington University Medical School, question the practice by many families of placing their children into the institutional settings of child-care centers.

Increasingly, parents are placing their children in some kind of child care during the day so that they are able to work to support the family economically. This is true not only for single parents but also for parents in a two-parent household who must work in order to live even modestly. In the past, the majority of children in child care were cared for in a family setting by a relative or a home day care with a few children. Today, many families have no relatives who stay at home during the day and are close by to whom they can turn for help. In addition, mothers used to take as much time as possible after the birth of a baby and stay at home during a large part of the child's infancy. Things have changed; due in large part to limited leave policies by employers, many women return to work within six weeks of giving birth and, when faced with choices for child care, find that they must place their infant in an institutional or chain-type day care facility.

These day care centers usually serve children of varying ages, from infancy to four or five years of age, and often have after-school programs for elementary school children. These centers often have many rooms and are housed in a large building with as many as 20 caregivers. Child-caregivers must meet minimum, state-imposed licensing standards, but because of the low pay and no benefits, the child-care industry is plagued with a high turnover rate. Thus, caregivers might change many times during a child's stay, depending upon the center's pay structure and the administration's philosophy of quality care. These types of centers look somewhat institutional because of their large building size, numerous rooms, and large number of personnel. Many object to the institutional-type child-care centers because they do not have the home-type atmosphere that one usually associates with the quality of care expected for very young children.

An April 2001 release of the results from a longitudinal study by the National Institute of Child Health and Human Development, a federal agency that has been studying children in child-care settings for 10 years, made headlines and caused a furor in the child-care industry. Some conclusions of the study, many say, were taken out of context and sensationalized by the press. It was reported that children who attended day care were found to be more aggressive than their stay-at-home counterparts. In actuality, the level of aggression for day care children was still within the normal range of behavior. These kinds of misinterpretations and partial facts create confusion for parents who are just trying to do the best they can for their children. American society asks parents to work to support their families but then asks them to stay home to take care of their children. This dichotomy of thinking and expectations makes it difficult to feel good about any choice made related to child care.

The quality of child care appears to be one of the most important issues in the debate over whether or not to send young children to child-care centers. Low adult-child ratios, competent and caring caregivers, and clean and nurturing environments are what contribute to quality child care. Is this type of setting preferable over being at home with a parent who does not want to be there and who does nothing to stimulate a child intellectually or emotionally? Consider another alternative—poor-quality child care, with multiple caregivers who have no training and no desire to work with young children in a dirty, nonstimulating environment. Contrast this scenario with a child's being at home with a parent who loves the child and provides educational materials and one-on-one interaction most of the day. These are the extremes that are presented when the question of how and where to best care for young children arises.

Another factor that confounds this argument is how much time and what quality of time parents who use day care spend with their children when they are at home. Mediocre out-of-home care can be mitigated by a stimulating home environment when children and parents are together. On the other hand, a poor, nonnurturing home environment, which could be devastating for a child's development, can be supplemented positively by a quality child-care experience.

What is a parent to do? Parents must work to support their families, and they must find a safe place to leave their children. Is a large institutional-like setting appropriate for infants and toddlers who need the security of a close, warm environment? Will these young children be harmed by having several caregivers within a week, or is institutional child care the best environment for children? This is the dilemma discussed in the following two selections. T. Berry Brazelton and Stanley I. Greenspan, long respected in the world of child development, voice their concerns about America's youngest children being enrolled in day care at an alarmingly high rate. In contrast, the Perry Preschool Project results, which are detailed by Greg Parks, indicate that child care is beneficial for children. Longitudinal data from the Perry Preschool Project span over 40 years and show the program to have been beneficial for the children who attended the center.

YES

Greg Parks

The High/Scope Perry Preschool Project

The Office of Juvenile Justice and Delinquency Prevention (OJJDP) recently published *Costs and Benefits of Early Childhood Intervention* (Greenwood, 1999), a Fact Sheet reviewing the benefits of early childhood intervention in the prevention of later delinquency. Among the most notable and longstanding secondary prevention programs considered was the High/Scope Perry Preschool Project of Ypsilanti, MI.[1] This [selection] examines this successful program model, which demonstrates a potential link between early childhood intervention and delinquency prevention.

The High/Scope Perry Preschool Project is a well-established early childhood intervention that has been in operation for almost 40 years. A review of the program's findings is useful at this time in light of the field's growing knowledge of risk factors associated with juvenile delinquency, including early childhood risk factors that may be diminished by secondary prevention programs targeted at high-risk populations. Juvenile justice research has made great strides in identifying risk factors that may be precursors to delinquency. Although the problem of delinquency increases with the number of risk factors, specific risk factors appear to vary according to a child's stage of development and may be reduced with appropriate preventive measures. These developmental differences for risk factors indicate the need for targeted interventions that address specific age-related factors (Wasserman and Miller, 1998). Given this link between early risk factors and later delinquency, it is important for practitioners to plan intervention programs for high-risk youth early in a youth's life so that he or she can develop a strong foundation for later development.

Background

The High/Scope Perry Preschool Project, which began in 1962, is the focus of an ongoing longitudinal study—conducted by the High/Scope Educational Research Foundation—of 123 high-risk African American children.[2] Participants were of low socioeconomic status, had low IQ scores (between 70 and 85, the range for borderline mental impairment) with no organic deficiencies (i.e., biologically based mental impairment), and were at high risk of failing school.

From *Juvenile Justice Bulletin,* a publication of the Office of Juvenile Justice and Delinquency Prevention/National Institute of Justice, (October 2000) pp. 1–6. References omitted.

Fifty-eight of these 3- and 4-year-old children were assigned to the program group, and 65 of these children were assigned to a control group that did not go through the program. The groups were matched according to age, IQ, socio-economic status, and gender. There were no differences between the groups with regard to father absence, parent education level, family size, household density, or birth order. Researchers collected followup data annually when the children were between ages 4 and 11 and at ages 14, 15, and 19 and collected age 27 data from 1986 to 1991 (Schweinhart, Barnes, and Weikart, 1993; Schweinhart and Weikart, 1995).[3]

The High/Scope Perry Preschool Project's high-quality educational approach is based on an active learning model that emphasizes participants' intellectual and social development. Children attended the preschool Monday through Friday for 2.5 hours per day over a 2-year period. During that same period, a staff-to-child ratio of one adult for every five or six children enabled teachers to visit each child's family in their home for 1.5 hours each week. In addition, parents participated in monthly small group meetings with other parents, facilitated by program staff.

Although it was initiated as an educational intervention, the High/Scope Perry Preschool Project has demonstrated a number of other positive outcomes, including a significantly lower rate of crime and delinquency and lower incidence of teenage pregnancy and welfare dependency. Overall, the program group has demonstrated significantly higher rates of prosocial behavior, academic achievement, employment, income, and family stability as compared with the control group. The success of this and similar programs demonstrates intervention and delinquency prevention in terms of both social outcome and cost-effectiveness and has a number of useful implications for policy, practice, and ongoing research. This Bulletin reviews the program outcomes, describes the early childhood risk factors that can be targeted with intervention, and explores the relationship between program components and risk factors.

Program Outcomes

Outcomes of the High/Scope Perry Preschool longitudinal study can be divided into three major categories: social responsibility, scholastic success, and socioeconomic success (Schweinhart et al., 1985). Social responsibility variables include delinquency, marital status, and pregnancy. Scholastic success is determined by a number of factors including graduation rate, grade point average, and postsecondary education, whereas socioeconomic success is measured in terms of employment, earnings, and welfare assistance. Cost-benefit is included as an additional outcome because of the long-term savings to society as a result of program success.

Social Responsibility

Delinquency   Data collected from police and court records show that juvenile delinquency was significantly lower for the High/Scope Perry Preschool program group as compared with the control group, including fewer arrests and fewer juvenile court petitions (Schweinhart, Barnes, and Weikart, 1993;

Schweinhart and Weikart, 1995). Only 31 percent of the program group had ever been arrested, compared with 51 percent of the control group. In addition to police and court records, data collected from respondents at age 19 were used as an overall indicator of delinquency. When study participants were 19 years old, researchers found significant differences between the program and control groups. The program group had fewer arrests overall than the control group (averages of 1.3 versus 2.3 arrests per person), fewer felony arrests (averages of 0.7 versus 2.0 arrests per person), and fewer juvenile court petitions filed (averages of 0.2 versus 0.4 petitions per person).

Like the criminal record data, a misconduct scale based on teacher-report data and self-report data from the 19-year-old respondents demonstrates a significant difference between the program and control groups, as reflected by the following results for the program group:

- Lower overall scores for total misconduct and serious misconduct at ages 15 and 19.
- Lower incidence of fighting and other violent behavior.
- Lower incidence of property damage.
- Fewer police contacts.

Data collected from respondents at age 27 indicate significant differences between the program group and control group for adult arrests: the control group underwent more than twice as many arrests as the program group (averages of 4.0 versus 1.8 arrests per person). Thirty-six percent of the control group accounted for 98 felony arrests between ages 19 and 27, while 27 percent of the program group accounted for 40 felony arrests during the same period. Thirty-five percent of the control group were considered frequent offenders (defined as five or more arrests), compared with only 7 percent of the program group. In addition, 25 percent of the control group had been arrested for drug-related offenses, versus 7 percent of the program group. The control group also averaged more months on probation (6.6 versus 3.2 months) and had more than twice as many of its members placed on probation or parole for longer than 18 months (20 percent versus 9 percent).

Marital status and pregnancy   Marital status among the males was the same for both groups, with 26 percent married at age 27, although program group males, on average, had been married for a longer period (6.2 versus 3.3 years). Marital status among the females differed significantly, with 40 percent of program group females married, compared with 8 percent of the control group females. Although fewer females in the program group were parents (64 percent versus 75 percent), significantly more of them were married, cohabiting parents (28 percent versus 8 percent). Fifty-seven percent of mothers in the program group gave birth out of wedlock, compared with 83 percent of mothers in the control group. In measures related to family stability, the program group scored significantly higher on a measure of closeness to family and friends (66 percent versus 48 percent) and the ability to maintain persistence at tasks (i.e., work or study hard all day) (47 percent versus 33 percent).

Scholastic Success

Participants in the High/Scope Perry Preschool study were characterized by better academic performance than those in the control group, as measured by higher graduation rates, better grades, higher standardized test scores, and fewer instances of placement in special education classes. In addition, the program group spent more time on homework and demonstrated more positive attitudes toward school at ages 15 and 19. More parents of program group members had positive attitudes regarding their children's educational experiences and were hopeful that their children would obtain college degrees. The program group demonstrated significant academic differences in the following areas:

- **Special education for mental impairment.** Only 15 percent of the program group had been placed in special education programs for mental impairment, compared with 34 percent of the control group.
- **Test scores.** Each year from ages 7 to 14, the mean achievement test scores of the program group were noticeably higher than those of the control group (an average difference of 16 percent). The difference in the final achievement test scores of the two groups at age 14 was particularly significant: the program group's scores were 29 percent higher than those of the control group.
- **Grade point average.** The mean high school grade point average of the program group was higher than that of the control group (2.09 versus 1.68).
- **Graduation from high school.** Seventy-one percent of the program group graduated from high school, compared with 54 percent of the control group. The difference was largely accounted for by graduation rates among females (84 percent and 35 percent, respectively).

Socioeconomic Success

Data collected at ages 19 and 27 indicate that the program group has been more successful socioeconomically than the control group. The data for age 19 reveal that significantly more program group members were employed (50 percent versus 32 percent) and self-reporting (45 percent versus 25 percent). These data also reflect that fewer program group members received welfare assistance (18 percent versus 32 percent). The data for age 27 reveal a continuation of significant economic differences characterized by more economic stability among the program group members, as measured by the following indicators:

- **Public assistance.** Fifteen percent of the program group were receiving public assistance, versus 32 percent of the control group.
- **Monthly earnings.** Twenty-nine percent of the program group had monthly earnings of $2,000 or more, versus 7 percent of the control group (36 percent versus 11 percent, respectively, when comparing only employed members in each group).

- **Household earnings.** When the income of the spouses of the study participants was taken into account, 47 percent of the program group had household income earnings of $3,000 or more per month, versus 17 percent of the control group.
- **Home ownership.** Thirty-six percent of the program group owned a home, versus 13 percent of the control group.
- **Automobile ownership.** Thirty percent of the program group owned a second car, versus 13 percent of the control group.

Cost-Benefit Analysis

A cost-benefit analysis of the High/Scope Perry Preschool study indicates a savings to the public of more than seven times the initial investment per child, with a return of $7.16 for every dollar spent (Barnett, 1983). When adjusted for inflation and a 3-percent discount rate, the investment in early childhood prevention resulted in a taxpayer return of $88,433 per child from the following sources:

- Savings in welfare assistance (prior to welfare reform).
- Savings in special education.
- Savings to the criminal justice system.
- Savings to crime victims.
- Increased tax revenue from higher earnings.

An independent reanalysis is provided in a recent RAND Corporation report (Karoly et al., 1998). This report found that eliminating the largest and least reliable savings category (savings to crime victims) still left a return of more than twice the initial investment. Savings to crime victims make up 65 percent of the total investment return in the earlier analysis (Barnett, 1993). Although victim savings should be considered a significant outcome and societal benefit of early childhood intervention, this factor is also distinct from the other factors that can be estimated based on direct governmental costs and savings. With victim savings factored out of the analysis, the largest savings category is in criminal justice costs (40 percent), followed by increased taxable revenue (26 percent), reduced educational services (25 percent), and reduced welfare costs (9 percent).

Early Childhood Risk Factors for Delinquency

An understanding of early childhood risk factors for delinquency is helpful to interpreting the success of the High/Scope Perry Preschool Project. One factor identified with risk for delinquency is poor language skills. (Stattin and Klackenberg-Larsson, 1993). As a component of overall mental development, language functions as an indicator of later intelligence and is a critical factor in the relationship between intelligence and delinquency. Additional early risk factors include poor attachment to caregivers (Egeland and Farber, 1984; Shaw and Bell, 1993), poor parenting skills (Hawkins et al., 1998; Loeber and Stouthamer-Loeber, 1986), and multiple family stressors (Fergusson and Lynskey, 1996; Shaw et al., 1998). These risk factors may not only directly affect delinquency but may also indirectly influence other factors that interact with delinquency, such as school- and community-related risk factors.

As demonstrated in the Prenatal and Early Childhood Nurse Home Visitation Program supported by OJJDP (Olds, Hill, and Rumsey, 1998), prenatal and early postnatal prevention are shown to reduce risk factors that contribute to the development of antisocial behavior in childhood. Early childhood intervention during the preschool years also offers an opportunity to halt the developmental trajectory toward delinquency and related behavioral disorders. Family support services help develop parenting skills, attachment, and coping mechanisms that have a positive effect on family stressors. A multicomponent approach to enhancing child development promotes protective factors and reduces risk factors by addressing the many systems and influences that affect a child's development.

Program Components and Related Risk Factors for Delinquency

The components of the High/Scope Perry Preschool Project affect a number of the early childhood risk factors associated with later delinquency and other behavioral problems. In addition to directly reinforcing early developmental processes in the educational setting, the program strengthens positive parenting skills.

The High/Scope Educational Research Foundation explains the effectiveness of the High/Scope Perry Preschool model in terms of empowerment, which includes developing skills for success by enabling children to be active and independent learners, helping parents to support the development of their children, and providing teachers with effective training and support (Schweinhart and Weikart, 1995).

Because an ongoing home-school relationship enhances socialization, involving parents early in the educational process is critical to the later success of participants in an early childhood intervention such as High/Scope Perry Preschool (Seitz, 1990). Weekly home visits by teachers and regular parent group meetings promote the strengthening of parent-child relationships and increase parent involvement in the educational process. A more recent OJJDP longitudinal study, the Rochester Youth Development Study (Thornberry et al., 1998), confirmed a significant relationship between parents' involvement in their children's lives and reduced delinquency.

In addition to enhancing parent attachment, parent involvement, and parenting skills, early childhood intervention aimed at both parents and children influences a child's attachment to school and later commitment to school success (Thornberry et al., 1998). Findings from the Rochester study confirm earlier research linking poor school attachment, commitment, and achievement to delinquent behavior and drug use (Krohn et al., 1995; Smith et al., 1995). Another OJJDP study, the Seattle Social Development Project (Hill et al., 1999), found that a lack of success in elementary school was linked to later gang membership. Even in the midst of multiple other factors placing youth at high risk for delinquency, school success (as indicated by higher standardized test scores, school commitment, attachment to teachers, college aspirations, and parent expectations) appears to be a protective factor against delinquency (Smith et al., 1995). Academic achievement outcomes of the High/Scope Perry Preschool study indicate that the program group was more successful than the control group in school-related factors that appear to protect against delinquency.

The positive outcomes of the High/Scope Perry Preschool study are the result of a cumulative effect that begins with increased school readiness (Berrueta-Clement et al., 1987; Zigler, Taussig, and Black, 1992). School readiness results in positive reinforcement from teachers in the early grades followed by enhanced academic performance in subsequent grades and an overall stronger commitment to school. A correlational analysis of the High/Scope Perry Preschool data reveals a strong association between school motivation in the early years and literacy scores at age 19 (Schweinhart, Barnes, and Weikart, 1993). School motivation is also higher correlated with the highest year of schooling completed, which is associated with higher monthly earnings in adulthood and fewer lifetime arrests.

Program and Policy Implications

The outcomes of the High/Scope Perry Preschool study demonstrate the value of prevention and early intervention efforts in promoting protective factors that reduce delinquency. The program was developed for high-risk children who stood to benefit the most from such an intervention. The intervention also affected multiple risk factors and was carried out in multiple domains (i.e., home and school). In an extensive review of early childhood interventions, Yoshikawa (1995) concluded that the combination of an early educational component with family support, as exemplified by the High/Scope Perry Preschool Project, is a determining factor in long-term effects on antisocial behavior. Other combination programs that have demonstrated long-term effects on delinquency include the Yale Child Welfare Project (Seitz and Apfel, 1994), Houston Parent Child Development Center (Johnson and Walker, 1987), and Syracuse Family Development Research Program (Lally, Mangione, and Honig, 1988). Single-component models, such as those that address only educational factors, have not been shown to demonstrate significant results.

In addition to the need to target appropriate populations and address multiple risk factors in multiple domains, program quality is essential to success. The High/Scope Perry Preschool model is based on a high-quality educational approach that assumes a low staff-to-child ratio, an active learning curriculum, and a home visitation component that engages parents in the educational process. Furthermore, teachers are well educated, adequately compensated, and well supported in their tasks.

Head Start, perhaps the largest and best-known early childhood intervention program, has recently made efforts to expand and improve its effectiveness by emphasizing family support, staff training, and performance standards (U.S. Department of Health and Human Services, 1999). The 1994 legislation reauthorizing Head Start incorporated a number of recommendations from the Advisory Committee on Head Start Quality and Expansion (1993), including increased parent involvement, a lower staff-to-child ratio, and increased mental health services.[4] Head Start has increased the emphasis on curriculum and child outcomes as a result of this reauthorization and has formed Head Start Quality Research Centers to respond to the need for additional research in the area of early childhood intervention. Further research is clearly needed to build on the limited existing knowledge base and assess the effectiveness of programs across various demographic groups, risk factors, and co-occurring factors that are related to delinquency, such as mental health issues and substance abuse (Yoshikawa, 1995).

Although the High/Scope Perry Preschool study's sample size was small in proportion to its eventual influence, its strong experimental design has contributed to its prominence in the field of early childhood education. Subsequent early childhood research that is carefully controlled and longitudinal in design remains limited. The limited research involving similar models that combine educational and family support components, however, supports the positive outcomes of the High/Scope Perry Preschool model. Subsequent independent evaluations of the programs that have implemented the High/Scope model have rated those programs significantly higher than comparison programs, with 58 percent of High/Scope programs versus 40 percent of comparison programs being rated as high quality (Epstein, 1993). In addition, 72 percent of children in High/Scope programs versus 57 percent of children in comparison programs scored high on measures of emotional, social, cognitive, and motor development.

Some targeted, multicomponent early childhood interventions have been demonstrated to exceed their costs in eventual savings and benefit to the public. However, implementing an effective prevention strategy requires a commitment to provide empirically based quality programming and to invest the up-front resources that will result in long-term savings and positive social change in the lives of children and families. The High/Scope Perry Preschool Project provides one such model for early childhood intervention that has proven successful when executed with quality and commitment to long-term results. The complexity of juvenile delinquency requires multiple strategies that address the problem at various stages of development; early childhood intervention is one promising component in the context of a more comprehensive approach, as recommended in OJJDP's *Comprehensive Strategy for Serious, Violent, and Chronic Juvenile Offenders* (Wilson and Howell, 1993). The High/Scope Perry Preschool model is worthy of consideration as an effective early childhood intervention as communities attempt to implement a comprehensive strategy that includes prevention, intervention, and graduated sanctions (Howell, 1995; Wilson and Howell, 1993).

Notes

1. Unlike primary prevention programs, which are directed at the general population, secondary prevention programs target children at risk for school failure or delinquency.

2. The original Perry Preschool no longer exists, but the High/Scope Educational Research Foundation—founded in 1970 by Perry Preschool researcher David Weikart—continues to collect followup data from the participants of the 1962 study. The foundation is an independent organization dedicated to nonprofit research, development, training, and public advocacy. Its principal goals are to promote the learning and development of children worldwide from infancy through adolescence and to support and train educators and parents as they help children learn. In a High/Scope program, students should learn through active involvement with materials, events, and ideas. The Foundation disseminates the High/Scope Preschool model worldwide.

3. Researchers are currently collecting followup data from the original program participants. Called the High/Scope Perry Preschool Midlife Study, researchers have already interviewed 30 of the 39- to 41-year-old participants. The interview emphasized health and the performance of the program participants' children. The researchers expect to complete the data collection by the end of 2001. This study is funded by the McCormick Tribune Foundation in Chicago, IL. [97% of the study participants still living were interviewed at age 40. Additional data were gathered from the subjects' school, social services, and arrest records. The study found that adults at age 40 who had the preschool program had higher earnings, were more likely to hold a job, had committed fewer crimes, and were more likely to have graduated from high school than adults who did not have preschool. The major conclusion of the mid-life phase is that high-quality preschool programs for young children living in poverty contribute to their intellectual and social development in childhood and their school success, economic performance, and reduced commission of crime in adulthood. This study confirms that these findings extend not only to young adults, but also to adults in midlife. It confirms that the long-term effects are lifetime effects. (Reference-www.highscope.org)]

4. Head Start Act Amendments of 1994. Pub. L. No. 103–252, tit. 1 § 108, Stat. 624 (1994).

T. Berry Brazelton and
Stanley I. Greenspan

 NO

The Irreducible Needs of Children: What Every Child Must Have to Grow, Learn, and Flourish

Children who are living with their biological parent or parents and are deprived of the ordinary experiences that would enable them to be warm, loving, and caring are often in families with multiple problems, such as mental illness or severe antisocial patterns in one or both parents. The children aren't provided opportunities for nurturance, interaction, or learning. Here, too, we see chaotic, impulsive, self-absorbed, aimless children with severe language, social, and emotional difficulties.

In reading this, one may sigh with a sense of relief thinking that in your community such patterns of multiple foster care placements or neglect and abuse are very rare. But there is another trend occurring, both in the United States and around the world—a new type of institutional care. This type of care is part of every community. Approximately 50 percent of young children are now reared for significant parts of the day by persons other than their biological parents. Here, we're not talking about after-school programs for school-aged children. We're talking about infants and toddlers in the first three years of life. From the 1970s through the 1990s, there has been a transformation of the attitudes of families towards raising their own children. During this time, there has been a huge increase in the number of families giving up the care of babies, toddlers, and preschoolers to others for 35 or more hours a week. In other words, large numbers of infants, toddlers, and preschoolers are spending the lion's share of their days in nonparental care.

More important than mere numbers are reports regarding the quality of this care. These are not encouraging. The most comprehensive study of the quality of day care reported that the vast majority of center-based care was not of high quality (over 85 percent was not of high quality for preschool children and over 90 percent was not of high quality for infants and toddlers). Similar reports have emerged around other non-parental child care arrangements, such as family day care. In addition, most states in the United States have very weak regulations governing care. New findings regarding day care options for mothers on welfare are especially alarming. These "Wave 1 Findings" are from the Growing Up in Poverty Project 2000. These findings suggest that day care for such families is of very poor quality (eg. instances of toddlers wandering aimlessly about). The findings about overall lack of care suggest that quality of care is an important contributor to a child's development.

The day care debate gets confused however by focusing only on research reports that maintain it's the quality of care that counts, not whether children are in institutional day care or family day care or cared for by parents. The reports stress that the quality of nurturance, interaction, and sensitivity to the child's cues are what's associated with their development status. It is true, and makes common sense, that quality would be an important variable and certainly, as indicated above, there's no guarantee that biological parents will always provide good quality care. But, what tends to get obscured in these academic discussions is the fact that at present most nonparental care (as revealed in a number of studies, including the study that documented that quality counts) is not of high quality.

We do know that quality child care is essential to the optimal development of small children. In our present setup, as indicated above, only 10% or less of infants and toddlers have access to high quality day care. The rest wind up with care that anyone with real options would not trust. Nor do the parents of these children. When a parent must leave a small child in less than optimal child care, that parent is bound to grieve. The grieving can take many forms: denial, detachment from the child, and anger and/or depression at the workplace that demands the separation. If we want motivated workers we need to offer them optimal child care or flexible hours that permit parental sharing of care.

With over half the nation's children receiving one form or another of nonparental care, the question is whether we want to allow a type of care that is not providing children the needed nurturance and social and intellectual interaction. We have to ask whether this nurturance is possible in settings where caregivers are caring for four or more babies (and later six or more toddlers), are paid minimal wage, and given little training and little incentive to avoid staff turnover (among those who can get better jobs). . . .

Even when children are cared for at home for the first few years, there still are worrisome trends. There has been a shift towards more impersonal, rather than emotionally nurturing types of care–giving for infants, toddlers, preschoolers, and children. A recent report from the Kaiser Foundation revealed that on average, children are spending five to six hours a day in front of the TV or computer screen. During this time, children are not receiving nurturing warmth or age-appropriate social or intellectual interactions.

But this is just one sign of the movement towards impersonal care. Many families are overly scheduled. Both parents are working to make ends meet or to improve the family's economics, leaving little relaxed family time. Education is becoming more impersonal as it is, more technologically oriented, losing the personal touch. Families in their own relationships with one another are also moving towards more impersonal modes of communication. E-mails are replacing lunches together and time in front of the screen is replacing many other forms of personal interaction. Recreation as well as work is taking place in a more impersonal atmosphere, with less interaction among and within families.

One of us (S.I.G.) was recently struck by how pervasive this shift is towards impersonal modes of care. A visit within the same week to two very different settings attempting to provide nurturing care revealed some striking similarities in what might be called "institutional love."

In the first setting, a woman sat in the corner of the room looking at the floor. Around her crawled four babies who seemed to relate only to their own bodies and the objects they can see or touch. One of them got her hand caught in a toy. The woman went to her, pulled her hand free, said, "O.K." and then moved silently back to her chair. Another baby banged on his half-filled bottle of milk. The woman picked him up, put him stiffly on her lap and faced him towards the wall while the baby sucked down the rest of his milk. When the baby was finished, she put him back on the floor without a word. The room was quiet. There were no signs of the familiar gestures, sounds, and expressions that tie people together.

Was this an overwhelmed, economically disadvantaged mother in a worrisome family situation? Or an over-stressed home day care facility in a poor neighborhood? No, in fact this was a scene in an upper-middle class day care center for infants and toddlers. The woman was an aide earning the minimum wage. The director of the private, well-run, fully accredited center said, "She is the norm."

In another room in the same center, a smiling woman animatedly exchanged words, grunts, smiles, laughs, and gestures with five toddlers as they rolled trucks back and forth and giggled at one another. The children pointed at, crawled over, and made sounds at each other and the woman caring for them. Using subtle movements of hand, face, and voice she engaged all five toddlers at once.

"Who is she?" S.I.G. asked.

"Oh, she is the assistant director, substituting for one of the aides who is sick," replied the director.

"Is it possible to have more of the staff that cares directly for the babies show her warmth and interactive skills?" S.I.G. asked.

"Occasionally we have caregivers similar to her, but in general we don't and people with her skills quickly get to higher levels. We can't afford to pay someone like her to spend time with the infants," the director responded.

A few days later, in the second setting, S.I.G. saw similarly unresponsive aides sitting in their chairs. One was telling an elderly woman, "Sit down and stop babbling or you won't get your ice cream." In another room, six other elderly women were sitting and staring silently into space while two more aides sat behind their table looking bored and indifferent. A woman pleaded unsuccessfully for a back rub and later confessed, "I just need some human touch." Another woman brightened up when an aide talked to her and was unnecessarily thankful for the little conversation.

This setting is one of the city's best institutions for the elderly. Here, too, the food, cleanliness and medical care are excellent.

This is "institutional love." It is provided at either end of the lifespan for both the poor and the well-to-do, for those who, because of their age and helplessness, need to depend on others for their care. We all know what this kind of care is like. What we don't want to think about is that this care is what we are providing for those we love.

Surely, one may rationalize, with enough money we can have good services. In fact, in some workplaces parental involvement in on-site day care creates a sense of an extended family. "Cooperative" nursery schools benefit from parent participation. A compassionate head nurse in a home for the elderly may instill a personal touch. But, sadly, these are the exceptions. The irony is that if we as a society keep this up, in 80 years the current infants will be back in these impersonal surroundings and it will feel strangely familiar.

One of us (S.I.G.) has questioned whether we are creating a new view of human nature reflected in our impersonal child care policies and interaction patterns, a concrete, materialistic one. In this view, we are more concerned with the brain than the mind and with biology and genetics than experience. . . .

Ongoing Nurturing Relationships

Day Care

SIG: If parents have options and are able to provide high-quality care themselves, I find it best not to have infants or toddlers (in the first two years) in full-time, 30–40-plus-hour-a-week day care. Current research and my own clinical observations suggest that most day-care centers do not provide high-quality care. The quality of interaction between caregivers and babies is often less than optimal. Also, the current ratios of four babies per caregiver in the first year and six in the second year, coupled with high staff turnover, minimum wages, insufficient training, and the expectable change of caregivers each year, make it difficult to provide high-quality, ongoing, nurturing care in those early years.

The question is, are parents able to shift back to caring for their babies and using day care less?

TBB: I would prefer if day care for babies and toddlers weren't necessary, but I think that there is a large portion of the population right now who can't take the full-time care of their infants.

SIG: Is one reason why parents can't do this a difference in the way people are growing up these days?

TBB: Expectations are changing. It's like what is happening to marriage in a society where the divorce rate is going up to 50 percent. The expectations for marriage have changed. I think the same thing is happening to the way mothers perceive staying at home. In an earlier generation, most mothers were expected to stay at home, and it was easier for them to do so. Now we've changed that expectation entirely, and it's hard to reverse it.

SIG: From the child's point of view, however, let's look at the first year of life in full-time day care—40 or more hours a week. How do you think babies develop relationships in this circumstance?

TBB: Babies can make can make multiple attachments that are meaningful. Certainly I would hope that the parents come first and the baby makes secondary attachments to everybody else. I visited a day–care center recently at a time when all the mothers were there. After a while, only one mother was left and all the children gravitated to her. I turned to the very talented day–care people there and said, "They really seem to desert you, don't they?" They said,

"When there's a mother here, we don't even exist." The children were already differentiating among caregivers. It doesn't even have to be their mother; it just has to be a mother.

SIG: That's not so great. In a number of day-care centers, when the children are mobile, I see a lot of emotionally hungry children. Children come up to any new adult and hang on. Some of that reaching out for any mother is simply reaching out to anyone who will give them some attention. It's a little indiscriminate. We see that in institutions such as orphanages where there is emotional deprivation. A minute here and there of reciprocal interaction, sometimes around feeding or diapering, is not enough to provide the needed security and sense of being cared for.

If we are going to give parents flexible options, we need both to improve day care and to reduce the number of hours per week children spend in day-care situations.

TBB: Again, I think it needs to be a case-by-case decision, weighing this or that, rather than simply telling people what to do. Some parents are better parents if there is an outlet for them. But we do need to provide the child with an optimal secondary caregiver.

SIG: When I talk to college students, I often ask them how they see their lives in terms of having children. As they think about a career and getting married, are they taking into account child-rearing, as well as the demands of a profession? Are they engaged to a neurosurgeon or are they going to be neurosurgeons themselves? Are they planning on having several children? Having two neurosurgeons in the family along with four children may be more difficult and demanding than they can possibly imagine. On the other hand, if two people are getting married and both want careers, and one of them is a writer and the other a psychologist, they may have more control of their time. Each one could work two-thirds time or one could work halftime and they could get child care for the limited remaining hours. But a lot of these potential parents haven't thought this out. They want children and a good career and see no problem. What they're being led to believe now is that full-time day care in the first years of life is as good as if not better than what they can provide: "I'll have a baby, take a two month leave of absence, put the baby in day care, and I'll be a lawyer and my spouse will be a lawyer. We'll work until 8:00 at night. We'll pick up the baby, come home, and play for an hour." In families like this I see children not getting their basic needs for nurturing met.

TBB: When I see a family like that I see a lot of grieving. That kind of treatment of the child is ignoring the child's interests to such an extent that there must be a lot of denial. Something is so painful that these parents have to hide behind defenses.

SIG: But do we support this type of denial or help parents out of it? As new parents make their decisions early on, some parents intuitively plan for the flexibility to be home more; sometimes it's the mom and sometimes it's the dad who stays home. The parents who are more ambivalent and tend to use denial often look around for guidance. But they're getting a lot of misinformation. They're told it doesn't make a difference. If parents-to-be knew more about this need for a continuous, close relationship, they might plan more realistically. They would see how hard it is to have such relationships with two full-time jobs and full-time day care. If parents see the options, they could make choices. If they have a caregiver at home and pick well, they have a greater likelihood, if they can afford it, of having the same caregiver being with them for a number of years. In day care, by design, the caregivers change each year. Turnover is so great, though, that there may be another change or two changes even within one year. There may be three changes of caregivers by the time a baby has had a year of day care. Minimum wages, lack of training, and so on contribute to this. The caregiver in a day-care setting is not like a *meta peleth* in a kibbutz in Israel, who is a stable person in a child's life, with him for four or five years. It doesn't have to be the mother. It could be the father or the grandfather or grandmother. The child needs a caregiver in his or her life who's going to be there for the long haul.

TBB: To improve day care, I see three babies per adult as the absolute maximum for the first year of life. But now the norm is four babies per caregiver. Imagine a mother with triplets and how hard it is for her to care for all three babies at the same time.

SIG: Would you recommend, Berry, that a baby should keep the same care givers for the first three or four years? One group of caregivers, for example, would follow a group of children who started as infants on up through their toddler years.

TBB: This would work as long as the caregiver really liked each baby, but suppose she didn't like one? Couldn't it be moved to another caregiver's group? Caregivers and babies, like parents, could be evaluated for "goodness of fit" between them. Also, when you go up into the second and third years, and taking care of four children becomes possible, a fourth child will be added to the group of three. The fourth baby wouldn't necessarily get the same caregivers.

SIG: The extra children in the group might come from outside, perhaps from home. To make this work, you'd have to have expanding entry into day care at the second and third years, with each class being larger than the last. More children are in day care by age three than in the first two years of life. Then we have to create incentives for the staff of day-care centers to stay on, giving better wages and training.

TBB: We have to increase wages to a decent level, and we need to improve their status. At present, they are thought of as "baby-sitters" with some scorn.

SIG: That's what we need to correct. We need to get across all that's involved in meaningful care of a child: creating ongoing dialogues, reflecting and accepting a variety of emotions. You can sometimes find people who are warm and nourishing and emotionally responsive, even though they haven't been given a chance to educate themselves. Sometimes you can find young people who want to get experience with children and who are naturally sensitive and flexible.

TBB: Day-care staff need constant refueling. It's a demanding job, taking care of somebody else's children. If parents and day–care personnel could handle their natural, inevitable gatekeeping, parents could become peer "fuelers" of the day–care personnel. The team (of parents and child care worker) could share the child's optimal development.

SIG: We need to see all this from the point of view of prevention. It's a public health issue.

TBB: When Congress was talking about that $22 billion for improving child care, I got a chance to go down to Washington, and told them that if they just turn the money over to the states, it will all get eaten up. You'd do better to give the money to states tied to choices based on the quality child care that we know how to produce, and to let them pick their choices. When it came to laying out choices that will work for the child, they said, "Oh, we have to do some research." I told them there was already plenty of research. What we need now is just the will to put the research into practice. They asked if I could tell them what programs work. I said not by myself, but I certainly could gather a bunch of colleagues who could tell you which ones we guarantee would work.

State governments can eat up revenues for child care at the top, if we're not careful. The one sector that could make a real difference and could afford to, and might be motivated to if we were smart enough, would be big business. If we could get them to set up a center in every business site that would contain preventive health care, child care, after-school care, and elder care, then maybe we could begin to reach a lot of people. I don't think we need to use the schools for this, but Ed Zigler at Yale has a model he calls the "School of the 21st Century," in which all these caregiving situations are gathered into school buildings that are not in use and made into centers for families in their communities. In our Touchpoints model, we are recommending that parent centers be established in every community where parents could receive child care, preventive health care, after-school care, and elder care. Parent resource centers, such as Family Support America, could be established for peer resources. Parents could then begin to feel a sense of community around them.

Our Touchpoints model has been developed at Children's Hospital in Boston to train multidisciplinary representatives from communities that are ready for change in an outreach, relational model. We want to improve preventive health care and child care with several goals. At each visit of parents and child, the provider (child care or medical care) identifies the strengths versus the failures of the parent. The child's development is the language between professional and parent. The parent is valued as the expert in the child's development. In this way, the passion of the parent is fostered. The relationship is transactional versus top-down. Each visit becomes an opportunity for sharing the child's new achievements and encouraging the child's development, both physical and psychological. Twenty-five centers have espoused our ideas, and they are changing communities to become parent-friendly. Our goal is to offer preventive outreach for the present 40 percent of underserved. We do know what to do. Can we do it? . . .

Relationships in Day Care

It is also important to consider now how these same principles can be applied to other contexts where children may find themselves such as family day care, makeshift baby-sitting arrangements, as well as institutional day care settings and care by relatives. These same standards for the nurturing care of children growing up in families apply to these other settings. In other words, a child in family day care or day care center should spend most of her time in facilitated activities or direct one-to-one interactions. However, in observations of day-care settings we found it rare that there were long interactive sequences between the caregivers and the babies.

Since it is so hard for caregivers to have long, nurturing interactions when caring for four or more babies (standard in most institutional day care), and because of the staff turnover that is characteristic of most institutional day-care settings, as well as the tendency to have staff change each year as children move from the infant room to the toddler room to the preschool room, we believe that in the first two years of life full-time day care is a difficult context in which to provide the ongoing, nurturing care by one or a few caregivers that the child requires. Part-time day care, on the other hand, may be quite helpful in giving mothers and fathers a chance to do other things and may not compromise either the security of ongoing nurturing care or the types of experiences we have described. But 35-plus hours a week for infants and toddlers makes it very difficult to have the consistency of caregiver and the depth of nurturance required, or the amount of facilitating interaction with the environment or direct interaction that we believe is healthy for infants and toddlers.

Because some families will need full-time day care in the early years, we must work to improve its quality. This means lower child/caregiver ratios, better training and salaries and maintaining the same caregiver from birth to roughly age 3. Although there is general agreement on the need to improve day care, improvements in the last 25 years have been modest. As we pointed out earlier, studies of the quality of available day care are not optimistic. We may be trying to rationalize a system that simply isn't providing the essentials of what children need. It may therefore be best to reconsider our assumptions. The best way these assumptions can be reconsidered is by each and every family having good and accurate information. With awareness we believe most will make a wise and enlightened choice.

Recommendations

In making the recommendations that follow, we are both mindful of the fact that there are many circumstances where nonparental care may be highly desirable or absolutely necessary. Single parents working to put food on the table, even if able to provide high-quality care themselves, may have no choice but to use out-of-home child care for 40-plus hours a week. Here, the goal would be to find the best care available and to work with the child care providers as a team to provide integrated care for that baby or toddler. There may be families where there is emotional stress in individuals or family stress that makes it highly desirable to have 30-plus hours of care provided by others. On balance this will provide a much stronger support system for this particular baby or toddler. Each circumstance has to be weighed individually, and parents have to make wise and enlightened choices regarding their own particular situation.

Continuous Relationships

- In the first three years, every child needs one or two primary caregivers who remain in a steady, intimate relationship with that child.
- During the infancy, toddler, and preschool years, children should always be in the sight of caregivers. There should be no time, other than when they are sleeping, that they are out of sight of caregivers.
- No more than one-third of infants', toddlers', and preschoolers' time should be spent in fully independent activities. The time that is spent in independent activities should be spent for 10 or 15 minutes here and there rather than a longer period in independent activities.
- The other two-thirds or longer time should be spent between two types of activities: those in which the caregiver facilitates interactions with the environment and direct interaction, such as cuddling, holding, shared pretend play, and funny face games. Infants and toddlers need at least four or more 20-minute or longer periods of direct interactive time. Preschoolers need at least three of these direct, interactive play opportunities. In a two-parent family, both parents should be part of these spontaneous, joyful games.
- During the facilitated time, caregivers are available to comment on, respond to, and help in the child's explorations, though also engaged in other activities, such as cooking or putting clothes in the washing machine. Some of this time a small child could be accompanying parents to the supermarket or being a junior chef. During the school years, when we consider available time, we are considering time minus schooltime, after-school activities, and peer playtime. Here, too, we recommend that of the available time two-thirds be spent with the caregiver being available for facilitating or directly interacting. The "facilitating" time could be spent helping a child with homework, hobbies, or other activities. The times of direct involvement, which should include at least two 20-minute periods (each parent should participate where possible) might mean imaginative play, games or other activities in which the child can take the lead.
- We recommend that working parents both be available for at least two-thirds of the evening hours, from 5:30 or 6:00 to 9:00, and that, if possible, in addition, one of the parents be available in the late afternoon when the children are home, often playing with peers or siblings, or involved in after-school activities. Also, the parents should be available enough so that they or the children don't have to be measuring each moment of time and the guidelines outlined above can be taken for granted.

Parental Leave

We recommend a leave of most of the first year of life for one parent.

Day Care

- We do not recommend full-time day care, 30 or more hours of care by nonparents, for infants and toddlers if the parents are able to provide high-quality care themselves and if the parents have reasonable options. We also recommend improving day care considerably by lowering ratios, improving training and wages, and, for children in full-time day care, having the same caregiver remain with the infant she cares for for three to four years. Those families that require day care will then have options for higher-quality day care than is now the case.

- In the first three years, a primary caregiver should be assigned to each child and should remain the same from year to year.
- For the first year there should be no more than three babies to one adult.
- For the second year, there should be no more than four toddlers to one adult.
- For the third and fourth years, there should be no more than five to eight children to one adult.

Group or Institutional Settings

- Various types of institutional arrangements, including children in group situations, need to follow the same guidelines outlined earlier for the family. Ongoing nurturing care with one or a few constant primary caregivers should include direct or "facilitated" interactions for at least two-thirds of the available time. In-service training, growing financial incentives with experience and training, and support structure to facilitate nurturing attitudes are all important components of satisfying this requirement for ongoing nurturing care in group or institutional settings.

EXPLORING THE ISSUE

Is Institutional Child Care Beneficial to Children?

Critical Thinking and Reflection

1. Parks asserts that single-component models are not successful in early childhood intervention and delinquency prevention. He contends that a multifaceted approach must be used in order to be successful. Do you agree or disagree? Support your answer with specific concepts discussed in the reading.
2. One of Brazelton and Greenspan's arguments is that many of the staff members in child-care facilities are not properly trained. How could a facility ensure that its staff members were properly trained?
3. Brazelton and Greenspan argue that the turnover rate in child-care facilities is high due to low wages. How can child-care centers increase wages and provide incentives for staff in order to avoid continual turnover?
4. What would you suggest to parents who do not want their children to be placed in a full-time day care setting, but would still like some time each day where their child is out of the home and interacting with other children and adults?
5. What are some strategies that you might suggest to parents who want to ensure that they spend quality time with their child even though they must rely on full-time child care in an institutional setting while they work?
6. What do you consider to be the most important aspect of child care: the setting it is provided in, or the quality of the care? Why?

Is There Common Ground?

The issue of child care is a touchy subject for debate. Is it an issue that should be debated in public or in a more private family setting? In most instances, choosing what kind of care a child will receive is a decision made by parents for financial or personal reasons. Does institutional child care hinder children from getting all the nurturing they need during their younger years? Or, does institutional child care provide the needed nurturing for children to grow to become productive adults? Parks and Brazelton and Greenspan may agree that the issue of child care is a complicated one, but they definitely disagree on how to confront this issue.

Perhaps if there were greater resources (e.g., more money to be able to hire more staff) available to child-care institutions, they could guarantee a high level of nurturing to children. Or, perhaps if the workplace could offer families greater flexibility in scheduling and leave policies, the families could afford to provide child care at home for a longer period of time. If both of these were in place, families would have the luxury of choosing either option and feeling more comfortable that they are doing the right thing for their children.

Additional Resources

American Academy of Child & Adolescent Psychiatry. (2002, November). Making Daycare a Good Experience. Retrieved on March 2, 2011, from http://www.aacap.org/cs/root/facts_for_families/making_day_care_a_good_experience.

An article posted on the Internet that provides tips and suggestions for helping parents select a day care that is optimal for their child(ren).

keepkidshealthy.com. (2001, February). Day Care Issues. Retrieved on March 2, 2011, from http://www.keepkidshealthy.com/welcome/daycare.html.

An article posted on the Internet that discusses the types of day care available, tips on how to select the right day care, and advice for transitioning a child to a day care setting.

Pendley, J. (2010, November). Choosing Child Care. Retrieved on March 2, 2011, from http://kidshealth.org/parent/positive/family/child_care.html.

An article posted on the Internet that discusses the types of day care available and offers advice to parents on how to select the right care for their child(ren).

Zolten, K. & Long, N. (1997). How to Select Daycares. Retrieved on March 2, 2011, from http://www.parenting-ed.org/handout3/General%20Parenting%20Information/daycare.htm.

An article posted on the Internet that discusses the types of day care available, benefits and challenges of the different types, and advice for how to select the day care that is right for a child.

ISSUE 2

Does Maternal Employment Have Negative Effects on Children's Development?

YES: Wen-Jui Han, Jane Waldfogel, and Jeanne Brooks-Gunn, from "The Effects of Early Maternal Employment on Later Cognitive and Behavioral Outcomes," *Journal of Marriage and Family* (February 2001)

NO: Thomas M. Vander Ven, Francis T. Cullen, Mark A. Carrozza, and John Paul Wright, from "Home Alone: The Impact of Maternal Employment on Delinquency," *Social Problems* (May 2001)

Learning Outcomes

After reading this issue, you should be able to:

- Summarize the effects that maternal employment can have on children.
- Discuss ethnic differences that are present in outcomes for children whose mothers work.
- Explain why some researchers believe there is a link between maternal employment and delinquency.

ISSUE SUMMARY

YES: University professors and researchers Wen-Jui Han, Jane Waldfogel, and Jeanne Brooks-Gunn from Columbia University conclude that maternal employment in the first year of a child's life has a significant negative effect on verbal ability at age 3 or 4 and lowered math achievement when children were 7 to 8. When ethnicity was controlled for, these negative effects were found for white children, but not for African-American children.

NO: University professors and researchers Thomas M. Vander Ven, Francis T. Cullen, Mark A. Carrozza, and John Paul Wright found that mother's employment in the first year of the baby's life had no effect on child delinquency when the child got older.

The number of women who combine work and motherhood has risen steadily in the past 35 years or so. Fifty-six percent of married mothers with a child under age 1 are employed, and 59 percent of unmarried mothers with a child under 1 are employed. The percentages of women entering the labor force increases as their children get older. Sixty-two percent of married mothers with a child aged 2 are working, and 75 percent of unmarried moms with a child aged 2 are working. Attitudes toward maternal employment have changed somewhat because of societal changes. It has become more socially acceptable today for moms to work. As more women obtain high-profile jobs in politics and corporations, more workplace assistance programs have been developed. These include on-site child care, flexible work hours, and allowing moms to work from home via computer technology. The realization that it is an economic necessity for single moms as well as both parents in a dual-parent household to work has created more of an acceptance for working mothers. Many families need two incomes to make ends meet.

Time-saving appliances such as self-cleaning ovens, dishwashers, and microwave ovens have given working moms more time to spend with their children. Obtaining food for dinner from the growing number of restaurants offering drive-through or pick-up service has also relieved working moms from the hassle of running home from work to make dinner.

Of course, these time-saving means are only available to those who can afford them. Women with lower wages still struggle to balance work and family time. Welfare reform created a predicament for those who believed mothers should stay at home with their infants. With no governmental monetary support, how does a single mom stay at home with her children and still make a living for her family?

As more women moved into the workforce in the 1960s, research on maternal employment's effects on children became a popular topic of study. For the past 20 years, maternal employment has evolved from being studied as a single factor affecting children's development to being studied as a more complex issue. It was once thought that maternal employment had a direct single influence on children. Now researchers agree that maternal employment is more than a question of whether or not the mother works. The issue needs to be studied within the context of the family, the society, and cultural norms. Researchers do agree that maternal employment's effects on children need to be examined through the interaction of multiple variables, such as child-care quality, control over work situation, and family and societal support systems. They do not, however, agree on which sets of variables combine to give an accurate picture of how a mother's employment affects children's development. Study on maternal employment's effects must face the complicated task of simultaneously answering these questions. What quality of child care does the child receive? How does the mother feel about working? What societal and family support do the mother and child receive?

Researchers are not only divided on what variables to study, there is also a lack of agreement about what methods to use in studying maternal employment effects. For example, some researchers combine several social classes to study the interactive effects of working mothers with child-care arrangements, whereas others examine only one social class and how it intersects with the mother's personality traits and type of work and family environment. It is difficult to control for all characteristics that may affect the outcome of studies on maternal employment. Researchers suggest that more studies be conducted on a larger population so that they might generalize the results for the population as a whole. It is also suggested that the research methods include a larger diversity of ethnic groups and social classes to gain a better understanding of how maternal employment affects a child's development and behavioral outcomes.

The effects of maternal employment on children are determined by many factors such as mother's work satisfaction and morale, amount of and control over work, and mother's perception of quality versus quantity time with her children. Depending on which studies one reads, how the data were collected, and which combination of variables was studied, different conclusions are reported. For example, some studies show that working moms spend more quality time with their children than nonworking moms, while other studies show exactly the opposite results.

Research on maternal employment continues to become more refined, yet the question still remains: Should moms stay home with their babies? Often women who have the opportunity to do so will drop out of the workforce for at least the first few years to stay home and care for their children in order to make a connection. The concept that mother-child attachment in the first few years is critical to the child's later development has been established from years of significant research. Conversely, other research suggests that quality child-care providers may be able to meet the same attachment needs that mothers previously met. In addition, research shows that being exposed to a variety of quality caregivers, including other family members, fosters positive personality characteristics and independence in the child later on.

Young children want to be with their parents and need their parents to care for them. In an ideal world, most people want babies to be cared for by someone who loves them. In all but extreme abuse cases, this is generally the mom or dad. In our society, those who want to stay at home and care for their children should have the opportunity to do so. Yet, the economic environment prevents this from happening. Perhaps another way to look at the issue of maternal employment's effects on children's development is to develop ways to allow moms who want to stay home to raise their children to do so and to give social support to those moms who want to work outside the home.

In the YES selection, Wen-Jui Han, Jane Waldfogel, and Jeanne Brooks-Gunn argue that maternal employment has negative effects on children. They found that mothers' working was associated with their children's lower scores on verbal ability and lower math achievement scores. In the NO selection, Thomas Vander Ven, Francis Cullen, Mark Carrozza, and John Wright assert that maternal employment does not affect children's development. They found that maternal employment during the child's first year of life had no relationship to subsequent child delinquency.

28

YES

Wen-Jui Han, Jane Waldfogel, and Jeanne Brooks-Gunn

The Effects of Early Maternal Employment on Later Cognitive and Behavioral Outcomes

Recent trends in labor force participation have given new urgency to understanding the effects of early maternal employment—employment begun in the child's 1st year of life—on child outcomes. Women with infants have had the fastest growth in labor force participation of any group in the United States. With welfare reform, even more mothers will be working in the labor market before their child's first birthday. These trends are of potential concern given prior research that has found negative effects of early maternal employment on outcomes for children.

Several studies have used data from the 1986 wave of the National Longitudinal Survey of Youth (NLSY) to investigate the effects of maternal employment in the 1st year on children's cognitive and behavioral outcomes as assessed at ages 3 or 4. In this article, we revisit these same children 2 and 4 years later, when they are aged 5 and 6 and aged 7 and 8, to see whether the effects that earlier studies found at ages 3 and 4 would persist. We also wanted to better understand what might cause these effects and how they might be moderated.

With one exception, all the NLSY studies to date have analyzed children at young ages or at one point in time. In a recent study, Harvey analyzed all the children in the NLSY born in 1980 or later. Her study is exceptional in that it assesses some outcomes as late as age 12 and at several different points in time. Unlike our study, however, Harvey's was not longitudinal in design. In our study, we follow one group of children from ages 3 and 4, to ages 5 and 6, and to ages 7 and 8. We are thus able to show whether the effects that many studies have found at a point in time persist over time or whether they attenuate. Another point of difference between our study and Harvey's is that she analyzes White, African American, and Hispanic children together. If there are important differences in the effects of early maternal employment across racial and ethnic groups, as some prior research has found and as we have found here, then analyzing children separately is likely to yield more accurate estimates.

Research on maternal employment and child outcomes has been conducted within several theoretical frameworks. The first is attachment theory,

From *Journal of Marriage and Family*, vol. 63, February 2001, pp. 336–354 (refs. omitted). Copyright © 2001 by National Council on Family Relations. Reprinted by permission of Wiley-Blackwell.

which posits that children whose mothers are absent during critical periods of early child development are less likely to develop secure attachments with their mothers. Attachment theory had in mind extended round-the-clock separations due to hospitalizations, illness, incarceration, and so on, and debate continues about whether maternal employment in the 1st year of life constitutes a comparable absence. Early studies conducted in the 1970s and 1980s, for the most part with small samples of primarily middle-class White children, found some evidence that maternal employment in the 1st year is associated with insecure attachment, but the effects were small. The most recent research, with a larger and more heterogeneous sample, does not find similar negative results. This discrepancy in findings may reflect in large part the differential selection of mothers into employment in the 1990s as compared with earlier decades when it was less common for mothers of infants to work.

Security of attachment to the mother is not the only child outcome of interest in the debate about maternal employment. Studies informed by child developmental psychology have paid particular attention to socioemotional adjustment (primarily behavior problems) and cognitive outcomes (primarily receptive verbal ability or early achievement test scores). Research on such outcomes has focused on large samples of children, with the bulk of studies analyzing data from the NLSY. These studies have found that maternal employment in the 1st year of life has a different effect on later emotional adjustment than does employment begun thereafter. There is also evidence that employment begun in the 1st year of life may have negative effects on cognitive development for some groups, whereas employment after the 1st year of life seems to have positive effects.

The few studies that have been able to control for child-care quality when examining maternal employment effects find that it plays an important mediating role, as does the type of care. High-quality care, if available to some low-income children, may make a bigger difference in their development than it does in high-income families. It may also matter how many hours the mother works.

Child and family characteristics also can mediate the effects of early maternal employment. The child's age when the mother begins work is obviously a critical mediating factor, but so, too, are factors such as the child's characteristics, family background, and current living situation. Moreover, the effects of early maternal employment may be moderated by family characteristics. For instance, family income is an important variable in its own right; mothers in low-income families may experience greater financial strain and hardship, which are in turn negatively associated with parental psychological functioning and parenting behavior. These effects may be more pronounced in low-income families where mothers are working than in families where they are not. In addition, low-income families may be less able to purchase high-quality and stable child care than more affluent families. Therefore, one might expect greater negative effects of maternal employment in low-income than in middle- or high-income families. Nonetheless, if children from high-income families have more to lose when they are separated from their mothers because their mothers are more nurturing or more cognitively skilled, then we might instead expect high-income children to be more vulnerable to the effects of early maternal employment.

Taken together, previous empirical findings and theory generate a rich set of hypotheses as to the likely effects of maternal employment in the 1st year on children's later cognitive and behavioral outcomes, the causes of these effects, and the potential buffers of them. We list the major hypotheses below and indicate which ones we will and will not test in this article. The premise of all these hypotheses is that all development is contextualized; any effects of early maternal employment are likely to vary as a function of context.

> Hypothesis 1: Children of mothers who work in the 1st year of life will have poorer long-term cognitive and behavioral outcomes because the time they would have spent with a cognitively stimulating and nurturing mother is spent instead with a substitute caregiver who is less cognitively stimulating and nurturing (because she or he has lower cognitive skills than the mother, because she or he is less motivated to stimulate and nurture the child, or because she or he is less able to give the child one-on-one attention).

We will test this hypothesis by estimating the effect of 1st-year maternal employment on later child cognitive and behavioral outcomes. We will also test several extensions of this hypothesis.

1. If there are racial or ethnic differences in mother-child interactions in the 1st year and/or in substitute caregiving arrangements in the 1st year, then the effects of maternal employment on child outcomes may differ by racial or ethnic group. We will test this by analyzing non-Hispanic White and African American families separately.
2. If children are more sensitive to maternal absences due to employment early in the 1st year of life than later, then effects of employment should be largest when it occurs earlier in the 1st year. We will test this by examining the quarter of the 1st year in which employment was initiated.
3. If the effects of employment are cumulative, the effects should be largest when mothers work longer hours. We will test this by comparing effects of full-time and part-time employment.
4. If boys are generally more vulnerable in the 1st year of life, then the effects of maternal absence in the 1st year should be larger for boys than for girls. We will test this by comparing the effects of 1st-year employment for boys and girls.
5. If the effects of 1st-year employment are due to the loss of the mothers' cognitive stimulation, then the effects should be more pronounced for children whose mothers have higher cognitive ability themselves. We will test this by comparing the effects of 1st-year maternal employment for children whose mothers have differing levels of cognitive ability (as measured by the AFQT).
6. It is unclear a priori how the effects of early maternal employment might vary by family income. If the effects of 1st-year employment are due to the absence of the mother, then the effects might be most pronounced for children from higher income families in which the

mothers might be more stimulating. If the effects of 1st-year employment are due to the low quality of the care in which the child is
placed, however, and if income is correlated with quality of child
care, the effects might be most pronounced for children from lower
income families. We will test these competing hypotheses by comparing the effects of early maternal employment for children from
families of differing income levels.

7. If the effects of 1st-year employment are due to the low quality of
care in which children are placed, then the effects should be most
pronounced for children in the lowest quality care. We cannot test
this directly because we lack data on child-care quality. Instead, we
will control for child-care type, which may be correlated with quality.

Hypothesis 2: Children of mothers who work in the 1st year of life will
have poorer long-term cognitive and behavioral outcomes because during the time the mother is with the child, she is tired and stressed and
therefore is less nurturing and stimulating.

We will test this hypothesis by comparing families of different income
levels because working mothers in low-income families may face more strain
and hardship than those in higher income families. We also would like to test
this hypothesis by controlling for the home environment in the 1st year of
life, but we have no measures of this (we only have measures of the concurrent
home environment starting at age 3).

Hypothesis 3: Children of mothers who work in the 1st year of life
may have poorer long-term cognitive or behavioral outcomes because
of other omitted factors that are correlated with mothers' employment
(e.g., single parenthood, fathers not working, mothers entering and
exiting the labor force).

We test this hypothesis by controlling for an extensive set of child and
family characteristics, including single parenthood and by comparing the
effects of 1st-year maternal employment in families where fathers do or do
not work and in families where mothers work continuously compared with
families where mothers transition in and out of the labor market.

There are several other hypotheses that we are not able to test with the
data at hand. These include hypotheses that focus on child-care characteristics, such as stability and quality; job characteristics, such as low wages, poor
working conditions, low satisfaction, and nonstandard working hours; and
maternal mental health and role strain.

Implicit in each of our hypotheses is the idea that the effects of early
maternal employment on cognitive or behavioral outcomes might be sustained. That is, we might see effects persisting to the latest year when we
observe our sample, at ages 7 and 8. This possible persistence of effects raises
the question of whether these effects might be moderated by subsequent experiences. Although a full examination of moderating effects is beyond the scope
of this study, we do control for subsequent maternal employment, years spent
living in a single-mother family, and whether the family was ever poor. We

also explicitly examine whether the quality of the home environment starting at age 3 has a moderating effect, given prior evidence on the importance of home environment for child development.

Data and Method
Data

Our main samples are composed of all the White and African American children in the NLSY whom we can follow, with no missing data on any outcome variables, from ages 3 and 4 in 1986 to ages 7 and 8 in 1990. Because there are missing data on PIAT scores for some children and because a number of children (the children of the disadvantaged White oversample) were dropped in 1990, the resulting samples are quite small ($n = 244$ for Whites, $n = 218$ for African Americans). Following Baydar and Brooks-Gunn (1991), we do not analyze Hispanic children because the tests, which were mainly administered in English, may not be reliable for them.

Our sample of children is not a random sample of all children born in 1982 and 1983. Rather, it represents children born in those years to the young women in the NLSY, who ranged in age from 17 to 26 at the time of their child's birth. Consequently, our sample consists of children of relatively young mothers, who will tend to have lower educational levels and lower incomes.

We also conducted supplementary analyses of a somewhat larger sample, the non-Hispanic White children whom we can follow with no missing data from age 3 and 4 in 1986 to age 5 and 6 in 1988; the main difference is that this sample includes children from the White disadvantaged oversample that was dropped in 1990. The results from this larger sample are consistent for the most part with the results for our main sample.

Measures

Maternal employment.   We use the detailed maternal employment information in the NLSY to establish the employment status of a mother during each year of her child's life. The following six measures were constructed: employed during the 1st year of life (coded as 1 if the mother worked any hours at all during the child's 1st year); employed during the 2nd or 3rd year; employed after age 3 up to the year before assessment; currently working; quarter of the 1st year that maternal employment began; and full-time–part-time work in the 1st year, with full-time defined as working 21 or more hours per week. The usual cut-off point of 35 hours for full-time was not used because we assume that very young children are more sensitive to the quantity of time a mother spends with them than are school-aged children. In addition, scholars have found that mothers working more than 20 hours are associated with poorer cognitive outcomes for children.

Parental presence and work status.   Six categories were constructed to represent all possible combinations of the mother's working status and father's presence and working status in the 1st year of a child's life: working mother and no father (7.0%), working mother and nonworking father (2.5%), working mother and working father (43.9%), nonworking mother and no father (7.8%), non-working mother and nonworking father (0.8%), and nonworking mother and working father (38.0%).

Home environment. The Home Observation for Measurement of the Environment-Short Form was used. This scale, which was scored by either maternal report or interviewer observation, measures the degree to which the child's home environment provided emotional support and cognitive simulation. The earliest information is from 1986 when the children were aged 3 to 4. We use information from the 1986, 1988, and 1990 HOME scores to investigate the effects of contemporary HOME environment on children's achievements. The mean scores for Whites and Blacks were 103 (with *SD* of 13) and 92 (with SD of 14), respectively.

Child care. Child-care arrangements during the first 3 years of a child's life were asked of the mothers retrospectively at the time of the 1986 survey. We categorize the primary child-care arrangement during the 1st year of the child's life as follows: parental care (care by mother or father); relative care (care by sibling, grandparent, or other relative); nonrelative care (care by someone other than a relative, whether in home or not); or center care (day-care center, group care center, nursery school, or preschool). As noted earlier, an important limitation of the NLSY data on child care is the absence of information pertaining to the quality of child care. Thus, our child-care results must be interpreted with caution.

Sociodemographic variables. Children and families' sociodemographic characteristics have substantial effects on children's cognitive ability, as evidenced by previous studies. Thus, we also controlled for gender, having older siblings, ever having lived in poverty, and years living in a single-parent family. To compare families at various income levels, three dummy variables were constructed to represent poverty (income-to-needs ratio ≤ 1), low income (income-to-needs ratio > 1 and ≤ 2), and middle income and higher (income-to-needs ratio > 2) in the 1st year of life. Mother's cognitive ability, as measured by the Armed Forces Qualification Test (AFQT; Bock & Mislevy, 1981) score, was included to not only capture the effect of mother's intelligence on a child's cognitive outcomes, but also to control for its possible effect on selection into the labor force.

Child's achievement and receptive vocabulary outcomes. The Peabody Picture Vocabulary Test-Revised was used to measure children's verbal ability at ages 3 and 4, and the Peabody Individual Achievement Test. Math and Reading Recognition are used to measure math and verbal achievement respectively for children at ages 5 and 6 and at ages 7 and 8. Thus, we are using different tests to compare children's cognitive outcomes at different points in time. Because the PPVT-R correlates significantly with other measures of verbal intelligence and with measures of reading and math achievement, however, these variables should allow us to assess the influence of maternal employment on the cognitive development of a child over time while still using tests that are appropriate to the age of the child. The PPVT-R test assesses vocabulary knowledge in children aged 3 years and older. The PIAT-Math measures achievement in mathematics and the PIAT-Reading Recognition assesses the attained reading knowledge of children aged 5 years or older. (We do not use PIAT-Reading Comprehension because many 5- to 6-year-olds have missing values, as their scores were lower than the national PIAT sample. The mean of PPVT-R score for Whites is 96.55 (*SD* 16.40), and it is 73.66 (*SD* 18.47) for Blacks. The mean of PIAT-Math score for Whites is about 102 (*SD* 12), and it is about 95 (*SD* of 12) for Blacks. The mean of PIAT-Reading Recognition for Whites is about 106 (*SD* 13), and it is about 101 (*SD* 11) for Blacks.

Behavioral problems.   The Behavioral Problems Index measures six dimensions of behavior problems (antisocial behavior, anxiousness/depression, headstrongness, hyperactivity, immaturity, and dependency). We use the total BPI score, as well as two subscales (internalizing and externalizing problems). This measure was collected only for children aged four or older. The two subscales used in the analysis have Cronbach's alpha of .70 and .84.

Empirical Strategy

Our statistical procedure is multiple regression, estimated using ordinary least squares. We regress the child's PPVT-R score at ages 3 or 4 and the PIAT-Math and Reading Recognition scores at ages 5 or 6 and at ages 7 or 8 on a set of demographic and socioeconomic family background variables, together with alternative sets of variables describing the mother's employment behavior over the child's early lifetime. We examine not only the impact of early maternal employment per se, but also the impact of the timing and the extent of early maternal employment. We also examine some moderating effects. We then turn to similar models where we estimate the effects of early maternal employment on the BPI and its two subscales.

Empirical Results

Does Early Maternal Employment Affect Cognitive Outcomes, and Do These Effects Vary by Race or Ethnicity?

. . . Consistent with previous studies, maternal employment in the 1st year of life has a significant negative effect on the PPVT-R score at age 3 or 4, reducing the score by 7 points at those ages. The results for the White children at age 5 to 6 and age 7 to 8 indicate that the negative effects of 1st-year maternal employment persist over time. Looking at the PIAT results, having a mother who worked in the 1st year lowers math achievement by 5 points at age 7 to 8 and lowers reading recognition by about 5 points at both age 5 to 6 and age 7 to 8. Subsequent maternal employment, in contrast, is mainly positive; in particular, having a mother who worked in the 2nd or 3rd year largely offsets the effects of 1st-year employment for reading at age 5 to 6 and age 7 to 8.

The results for African Americans . . . are quite different, with no significant effects of maternal employment on cognitive outcomes in any of the models. We also found no significant effects for African Americans in any of the other models that we ran, providing some support for the notion that there are important racial or ethnic differences at work here. Therefore, the rest of our analyses are reported for White children only.

Do the Effects of Early Maternal Employment Vary by When the Employment Began?

The existence of negative effects of 1st-year maternal employment for some children raises the question of whether these effects are more pronounced if they occur during earlier periods within the 1st year. . . . With everything else held constant, timing within the 1st year may matter. The results for PPVT-R at age 3 to 4 suggest that starting employment before the 4th quarter of the year could lower a child's PPVT-R score by 7 points, whereas starting employment in the 4th quarter has no significant effect. The results for other outcomes at other ages further indicate that the strong negative effect for White children of the mother entering the labor force before the 4th quarter persists over time.

Do the Effects of Early Maternal Employment Vary by the Mothers' Hours?

We also examined whether the effects of maternal employment varied by women's full-time versus part-time working status in the 1st year. The results . . . suggest that the effects of working part-time in the 1st year are not significantly different than the effects of working full-time. The analysis was also reestimated using mother's continuous working hours; the results are not significant.

Do the Effects of Early Maternal Employment Vary by the Child's Gender?

We also examined whether the effects of maternal employment varied by the child's gender. . . . We found no significant differences in the effects of maternal employment on cognitive outcomes by gender.

Do the Effects of Early Maternal Employment Vary by Mothers' Cognitive Ability?

To further test the hypothesis that it is the absence of a cognitively stimulating mother that leads to lower outcomes for children whose mothers work in the 1st year and that children of the more highly skilled mothers would be more affected, we use data on mothers' AFQT scores to divide our sample into quartiles of cognitive ability. We use AFQT rather than educational attainment because these scores are strongly associated with children's cognitive scores and are likely to be a better measure of these relatively young mothers' cognitive ability than their educational attainment at the time of the birth.

. . . The results of the *F* tests . . . indicate that 1st-year maternal employment has statistically significant negative effects in one of five models for children of mothers in the top quartile of AFQT scores, in three of five models for children of mothers in the 2nd quartile, and in two of five for children of mothers in the 3rd quartile; there are no significant effects for children of mothers in the lowest quartile. This pattern of results is consistent with the hypothesis above in that we find some significant effects of early maternal employment for children whose mothers are moderately to highly skilled but no significant effects for children whose mothers are very low skilled (with a mean AFQT of 41).

Do the Effects of Early Maternal Employment on Cognitive Outcomes Vary by Family Income?

As we saw earlier, children from low-income families may be more affected by early maternal employment if their mothers are more stressed or if they are placed in poorer quality child care. At the same time, children from high-income families might be more affected if they have more to lose from the absence of their mother. We tested whether the effects of early maternal employment vary by family income. . . . The *F* tests . . . indicate that 1st-year maternal employment has statistically significant negative effects in all five models for children of low-income families, compared with three of five models for middle-income families and two of five for high-income families. Thus, maternal employment has the most significant effects on cognitive outcomes for children in low-income families, as we would expect if income is correlated with child-care quality and if low child-care quality is part of the reason for the adverse effects of early maternal employment, or if mothers who work in low-income families experience greater financial strain and hardship.

Do the Effects of Early Maternal Employment Vary by Child-Care Type?

Given these results, it would be of particular interest to control for child-care quality. As noted earlier, however, we cannot do so with the NLSY. The best we can do is to control for the type of child care the child attended during the 1st year. . . . We find that relative care, nonrelative care, and center care have positive effects on PPVT-R at age 3 to 4 compared with the reference category, parental care, which might suggest that quality child care can compensate to some extent for early maternal employment.

Do Other Factors Such as Fathers' Employment Status, Single Motherhood, or Mothers' Subsequent Employment Patterns Account for the Effects of Early Maternal Employment?

Bearing in mind that these children were born in 1982 or 1983, a time when maternal employment was less typical than it is today and when the United States was undergoing a recession, . . . we tested the hypothesis that mothers' employment might be associated with fathers' employment status and that this might affect child outcomes. . . . [C]hildren from two-parent families whose mothers worked in the 1st year have lower cognitive scores than the reference group (children in two-parent families whose mothers did not work in the 1st year and whose fathers did). . . . [T]he negative effects of 1st-year maternal employment are largest for children whose fathers were present but not working, however, suggesting that there is a connection between mothers' and fathers' work in the 1st year and outcomes for children. . . . [We] compared children in single-mother families where the mother did or did not work in the 1st year. We find no significant differences between these groups (both have lower PPVT-R scores than the reference group at age 3 to 4 and lower PIAT-Math scores at age 7 to 8).

[We] examined the impact of mothers' subsequent employment status by categorizing women according to their employment across the first 3 years of the child's life. The results show that only for those women who worked in the 1st year and then left the labor force is there a significant long-term negative effect of that 1st-year employment; for those who worked in the 1st year and continued working, the effect of 1st-year employment, although still negative, is not significant after the 1st year. . . . [A]lthough White children might have higher cognitive scores at ages 3 to 4 if their mothers delayed entry into the labor force into the 2nd or 3rd year, this difference is no longer significant by the time they are age 5 to 6 and 7 to 8. This result lends some support to the hypothesis that factors other than 1st-year maternal employment (e.g., entry and exits) may account for some of the effects of maternal employment.

Does Contemporary Home Environment Moderate the Effects of Early Maternal Employment?

To test for the moderating effect of the quality of home environment, we added the contemporary HOME score to the model. In results not shown, although the home environment does have a significant positive effect on children's cognitive outcomes, no significant result was found for the interaction between HOME score and early maternal employment, and the addition of HOME scores did not reduce the effect of early maternal employment.

Does Early Maternal Employment Affect Behavioral Outcomes?

In analyses using the total BPI score . . . we find no statistically significant effects of maternal employment on White children's behavioral problems, but timing seems to matter when they are 7 to 8 years old. Specifically, entering the labor force before the 4th quarter of the 1st year has a significant effect on children's behavioral outcomes (the higher the score, the more problems).

. . . [We] compare the difference between internalizing and externalizing problems. The results indicate that 1st-year maternal employment, and entering the labor force early in the 1st year, have a significant effect only on externalizing problems, with effects at age 4 and again at ages 7 to 8.

In results not shown, we interacted gender with maternal employment but found no significant differences in these behavioral problem models; when we interacted family income with early maternal employment, we found that children in high-income families exhibit more externalizing problems at age 4 if their mothers worked in the 1st year.

Discussion and Conclusions

The empirical results in this study indicate that early maternal employment has a significant negative effect on White children's cognitive outcomes at age 3 or 4 and that these effects persist to age 7 or 8 in some instances but not in others. We found no significant effects of early maternal employment on cognitive outcomes for African American children, suggesting that the effects of early maternal employment do vary by racial and ethnic group. We can only speculate as to the reason for this difference, but one possibility is that it reflects the fact that employment of mothers of young children has been traditionally more common in African American families and therefore may be seen as more normative; that is, the context in which early maternal employment occurs may differ for different groups.

Given the small size of our sample, our results are somewhat tentative, but we found evidence that the effects we find among White children may be more pronounced for some children than others. Specifically, we found that the effects may be more pronounced for children whose mothers start work early in their 1st year of life. But we found no significant differences between children whose mothers worked full-time or part-time in the 1st year. We also found no significant differences in the effects of early maternal employment for boys and girls.

With regard to the mother's level of cognitive ability, we found some significant effects of early maternal employment on cognitive outcomes for children of mothers who had moderate to high AFQT scores. We found no significant effects for children of mothers who had very low AFQT scores (in the bottom quartile), however; these children have lower cognitive scores, as expected, but this was the case whether or not their mothers worked. This pattern of results lends some support to the hypothesis that it is the loss of a cognitively stimulating mother that accounts for some of the ill effects of early maternal employment on cognitive outcomes for children.

Comparing children from poverty, low-income, and moderate- and high-income families, we found the most significant effects of early maternal employment for the children from poverty-income families. These stronger effects may be due to the low quality of the child care they attend, to turbulence in their child-care arrangements, to the strain and hardship their mothers experience when they are working, or to a combination of these factors. We were not able to assess the impact of child-care quality because of the limitations of the NLSY data.

We found no support for the hypothesis that the effects of early maternal employment might be due to the correlation between employment and single motherhood. We did find, however, that controlling for fathers' employment status and for mothers' subsequent employment status did make a difference. Children whose mothers worked in the 1st year and whose fathers were present but did not work, and children whose mothers worked in the 1st year and then dropped out of the labor market, fared worse in terms of their long-run cognitive outcomes than did other children whose mothers worked in the 1st year of life.

Turning to moderating effects, we found that the effects of early maternal employment may be buffered for children whose families provide a nurturing and stimulating home environment. Whether they might also be buffered for children whose child-care settings are nurturing and stimulating is an important question but one that we are not able to address with the data at hand.

We also found some negative effects of 1st-year maternal employment on behavioral problems for White children, mainly at ages 7 to 8. The effects seem to be concentrated in the area of externalizing problems. We found no significant effects of 1st-year maternal employment on behavioral outcomes for African American children, again suggesting important racial and ethnic differences.

The question remains: Why are there negative effects of 1st-year maternal employment, and why do these effects persist over time for some children but not others? This study included an extensive set of controls. Nonetheless, we were still unable to control for some characteristics that might help explain the persistent effects for some children of maternal employment in the 1st year. For instance, information on the quality of child care, as well as the quality of time mothers spend with their infants, would be helpful, given previous findings on the positive effects of high-quality child care on children's cognitive outcomes.

The significant negative effects of early maternal employment found for some children in this study were not found in Harvey's recent work. The differences between these two sets of results primarily reflect the different approaches used in these two studies. The samples were different: Harvey used a larger sample but did not follow the same children over time, whereas we followed a longitudinal sample that was of necessity smaller. Most important, our study analyzed non-Hispanic White and African American children separately, whereas her study pooled Whites, African Americans, and Hispanics together. When we pooled the three racial and ethnic groups (results not shown), we, too, found much weaker links between 1st-year maternal employment and later outcomes.

The generalizability of our results is limited in that we examined children of relatively young mothers. Analyses of a more representative sample of children should be undertaken. Despite these limitations, however, our study makes a unique contribution by assessing the effects of early maternal employment on children's cognitive and behavioral outcomes over time. Our findings that 1st-year maternal employment has negative effects on cognitive outcomes for White children and that these effects persist in some instances to ages 7 and 8 merit further research, as does the suggestion that there may be some longrun effects on behavioral problems for White children as well. The negative effects we found are fairly small. Nonetheless, if for some children these effects occur in addition to those associated with other risk factors, such as poverty or a nonemployed father, the cumulative effects may be of concern.

Proponents of family leave legislation have argued that such laws will improve maternal and child health. Our results suggest that giving parents the right to longer periods of parental leave might improve some children's cognitive and behavioral outcomes as well. In this regard, research on the impact on child outcomes of the recently adopted U.S. Family and Medical Leave Act, and of the more generous family leave legislation in place in other countries, would be welcome. Nonetheless, we are mindful that there is a good deal of variation in preferences and outcomes among families and that the effects of early maternal employment will depend on many contextual factors. Therefore, we also recommend more research on child-care quality and policy initiatives designed to raise the quality of child care provided to infants.

Thomas M. Vander Ven, Francis T. Cullen,
Mark A. Carrozza, and John Paul Wright

 NO

Home Alone: The Impact of Maternal Employment on Delinquency

In recent decades, American family life has been transformed dramatically. Family scholars debate the causes and consequences of these major changes, routinely clashing over whether family forms are changing for the better or whether our most important social institution is experiencing a moral and functional freefall.

One of the most profound changes is the unprecedented number of women who have entered the paid workforce since the 1950s. Census data show that female labor force participation rose from approximately 28 percent in 1940 to close to 60 percent in 1992. This wave of women entering the labor force was accompanied by a large increase in maternal employment. While only 16 percent of all children had working mothers in 1950, close to 70 percent of all mothers with dependent children work today. Recent estimates show that over half of those with children less than one year old are employed outside the home and over 60 percent of those with children younger than six are employed.

While the mass entrance of women and mothers into the labor market might be regarded as a sign of social progress, many Americans are worried about the trend and have been for some time. And in what may be seen as part of the "backlash" to feminist political victories, politicians, social critics, and parenting "experts" have frequently pointed to the working mother as the cause of many of our social problems.

While supporting empirical evidence is scarce, the political Right charges that feminist philosophies damage the American family by encouraging women to choose work and self-fulfillment over family obligations. Additionally, noted psychologists argue that the neglected child of the working mother may suffer from an attachment disorder, which is widely believed to be a major causal factor in the production of extreme child behavior problems. One pediatrician and TV personality warns that mothers should stay home to raise their infants or risk the disruption of the critical mother-child bonding period: "if he doesn't have that through infancy, it's hard to put it in later . . . and these kids that never get it . . . will become difficult in school, they'll never succeed in school, they'll make everybody angry, they'll become delinquents later and eventually they'll become terrorists."

From *Social Problems*, vol. 48. no. 2, May 2001, pp. 236–257 (refs. and notes omitted). Copyright © 2001 by University of California Press. Reprinted by permission via Rightslink.

Although there is no shortage of claims that maternal employment causes negative child outcomes, there is little evidence that this is the case. Recent research shows that the children of working mothers are no less attached than other children and that they experience no deficits in social, emotional, or behavioral functioning. While no work and family issue attracts more scholarly attention than the potential effects of maternal employment on children's development, few researchers have investigated the possible link between working mothers and delinquency.

In this context, we analyze the impact of maternal employment—of kids being left "home alone"—on delinquency using models that include different characteristics of maternal employment (e.g., hours, workplace controls), variations in maternal non-employment (e.g., welfare reliance), and child care arrangements. Our analysis is influenced by the research program of Parcel and Meneghan, who investigated the impact of various dimensions of parental work on a range of social, cognitive, and behavioral outcomes. Similarly, we test models that consider the number of hours usually employed, working conditions, and the timing of work. This more comprehensive measurement of maternal work improves upon past research on maternal employment and delinquency, where mother's work was simply divided into "working mother" and "nonworking mother" categories.

Furthermore, in an attempt to isolate the independent effects of maternal work, we simultaneously consider the impact of maternal resources (i.e., maternal cognitive skills, maternal education, family income), child care arrangements, and marital status. By controlling for maternal resources, we are better able to isolate the independent effects of maternal employment.

Maternal Employment and Delinquency

Previous Delinquency Research

Although there is a tremendous body of literature on the effects of maternal employment on child outcomes, studies on the link between maternal work and delinquency are relatively scarce. Early researchers tended to find a small positive effect of maternal employment on delinquency, which they usually assumed was the consequence of low maternal supervision. Most contemporary researchers found little or no connection between maternal work status and delinquency. Other studies suggest that delinquency is less common among the children of regularly employed mothers. In some cases, maternal work actually served as insulation against delinquent risks because working mothers effectively raised the family income, thus improving the living conditions of their children. Maternal employment, then, should be considered as an economic dimension of family life and may be most beneficial for children when the alternative is poverty or welfare dependency.

When examined closely, the extant literature on maternal employment and delinquency suggests that working conditions are an important factor that must be included in analytical models. Glueck and Glueck, for example, found that delinquency was highest among the children of occasionally employed mothers. This finding is provocative because occasional or sporadic work may be indicative of secondary labor market employment. Employment in the secondary labor market is often erratic and coercive due to the vulnerability of the low-skilled, uneducated workers at this level. Such employment may be criminogenic if coercive workplace experiences negatively shape parenting techniques.

In a related vein, Roy found that maternal work was related to delinquency in urban settings, but not in rural areas. This effect, also, may reflect important differences between working conditions in urban vs. rural communities. It may be that maternal work in urban centers and among minority populations is, on average, more likely to be coercive, secondary labor market work. In light of these findings, better measures of maternal employment—including measures for workplace controls and regularity of employment (part-time vs. full-time) are needed.

Maternal Employment and the Pathways to Delinquency

Concerns about the effects of maternal employment suggest that working mothers are less able to supervise, discipline, and nurture their children, which may contribute to misconduct or youth crime. The main pathway between maternal work and delinquency, then, would be a breakdown in parental responsibility. Generally, theories of delinquency divide parental responsibility into two broad categories: control and support. Guided by several strains of criminological thought, we include pathway variables that reflect both parental controls and parental supports in our analysis.

Parental control.   Control theories of delinquency emphasize the importance of both direct controls and indirect controls. Direct parental control is generally measured as the degree to which parents supervise or monitor their children's activities. Lax parental supervision has been identified as a powerful predictor of behavior problems.

The importance of indirect control mechanisms (e.g., attachment to parents) is also a common theme in criminological theory and research. Low parent-child bonding is also a well-documented path to delinquency. Thus, we trace the effects of maternal work on delinquency through both direct (i.e., supervision) and indirect parental controls (i.e., attachment).

The relationship between parental work and parent-child bonds is central to Colvin and Pauly's structural-Marxist theory of delinquency production. The authors argue that coercively controlled workers may be prone to harsh and erratic parenting styles, which include punitive discipline and lax supervision. Children who are socialized on a coercive and erratic schedule are likely to form alienated bonds to parents, which may contribute to behavior problems later on. Thus, we examine the path from workplace controls to modes of parental discipline (i.e., spanking), to supervision, and to attachment.

A breakdown in parental control may also be reflected in a child's association with delinquent peers. That is, if the children of employed mothers spend more time on average in peer interaction and if their peer relationships are less subject to parental review, we might find that delinquent peer association links maternal work to delinquency. As such, we evaluate this potential pathway by including delinquent peer association in our models.

Parental support. Cullen's social support perspective asserts that, in addition to social control, delinquency is reduced by the receipt by youths of parental social support. Because work commitment and working conditions may influence delinquency indirectly by affecting maternal support, we investigate this potential pathway by including measures of warm and responsive parenting in our models.

Similarly, Sampson and Laub suggest that social relations between individuals—between a parent and child, for example—should be seen as a form of social investment or social capital. According to this view, a parent-child relationship is a social and psychological resource that children "can draw on as they move through life transitions that traverse larger trajectories." While Hirschi depicts the parent-child bond as a psychological constraint or control on deviant impulses, Sampson and Laub describe the parent-child relationship as a matrix for support where children develop cognitive, social, and behavioral skills.

Parental support can result in the cognitive ability and emotional development a child needs to succeed in school and may lead to greater child attachment to school. Thus, if maternal employment prevents mothers from investing in children, it may indirectly result in negative school outcomes. This may be an important link between maternal work and delinquency, because low school attachment is a consistent predictor of delinquent involvement. Accordingly, we examine the indirect effect of maternal work on delinquency through school attachment.

Methodology

Sample

In the 1960s, the United States Department of Labor hired the Center for Human Resource Research at the Ohio State University to gather longitudinal data on the labor market experiences of four representative target groups among the U.S. population. A fifth cohort of men and women between the ages of 14 and 22 was identified in 1979. Known as the National Longitudinal Survey of Youth (NLSY), this project involved a multistaged stratified random sampling that produced 12,686 subjects, 11,404 of whom were interviewed annually about their occupational, educational, familial, and childbearing experiences.

By 1994, 10,042 children of sample mothers were identified to report on their home environment, family relations, and school experiences in addition to taking a number of inventories designed to measure cognitive and socio-emotional development. To investigate the relationship between maternal work and delinquency, we conduct our analysis on a sample of 707 adolescents who were between the ages of 12 and 14 in 1994. These children are the offspring of female respondents originally interviewed in 1979. Each of these respondents completed the Child Self-Administered Supplement (CSAS) in 1992 and in 1994. This self-report booklet collects information on a wide range of variables including child-parent interaction, peer relationships, and involvement in various delinquent activities.

Additionally, the children of the NLSY mothers were studied every other year beginning in 1986, so data on various developmental outcomes are available from early childhood up through early and middle adolescence for this sample. To study the effects of both early and current maternal employment on delinquency, we follow this sample from 1994 back to 1986 when study children were between the ages of 2 and 5 years old. We selected 1986 as the study year for early employment effects because it was the first year that NLSY researchers collected extensive data on parent-child interaction and family relations. We take advantage of the longitudinal nature of the NLSY data by controlling for 1994 employment when examining the effects of 1986 employment on 1994 delinquency. By controlling for current employment, it will lend support to any assertions that the effect of early employment is independent of the effect of current employment.

The NLSY data, while presenting great possibilities for research, have their shortcomings. One limitation of these data, for example, is that over 27 percent of the children who were between the ages of 10 and 14 in 1994 were born to mothers who were less than twenty years old when they gave birth to their children. As a result, many of these mothers are less-educated and are more likely to be members of a minority group than one would find in a representative sample where maternal age is normally distributed. Because early childbearers are more prone to having children with developmental deficits, such as low cognitive ability, and are at a greater risk for criminality, these children should be considered to be a high-risk group.

While other researchers use weighted data to correct for the large number of lower socioeconomic and minority women in the sample, we perform our analysis on the unweighted sample. The NLSY guide to Child Data strongly cautions against using weighted data across years because "analyzing data from persons interviewed in multiple years creates problems since the yearly weights are not appropriate to such a universe." Using the weighted data in regression equations that represent longitudinal effects, then, may result in substantial miscalculations of standard errors. Guo argued that bias can be reduced in the unweighted sample by controlling for those characteristics that are overrepresented, such as race, maternal education, and an assessment of mother's cognitive ability. Controls for each of these variables are included in each of our analytical models. As a check on our results, we also performed our main analyses using weighted data. The relationships between variables did not differ substantially when using the unweighted rather than the weighted sample. All reported results, hereafter, reflect the unweighted analysis.

. . . Correlation matrix analysis and tolerance tests did not detect the presence of multicollinearity between any two independent measures. Mean replacement was used to address missing values. The main analysis was also estimated without mean replacement. No substantial differences were found.

Dependent Variable: Delinquency

The 1994 CSAS includes nine highly correlated items that assess involvement in deviant and delinquent acts. Five of the items measure relatively minor to moderate acts of youth deviance: breaking parents' curfew, dishonesty (i.e., lying to a parent), school problems (i.e., parent came to school because of child behavior), truancy, and staying out all night. The other four items involve more serious acts of lawbreaking: alcohol abuse, vandalism (i.e., damaged school property on purpose), store theft, and violence (i.e., hurt someone badly enough to need bandages or a doctor). These nine items are summed to create our scale measuring youth deviance and delinquency (alpha = .78).

The respondents were asked to report on their involvement in each of these behaviors over the last twelve months. If the children reported that they had no involvement in any given act, that variable received a score of 0. If the respondent was involved in that activity over the past year, the variable received a score of 1. Measuring delinquent involvement in this way is common in the delinquency literature. We should note, however, that we also conducted our analyses using the same delinquency scale but with involvement measured by the number of times the respondent committed each act (i.e., the frequency score). The results of this investigation did not differ from results produced by the main analysis.

This measure of delinquency is skewed towards non-offending. Nearly 25 percent of the adolescent sample reported no involvement in any of the nine items used to create the scale. Furthermore, over 75 percent of the sample reported involvement in no more than three of the nine items used to construct the index. This variable is transformed into a new measure equal to the natural logarithm of the delinquency variable in order to increase the explainable variance in delinquency.

Independent Variables

Maternal employment status. A continuous measure of hours usually worked is used in this analysis. In past studies, investigators assigned missing values to work-hour variables for non-employed mothers, who were then excluded from the analysis. Thus, these studies focused on the effects of paid maternal employment among a sub-group of working mothers only. Other studies include non-employed mothers but as a dummy category that is used in equations with other dummy variables capturing increasing levels of time commitment to paid employment (e.g., part-time, full-time, over-time). Measuring maternal work hours via a series of dummy variables is arguably a good strategy for organizing information and for detecting non-linear effects. As Harvey points out, however, this method is problematic because the dummy categories are formed from continuous variables so there are infinite ways one could create categories and arbitrary boundaries between categories are often created. Moreover, using continuous variables does not prevent the detection of nonlinear effects. Based on this rationale, we use a continuous measure of hours worked in our primary analysis.

In order to compare nonworking mothers to working mothers on various pathway and delinquency variables, we assign nonworking mothers mean values for work hours. As suggested by Menaghan, et al., we run models where dummy variables are employed to capture employment status (i.e., welfare, coercive, technical, and bureaucratic work controls) while substituting mean values for the continuous variable measuring work-role conditions (i.e., hours worked) for nonworking mothers. Regression estimates for the continuous hours variable will reflect the effects for working mothers, and coefficients for the occupational class dummy variables will "reflect the contrast between that group and the reference category, evaluated at average conditions on the continuous variables."

One might argue that assigning the mean hours worked to non-employed mothers blurs the analysis since the main objective here is to examine the impact of real differences (e.g., the effects of zero hours of employment vs. the effects of forty hours of employment) in maternal work commitment. To bolster confidence in our measure of work hours, we conducted separate analyses where nonworking mothers were assigned zeros for work hours. No substantive differences in the results were found. Furthermore, consistent with Parcel and Menaghan's usual strategy, we also measure work hours with a series of dummy variables capturing part-time, full-time, and overtime work schedules in a separate analysis. Again, our results did not differ from results produced using the continuous measure of work hours. In all analyses, nonworking mothers (those who neither worked nor received welfare in the previous year) serve as the reference category.

To identify welfare-reliant mothers, we use a dummy variable, which is coded as 1 if the respondent reported that she did not work during the survey week and if the respondent answered affirmatively to the question, "Did you or your spouse receive income from AFDC in the past calendar year?" In this way, we distinguish between those who draw income primarily from welfare and those who may draw welfare but participate in the workforce as well.

Current employment is measured in 1992. We used the 1992 work variables and controls in the current effects model because the delinquency items ask respondents to report on delinquency involvement over the previous 12 months. Therefore, to approximate the temporal order of our conceptual model, we chose to measure employment status in the year preceding the reported delinquency.

Finally, we construct measures of father's employment to examine the relative effects of father's work as compared to mother's work. Father's work is measured as the paid employment of spouses who are co-residing with the family— biological fathers and stepfathers are counted equally. We assign them work hours values and occupational class classifications drawn from maternal reports in the NLSY data.

Occupational class.   We measure occupational class in two ways. First, following Parcel and Menaghan, we construct a 19-item-based occupational complexity scale by matching occupational titles reported by NLSY respondents to job descriptions reported in the Dictionary of Occupational Titles. As stated above, we estimate models using this measure of job complexity along with dummy variables for part-time, full-time and overtime hours. Our primary strategy, however, involves the use of a series of dummy variables capturing workplace controls, as outlined below, along with a continuous measure of work hours. We should note that our results did not differ when substituting the job complexity measure for our workplace control dummy variables.

Our primary measure of workplace conditions is developed based on the work of Mark Colvin. Drawing from Kohn and Edwards, Colvin links the workplace controls experienced by parents to the patterns and styles of control parents exert upon children. Unskilled, non-unionized employees (Fraction I workers) are subjected to "simple control" in the workplace, which is coercive and alienating. Simple control involves exacting worker compliance through the threat of job termination. This type of control is then reproduced in the home through erratic, harsh, and punitive parenting. Children who are raised under these conditions may be likely to form an alienated bond with authority, which frees them to behave in anti-social and delinquent ways.

Skilled laborers and craftspersons (Fraction II workers), who often belong to labor unions, experience greater job security and are controlled via "technical control"—the machine-paced atmosphere of manufacturing and industrial workplaces where workers are motivated to produce by wage increases and job security. Workers who are controlled by "technical control" will be more likely to control their children through extending and suspending rewards and punishments, which results in the formation of calculative bonds to authority in children. Such children are less likely to be involved in serious delinquency than the children of Fraction I workers.

Fraction III workers are those skilled workers, technicians, salaried professionals, and supervisory staff who experience greater self-direction, job complexity, and job security in the workplace. Fraction III workers are controlled in a bureaucratic fashion which relies on the power of normative pressure to control workers. These workers are heavily invested in the rules of the organization due to their favored status and, as a result, tend to be self-regulating employees. Due to high levels of autonomy in the workplace, Fraction III workers are positively bonded to authority, which they reproduce in their children through a steady and consistent style of parenting. Children of Fraction III workers are least likely to deviate from rules and laws due to their strong, normative bond with authority.

Colvin and Pauly's class fraction scheme provides a simple and parsimonious method for linking general job conditions to family life and to delinquency. For that reason, we measure working conditions by assigning each NLSY mother an occupational class value. First, using occupational codes in the NLSY data, we make an initial assessment about class fraction membership based on the presumed skill-level, autonomy, and job stability of each occupation. Fraction I workers are those unskilled, non-union workers found in agricultural labor, small-manufacturing firms, retail and food services, household domestic work, low-level clerical jobs (e.g., stock clerk) and sales (e.g., shoe sales, retail). All NLSY workers whose occupational titles fit the above description were placed in Fraction I. Those assigned to Fraction II include skilled blue-collar workers (e.g., welders, plumbers, steelworkers, auto assemblers), skilled clerical workers (e.g., secretaries), craftsworkers, and low-level supervisors (e.g., foreman). Fraction III status was assigned to professionals, technicians, managers, government workers, and proprietors.

Family income. Total family income is included in all models. By employing a family income measure, we are able to assess the impact of mother's employment experiences while controlling for the total standard of living of each family included in the analysis. Controlling for family income helps to isolate the independent effects of occupational variables in the analysis.

Child care. Following Parcel and Menaghan, we measure child care with a series of dummy variables. Dummy variables representing professional daycare settings, childcare provided by a relative (including fathers), and childcare provided by a non-relative are included.

Pathway Variables

The NLSY was designed primarily to study labor market experiences across the life course. Because it was not constructed as a criminological data set, some of our measures, although reasonable, are not ideal. Further, although scales are available to measure some variables, for other constructs we used one-item measures. In these instances, the results should be viewed with appropriate caution. All pathway variables are measured in 1986 for the early models and 1992 for the current models. All scales are constructed using a simple summing of the component items.

Supervision. Criminologists commonly operationalize parental supervision as the degree to which parents know the whereabouts of children when they are away from home and who they are with when away from home. We employ a similar measure of supervision found in the CSAS. The one-item measure is a four-point scale reflecting the child's report on how often "your mother knows who you are with when not at home."

Attachment. Attachment is often measured by items that relate to a child's feelings of closeness, love, or admiration for a parent. It is difficult to measure attachment among young children because they are unable to answer standard survey questions. The NLSY data, however, contain mother-reported items related to the insecure behaviors exhibited by children. Mothers were asked if their 2 to 5 year-olds were difficult to soothe or calm, anxious and or worried when left alone, prone to crying when left alone, or tended to need help with most things. Attachment in young children is often studied via mother-reported assessments of child behavior. Our insecure attachment index has a reliability of .61. To measure attachment in adolescence, we use a one-item question drawn from the CSAS that asks, "How close do you feel to your mother?"

Maternal support.   In the present analysis, we measure maternal support at two intervals—in 1986 when study children were in their pre-school years and in 1992 in early adolescence. Past researchers using the NLSY data captured expressive maternal support, from mother to children, with a warmth and responsiveness scale. Our warmth and responsiveness scale is an adaptation of the measure used by Menaghan, et al. This five-item index is drawn from interviewer observations of the warmth and responsiveness shown by mothers toward children. Interviewers observed whether or not mothers: spoke simultaneously to their child twice or more, responded verbally to child's speech (excluding scolding), answered child's questions or requests verbally, caressed, kissed, or hugged the child at least once, or conveyed positive feelings about the child. The reliability of the warmth and responsiveness scale is .79.

To examine maternal support in adolescence, we use a five-item index drawn from interviewer observations of maternal treatment of children in the home. This index is similar to the warmth and responsiveness scale used for pre-school children, but the items are tailored for school-age children. The items include whether mothers: encouraged the child to talk, answered child's questions, spoke with child, introduced the child to the interviewer by name, or used a loving voice toward child. The reliability of this scale is .76.

Spanking.   Punitive parenting, such as corporal punishment, is associated with negative behavioral outcomes in children. Some scholars argue that the causal relationship between physical discipline and child behavior has yet to be untangled. Child misbehavior and physical punishment, that is, are likely to be related reciprocally. Other researchers claim that early physical discipline is independently related to misbehavior later on. We measure early maternal spanking with an item that asks mothers to report the number of times they spanked their child during the last week. This NLSY item was used by previous researchers interested in the maternal characteristics associated with spanking.

Delinquent peer association.   Delinquent peer association is generally captured through survey questions tapping into the number of delinquent friends possessed by the respondent. Johnson, Marcos, and Bahr argue that the differential association process should not be seen simply in terms of the kinds of people one associates with, but should also consider the *situational pressures* that go along with associating with certain types. The process, then, is best evaluated by gaining measures on the amount of pressure to be delinquent exerted by one's friends. The CSAS asked youth to report whether they felt pressure from friends to try cigarettes, drugs, alcohol, skip school, or commit crime or do something violent. We combine these items into a scale ranging from 0 to 5, with 5 being the highest degree of delinquent pressure. The reliability of this scale is .79.

School attachment.   Following Wiatrowski, Griswold, and Roberts', we focus on level of satisfaction with school as the measure of school attachment. The response item—drawn from the CSAS—asks respondents to report their satisfaction with their school. The responses range from 1, meaning very dissatisfied, to 4, meaning very satisfied.

Maternal Resources

AFQT.   Mother's cognitive skills are estimated by her score on the Armed Forces Qualification Test, administered to all respondents in 1980. An AFQT score can be seen as an individual difference which is likely to influence a mother's life chances and those of her children similarly.

Maternal education.   Mother's educational attainment is measured as the highest grade completed by mothers as of 1992. When examining the effects of early maternal employment, education is equal to the highest grade completed as of 1986.

Structural and Family Background Factors

In all models we control for race, sex, and age of study children. Age is an interval measure and race and sex are dummy variables. Race is coded 1 = Black or Hispanic and 0 = White. In separate equations, the Black and Hispanic children were isolated from one another to examine any differences between these groups and between these groups and the white sub-group. No differences were found. Sex is coded 0 = male and 1 = female. Family structure is a measure of the presence of mother's spouse in the home. An "intact" family is a home where the mother is married and presently co-residing with her partner. Thus, biological fathers, stepfathers, and adoptive fathers are all counted equally. Intact Family is coded 0 = no marital partner in the home and 1 = marital partner present.

Neighborhood Disorder

There is a strong relationship between certain neighborhood traits, such as poverty and joblessness, and crime. Those who have unstable, low-paying, or coercively controlled jobs are more likely to live in an economically and socially impoverished community where informal controls on behavior are low. The children of sub-employed or welfare-reliant mothers may be doubly at-risk because of the effects of economic strain and because poverty constrains families to live in socially disorganized settings. Researchers interested in the negative effects of community breakdown focus on the rates of joblessness, poverty, and family breakdown in neighborhoods. Because the NLSY lacks data on the rates of these problems at the community level, we construct a measure of neighborhood disorder from maternal responses to items related to community disorder. Our scale is drawn from responses to questions about whether the neighborhood had a "problem" with crime and violence, lack of parental supervision, and abandoned or run-down buildings (alpha = .85).

Statistical Analysis

The analysis of the data is conducted through the use of ordinary least squares regression (OLS). Our strategy is to examine 1) the direct effects of maternal employment hours and of maternal employment conditions on delinquency and 2) the indirect effects of maternal work on delinquency through the delinquency pathway variables. In this model, non-employed, welfare-reliant, and employed mothers are all included. Because working conditions are captured via a series of dummy variables reflecting the three working class fractions, nonemployed mothers and welfare-reliant mothers are treated as occupational class categories.

The analytic strategy follows a three-equation process. In the first equation, we examine the direct effect of maternal employment on the delinquency pathways. In this equation, each pathway is regressed against the employment/non-employment variables while controlling for maternal resources and child characteristics (age, sex, and race).

The second equation involves regressing the delinquency index against the employment/non-employment variables with mother and child control measures. The results of this equation demonstrate the direct effects of employment on delinquency without taking the delinquency pathways into consideration.

In the third, and final, equation, the delinquency index is regressed against maternal employment and the delinquency pathways. This equation produces estimates for the direct effects of all preceding variables on delinquency. Furthermore, by using this strategy, the third equation produces estimates of the direct effect of maternal employment on delinquency, while controlling for the delinquency pathways.

As a complement to this main strategy, we also perform an Analysis of Moment Structures (AMOS) analysis on the main model. Structural modeling allows us to assess the total, direct, and indirect effects of maternal employment on delinquency and will serve as confirmatory evidence for the findings based on the OLS strategy.

Findings

The Impact of Early Maternal Employment on Early Pathways to Delinquency

. . . [The] results of regression models that examine the effects of early maternal employment status on insecure attachment, maternal warmth and responsiveness, and spanking, controlling for maternal resources, child characteristics, and child care arrangements [show] . . . few significant effects. Child's age is inversely related to insecure attachment, warmth and responsiveness, and mother's use of spanking. Increasing AFQT score is associated with less insecure attachment and increasing warmth and responsiveness. Finally, higher family income is related to less maternal use of spanking. None of the early employment variables are related to the early delinquency risks.

The Impact of Early Maternal Employment on Delinquency

. . . [A] multiple regression equation . . . examines the impact of early maternal employment status, with controls for mother and child background effects and child care arrangements, on the 1994 delinquency index. Current family income and current hours employed are also controlled to estimate the independent effects of early work.

. . . [C]hild's sex and child's age are both significant predictors of delinquency; females are less involved in delinquency than males, and increasing age is associated with greater involvement in delinquency. As the data show, none of the early employment variables, including welfare reliance, are significant predictors of delinquency in 1994. It should be noted, however, that a near significant effect of coercive maternal work on later delinquency appeared. When mothers were employed under coercive conditions in 1986, their children had greater involvement in delinquency in 1994. This relationship was significant at the .07 level of probability. Finally, current family income is inversely related to delinquency.

The impact of father's early and current employment status and work hours on delinquency was also examined. With professional fathers as the reference category, the effects of father's work were assessed. Controls for maternal resources, child characteristics, family income, and maternal work were included in the model. No significant effects on delinquency for either the early or current measures of paternal work were detected. Furthermore, the inclusion of paternal work measures did not change the relationships between mother's work and delinquency.

Early Maternal Employment, Early Pathways, and Delinquency

. . . [The] effects of early work, maternal resources, child characteristics, child care, and delinquency pathways on delinquency . . . [show] both child's sex and age remain significantly associated with delinquency. Introducing the pathway variables—spanking, warmth and responsiveness, and insecure attachment—does not diminish the influence of sex and age. Again, we should note that coercive maternal work during the child's early school years remains related to greater delinquency in 1994 at the .07 level. Current family income remains a significant predictor of delinquency.

Furthermore, none of the early pathway variables exhibited a significant influence on delinquent involvement. The addition of these variables did not contribute any additional explained variation over the model that consisted only of maternal resources, child characteristics, and maternal employment. In this sample, spanking, maternal warmth and responsiveness, and insecure attachment cannot be considered "pathways" to delinquency.

Current Maternal Employment and the Pathways to Delinquency

. . . [The] effects of current maternal work on five "pathways" to delinquency—supervision, delinquent peers, warmth and responsiveness, mother-child attachment, and school attachment . . . [show] older children are supervised less by mothers. . . . [Being] female is associated with greater maternal supervision, less delinquent peer association, higher attachment to mothers, and greater school attachment. Greater maternal AFQT and higher family income are linked to more warmth and responsiveness in parenting, while welfare reliance had the opposite effect. Increasing AFQT is also related to a closer mother-child bond in adolescence. Increasing family income positively influences school attachment.

Paid employment appears to share a complex relationship with maternal supervision. Employment hours are positively, but very weakly, related to supervision. This suggests that greater maternal involvement in the paid workforce results in a higher level of maternal supervision of children. On the other hand, being employed in a bureaucratically controlled setting reduces maternal supervision. Compared to non-employed mothers, female professionals are less involved in the supervision of their children. Finally, children living in a disorganized neighborhood are prone to more delinquent peer association.

The Impact of Current Maternal Employment and Delinquency

. . . [Only] child's age and child's sex are associated with delinquent involvement. According to the data, being older and being male are associated with greater involvement in delinquency. Consistent with the early employment model, none of the current employment categories exerts influence on delinquency.

The Impact of Current Maternal Employment and Delinquency

Pathways on delinquency. . . . [The] influence of mother's current employment status, delinquency pathways, and control variables on delinquency . . . shows three delinquency pathways exert direct influence on delinquency. Greater maternal supervision, lesser delinquent peer influence, and greater school attachment are associated with less delinquent involvement. That is, controlling for maternal resources, child characteristics, and mother's work, those children who are supervised more closely, those who have relatively fewer delinquent peer associations, and those more attached to school are less involved in delinquent activities. These pathways exert the most powerful influence on delinquency in the analysis.

The above analysis suggests that maternal employment had no direct effect on delinquency, but did have an indirect impact through its influence on maternal supervision. Specifically, maternal work hours are related to higher supervision, which reduces delinquency. On the other hand, working under bureaucratic controls was related to lower supervision and, thus higher delinquency. These indirect effects, though small in size, are worth noting. These findings were confirmed by an AMOS structural modeling analysis of the main model: the small effects of maternal hours and bureaucratic workplace controls on delinquency were accounted for entirely by their impact on supervision.

Discussion

Are the children of working mothers more likely to be delinquent than other children? According to past studies and to the results of our analysis, the answer is a qualified "No." The present study demonstrates that regardless of how this issue is examined, having a working mother has only a small and indirect effect on delinquency. This general pattern holds whether we considered maternal employment in a child's pre-school years or maternal work in adolescence. Furthermore, with the lone exception of maternal supervision, maternal employment has little influence on several known pathways to delinquency.

Like Parcel and Menaghan and more recent findings by Harvey, our research suggests that the widespread concern over the fates of working women and their children is largely unsupported. Rather than being a social problem whose untoward effects can be demonstrated empirically, the maternal employment-delinquency connection is better understood as a socially constructed problem. As a perceived social problem, the dark side of maternal employment has a long history in America. Fueled by scientific data on the link between early family processes and delinquency and by cherished popular beliefs in the sanctity of the "first relationship"—the coupling of mother and child—for decades politicians and social commentators have pointed to modern trends in female labor participation to explain social problems such as crime. But if the unprecedented entrance of mothers into the paid workforce is related to delinquency, it must be because working mothers fail their children by depriving them of the support and discipline they need. The current study adds to the growing literature that casts doubt on these assumptions.

Our findings suggest other notable conclusions. First, it is maternal and family resources, rather than the characteristics of maternal work, that most influence some well-known pathways to delinquency in our study. Maternal AFQT score, a measure of intellectual resources, affects both parental support and mother-child bonds in early childhood and in adolescence: mothers who draw from greater cognitive resources are more supportive in parenting and raise more securely attached children.

Although the AFQT measures an individual's intellectual capacity, it reflects the subject's developed abilities rather than a biologically assigned aptitude. The AFQT score varies with family of origin, geographic region, and years of schooling, which implies that, like maternal education, an AFQT score reflects relative social advantage or disadvantage. Our findings should be interpreted as further evidence that social disadvantage is reproduced partly through its effect on parent-child relations. Consistent with this theme, our analysis found that an important family resource, family income, exerts a positive influence on warm and responsive parenting in adolescence, while welfare reliance has the opposite effect. This relationship is consistent with past research that identified economic hardship as a strain on family functioning.

The most powerful predictors of delinquency in our analysis are maternal supervision, delinquent peer association, and school attachment. Adolescents who are supervised more closely, those who have fewer delinquent peers, and those who are more attached to school show less involvement in delinquency. This result supports a large body of research that identifies these factors as important to the production of antisocial behavioral patterns. We reiterate, here, our discovery that maternal employment had relatively little negative impact on these important pathways to delinquency.

In one instance, however, workplace controls had a small indirect effect on delinquency. Specifically, bureaucratic work controls were negatively related to maternal supervision and, thus, had a slightly positive effect on delinquency. One interpretation of this result is that professional mothers may invest more time in their careers than the average mother does which may diminish their ability to monitor children. On the other hand, the negative effect of bureaucratic controls on supervision may not reflect a difference in time spent with children so much as a difference in parenting style. The freedom and autonomy experienced by the professional parent may translate into a parenting style characterized by less overt supervision and greater attempts to equip children with internal normative controls.

Conversely, we found that maternal work hours were indirectly related to lower involvement in delinquency, through their positive effect on supervision. Again, although the effect is small, maternal work hours is actually related to greater supervision in our sample. This may be due to the stabilizing influence of steady employment on family life. As Wilson has argued, a job "constitutes a framework for daily behavior and patterns of interaction because it imposes disciplines and regularities" upon a parent.

Furthermore, while no maternal employment variable is related to delinquent peer association, neighborhood disorder is. This finding is consistent with social disorganization theory: the breakdown of informal neighborhood controls leaves children at a greater risk for being socialized in intimate delinquent peer groups. It is instructive that our analysis points to community breakdown, as it operates through delinquent peer influence, as a cause of delinquency rather than family breakdown related to the absence of a working mother.

Finally, if improving family life is a goal of crime control policy, it would make good sense to aim at addressing the structural factors that limit maternal and family resources and that contribute to community disorder. Our study suggests that policy debates should avoid ideological attacks on working mothers, which portray them as leaving their children "home alone," and concentrate instead on the economic and educational inequalities that weaken families and neighborhoods.

EXPLORING THE ISSUE

Does Maternal Employment Have Negative Effects on Children's Development?

Critical Thinking and Reflection

1. Vander Ven, Cullen, Carrozza, and Wright include several factors in their pathway to delinquency variable for children. In your opinion, which of these factors seem to have the greatest impact? Based on that, what would you suggest as protective factors for those issues?
2. Why do Han, Waldfogel, and Brooks-Gunn conclude that negative effects of maternal employment were found for white children, but not for African American children.
3. What are some creative ways that you can identify that would allow moms who want to stay home to raise their children to do so, as well as to give social support to those moms who want to work outside the home?
4. What do you consider to be the biggest influence on mothers' decision making about whether or not they should work outside of the home?

Is There Common Ground?

Han, Waldfogel, and Brooks-Gunn found that children whose mothers worked when they were infants had lower achievement on verbal and math skills. Vander Ven, Cullen, Carrozza, and Wright found no ill effects on children whose moms worked in the baby's first year. It is obvious that there are other factors to be considered.

Families must have discussions about the type of care that they want for their children, and how they can accommodate their lifestyles to obtain that care. And, society must take action to support mothers in whatever choice they make by providing quality child care for those who work and supportive leave policies and social support systems for those who do not.

Additional Resources

Columbia University School of Social Work. (2010). New Evidence on First-Year Maternal Employment and Child Outcomes. Retrieved on March 8, 2011, from http://www.columbia.edu/cu/ssw/news/jul10/maternity.html.

An article posted on the Internet that provides a more nuanced understanding of how maternal employment might impact children.

Parenthood in America. (1998). The Effects of the Mother's Employment on the Family and the Child. Retrieved on March 8, 2011, from http://parenthood.library.wisc.edu/Hoffman/Hoffman.html#top.

An article posted on the Internet that provides information on maternal employment trends throughout the years and discusses multiple factors that impact the effects of maternal employment on children.

USA Today (Society for the Advancement of Education). (2011). Positive Effects of Working Mothers—Brief Article. Retrieved on March 8, 2011, from http://findarticles.com/p/articles/mi_m1272/is_2659_128/ai_61586736/.

An article posted on the Internet that discusses some positive effects that have been identified for mothers who work.

ISSUE 3

Should Scientists Be Allowed to Clone Children?

YES: Kyla Dunn, from "Cloning Trevor," *The Atlantic Monthly* (June 2002)

NO: Robert A. Weinberg, from "Of Clones and Clowns," *The Atlantic Monthly* (June 2002)

Learning Outcomes

After reading this issue, you should be able to:

- Describe the goals that ACT hopes to accomplish through cloning.
- Summarize the political and monetary challenges that ACT faces.
- Discuss the ethical and moral concerns that cloning raises.

ISSUE SUMMARY

YES: Kyla Dunn, a former biotech researcher and now a reporter for PBS and CBS, details the six months that she spent with scientists inside the labs of Advanced Cell Technology (ACT), a group openly pursuing human cloning for medical purposes. Dunn outlines what the group hopes to accomplish through cloning, why the group believes that cloning is the best way to accomplish these goals, and the political and monetary trials that ACT faces.

NO: Robert A. Weinberg, a member of the Whitehead Institute for Biomedical Research and a biology professor at MIT, offers his concerns about what he calls the "cloning circus." Weinberg discusses the damage that many cloning groups have been doing to serious research and the impending dangers of reproductive cloning.

With several cloning groups claiming to have cloned humans, society's debate over cloning is becoming even more heated. On one side there are conservative politicians, clergymen, scientists, and many members of the American public who believe that cloning is ethically wrong. On the other side are other scientists who have invested their professional lives toward cloning research and people suffering from degenerative diseases whose lives may be saved through therapeutic cloning. Both selections in this issue discuss the distinction between therapeutic and reproductive cloning. Is one type of cloning "more ethical" than the other? One type of cloning would be used to heal people, but at the same time it would be destroying a human embryo. The other type of cloning would let the embryo live, but it could possibly tamper with the very essence of the propagation of the human race.

So, is cloning morally and ethically wrong? Is there really a difference between therapeutic and reproductive cloning? Could cloning possibly be the key to curing many diseases? Is the utilization of embryonic stem cells the only way to proceed with this science, or can adult stem cells be used? These are just a few of the myriad questions being asked about cloning. While some of the questions have definitive answers, the ethical debate over cloning does not have an easy or definite answer.

As you read the following selections, try to suspend the personal attitudes about cloning that you may have developed. Try to learn about the process of cloning, what it truly is intended to do, and what it could possibly accomplish. In addition, consider what could be the consequences of allowing cloning to occur. Some questions to consider include the following: Is a human life present in the group of indeterminable cells used for embryonic stem cell research? Would we be better off if the federal government decided to fund cloning research? Would we be better off if cloning was banned completely and totally? Is there truly a difference between the ethical dilemmas involved with therapeutic cloning and those involved with reproductive cloning?

In the following selections, Kyla Dunn gives us an inside look into the cloning labs of ACT and the circumstances of a boy whose life could possibly be saved by cloning. The scientists at ACT are trying to make medical breakthroughs that may cure many diseases. However, they must also deal with the pressure of finding adequate funding to continue their work. In addition, they live with the knowledge that on any day, governments around the world might ban their efforts altogether. Robert Weinberg contends that many cloning groups have made a "circus" out of the scientific research community. He heightens awareness of the problems with animal clones and the far-reaching consequences that these problems may have on human clones.

Can governments worldwide effectively stop the rapidly evolving technology and science of cloning? If human cloning were to be banned worldwide, would scientists throughout the world truly desist in their endeavors? Or, is the "cloning genie out of the bottle" with no possible way to return to the type of science that was practiced before cloning became possible?

YES

Kyla Dunn

Cloning Trevor

At 9:00 in the evening on January 29, just as President George W. Bush was about to begin his first State of the Union address, I gathered with three anxious scientists in a small, windowless laboratory in Worcester, Massachusetts. We were at Advanced Cell Technology—a privately owned biotechnology company that briefly made international headlines last fall by publishing the first scientific account of cloned human embryos. The significance of the achievement was debatable: the company's most successful embryo had reached only six cells before it stopped dividing (one other had reached four cells, another had reached two)—a fact that led to a widespread dismissal, in the media and the scientific community, of ACT's "breakthrough." The work was largely judged to be preliminary, inconsequential, and certainly not worthy of headlines. Many people in political and religious circles, however, had a decidedly different view. They deemed ACT's work an ethical transgression of the highest order and professed shock, indignation, and horror. . . .

Skin cell to embryo—it's one of the most remarkable quick-change scenarios modern biology has to offer. It's also one of the most controversial. Since the announcement, in 1997, of the cloning of Dolly the sheep, attempts to use human cells for cloning have provoked heated debate in the United States, separating those who have faith in the promise of the new technology from those who envision its dark side and unintended consequences.

Crucial to the debate is the fact that human cloning research falls into two distinct categories: reproductive cloning, a widely frowned-on effort that aims to produce a fully formed child; and therapeutic cloning, a scientifically reputable procedure that takes place entirely at the microscopic level and is designed to advance medical therapies and cure human ailments. The two start out the same way—with a new embryo in a petri dish. But the scientists I was observing in the lab had no intention of creating a person. Instead they were embarking on an experiment that, if successful, would be a first step toward creating radical new cures for patients like the donor of the skin cell— Trevor Ross (not his real name), a two-year-old boy afflicted with a rare and devastating genetic disease.

The mood in the lab was tense in part because of the uncertain outcome of the experiment. But it was also tense because of concern over what President Bush might say about cloning in his address to the nation. A radio in one corner of the room was tuned to the broadcast as the scientists began their work, and they were listening carefully: in perhaps no other field of science are researchers as mindful of which way the political winds are blowing. The ACT scientists had good reason to be concerned—what they were doing that night might soon be made illegal.

On July 31 of last year, by a 100-vote margin, the U.S. House of Representatives passed the Human Cloning Prohibition Act of 2001, which would impose a ban on the creation of cloned human embryos for any purpose, whether reproductive or therapeutic. Both forms of cloning would be punishable by up to ten years in prison and a million-dollar fine. The House passed the measure over the objections of a long list of biomedical organizations (including the Association of American Medical Colleges and the American Society for Cell Biology) and patients' advocacy groups. . . .

Politics and religion, it seemed, were trumping science. Therapeutic-cloning research was already ineligible for federal funding in the United States. In 1995 Congress had passed legislation barring the use of federal funds for any experiment in which a human embryo is either created or destroyed, thus making official a de facto ban that had been in existence since 1975. . . . As a result, the burden of moving many areas of important medical research forward has fallen on the private sector, a situation that by many accounts has severely hobbled research into treatments for infertility—and even disorders such as childhood cancer and birth defects. These research areas, like therapeutic-cloning research, demand the kind of long-term study and financial commitment that only the federal government can provide. This past summer human therapeutic cloning already fell squarely under the federal-funding ban, yet Congress was now going further, considering making that research illegal. . . .

Last fall, with the prospect of a Senate vote looming, I decided to take a considered look at cloning research. The time seemed right: it was a unique moment in what could be the development of a major new medical technology, an odd period of legislative limbo in which the first halting steps were being taken toward creating cloned human embryos just as such efforts were in imminent danger of being outlawed. . . .

Progress Measured in Eggs

"That's Trevor's cells," Jose Cibelli told me in the ACT cloning lab on January 23. Cibelli is the vice-president of research at ACT, and the scientist in charge of its therapeutic-cloning attempts. He's a gentle, compact man with dark hair, a trim moustache and goatee, and a vaguely worried expression. A native of Argentina, he speaks quietly and with a thick accent. . . .

The cells had come from a round plug of Trevor's skin, three millimeters across, and had arrived at ACT just five days before. The Rosses' dermatologist had chosen a crease between Trevor's buttock and thigh, where a scar would not be likely to show, and had punched down with a circular razor blade—past the dead cells of the epidermis and into the dermis, where fibroblasts grow and thrive. . . .

Cibelli now had fibroblasts for potential therapeutic-cloning experiments stored away at ACT from five patients: one with a spinal-cord injury, one with diabetes, two with healthy but aging bodies, and Trevor. But skin cells are the easy part—they're plentiful, hardy, easy to obtain and work with. Eggs are much trickier, and Cibelli had thus started measuring the likelihood of progress not in years but in eggs. "When do I think we'll get this to work?" he asked me rhetorically. "About two hundred eggs from now."

"We've gotten a handful of eggs so far," he had earlier explained. "It's a whole different game when you're talking about animal embryology versus human embryology." In the cow-cloning lab next door, for example, ACT receives 1,400 eggs on a typical day. But whereas cow eggs are available in abundance from slaughterhouses, human eggs must be obtained from young women who have undergone two weeks of hormone injections, regular visits to a doctor, and a nontrivial surgical procedure. All told, it costs ACT about $22,000 to take an egg-donation procedure from start to finish. "And the number is so small," Cibelli added. "I mean, you get ten eggs! Instead of working with a hundred embryos, I'm working with one." From July to October of last year, ACT collected a total of seventy-one eggs from seven donors—of which only nineteen were designated for cloning. That didn't leave much room for error, or much chance to tinker with conditions that might improve the chances of success. . . .

At five days of development a human embryo is smaller than a grain of sand. It's a perfectly round ball with a fluid-filled core. The internal architecture of the ball, however, is somewhat lopsided. Huddled against one wall of its interior is a group of cells known as the inner cell mass. The outside of the ball is destined to become the placenta and associated membranes; the inner cell mass is what forms a baby. But after only five days of development no cell's fate has yet been determined—it's impossible to tell which cells will become blood or muscle, skin or brain, gut or liver. All that is present is the simple raw material from which the more than 200 cell types in a human body will eventually be built.

If the inner cell mass of an embryo is removed at this early stage, it can yield cells known as human embryonic stem cells—which retain the ability to form any cell or tissue in the body. In a sense they are immortal, in that they can divide indefinitely in the lab, producing large quantities of cells. With the right coaxing those cells can theoretically be converted into an unlimited supply of tissue for transplant: new heart muscle for heart-attack survivors; insulin-secreting cells for diabetics; neurons to treat those suffering from spinal-cord injuries, the effects of stroke, or Parkinson's disease. Tissue engineers hope someday to build even more complex structures from these stem cells: new blood vessels for bypass surgery, new liver tissue, even new kidneys—all from what began as a loose collection of cells in a lab dish. They dream of a future in which all kinds of organs and tissues can be custom made to replace those ravaged by disease, injury, or a lifetime of hard use. . . .

A Radical Hope

Adrienne and Ben Ross (all names of the family members have been changed) first came to ACT late last October, ten months after their son, Trevor, and two of his cousins had received a diagnosis of X-linked adrenoleukodystrophy

(ALD), a relatively rare and underdiagnosed genetic disorder that can abruptly ravage the white matter of the brain, with devastating and often fatal results.

. . . Boys with ALD who are lucky enough to escape childhood cerebral onset are almost certain to suffer a degeneration of the spinal cord in adult-hood, which can lead to such symptoms as muscle spasms in the legs, loss of bladder control, and general weakness and stiffness. Although symptoms in adults can vary a great deal in severity, a third of adults with the disease also develop brain involvement and are reduced to a vegetative state or die within three to four years of onset. . . .

Currently, the best treatment for childhood cerebral onset of ALD is a bone-marrow or umbilical-cord-blood transplant from a healthy, well-matched donor. . . . Compatible transplant donors are extraordinarily hard to find, however—and even when suitable donors are found, the transplants don't always take. Sometimes transplants don't work because a patient's immune system rejects the transplanted cells as foreign. In other cases mature immune cells in the transplanted material actually reject and attack their new host, a life-threatening condition known as graft-versus-host disease. . . .

The Rosses had sought out ACT with the radical hope that therapeutic cloning might someday allow doctors to create a transplant that would carry no risk of rejection. The work of a bone-marrow transplant is actually done by hematopoietic stem cells—cells in the marrow that restock our blood and immune systems throughout life, serving as a reservoir of new components as old ones wear out. HSCs are also the cells that have rescued patients with ALD. What the Rosses were exploring with ACT was the idea of coaxing human embryonic stem cells, taken from cloned embryos, into forming HSCs that might someday save Trevor. . . .

⁛

What therapeutic cloning should allow scientists to do, [Michael] West explained, is provide a pure population of genetically modified cells. Use one modified cell for cloning, and the entire cloned embryo will then carry that modification. So will embryonic stem cells derived from it, and any therapeu-tic tissues they produce. Alternatively, scientists could do the modification in embryonic stem cells after cloning, and then grow a limitless supply of tissue from one properly modified cell. "We can give the patient cells that all have the same precise targeted modification," West said. "One hundred percent. We won't do that with gene therapy in our lifetime."

A therapy for Trevor isn't the only thing at stake. The stem cells derived from cloned embryos bearing an ALD mutation could be powerful research tools. In fact, scientists consider creating cloned embryos that match patients with a genetic predisposition to disease to be one of the most important thera-peutic applications of the technology, because, for one thing, it would allow diseased tissues of all kinds to be created and studied in the lab. But such work is rarely discussed in the political debate about cloning.

As she listened to West spin out optimistic future scenarios, Adrienne began to wonder if they would be able to proceed—or if using Trevor's cells for cloning would be pushing the bounds of the law as well as of science. "Can you clarify for me?" she asked, interrupting West. "On the cloning side, if you're not using federal funds, can you do what you want?"

It's understandable that she would wonder. The House's anti-cloning legislation was designed to make everything Mike West and the Rosses were discussing that day illegal. If the Senate were to pass the bill, not only could ACT's scientists be prosecuted for attempting therapeutic cloning for Trevor but Adrienne and Ben could be prosecuted for participating in such an attempt. One provision of the legislation would make it illegal even to "import" a life-saving medical therapy developed elsewhere in the world through cloning.

Adrienne's question was a sore point for West. "Yeah, we're free to do what we want," he answered simply.

"But now they're looking to try to ban that?" Adrienne asked.

West hesitated. "Well, I don't know," he said. "The Senate at some point will take this up, and my honest, best read is, I don't believe the Senate will pass it." Still, he admitted, anything could happen. "We could lose," he said, "and that would be tragic." . . .

A Public-Relations Disaster

A few weeks later ACT took a risk that could have put the company out of business—and, worse, could have closed the door on the budding field of therapeutic-cloning research. On November 9 the company e-mailed a hastily written scientific paper to *e-biomed: The Journal of Regenerative Medicine,* an online publication known for its quick turn-around time. The paper announced dryly that in ACT's lab "three somatic cell-derived embryos developed beyond the pronuclear stage." Robert Lanza, ACT's vice-president of medical and scientific development, called before the report came out to give me a translation. "The news is going to be that we have the world's first cloned human embryos," he said. "I just want to give you a heads-up—because when we make this announcement, it might bump the war [on terrorism] off the front page."

On almost every level the announcement was premature. ACT's original goal had been to publish in a prestigious journal like *Science* or *Nature,* when the company had what it is really after: human embryonic stem cells derived from a cloned embryo. ACT had nothing like that—it had managed only to sustain a cloned embryo to the six-cell stage of development.

At first, ACT's scientists say, they were uncertain whether they should publish such preliminary data. But given that they were working in an ethically fraught area of science, they decided to be as open as possible about their progress.

After Lanza called me about the imminent publication of ACT's cloning paper, I traveled to his house, on an island in a pond in central Massachusetts, to discuss the announcement. . . . He, West, and Cibelli form ACT's core triumvirate. As we sat at his kitchen table, Lanza told me that rumors in the scientific community were starting to make him nervous. Apparently the mavericks of the cloning world—those trying to produce a baby—were possibly on the verge of getting some preliminary results. "If they should come out and make some sort of an announcement first," Lanza said, "it could do severe damage. Because when it breaks, if their goal is reproductive cloning, all of the research will be banned. It will be killed—and it won't matter what we say, because no one's going to listen anymore." Last year, in fact, the outrage surrounding the mavericks' activities had directly contributed to the passage of the House anti-cloning bill.

But ACT itself also bore responsibility. On July 12, just weeks prior to the bill's passage, *The Washington Post* had broken the news that ACT was trying to create cloned human embryos as a source of stem cells—making it the only group in the country to acknowledge such plans publicly. The uproar that followed was still fresh in congressional minds at the time of the vote. Congressman Bart Stupak, of Michigan, one of the bill's co-sponsors, alluded on the day of the vote not only to the renegades but also to ACT. "The need for action is clear," he told his colleagues. "Research firms have announced their intentions to clone embryos for research purposes and then discard what is not needed."

A week before the publication of ACT's paper in *The Journal of Regenerative Medicine,* I called Thomas Okarma, the current chief executive officer of Geron, to get his views on ACT and its reputation. Despite his commitment to stem-cell and therapeutic-cloning research, Okarma was harshly critical of ACT. "They've done more harm to the field than good, I'm afraid," he told me. The most glaring example, he said, was ACT's announcement, just after Mike West joined the company, in the fall of 1998, that it was attempting to fuse human skin cells with cow eggs whose nuclear DNA had been removed. The motivation was sound: ACT was essentially hoping to do therapeutic cloning without the difficulty and expense of using human eggs—reviving experiments Jose Cibelli had started as a graduate student, in 1996, with his own cells. But, in the interest of "transparency" West released details to *The New York Times* and *48 Hours,* and two days after the news broke, President Bill Clinton, "deeply troubled" by the work, asked the head of his National Bioethics Advisory Commission to investigate. By an unfortunate coincidence, one week before the *48 Hours* broadcast, scientists had announced that they had derived human embryonic stem cells for the first time—news that made ACT's announcement seem like me-too publicity.

The cow-human embryos turned out to be "just plain duds," according to West, and ACT has never generated enough data for a significant scientific paper. (Members of the scientific community had predicted this outcome, although researchers in China have recently claimed success using rabbit eggs.) But the damage was done, because the public entirely misinterpreted the experiments. "Religious fundamentalists who, you know, are against reproductive and therapeutic cloning anyway, are using this example," Okarma told me. "'My God,' they say, 'these people are going to make chimeric creatures—mixing cows and humans.' It creates a fantasied negative scenario that casts an umbra on all of us working in the field, and makes it harder for the field to advance. And it's well documented in the scientific literature that fusing cells from two such distantly related species will not work." Okarma was not alone in dismissing ACT: the company's "publication by press release" was widely attacked by other scientists as irresponsible and insubstantial.

He added, "It's not in the same category as the Raëlians"—a religious group, inspired by "revelations" from extraterrestrials, that is working on reproductive cloning—"because there are certainly legitimate scientists at ACT trying to do this work, okay? But from the perspective of the regulatory bodies, they are in the same spaceship." . . .

"An Incredible Gift to Mankind"

. . . The most frequent refrain among political opponents of therapeutic cloning, and of human embryonic-stem-cell research in general, is that adult stem cells are a better choice for the development of medical therapies. Like cells from cloned embryos, adult stem cells are a perfect genetic match for a patient. Unlike embryonic cells, however, they can be found in the tissues of the patient's own body—a fact that prompted Senator [Sam] Brownback [of Kansas], after ACT's announcement, to insist on CNN that adult-stem-cell research is "a much better route to go." Opponents of therapeutic cloning wonder why there's a need to work with embryonic cells at all, since adult stem cells aren't rejected by the immune system, can produce a wide variety of body tissues, and do not require destroying embryos.

A report released by the NIH last July provided some answers, pointing out most adult stem cells are rare, may be difficult or dangerous to harvest from patients, and have a limited capacity to divide in the laboratory, which means that they can't yet be grown in large enough quantities to be of therapeutic value. What's more, adult stem cells have not been found for all types of tissue. . . .

"When there's this ethics debate about adult versus embryonic stem cells and cloning," Mike West told me, "I don't think what's properly weighed in the balance is the amazing breakthrough that this is. I mean, the idea that you can take a person of any age—a hundred and twenty years old—and take a skin cell from them and give them back their own cells that are young! Cells of any kind, with any kind of genetic modification! That's such an incredible gift to mankind! For the U.S. Congress to spend two hours and debate this and say, 'Oh, we'll make all this illegal,' to me is unbelievable. They don't understand." He shook his head. "We've never been able to do anything like this before."

Malcolm Moore's [a specialist in blood-cell development at the Memorial Sloan-Kettering Institute, in Manhattan] main concern is that Congress will shut the door on this research before its full benefits are known—if they indeed exist. "Basically," he told me, "my plea is, don't close down an avenue of research that might be of value in the future in the treatment of human disease. Time, science, and medical practice will be the ultimate proofs of whether these strategies are going to benefit mankind."

Bob Lanza put things more enthusiastically. "I'd stake my life on it," he said. "If this research is allowed to proceed, by the time we grow old, this will be a routine thing." He pounded the table we were sitting at, for emphasis. "You'll just go and get a skin cell removed at the doctor's office, and they'll give you back a new organ or some new tissue—a new liver, a new kidney— and you'll be fixed. And it's not science fiction. This is very, very real."

Breaching the Zona Pellucida

. . . If and when Trevor's skin cell fused with the empty egg, what exactly was going to be created? "You are creating people," Sam Brownback has insisted. "You're creating humans." Opponents of therapeutic cloning believe that embryos deserve governmental protection before they have even divided from one cell into two (although not even the world's major religions agree on when a human life begins).

Positions like Senator Brownback's frustrate Mike West. "I'm just very disappointed," he said to me. "I'm sad, because even the critics admit that millions of human beings and their fate in the hospital may be contingent on this research." As a young man, West was an evangelical Christian and a creationist. He protested outside abortion clinics. But swayed by the scientific evidence for evolution, he eventually abandoned the biblical view of creation. Science now dictates his view of the earliest human embryos as well. "You can be as pro-life as you can get," he told me, "but you can't say that making and destroying a pre-implantation embryo is the destruction of a human. Because it isn't. If it was a human life, I wouldn't touch it. Absolutely not." He went on, "A human individual does not begin at conception. It begins at primitive-streak formation."

The "primitive streak" appears after fourteen days of embryonic development in utero. It's like an arrow drawn on the embryo, one that delineates head and tail, front and back. Until then how many individuals, if any, that tiny ball of tissue will produce is entirely unclear. During the first two weeks of development one embryo can still split into two, a process that produces identical twins. Remarkably, two embryos can also fuse into one, eventually resulting in a single person whose body is a patchwork of two genotypes (with each eye a different color, perhaps, or mottled, two-tone skin). Not until the appearance of the primitive streak are the beginnings of a human individual sketched out. At that point, according to West, "There is no brain, no sensation, no pain, no memory, nothing of that. But it is an individualized human in a very early stage, and I advocate we don't touch that. But before then— they're wrong. It is just cells, it is a kind of raw material for life: the cellular life out of which human life arises."

West's line of thinking is fully consistent with the conclusions laid out by the NIH Human Embryo Research Panel in 1994. "If the President and members of Congress really understood what these little balls of cells were," West went on, "they would have a completely different view."

Adrienne Ross has a blunter assessment. "To me," she told me, "it's like, how dare they tell me that I cannot save my son's life? It's as simple as that. You know, if you want to practice your religion, practice your religion. But not when it interferes with other people's lives." She continued, "They're telling me, 'Let your child die, because my religious belief is more important than your child's life.' They can make their choices for their own embryos and they can make their choices for their own children. But they have no right to stop me from saving my son's life."

A Shot in the Dark

. . . In the United States the broad consensus in the scientific community is that therapeutic-cloning research merits significant exploration, and that real progress is likely only with government funding and support. "Such research," Harold Varmus, the former NIH director, wrote last year in *The New York Times,* "is vital not just to biotechnology companies and their investors, but to the nation as a whole. By structuring our system so that only those with private funds or a commercial motive do this pioneering work, we curb our full capacity to expand our scientific understanding." To put it another way: as long as a federal-funding ban remains in place, the organizations most likely to move forward with therapeutic-cloning research will be companies like ACT—which, despite generally noble intentions, are bedeviled by the need to raise money, generate buzz, and please investors. . . .

What is clear is that the potential fruits of therapeutic-cloning research will not come soon enough for Trevor Ross. In February, doctors detected the first signs of childhood cerebral onset of ALD. All hopes of developing an experimental cure for Trevor were dashed; time had run out. The Rosses immediately scheduled a more traditional cord-blood transplant, fully aware of the risks and of the odds of failure.

Robert A. Weinberg

Of Clones and Clowns

$\mathbf{B}$iologists have been rather silent on the subject of human cloning. Some others would accuse us, as they have with predictable regularity in the recent past, of insensitivity to the societal consequences of our research. If not insensitivity, then moral obtuseness, and if not that, then arrogance—an accusation that can never be disproved.

The truth is that most of us have remained quiet for quite another reason. Most of us regard reproductive cloning—a procedure used to produce an entire new organism from one cell of an adult—as a technology riddled with problems. Why should we waste time agonizing about something that is far removed from practical utility, and may forever remain so?

The nature and magnitude of the problems were suggested by the Scottish scientist Ian Wilmut's initial report, five years ago, on the cloning of Dolly the sheep. Dolly represented one success among 277 attempts to produce a viable, healthy newborn. Most attempts at cloning other animal species—to date cloning has succeeded with sheep, mice, cattle, goats, cats, and pigs—have not fared much better.

Even the successes come with problems. The placentas of cloned fetuses are routinely two or three times larger than normal. The offspring are usually larger than normal as well. Several months after birth one group of cloned mice weighed 72 percent more than mice created through normal reproduction. In many species cloned fetuses must be delivered by cesarean section because of their size. This abnormality, the reasons for which no one understands, is so common that it now has its own name—Large Offspring Syndrome. Dolly (who was of normal size at birth) was briefly overweight in her young years and suffers from early-onset arthritis of unknown cause. Two recent reports indicate that cloned mice suffer early-onset obesity and early death.

Arguably the most successful reproductive-cloning experiment was reported last year by Advanced Cell Technology, a small biotech company in Worcester, Massachusetts. Working with cows, ACT produced 496 embryos by injecting nuclei from adult cells into eggs that had been stripped of their own nuclei. Implanting the embryos into the uteruses of cows led to 110 established pregnancies, thirty of which went to term. Five of the newborns died shortly after birth, and a sixth died several months later. The twenty-four surviving calves developed into cows that were healthy by all criteria examined. But most, if not all, had enlarged placentas, and as newborns some of them suffered from the respiratory distress typical of Large Offspring Syndrome.

The success rate of the procedure, roughly five percent, was much higher than the rates achieved with other mammalian species, and the experiment was considered a great success. Some of the cows have grown up, been artificially inseminated, and given birth to normal offspring. Whether they are affected by any of the symptoms associated with Large Offspring Syndrome later in life is not apparent from the published data. No matter: for $20,000 ACT will clone your favorite cow.

Imagine the application of this technology to human beings. Suppose that 100 adult nuclei are obtained, each of which is injected into a human egg whose own nucleus has been removed. Imagine then that only five of the 100 embryos thus created result in well-formed, viable newborns; the other ninety-five spontaneously abort at various stages of development or, if cloning experiments with mammals other than cows are any guide, yield grossly malformed babies. The five viable babies have a reasonable likelihood of suffering from Large Offspring Syndrome. How they will develop, physically and cognitively, is anyone's guess. It seems unlikely that even the richest and most egomaniacal among us, intent on recreating themselves exactly, will swarm to this technology.

❧

Biological systems are extraordinarily complex, and there are myriad ways in which experiments can go awry or their results can be misinterpreted. Still, perhaps 95 percent of what biologists read in this year's research journals will be considered valid (if perhaps not very interesting) a century from now. Much of scientists' trust in the existing knowledge base derives from the system constructed over the past century to validate new research findings and the conclusions derived from them. Research journals impose quality controls to ensure that scientific observations and conclusions are solid and credible. They sift the scientific wheat from the chaff.

The system works like this: A biologist sends a manuscript describing his experiment to a journal. The editor of the journal recruits several experts, who remain anonymous to the researcher, to vet the manuscript. A month or two later the researcher receives a thumbs-up, a thumbs-down, or a request for revisions and more data. . . .

We participate in the peer-review process not only to create a sound edifice of ideas and results for ourselves; we do it for the outside world as well—for all those who are unfamiliar with the arcane details of our field. Without the trial-by-fire of peer review, how can journalists and the public possibly know which discoveries are credible, which are nothing more than acts of self-promotion by ambitious researchers, and which smack of the delusional?

The hype about cloning has made a shambles of this system, creating something of a circus. Many of us have the queasy feeling that our carefully constructed world of science is under siege. The clowns—those who think that making money, lots of it, is more important than doing serious science—have invaded our sanctuary.

The cloning circus opened soon after Wilmut, a careful and well-respected scientist, reported his success with Dolly. First in the ring was Richard Seed, an elderly Chicago physicist, who in late 1997 announced his intention of cloning a human being within two years. Soon members of an international religious cult, the Raëlians (followers of Claude Vorilhon, a French-born mystic who says that he was given the name Raël by four-foot-high extraterrestrials, and who preaches that human beings were originally created by these aliens), revealed an even more grandiose vision of human cloning. To the Raëlians, biomedical science is a sacrament to be used for achieving immortality: their ultimate goal is to use cloning to create empty shells into which people's souls can be transferred. As a sideline, the Raëlian-affiliated company Clonaid hopes to offer its services to couples who would like to create a child through reproductive cloning, for $200,000 per child.

Neither Seed nor the Raëlians made any pretense of subjecting their plans to review by knowledgeable scientists; they went straight to the popular press. Still, this wasn't so bad. Few science journalists took them seriously (although they did oblige them with extensive coverage). Biologists were also unmoved. Wasn't it obvious that Seed and the Raëlians were unqualified to undertake even the beginnings of the series of technical steps required for reproductive cloning? Why dignify them with a response?

The next wave of would-be cloners likewise went straight to the mainstream press—but they were not so easily dismissed. In March of last year, at a widely covered press conference in Rome, an Italian and a U.S. physician announced plans to undertake human reproductive cloning outside the United States. The Italian member of the team was Severino Antinori, a gynecologist notorious for having used donor eggs and *in vitro* fertilization to make a sixty-two-year-old woman pregnant in 1994. Now he was moving on. Why, he asked, did the desires of infertile couples (he claimed to have 600 on a waiting list) not outweigh the concerns about human cloning? He repeatedly shouted down reporters and visiting researchers who had the temerity to voice questions about the biological and ethical problems associated with reproductive cloning.

The American member of the team was Panayiotis Zavos, a reproductive physiologist and an *in vitro* fertilization expert at the Andrology Institute of America, in Lexington, Kentucky. "The genie is out of the bottle," he told reporters. "Dolly is here, and we are next." Antinori and Zavos announced their intention of starting a human cloning project in an undisclosed Mediterranean country. Next up was Avi Ben-Abraham, an Israeli-American biotechnologist with thwarted political ambitions (he ran unsuccessfully for the Knesset) and no reputable scientific credentials, who attempted to attach himself to the project. Ben-Abraham hinted that the work would be done either in Israel or in an Arab country, because "the climate is more [receptive to human cloning research] within Judaism and Islam." He told the German magazine *Der Spiegel*, "We were all created by the Almighty, but now we will become the creators."

Both Antinori and Zavos glossed over the large gap between expertise with established infertility procedures and the technical skills required for reproductive cloning. Confronted with the prospect of high rates of aborted or malformed cloned embryos, they claimed to be able to weed out any defective embryos at an early stage of gestation. "We have a great deal of knowledge," Zavos announced to the press. "We can grade embryos. We can do genetic screening. We can do [genetic] quality control." This was possible, he said, because of highly sensitive diagnostic tests that can determine whether or not development is proceeding normally.

The fact is that no such tests exist; they have eluded even the most expert biologists in the field, and there is no hope that they will be devised anytime soon—if ever. No one knows how to determine with precision whether the repertoire of genes expressed at various stages of embryonic development is being "read" properly in each cell type within an embryo. Without such information, no one can know whether the developmental program is proceeding normally in the womb. (The prenatal tests currently done for Down syndrome and several other genetic disorders can detect only a few of the thousands of things that can go wrong during embryonic development.)

Rudolf Jaenisch, a colleague of mine with extensive experience in mouse reproductive cloning, was sufficiently exercised to say to a reporter at the *Chicago Tribune,* "[Zavos and Antinori] will produce clones, and most of these will die in utero . . . Those will be the lucky ones. Many of those that survive will have [obvious or more subtle] abnormalities." The rest of us biologists remained quiet. To us, Antinori, Zavos, and Ben-Abraham were so clearly inept that comment seemed gratuitous. In this instance we have, as on other occasions, misjudged the situation: many people seem to take these three and their plans very seriously indeed. And, in fact, this past April, Antinori claimed, somewhat dubiously, that a woman under his care was eight weeks pregnant with a cloned embryo.

❧

In the meantime, the biotechnology industry, led by ACT, has been moving ahead aggressively with human cloning, but of a different sort. The young companies in this sector have sensed, probably correctly, the enormous potential of therapeutic (rather than reproductive) cloning as a strategy for treating a host of common human degenerative diseases.

The initial steps of therapeutic cloning are identical to those of reproductive cloning: cells are prepared from an adult tissue, their nuclei are extracted, and each nucleus is introduced into a human egg, which is allowed to develop. However, in therapeutic cloning embryonic development is halted at a very early stage—when the embryo is a blastocyst, consisting of perhaps 150 cells— and the inner cells are harvested and cultured. These cells, often termed embryonic stem cells, are still very primitive and thus have retained the ability to develop into any type of cell in the body (except those of the placenta). . . .

Therapeutic cloning has the potential to revolutionize the treatment of a number of currently untreatable degenerative diseases, but it is only a potential. Considerable research will be required to determine the technology's possibilities and limitations for treating human patients.

Some worry that therapeutic-cloning research will never get off the ground in this country. Its proponents—and there are many among the community of biomedical researchers—fear that the two very different kinds of cloning, therapeutic and reproductive, have merged in the public's mind. Three leaders of the community wrote a broadside early this year in *Science,* titled "Please Don't Call It Cloning!" Call therapeutic cloning anything else— call it "nuclear transplantation," or "stem cell research." The scientific community has finally awakened to the damage that the clowns have done.

This is where the newest acts of the circus begin. President George Bush and many pro-life activists are in one ring. A number of disease-specific advocacy groups that view therapeutic cloning as the only real prospect for treating long-resistant maladies are in another. In a third ring are several biotech companies that are flogging their wares, often in ways that make many biologists shudder.

Yielding to pressure from religious conservatives, Bush announced last August that no new human embryonic stem cells could be produced from early human embryos that had been created during the course of research sponsored by the federal government; any research on the potential applications of human embryonic stem cells, he said, would have to be conducted with the existing repertoire of sixty-odd lines. The number of available, usable cell lines actually appears to be closer to a dozen or two. And like all biological reagents, these cells tend to deteriorate with time in culture; new ones will have to be derived if research is to continue. What if experiments with the existing embryonic-stem-cell lines show enormous promise? Such an outcome would produce an almost irresistible pressure to move ahead with the derivation of new embryonic stem cells and to rapidly expand this avenue of research.

How will we learn whether human embryonic stem cells are truly useful for new types of therapy? This question brings us directly to another pitfall: much of the research on human embryonic stem cells is already being conducted by biotech companies, rather than in universities. Bush's edict will only exacerbate this situation. (In the 1970s a federal decision effectively banning government funding of *in vitro* fertilization had a similar effect, driving such research into private clinics.)

Evaluating the science coming from the labs of the biotech industry is often tricky. Those who run these companies are generally motivated more by a need to please stock analysts and venture capitalists than to convince scientific peers. For many biotech companies the peer-review process conducted by scientific journals is simply an inconvenient, time-wasting impediment. So some of the companies routinely bypass peer review and go straight to the mainstream press. Science journalists, always eager for scoops, don't necessarily feel compelled to consult experts about the credibility of industry press releases. And when experts are consulted about the contents of a press release, they are often hampered by spotty descriptions of the claimed breakthrough and thus limited to mumbling platitudes.

ACT, the company that conducted the successful cow-cloning experiment and has now taken the lead in researching human therapeutic cloning, has danced back and forth between publishing in respectable peer-reviewed journals and going directly to the popular press—and recently tried to find a middle ground. . . . Last fall, with vast ambitions, ACT reported that it had conducted the first successful human-cloning experiment. In truth, however, embryonic development went only as far as six cells—far short of the 150-cell blastocyst that represents the first essential step of therapeutic cloning. Wishing to cloak its work in scientific respectability, ACT reported these results in a fledgling electronic research journal named *e-biomed: The Journal of Regenerative Medicine.* Perhaps ACT felt especially welcome in a journal that, according to its editor in chief, William A. Haseltine, a widely known biotech tycoon, "is prepared to publish work of a more preliminary nature." It may also have been encouraged by Haseltine's stance toward cloning, as revealed in his remarks when the journal was founded. "As we understand the body's repair process at the genetic level, we will be able to advance the goal of maintaining our bodies in normal function, perhaps perpetually," he said.

Electronic publishing is still in its infancy, and the publication of ACT's research report will do little to enhance its reputation. By the usual standards of scientific achievement, the experiments ACT published would be considered abject failures. Knowledgeable readers of the report were unable to tell whether the clump of six cells represented the beginning of a human embryo or simply an unformed aggregate of dying cells. . . .

≈≈≈

No one yet knows precisely how to make therapeutic cloning work, or which of its many claimed potential applications will pan out and which will not. And an obstacle other than experimental problems confronts those pushing therapeutic cloning. In the wake of the cloning revolution a second revolution has taken place—quieter but no less consequential. It, too, concerns tissue-specific stem cells—but ones found in the tissues of adults. These adult stem cells may one day prove to be at least as useful as those generated by therapeutic cloning. . . .

Until two years ago the dogma among biologists was that stem cells in the bone marrow spawned only blood, those in the liver spawned only hepatocytes, and those in the brain spawned only neurons—in other words, each of our tissues had only its own cadre of stem cells for upkeep. Once again we appear to have been wrong. There is mounting evidence that the body contains some rather unspecialized stem cells, which wander around ready to help many sorts of tissue regenerate their worker cells.

Whether these newly discovered, multi-talented adult stem cells present a viable alternative to therapeutic cloning remains to be proved. Many of the claims about their capabilities have yet to be subjected to rigorous testing. Perhaps not surprisingly, some of these claims have also reached the public without careful vetting by peers. Senator Sam Brownback, of Kansas, an ardent foe of all kinds of cloning, has based much of his case in favor of adult stem cells (and against therapeutic cloning) on these essentially unsubstantiated scientific claims. Adult stem cells provide a convenient escape hatch for Brownback.

Their use placates religious conservatives, who are against all cloning, while throwing a bone to groups lobbying for new stem-cell-based therapies to treat degenerative diseases.

Brownback would have biologists shut down therapeutic-cloning research and focus their energies exclusively on adult stem-cell research. But no one can know at present which of those two strategies is more likely to work. . . .

Precisely this issue was debated recently by advisory committees in the United States and Germany. The U.S. committee was convened by Bruce Alberts, the president of the National Academy of Sciences and a highly accomplished cell biologist and scientific educator. Quite naturally, it included a number of experts who are actively involved in exploring the advantages and disadvantages of stem-cell therapies. The committee, which announced its findings in January, concluded that therapeutic cloning should be explored in parallel with alternative strategies.

For their trouble, the scientists were accused of financial self-interest by Steven Milloy of Fox News, who said, "Enron and Arthur Andersen have nothing over the National Academy of Sciences when it comes to deceiving the public . . . Enter Bruce Alberts, the Wizard of Oz–like president of the NAS . . . On his own initiative, Alberts put together a special panel, stacked with embryonic-stem-cell research proponents and researchers already on the taxpayer dole . . . Breast-feeding off taxpayers is as natural to the NAS panel members as breathing." . . .

President Bush, apparently anticipating the NAS panel's conclusion, has appointed an advisory committee all but guaranteed to produce a report much more to his liking. Its chairman, Leon Kass, has gone on record as being against all forms of cloning. (Earlier in his career Kass helped to launch an attack on *in vitro* fertilization.)

Meanwhile, a coalition of a hundred people and organizations recently sent a letter to Congress expressing their opposition to therapeutic cloning—among them Friends of the Earth, Greenpeace, the Sierra Club, the head of the National Latina Health Organization, and the perennial naysayer Jeremy Rifkin. "The problem with therapeutic cloning," Rifkin has said, "is that it introduces commercial eugenics from the get-go." Powerful words indeed. Few of those galvanized by Rifkin would know that therapeutic cloning has nothing whatsoever to do with eugenics.

⁕

Usually progress in biology is held back by experimental difficulties, inadequate instruments, poorly planned research protocols, inadequate funding, or plain sloppiness. But in this case the future of research may have little connection with these factors or with the scientific pros and cons being debated earnestly by members of the research community. The other, more public debates will surely be the decisive ones.

The clashes about human therapeutic cloning that have taken place in the media and in Congress are invariably built around weighty moral and ethical principles. But none of us needs a degree in bioethics to find the bottom line in the arguments. They all ultimately converge on a single question: When does human life begin? Some say it is when sperm and egg meet, others when the embryo implants in the womb, others when the fetus quickens, and yet others when the fetus can survive outside the womb. This is a question that we scientists are neither more nor less equipped to decide than the average man or woman in the street, than a senator from Kansas or a cardinal in Cologne. (Because Dolly and the other cloned animals show that a complete embryo can be produced from a single adult cell, some biologists have proposed, tongue in cheek, that a human life exists in each one of our cells.) Take your pick of the possible answers and erect your own moral scaffolding above your choice.

EXPLORING THE ISSUE

Should Scientists Be Allowed to Clone Children?

Critical Thinking and Reflection

1. A huge issue in the debate over cloning is the differences between therapeutic and reproductive cloning. What are the differences and commonalities between the two? Is it the end result many people are against (the human clones from reproductive cloning) or the method used to get there (the making of human embryos, used with both types of cloning).
2. Many people have previous ideas about cloning from what they have heard on television or read in magazine articles. Think about the previous notions you had about cloning and what you learned from these articles that you did not previously know. Did either of these articles change your position on cloning?
3. The NIH Human Embryo Research Panel concluded that human life begins approximately 14 days after conception. Until then there are only undifferentiated cells. What are your thoughts about this conclusion? Also, do you believe it makes a difference whether it was a sperm and an egg or a skin cell and an egg?

Is There Common Ground?

The future will ultimately tell us whether we will make a mistake by either allowing cloning and tampering with the natural order of things or by dismissing cloning as science fiction and consequently watching many people die whose lives could have been saved.

Perhaps someday there can be a middle ground where scientists can find a way to obtain the materials that they need in a manner that does not violate the ethical or moral challenges being posed to them by the opposing side.

Additional Resources

American Medical Association. Stem Cell Issues. Retrieved on March 22, 2011, from http://www.ama-assn.org/ama/pub/physician-resources/medical-science/genetics-molecular-medicine/related-policy-topics/stem-cell-research/human-cloning.page.

An article posted on the Internet that provides information about stem cell research, human cloning, and legislation that affects it.

Human Cloning Foundation. Retrieved on March 22, 2011, from http://www.humancloning.org/.

A Web site with information about benefits and myths concerning human cloning.

Human Genome Project Information. Cloning Fact Sheet. Retrieved on March 22, 2011, from http://www.ornl.gov/sci/techresources/Human_Genome/elsi/cloning.shtml.

National Conference of State Legislatures. Human Cloning Laws. Retrieved on March 22, 2011, from http://www.ncsl.org/default.aspx?tabid=14284.

A Web site that describes the laws of the 15 states that have addressed human cloning.

ISSUE 4

Do Federal Laws Make Transracial Adoptions More Commonplace?

YES: Ezra E. H. Griffith and Rachel L. Bergeron, from "Cultural Stereotypes Die Hard: The Case of Transracial Adoption," *The Journal of the American Academy of Psychiatry and the Law* (November 3, 2006)

NO: Elizabeth Bartholet, from "Commentary: Cultural Stereotypes Can and Do Die: It's Time to Move on with Transracial Adoption," *The Journal of the American Academy of Psychiatry and the Law* (November 3, 2006). **Diane H. Schetky**, from "Commentary: Transracial Adoption—Changing Trends and Attitudes," *The Journal of the American Academy of Psychiatry and the Law* (November 3, 2006).

Learning Outcomes

After reading this issue, you should be able to:

* Describe some of the reasons that adoptions are necessary in America.
* Discuss the reasons that transracial adoptions might be preferable to institutional care.
* Discuss the arguments against transracial adoption, specifically what researchers argue the challenges might be.

ISSUE SUMMARY

YES: Ezra Griffith and Rachel Bergeron, formerly professors at Harvard Law School, suggest that there is a cultural preference for race matching in adoptions. As a result, federal statutory attempts to omit race as a factor in child placement decisions have not been effective.

NO: Elizabeth Bartholet, the Morris Wasserstein Professor of Law and faculty director of the Child Advocacy Program at the Harvard Law School, and Diane Schetky, clinical professor of psychiatry at the Maine Medical Center, state that the current law is clear and effective in prohibiting adoptions based on race. They suggest that in the future, the need for legislation in this area will diminish even further.

Our society has always preferred finding loving and caring adoptive parents for children rather than placing them in institutions. A family unit not only socializes a child but provides a child with nurturance, a sense of security, and unconditional love. Unfortunately, there are hundreds of thousands of children in America who, for various reasons, are not with their biological families. These children are mostly nonwhite, minority children. Although the research literature suggests that, regardless of the race of the parents or children, all children do better in adoptive families than in institutions, there still seems to be a "concern" about placing children transracially.

Transracial adoption typically refers to a family in which a minority child (e.g., Asian American, Native American, African American, or Latino) or a child with a mixed racial background is adopted by an Anglo-American couple. These adoptions account for about 15 percent of all adoptions in the United States annually. Due to world events, transracial adoption became more commonplace in the United States in the late 1940s. Children with mixed backgrounds came from Europe and Asia after World War II. After the Korean War, Korean-American children and refugee Chinese children were adopted by Anglo-American couples in the United States. Finding adoptive homes for Native American children followed. The movement to place African American children with Anglo-American families is the most recent evolution of transracial adoption.

The Multi-Ethnic Placement Act of 1994 and the 1996 amendments to that act forbade using race as a sole factor when determining if a family can adopt a child. The National Association of Black Social Workers (NABSW) strongly opposes transracial adoption because they believe the adopted child will have many problems dealing with his or her ethnic identity or ethnic community. Other organizations disagree and base their support of transracial adoptions on the principle of adoption being in the best interest of the child. The only time a transracial adoption process can be delayed because of race is if mental health professionals determine the prospective adoptee is a special case and an intra-racial adoption is in that child's best interest. It should be noted that there is virtually no information related to the issue of minority families adopting white children. This has occurred, but only in rare instances over the generations. Although it is likely that the research literature would come to similar conclusions about the welfare of these adopted children, there is a need for research on this type of transracial adoption as well. At this time it is not possible to say if society could embrace such adoptions without any "concern."

The following two sections describe the debate between restricting transracial adoptions and making transracial adoptions more commonplace via federal law. Despite the law, should race be a factor that is considered in adoption? Do you agree that attitudes and trends *have* changed and the controversy over transracial adoptions is no longer as large an issue as it was a decade or two ago?

YES

Ezra E. H. Griffith and
Rachel L. Bergeron

Cultural Stereotypes Die Hard: The Case of Transracial Adoption

The adoption of black children by white families, commonly referred to as transracial adoption in the lay and professional literature, is the subject of a debate that has persisted in American society for a long time. On one side of the divide are those who believe that black children are best raised by black families. On the other are the supporters of the idea that race-matching in adoption does not necessarily serve the best interests of the child and that it promotes racial discrimination.

Coming as it does in the midst of myriad other discussions in this country about black-white interactions, transracial adoption has occupied an important place in any debate about adoption policy. But in addition, as can be seen in language utilized by the Fifth Circuit Court in a 1977 case, there is a long-held belief that since family members resemble one another, it follows that members of constructed families should also look like each other so as to facilitate successful adoption outcomes. . . .

In utilizing this language, the court acknowledged that transracial adoption ran counter to the cultural beliefs that many people held about the construction of families. Still, the court concluded that while the difficulties attending transracial adoption justified the consideration of race as a relevant factor in adoption proceedings, race could not be the sole factor considered. With a bow to both sides in the transracial adoption debate, the argument could only continue.

As the debate marches on, mental health professionals are being asked to provide expert opinions about whether it would be preferable for a particular black child to be raised by a black family or by a family or adult of a different ethnic or racial group. There are, of course, different scenarios that may lead to the unfolding of these adoption disputes. For example, the question may arise when a black child is put up for adoption after having spent a number of months or years in an out-of-home placement. The lengthy wait of black children for an adoptive black family may understandably increase the likelihood of a transracial adoption. In another situation, the death of a biracial child's parents, one of whom was white and the other black, may lead to competition between the white and black grandparents for the right to raise the child. In a third possible context, the divorce of an interracial couple may result in a

From *The Journal of the American Academy of Psychiatry and the Law,* vol. 34, no. 3, November 3, 2006, pp. 303–314 (excerpts). Copyright © 2006 by American Academy of Psychiatry and the Law. Reprinted by permission via S&S Management, Inc.

legal struggle for custody of the biracial child, with race trumpeted at least as an important factor if not the crucial factor to be considered in the decision about who should raise the child. . . .

We have already alluded to two significant factors that have played a role in the evolution of adoption policy concerning black children, particularly with respect to the question of whether race-neutral approaches make sense and whether transracial adoption is good practice. One factor has been judicial decision-making. In a relatively recent review, Hollinger reminded us that, in general, racial classifications are invalidated unless they can survive the "strict scrutiny" test, which requires meeting a compelling governmental interest. Hollinger suggested that the "best-interest-of-the-child" standard commonly used in adoption practice would serve a substantial governmental interest. Such argumentation would allow the consideration of race as one element in an adoption evaluation. Following this reasoning, while race-neutral adoption may be a lofty objective, the specific needs of a particular child could legally allow the consideration of race.

The second factor to influence the evolution of adoption policy in this arena has been the academic research on transracial adoption. This work has cumulatively demonstrated that black children can thrive and develop strong racial identities when nurtured in families with white parents. Transracially adopted children also do well on standard measures of self-esteem, cognitive development, and educational achievement. However, neither judicial decision-making nor scholarly research has settled the debate on transracial adoption policy.

In this article, we focus on a third factor that emerged as another mechanism meant to deal with transracial adoptions and the influential race-matching principle. These statutory efforts started with the Multiethnic Placement Act, which Hollinger stated "was enacted in 1994 amid spirited and sometimes contentious debate about transracial adoption and same-race placement policies." We will point out that even though the statutory attempts were meant to eliminate race as a controlling factor in the adoption process, their implementation has left room for ambiguity regarding the role that race should play in adoption proceedings. Consequently, even though the statutes were intended to eliminate adoption delays and denials because of race-matching, they may have allowed the continued existence of a cultural stereotype—that black children belong with black families—and may have facilitated its continued existence. This article is therefore principally about statutory attempts in the past decade to influence public policy concerning transracial adoption. Secondarily, we shall comment on potential implications of these developments for the practice of adoption evaluations. . . .

Brief Review of Race-Matching in Adoption

Feelings about who should raise a black child have run high in the United States for a long time. These feelings come from different groups for different reasons. Kennedy presented a number of historical cases to illustrate this. Among the cases he described, Kennedy told the early 1900s story of a white girl who was found residing with a black family. The authorities concluded that the child had been kidnapped and rescued her. They then placed her with a white family. When it was learned later that the child was black, she was returned to the black family because it was not proper for the black child to be living with a white family. This case, along with others described by Kennedy, is part of the fabric of American racism and racial separatist practices. Kennedy also pointed to the practice during slavery of considering "the human products of interracial sexual unions" as unambiguously black and the mandate that they be reared within the black slave community as an attempt to undermine any possibility of interracial parenting.

Whites have not been the only ones to support the stance of race-matching—the belief that black or white children belong with their own group. In 1972, the National Association of Black Social Workers (NABSW) stated unambiguously that white families should never be allowed to adopt black children. The NABSW opposed transracial adoption for two main reasons: the Association claimed that transracial adoption prevents black children from forming a strong racial identity, and it prevents them from developing survival skills necessary to deal with a racist society.

Since its 1972 statement, the NABSW has remained steadfast in its opposition to transracial adoption. In testimony before the Senate Committee on Labor and Human Resources in 1985, the President of the NABSW reiterated the Association's position and stated that the NABSW viewed the placement of black children in white homes as a hostile act against the black community, considering it a blatant form of race and cultural genocide.

In 1991, the NABSW reaffirmed its position that black children should not be placed with white parents under any circumstances, stating that even the most loving and skilled white parent could not avoid doing irreparable harm to an African-American child. In its 1994 position paper on the preservation of African-American families, the NABSW indicated that, in placement decisions regarding a black child, priority should be given to adoption by biological relatives and then to black families. Transracial adoption "should only be considered after documented evidence of unsuccessful same race placements has been reviewed and supported by appropriate representatives of the African American community." . . .

Race-matching has been and remains an influential and controversial concept regarding how best to construct adoptive families. Matching, in general, has been a classic principle of adoption practice, governing non-relative adoptions for much of the 20th century. Its goal was to create families in which the adoptive parents looked as though they could be the adopted child's biological parents. Matching potential adoptive parents and children on as many physical, emotional, and cultural characteristics as possible was seen as a way of insuring against adoptive failure. It was not uncommon for potential adoptive parents to be denied the possibility of adoption if their hair and eye color did not match those of a child in need of adoption. Differences among family members in constructed families were seen as threats to the integration of an adopted child and the child's identification with the adoptive parents. Race, along with religion, was considered the most important characteristic to be matched, and it continued to be important even as the matching concept regarding other characteristics began to shift. . . .

Matching, of course, continued to influence child placement decisions outside of adoption agencies, as evidenced by the comments of the Drummond court. Following that court's decision, the general rule has been that trial courts may consider race as a factor in adoption proceedings as long as race is not the sole determinant.

Statutory Attempts at Remedies

. . . The Black Social Workers had a quick and striking effect on transracial adoption policy. Following the appearance of the paper, adoption agencies, both public and private, either implemented race-matching approaches or used the NABSW position to justify already existing race-matching policies. As a result, the number of transracial adoptions were estimated to drop significantly—39 percent within one year of the publication of the NABSW statement. Although robust data were lacking, it was thought that the number and length of stay of black children in out-of-home placements increased as social workers and other foster care and adoption professionals, believing that same-race placements were in the best interest of the child, searched for same-race foster and adoptive parents. Agencies and their workers had considerable discretion in deciding the role race played in placement decisions. States, while generally requiring that foster care and adoption decisions be made in the best interest of the child, varied in their directions regarding the extent to which race, culture, and ethnicity should be taken into account in making the best-interest determination.

While race-matching policies were not the sole determinant of increasing numbers of black children in institutions and out-of-home placements, there was growing concern that such policies, with their focus on same-race placement and their exclusion of consideration of loving, permanent interracial homes, kept black children from being adopted. Because he was concerned that race had become the determining factor in adoption placements and that children were languishing in foster care homes and institutions, Senator Howard Metzenbaum introduced legislation to prohibit the use of race as the sole determinant of placement. Senator Metzenbaum believed that same-race adoption was the preferable option for a child, but he also believed that transracial placement was far preferable to a child's remaining in foster care when an appropriate same-race placement was not available.

Multiethnic Placement Act

Congress passed the Howard Metzenbaum Multiethnic Placement Act (MEPA) and President Clinton signed it into law on October 20, 1994. MEPA's main goals were to decrease the length of time children had to wait to be adopted; to prevent discrimination based on race in the placement of children into adoptive or foster homes; and to recruit culturally diverse and minority adoptive and foster families who could meet the needs of children needing placement. In passing MEPA, Congress was concerned that many children, especially those from minority groups, were spending lengthy periods in foster care awaiting adoption placements. Congress found, within the parameters of available data, that nearly 500,000 children were in foster care in the United States; tens of thousands of these children were waiting for adoption; two years and eight months was the median length of time children waited to be adopted; and minority children often waited twice as long as other children to be adopted.

Under MEPA, an agency or entity receiving federal funds could not use race as the sole factor in denying any person the opportunity to become an adoptive or foster parent. Furthermore, an agency could not use race as a single factor to delay or deny the placement of a child in an adoptive or foster care family or to otherwise discriminate in making a placement decision. However, an agency could consider a child's racial, cultural, and ethnic background as one of several factors—not the sole factor—used to determine the best interests of the child. . . .

So, under MEPA, agencies could consider a child's race, ethnicity, or culture as one of a number of factors used to determine the best interests of the child, as long as it was not the sole factor considered, and they could consider the ability of prospective parents to meet the needs of a child of a given race, ethnicity, or culture.

Following the passage of MEPA, the Department of Health and Human Services (DHHS), Office of Civil Rights, provided policy guidance to assist agencies receiving federal financial assistance in complying with MEPA. The guidance permitted agencies receiving federal assistance to consider race, culture, or ethnicity as factors in making placement decisions to the extent allowed by MEPA, the U.S. Constitution and Title VI of the Civil Rights Act of 1964.

Under the Equal Protection Clause of the Fourteenth Amendment, laws or practices drawing distinctions on the basis of race are inherently suspect and subject to strict scrutiny analysis. To pass such analysis, classifications or practices based on race have to be narrowly tailored to meet a compelling state interest. The Supreme Court has not specifically addressed the question of transracial adoption. It has considered race as a factor in a child placement decision in the context of a custody dispute between two white biological parents when the mother, who had custody of the child, began living with a black man, whom she later married. The Court found the goal of granting custody on the basis of the best interests of the child to be "indisputably a substantial government interest for purposes of the Equal Protection Clause." The DHHS guidance on the use of race, color or national origin as factors in adoption and foster care placements addressed the relevant constitutional issues and indicated that the only compelling state interest in the context of child placement decisions is protecting the best interests of the child who is to be placed. So, under MEPA, consideration of race or ethnicity was permitted as long as it was narrowly tailored to advance a specific child's best interests. Agencies receiving federal funds could consider race and ethnicity when making placement decisions only if the agency made a narrowly tailored, individualized determination that the facts and circumstances of a particular case required the contemplation of race or ethnicity to advance the best interests of the child in need of placement. Agencies could not assume that race, ethnicity, or culture was at issue in every case and make general policies that applied to all children. The guidance also specifically prohibited policies that established periods during which same-race searches were conducted, created placement preference hierarchies based on race, ethnicity, or culture, required social workers to justify transracial placement decisions or resulted in delayed placements to find a family of a particular race, ethnicity, or culture.

The DHHS policy guidance did address MEPA's permissible consideration of the racial, cultural, or ethnic background of a child and the capacity of the prospective foster or adoptive parents to meet the needs of a child of this background as one of a number of factors in the best-interest-of-the-child determination. The guidance allowed agencies to assess the ability of a specific potential adoptive family to meet a specific child's needs related to his or her racial, ethnic, or cultural background, as long as the assessment was done in the context of an individualized assessment. . . .

However, agencies were not allowed to make decisions based on general assumptions regarding the needs of children of a specific race, ethnicity, or culture or about the ability of prospective parents of a specific race, ethnicity, or culture to care or nurture the identity of a child of a different race, ethnicity, or culture.

To increase the pool of potential foster or adoptive parents, MEPA also required states to develop plans for the recruitment of potential foster and adoptive families that reflected the ethnic and racial diversity of the children needing placement. The recruitment efforts had to be focused on providing all eligible children with the opportunity for placement and on providing all qualified members of the community with an opportunity to become an adoptive or foster parent. As a result, while MEPA sought in a reasonable way to recruit a broad racial and cultural spectrum of adoptive families, the law was at the same time underlining the idea that there was something special about a black child's being raised by a black family.

Those who objected to the permissive consideration of race in MEPA asserted that it allowed agencies to continue to delay adoptions of minority children based on race concerns. They also argued that race-matching policies could and did continue under MEPA. Social workers could, for example, use race as a factor to support a finding that a transracial adoption was not in a given child's best interest. Supporters of MEPA reached their own conclusion that it did not accomplish its goal of speeding up the adoption process and moving greater numbers of minority children into foster care or adoption placements and that the permissive consideration of race allowed agencies legitimately to continue race-matching to deny or delay the placement of minority children with white adoptive parents. Senator Metzenbaum himself agreed with this conclusion about MEPA and worked for its repeal. As we shall see later, the arguments and counterarguments about the effectiveness of MEPA were being made in the absence of robust data.

The Interethnic Adoption Provisions

MEPA was repealed when on August 20, 1996, President Clinton signed the Small Business Job Protection Act of 1996. Section 1808 of the Act was entitled "Removal of Barriers to Interethnic Adoption" (The Interethnic Adoption Provisions; IEP). MEPA's permissible consideration provision was removed and its language changed. . . .

Under the IEP, states were still required to "provide for the diligent recruitment of potential foster and adoptive families that reflect the ethnic and racial diversity of children in the State for whom foster and adoptive homes are needed."

Failure to comply with MEPA was a violation of Title VI of the Civil Rights Act of 1964; failure to comply with the IEP is also a violation of Title VI. Under MEPA, an agency receiving federal assistance that discriminated in its child placement decisions on the basis of race and failed to comply with the Act could forfeit its federal assistance and an aggrieved individual had the right to bring an action seeking equitable relief in federal court or could file a complaint with the Office of Civil Rights. The IEP added enforcement provisions that specified graduated fiscal sanctions to be imposed by DHHS against states found to be in violation of the law and gave any individual aggrieved by a violation the right to bring an action against the state or other entity in federal court.

The Department of Health and Human Services issued two documents to provide practical guidance for complying with the IEP: a memorandum and a document in question-and-answer format. According to the guidance, Congress, in passing the IEP, clarified its intent to eliminate delays in adoption or foster care placements when they were in any way avoidable. Race and ethnicity could not be used as the basis for any denial of placement nor used as a reason to delay a foster care or adoptive placement. The repeal of MEPA's "permissible consideration" provision was seen as confirming that strict scrutiny was the appropriate standard for consideration of race or ethnicity in adoption and foster care placements. DHHS argued that it had never taken the position that MEPA's permissible consideration language allowed agencies to take race into account routinely in making placement decisions because such a view would be inconsistent with a strict scrutiny standard. It reaffirmed that any decision to consider race as a necessary element in a placement decision has to be based on concerns arising out of the circumstances of the particular situation. . . .

The guidance again made clear that the best interest of the child is the standard to be used in making placement decisions. So, according to the guidance, the IEP prohibits the routine practice of taking race and ethnicity into consideration ("Public agencies may not routinely consider race, national origin, and ethnicity in making placement decisions"), but it allows for the consideration of race, national origin, and ethnicity in certain specific situations ("Any consideration of these factors must be done on an individualized basis where special circumstances indicate that their consideration is warranted"). Once again, such language seems to suggest that, in certain contexts, the adoptive child may well benefit from placement in a same-race family.

The DHHS guidance seemed to frame the possibility for adoption agencies to continue the practice of race-matching. For example, while warning that assessment of a prospective parent's ability to serve as a foster or adoptive parent must not act as a racial or ethnic screen and indicating that considerations of race must not be routine in the assessment function, the guidance conceded that an important aspect of good social work is an individualized assessment of a prospective parent's ability to be an adoptive or foster parent. Thus, it allows for discussions with prospective adoptive or foster care parents about their feelings, preferences, and capacities regarding caring for a child of a particular race or ethnicity. . . .

Discussion

In considering the best interests of a child who is being placed for adoption, DHHS is suggesting that there could be special circumstances uniquely individualized to the child that require consideration of ethnicity and race of the potential adoptive parents. Presumably this should not be done routinely and should not be seen as serving as a proxy for a consistent and mundane contemplation of ethnicity or race in the adoption context. Undoubtedly, what constitutes special circumstances in the practices of any given adoption agency is likely to be a matter of interpretation. While agencies can readily assert what their routine practices are, much may turn on how vigorously supervised are the claims that special circumstances exist with respect to a particular black child that dictate consideration of ethnicity and race in that child's case. As a practical result, while it appears no one is now allowed to claim that every black child needs a black family, it may still be reasonable and practicable to claim that a black child requires adoption by a black family, as dictated by consideration of the best interests of that child. For example, Kennedy has raised the possibility that an older child might say he or she wanted to be adopted only by a black family. Such a context could indeed make it difficult for the child's wish to be refused outright, without any consideration whatsoever.

Such reasoning is articulated starting from the point of view of the child. Giving consideration to the interests of the potential adoptive parent is another matter. In other words, what should we consider about the adoptive parent's interest in raising black children and the parent's ability to do so? The opinions about this matter remain divided. Kennedy and Bartholet have proposed that prospective adoptive parents be allowed to state a preference for adopting a child from a particular ethnic group. This is, in their view, permissible race-matching that ultimately serves the best interests of the child. After all, what would be the use of forcing a family to adopt a child they really did not want? In addition, both authors also have argued that state intervention in such racial selectivity in the formation of families would be akin to imposing race-based rules on the creation of married couples. However, Banks has opposed this accommodationist stance, where in practice adoption agencies would simply show prospective adoptive parents only the class of ethnic children the adoptive parent was interested in adopting. Banks thought this merely perpetuated the status quo, as white adoptive parents had little interest in black children. This would result in black children's continuing to languish in out-of-home placements, and their time spent awaiting adoption would remain prolonged.

Kennedy and Bartholet were permissive in their attitude toward the racial selectivity of prospective adoptive parents, respecting parents' choice to construct families as they wish.

There has been and continues to be strong support for the belief that black children belong with black adoptive parents. It is not only the NABSW, which has called for the repeal of the IEP, that has taken this position. For example, in a 1998 letter to the Secretary of the Department of Health and Human Services, a former executive director of the Child Welfare League of America strongly disagreed with the DHHS's interpretation of MEPA/IEP, stating that prohibiting any consideration of race in adoptive and foster care placement decisions contradicts best-practice standards in child welfare. . . .

The CWLA, in its most recent *Standards of Excellence for Adoption Services* (2000), reiterated its belief that race is to be considered in all adoptions and that placement with parents of the same race is the first choice for any child. Other placements should be considered only after a vigorous search for parents of the same race has failed. . . .

In its most recent policy statement on foster care and adoption (2003), the National Association of Social Workers also reiterated its position that consideration of race should play a central role in placement decisions. . . .

Others have espoused the view that inracial adoption is the preferred option for a black child because black families inherently possess the competence to raise children with strong black identities and the ability to cope with racism. While questions of cultural competence to raise a black child often arise about prospective white adoptive parents, no such questions are posed about prospective black adoptive parents. The competence of black families to raise black children is regularly referred to as though black families are culturally identical or homogeneous and all are equally competent to raise black children and equip them to live in our society. We may all think about black cultural competence as though it is a one-dimensional concept. Indeed, we may all be referring simply to stereotypical indicators of what we think it means to be black. We may be referring to our own personal preferences for the stereotypic activities of black people: involvement in a black church; participation in a community center where black-focused programs are operating; viewing movies with a clearly black theme; reading literature authored by blacks. What is rarely considered is that some black families are drawn to rap music, others to jazz greats, and still others to traditional classical music. Indeed, some families obviously manage to exhibit an interest in all these genres of music. With respect, therefore, to even these stereotyped indicators of what it means to be black, black families vary in the degree of their attachment to the indicators. This is to say that blacks differ in their level of commitment to the salience of black-oriented culture in their individual and family lives. As a result, there is considerable cultural heterogeneity among black families.

Such variability may well lead to differences in black families' ways of coping with racism.

To date, the statutory attempts to deal with transracial adoptions have not been considered as spectacularly successful, especially in the case of MEPA. Nevertheless, efforts have been made to limit the routine consideration of race and ethnicity in adoption, with the result that black children may be remaining for shorter periods in undesirable out-of-home placements. (National data are not yet able to demonstrate clear trends.) However, DHHS guidance still permits consideration of race and ethnicity in specific cases, with the apparent concession that some black children may need a black family for the realization of the child's best interests.

The burden is on forensic psychiatrists and other mental health professionals who perform adoption evaluations to point out cogently and logically two points: first, whether race is a factor that is relevant in the adoption evaluation; and second, whether there is something unique or particular about that adoption context that requires race to be considered. It will require special argumentation for the evaluator to claim that a particular black child could benefit more from placement with a black family than with a non-black family. As stated earlier, the evidence is clear that black children can do well in transracial placements. The pointed objective, therefore, in future evaluations will be to show that a particular black child has such unique and special needs that he or she deserves particular consideration for placement in a black family. It will be interesting to see whether our forensic colleagues, in striving for objectivity, will consider the factor of race in their evaluations only when something unique about that particular adoption context cries out for race to be considered so that the best-interest-of-the-child standard can be met. It seems clear that forensic professionals must be careful not to state that they routinely consider race in their adoption evaluations unless they intend to argue clinically that race is always relevant. And even then, they should be cautious about not articulating a general preference for inracial over transracial adoptions.

Despite federal statutory attempts to remove race as a controlling factor in adoption and foster care placement decisions, the debate over transracial adoption is not over. Indeed, strains of the debate are evidenced in the statutes and their implementation guidelines and the argument continues among our mental health colleagues. . . .

Elizabeth Bartholet and
Diane H. Schetky

Commentary: Cultural Stereotypes Can and Do Die: It's Time to Move on with Transracial Adoption

Ezra Griffith and Rachel Bergeron write in their article, "Cultural Stereotypes Die Hard: The Case of Transracial Adoption," that the controversy that has long surrounded transracial adoption is ongoing and that the law is significantly ambiguous. Accordingly, they say that psychiatrists and other mental health professionals are faced with a challenge in deciding on the role that race should play in adoption evaluations for purposes of foster and adoptive placement decisions.

I agree that the controversy is ongoing, but think that the law is much clearer than Griffith and Bergeron indicate and that it provides adequate guidance as to the very limited role that race is allowed to play. However, because of the ongoing controversy, many players in the child welfare system are committed to law resistance and law evasion. The challenge for mental health professionals is to decide how to respond to conflicting pressures and whether to use their professional skills to assist in good faith implementation of the law or in efforts to undermine the law. The challenge is a real one, because those committed to undermining the law do so in the name of the ever popular best-interests-of-the-child principle, arguing that best practices require consideration of race in placement decisions. However, in my view the choice should be clear, not simply because the law exists, but because the law takes the right position—right both for children and for the larger society.

Griffith and Bergeron acknowledge that, after a period in which race-matching was common and court-made law allowed at least some regular use of race in the placement process, the U.S. Congress passed laws governing these matters: the 1994 Multiethnic Placement Act and the 1996 amendments to that Act (here referred to collectively as MEPA and, when it is important to distinguish between the original 1994 Act and the amended Act, referred to as MEPA I and MEPA II, respectively). However they say that these laws "may still leave the door open to continued race-matching. . . ." They go on to say:

> [E]ven though the statutory attempts were meant to eliminate race
> as a controlling factor in the adoption process, their implementation

From *The Journal of the American Academy of Psychiatry and the Law,* vol. 34, no. 3, November 3, 2006, pp. 315–320 (excerpts). Copyright © 2006 by American Academy of Psychiatry and the Law. Reprinted by permission via S&S Management Services, Inc.

has left room for ambiguity regarding the role that race should play in adoption proceedings. Consequently, even though the statutes were intended to eliminate adoption delays and denials because of race-matching, they may have allowed the continued existence of a cultural stereotype—that black children belong with black families—and may have facilitated its continued existence.

Griffith and Bergeron accurately describe how MEPA I allowed the use of race as one factor in placement, so long as it was not used categorically to determine placement or to delay or deny placement:

> An agency . . . may consider the cultural, ethnic, or racial background of the child and the capacity of the prospective foster or adoptive parents to meet the needs of a child of this background as one of a number of factors used to determine the best interests of a child.

And they describe how MEPA II removed that section of the law, and made related amendments designed to limit the use of race. They note that the U.S. Department of Health and Human Services (DHHS), the MEPA enforcement agency, interprets the law to require strict scrutiny as the standard by which to judge use of race in placements and quote one of the guidance memoranda issued by DHHS. . . .

But they conclude that the DHHS guidance "seemed to frame the possibility for adoption agencies to continue the practice of race-matching," and "allows for discussions with prospective adoptive or foster care parents about their feelings, preferences, and capacities regarding caring for a child of a particular race or ethnicity." They go on to cite the positions of the National Association of Black Social Workers, the Child Welfare League of America, the National Association of Social Workers, and some others, all arguing for a systematic preference for race-matching.

While Griffith and Bergeron raise some questions about the wisdom of assumptions made by race-matching proponents that all blacks will be culturally competent to raise black children in a way that no whites will be, they conclude with a message that seems to emphasize the difficulty of the challenge faced by mental health professionals in deciding just how much weight to give race in their placement evaluations. They state that MEPA has not been considered "spectacularly successful," and that DHHS guidance permits some consideration of race in specific cases. . . .

In their final two paragraphs Griffith and Bergeron cite the Adoption and Race Work Group, assembled by the Stuart Foundation, as evidence of the ongoing debate within the mental health community, noting its conclusion that "race should not be ignored when making placement decisions and that children's best interests are served—all else being equal—when they are placed with families of the same racial, ethnic, and cultural background as their own."

There are several problems with the message that this article by Griffith and Bergeron sends to their colleagues. First, the law is much clearer than they indicate. MEPA II did, as they point out, eliminate the provision in MEPA I that had allowed race as a permissible consideration. MEPA II also eliminated related language indicating that some use of race might be permissible—language in MEPA I forbidding agencies to "categorically deny" placement, or delay or deny placement "solely" on the basis of race—and substituted language that tracked the language of other civil rights statutes, simply prohibiting discrimination. As I discuss elsewhere:

> The intent to remove race as a factor in placement decisions could hardly have been made more clear. The legislative history showed that the race-as-permissible-factor provision was removed precisely because it had been identified as deeply problematic. The simple antidiscrimination language substituted had been consistently interpreted in the context of other civil rights laws as forbidding *any* consideration of race as a factor in decision-making, with the increasingly limited exception accorded formal affirmative action plans.

While it is true that DHHS issued a 1997 Guidance Memorandum allowing consideration of race in some circumstances, that Guidance makes clear that race cannot be used in the normal course but only in exceedingly rare situations. . . .

Moreover, when the Guidance states that use of race in placement is governed by the strict scrutiny standard, it invokes a standard known in the legal world as condemning as unconstitutional under the Federal Constitution almost all race-conscious policies.

MEPA's prohibition of racial matching is controversial within the child welfare world, with some arguing for its repeal and others for "interpretations" that would allow for race-matching in blatant disregard for the clear meaning of the law. The positions taken by the Child Welfare League of America, the National Association of Social Workers, and the National Association of Black Social Workers, cited by Griffith and Bergeron, illustrate these organizations' disagreement with the law. The Report issued by the Stuart Foundation's Adoption and Race Work Group, relied on by Griffith and Bergeron in their concluding paragraphs, illustrates the commitment by many who disagree with the law to evade its restrictions. As I wrote when asked for my comments on this Group's preliminary draft report, which became the final report with no significant changes in tone or substance:

> From start to finish [the Report] reads like a justification for the present race-matching system, and an argument for continuing to implement essential features of that system in a way designed to satisfy the letter but not the spirit of [MEPA]. . . .
>
> The general thrust of the Report in terms of policy direction, together with its specific Recommendations, read to me like the advice prepared by clever lawyers whose goal it is to help the client avoid the clear spirit of the law. The general idea seems to be to tell those in a position to make and implement policy, that this is a bad law, based on a misunderstanding of the needs of black children, but that since it is less than crystal clear, it will be possible to retool and reshape current

policies and practices so that they look quite different but accomplish much the same thing.

The fact that there is ongoing controversy about and resistance to this law matters. Law is not self-enforcing. It relies on people, nonprofit organizations, and government entities to demand enforcement.

However, just as controversy affects law, so law also affects controversy. The fact that federal law now states that race-matching is equivalent to race discrimination matters in a nation that has committed itself in significant ways to the proposition that race discrimination is wrong. Moreover this particular law mandates powerful penalties, specifying an automatic reduction of a set percentage of the federal funds provided to each state for foster and adoption purposes, for any finding of violation. This changes the risk assessment enterprise for typically risk-averse bureaucrats. Acting illegally can get you into trouble, especially if millions of dollars of financial penalties are at stake. While in the years after MEPA's passage I was one of the most vocal critics of the absence of MEPA enforcement activity, as the years went by I began to get the sense in my travels around the country speaking on these issues that social work practice was adjusting, albeit slowly, to MEPA's demands.

The dramatic new development is on the enforcement front. The U.S. Department of Health and Human Services (DHHS), designated as the enforcement agency for MEPA, has finally moved beyond the tough-sounding words that it issued providing interpretive guidance, to take action—action in the form of decisions finding states in violation of the law and imposing the financial penalties mandated by MEPA for such violations. Griffith and Bergeron make no mention of this development, but it seems likely to have a major impact on child welfare agencies nationwide and accordingly seems likely to change the context in which mental health professionals will work in making placement evaluations and the pressures on them with respect to the race factor. The first such enforcement decision involved Hamilton County, Ohio. In 2003, after a four-and-one-half-year investigation, DHHS's Office for Civil Rights (OCR) issued a Letter of Findings, concluding that Hamilton County and Ohio had violated MEPA as well as Title VI of the 1964 Civil Rights Act (42 U.S.C. Sec. 2000(d)), and DHHS's Administration for Children and Families (ACF) issued a Penalty Letter imposing a $1.8 million penalty. In its extensive Letter of Findings, DHHS confirmed that under MEPA as well as Title VI, strict scrutiny is the standard, and child welfare workers have extremely little discretion to consider race in the placement process. DHHS found that MEPA prohibits any regular consideration of race in the normal course, any regular consideration of race in the context of a transracial placement, and any differential consideration of transracial as compared with same-race placements. Moreover, the Letter stated that MEPA prohibits the variety of policies and practices used to assess transracial placements with a view toward the prospective parents' apparent ability to appropriately nurture the racial heritage of other-race children. More specifically, DHHS found illegal administrative rules requiring that: (1) home-studies of prospective adoptive parents seeking "transracial/transcultural" placements include a determination of whether a prospective parent is able to "value, respect, appreciate and educate a child regarding a child's racial, ethnic and cultural heritage, background and language and . . . to integrate the child's culture into normal daily living patterns"; (2) assessments be made of the racial composition of the neighborhood in which prospective families live; and (3) prospective parents prepare a plan for meeting a child's "transracial/transcultural needs." DHHS stated that, in enacting MEPA II, Congress "removed the bases for arguments that MEPA permitted the routine consideration of race, color, or national origin in foster or adoptive placement, and that MEPA prohibited only delays or denials that were categorical in nature." In the consideration of particular Hamilton County cases, DHHS regularly faulted child welfare workers for demanding that home-studies reflect a child's cultural needs, asking for additional information on racial issues, and inquiring into and relying on prospective parents' statements about their racial attitudes (e.g., intention to raise the child in a "color-blind" manner), the degree of contact they had with the African-American community, the level of racial integration in their neighborhood or school system, their plans to address a child's cultural heritage, their level of realism about dealing with a transracial placement, the adequacy of their training in areas like hair care, their unrealistic expectations about racial tolerance, their apparent ability to parent a child of another race, their willingness to relocate to a more integrated community, their apparent ability to provide a child with an understanding of his heritage, and their readiness for transracial placement.

In rejecting one of Ohio's defenses, based on allegedly inadequate advice on the operation of MEPA, DHHS found that the guidance issued in the form of various memoranda from 1995 through 1998 was fully adequate in clarifying the prohibition against any special requirements related to transracial placements.

The subsequent DHHS decision imposing the $1.8 million penalty took issue additionally with Ohio's apparent attempt to circumvent the law by a new administrative rule providing that an agency determination that race should be considered would trigger a referral for an opinion from an outside licensed professional (psychiatrist, clinical psychologist, social worker, or professional clinical counselor). The professional was to be required to provide an "individual assessment of this child that describes the child's special or distinctive needs based on his/her race, color, or national origin and whether it is in the child's best interest to take these needs into account in placing this child for foster care or adoption." DHHS faulted the process for signaling to the professional that the agency thinks race should be a factor, for the professional's lack of training regarding the legal limitations on considering race and for asking the professional whether race should be considered, while failing to require any finding by the professional: "that there is a compelling need to consider race; that such consideration is strictly required to serve the best interests of the child; and that no race-neutral alternatives exist." DHHS also noted that Ohio had indicated its desire for state approval to obtain opinions from professionals known to be opposed to transracial adoptions. DHHS concluded that the rule was "readily susceptible to being used to foster illegal discrimination."

In 2005, DHHS made a second enforcement decision, involving South Carolina, with OCR issuing a Letter of Findings concluding that the state's Department of Social Services had violated both MEPA and Title VI, and ACF issuing a Penalty Letter imposing a penalty of $107,481. In its Letter of Findings in this case, DHHS again emphasized that strict scrutiny is the standard and that the law forbids any regular consideration of race, allowing its consideration only on rare occasions and even then only to the degree it can be demonstrated to be absolutely necessary. DHHS found illegal South Carolina's practice of treating prospective parent racial preferences with greater deference than other preferences: "By treating race differently from all other parental preferences . . . [the agency] establishes its own system based on racial preference. . . ." DHHS also found illegal the agency's practice of deferring to birth parents' racial preferences, stating that the law requires agencies to make placement decisions "independent of the biological parent's race, color or national origin preference." Furthermore, DHHS found illegal the agency's practice of treating transracial adoptions with greater scrutiny, faulting, for example, the inquiries into prospective parents' ability to adopt transracially, and ability to nurture a child of a different race, as well as inquiries into the racial makeup of such parents' friends, neighborhoods, and available schools. And finally, DHHS found to be illegal various other ways in which the agency took race into consideration, including use of race as a "tie-breaking" factor, matching for skin tone, and use of young children's racial preferences—"the routine deference to and wide range of reasons given for . . . following the same-race preferences of young children undermines any claim that these placement decisions are truly individualized." In addition, DHHS made findings of violations in several individual cases, including that of a black couple interested in adopting a Hispanic child, in which the agency was faulted for inquiry into the couple's ability to meet the child's cultural needs. DHHS specified that any acceptable corrective action plan by the state would have to include, *inter alia*, support and encouragement for parents interested in adopting transracially, the creation of progressive disciplinary action, including termination, for staff continuing to use race improperly, the development of whistle-blower protection for staff who reported the use of race by others, and monitoring and reporting requirements designed to ensure future compliance with the law. The ACF Penalty Letter noted that, having reviewed and concurred in the OCR's Letter of Findings, it was imposing the penalty mandated by MEPA.

While these are the only cases in which Letters of Findings and Penalty Letters have been issued, DHHS's OCR has engaged in compliance efforts in several other cases, resulting in agreements by various state agencies to modify their practices in accord with OCR's demands. In addition DHHS's ACF has through various policy statements reenforced its commitment to rigorous enforcement of MEPA.

DHHS's recent enforcement action constitutes a shot across the bow for all state agencies involved in foster and adoptive placement throughout the nation. The opinions in the two cases in which financial penalties were imposed are as clear as they can be that, at the highest ranks, DHHS believes that MEPA and the various MEPA-related guidance memoranda that DHHS has issued mean that race cannot lawfully be taken into account in any routine way in placement decisions, that it is only in the exceptional cases that race can be considered, and even then that authorities will have to be very careful to demonstrate that compelling necessity demands such consideration, consistent with the strict scrutiny standard.

While DHHS guidance had in my view made all this clear previously, the fact that OCR has now taken enforcement action finding MEPA violations, with ACF imposing financial penalties, raises the stakes in a way that agency directors and agency workers will not be able to ignore. Penalties for MEPA violations are mandated under the law, and they are very severe, reducing by set percentages the federal funds on which states are absolutely dependent to run their child welfare systems. A 1997 DHHS Guidance Memorandum noted that in some states MEPA's penalties could range up to more than $3.6 million in a given quarter and could increase to the $7 to $10 million range for continued noncompliance. State agencies act at their peril in ignoring this law. So, too, do agency workers, since their supervisors are not likely to be pleased with action that puts the state's child welfare budget at risk.

Some will no doubt continue to resist and evade the law, but I predict that such conduct will diminish over time as the law becomes more established in people's minds as simply part of the nation's basic civil rights commitment. While some have called for MEPA's repeal there has been no significant move in this direction.

My hope is that mental health professionals will join ranks with those interested in following the law in good faith, rather than with those interested in evading its mandate. I say this not simply because MEPA is the law, but because I believe it is a good law, one that serves the interests both of children and of the larger society. Griffith and Bergeron note that black children "can" do well in white families, but I believe the social science evidence provides much stronger support for MEPA than that. By now, there is a significant body of studies on transracial adoptees, many of which are good, controlled studies, comparing them to same-race adoptees. My review of these studies and that of others besides me, reveals no evidence that any harm comes to children by virtue of their placement across color lines. By contrast, there is much evidence that harm comes to children in foster or institutional care when they are delayed in adoptive placement or denied adoption altogether, and there is much evidence that race-matching policies result in such delay and denial. In addition, there is evidence that even when child welfare systems purport to use race as only one factor in decision-making, rather than as a categorical factor justifying delay and/or denial of adoptive placement, race ends up being used in ways that result in just such delay and denial. This latter was, of course, the main reason Congress amended MEPA I to eliminate race as a permissible consideration—Senator Metzenbaum, the law's sponsor, became convinced that MEPA I was not succeeding in eliminating the categorical use of race because its permission to use race as one factor was being abused, something that many of us who supported MEPA II had thought was inevitable, based on experience.

So, it seems to me clear that MEPA serves the interests of children, by helping black children in particular to find placements in loving homes of whatever color as promptly as possible. MEPA also seems to me to serve the interests of the larger society, by combating in a small but significant way the notion that race should divide people. Race-matching is the direct descendant of white supremacy and of black separatism. For the state to promote the formation of same-race families and discourage the formation of interracial families, as it does when it endorses race-matching, is wrong in my view for the same reasons that barriers to interracial marriage were wrong. The U.S. Supreme Court struck down those marriage barriers in 1967 in *Loving v. Virginia*. Congress took an important step in passing MEPA II to bring our nation's child welfare policies in line with the rest of our civil rights regimen. This law makes the statement that while race, of course, does matter in myriad ways in our society, it does not and should not define people's capacity to love each other.

~~~

Commentary: Transracial Adoption— Changing Trends and Attitudes

. . . The increase in transracial adoptions of African-American children in the United States arose in response to the paucity of white babies available for adoption and pressures on public agencies to free children in foster care for adoption. The majority of single teenage mothers now choose to keep their babies. There is increased use of kinship care or adoption, and heightened use of birth control, all of which result in fewer newborn babies being available for adoption. In my state of Maine, the rate of teenage pregnancies has plummeted and is now one of the lowest in the nation. The option of seeking infants from abroad is fraught with uncertainty—concerns about health problems and attachment disorders, delays, expenses, and policies regarding adoptions by foreigners that keep shifting in many nations. Yet another attraction for parents considering adopting African-American babies is the shorter waiting period.

In many parts of the United States and other countries, communities have become more accepting of racially mixed families. In as much as African-American children tend to stay longer in out-of-home care than do white children, freeing them for adoption by white families became a means of alleviating this situation. In the 1990s, public agencies were under a mandate to hasten the exit of children from foster care into permanent care and the Adoption and Safe Families Act of 1995 offered incentives to states that increased adoption of children in foster care. This, combined with the Multiethnic Placement Act, resulted in a dramatic decrease in the number of children in foster care and those awaiting adoption. As of 2001, 14 percent of all adoptions were transracial, although most of them were international adoptions.

As noted by Griffith and Bergeron, the pendulum of statutes regarding transracial adoptions has been swinging like the chapper of a ringing bell. The common thread that runs throughout these debates and dialogues is the concept of adhering to the child's best interests. This guidepost dates back to a 1925 decision by judge Cardozo who first coined the term *best interests*. Goldstein *et al.* would later elaborate on this concept in their book, *Beyond the Best Interests of the Child,* in which they applied psychoanalytic concepts to the resolution of custody disputes. The best-interest standard has held up well over time and continues to be used by courts in determining child custody determinations. Most states further delineate a list of factors to be considered in making custody recommendations to the court.

Caseworkers and forensic mental health professionals have always had to be mindful of their potential biases in making custody recommendations. Such biases might pertain to potential adoptive parents' socioeconomic status, education, lifestyle, or sexual orientation. The issue of transracial adoptions may bring out even stronger feelings that threaten the objectivity of those making recommendations and final decisions about adoptions. Resistance to transracial adoptions is reminiscent of the opposition to adoption by same-sex couples. There used to be great concern that children adopted into these families would be stigmatized, proselytized into the gay lifestyle, and deprived of adequate role models. Some professionals in child welfare were adamantly opposed on moral grounds. And yet, follow-up studies have consistently shown that children raised by same-sex couples are no different from children raised by heterosexual parents. Eventually, adoption agencies began to see same-sex couples as a valuable resource for hard-to-place children such as those with AIDs or other serious medical or mental problems and older children with histories of failed adoptions. With time, society has become more accepting of these alternative families and their children. These families have, in turn, demonstrated their parenting skills with some of the most challenging children.

Griffith and Bergeron raise the question of the importance of African-American culture in the adoptee's life. I recall many years ago testifying in the Northwest regarding the placement of a child who was part Native American and part Latino. Strong arguments were put forth on the importance of preserving his Native-American heritage, yet no one was arguing for his Latino heritage. Concern for the well-being of African-American children unable to be returned to their birth parents is a relatively new phenomenon. Certainly, few people advocated for them or for white children in the mid-20th century when it was not unusual for children to languish in foster care for up to five years and then be too old or too emotionally damaged to be deemed adoptable. The hue and cry of professionals opposed to transracial adoption was in part related to fears that African-American children raised by whites would not be able to defend themselves against prejudice in a racist society. However, one must also ask whether life in the impermanence of foster care with multiple placements and the risk of further abuse or neglect better prepare them to live in a racist society. Of note, private adoption agencies began placing African-American children with white families long before public agencies did so, as the costs of recruiting African-American families was too high. The numbers were small, but there was little protest and somehow this practice passed under the radar screen.

Norris and Ferguson note that the 1960s and 1970s saw the decimation of many minority families due to substance abuse, incarceration, the HIV epidemic, higher mortality rates, and unemployment due to racism. The net result of these forces was more children of color in foster care. In addition, African-American families often failed to meet the criteria for adoption eligibility. The Adoption Assistance and Child Welfare Act of 1980 provided some relief to families that could not afford to adopt. Simon conducted a 20-year study of 200 white parents and their predominantly African-American adopted children and found that most of the children were happy with their racial identity and racial awareness and happy with themselves. Twenty percent of the group studied experienced some problems in their preteen and adolescent years. This is not a very high percentage, considering the problems faced by most teens and, in particular, adopted teens who have a more difficult time coming to terms with their identity as they approach this phase of development.

The problems faced by children in transracial families should be approached on a developmental level. Ethnoracial awareness does not begin until sometime between the ages of three and five years. My eldest son who, at age three, would insist that our African-American nanny was part of our family and shared our last name brought this point home to me. One day, he was looking out the window at the park across the street and said excitedly, "Mommy, look! There are three black people out there!" Thinking he finally was beginning to note racial differences, I looked out the window and saw three nuns walking in their black habits. As adopted children become aware that their color is different from that of their parents, this might actually facilitate conversations about adoption earlier than in homogenous families, and there is less likely to be secrecy about the adoption.

As noted, problems with racial identity may not surface until adoptees enter their preteen and adolescent years. White families who welcome African-American children into their homes to play with their children may become less welcoming once their children are of dating age. African Americans raised in predominantly white communities may have difficulty fitting in with other African Americans once they leave home. I treated an African-American teenager from an affluent white community where she was well accepted in her predominantly white high school. She related how difficult she found it relating to the African-American students at her college who viewed her as an "Oreo": black on the outside and white inside. She commented on how she had felt like neither fish nor fowl in her new environment. Although not adopted, she faced dilemmas similar to those faced by adoptees who grew up in cultures where they are very much in the minority.

For many years, adoption agencies tried to match children with families who shared similar physical attributes. This effort coincided with secrecy about adoption, the shame of infertility, and even the need to protect a child from knowledge of his illegitimacy. Families now speak more openly of adoption and even practice open adoptions. My brother was carefully matched to my family's phenotype, but aside from both of us being tall and Anglo-Saxon in appearance, we have little in common. Biological siblings may look very different from one another and even their parents. Why must there be so much emphasis on sameness? Rainbow families have demonstrated that there is much more to being family than external appearances. Diversity might actually facilitate individuation and separation in children.

Cultural competence and capacity are routinely screened for in white parents wishing to adopt African-American children. In addition, there are many books and Web sites available to help these parents, once they have been approved to adopt, on how best to raise children of a different race and preserve their cultural roots. There is much emphasis on the need for adoptive parents to expose their adopted children to their African-American culture. While I do not take issue with this, I think there is a much broader need to instill appreciation of African-American culture among all school children and their parents. Tolerance, understanding, and respect should be taught early and reinforced at home. The magazine *Teaching Tolerance* published by the Southern Poverty Law Center has had significant impact on our school systems in this regard. Our culture is rapidly changing, and the fear that African Americans in white families will not be able to handle discrimination seems like an outdated notion. The onus should not be put on adoptees to learn to deal with discrimination but rather on society to end discrimination. African-American children in white families may play an important role in helping other children and their parents overcome racial stereotypes.

EXPLORING THE ISSUE

Do Federal Laws Make Transracial Adoptions More Commonplace?

Critical Thinking and Reflection

1. Griffith and Bergeron believe that transracial adoption should be less commonplace because more and more children are being considered "special cases." Define what makes a child a special case and why it would be harmful for children in these special cases to be adopted transracially.
2. Bartholet suggests that by allowing race as a factor in adoptions, American society is allowing racial discriminations, which our country has been fighting to eliminate. Support or refute this statement and explain why making reference to content from the articles.
3. Take a stance, pro or con, regarding transracial adoption. Explain your position citing evidence from either the Griffith and Bergeron or the Bartholet selections to support your position.

Is There Common Ground?

The Multiethnic Placement Act is intended to provide an effective support for transracial adoption. It seeks to eliminate the consideration of race in the placement of children except in exceptional cases. Legislation such as this is intended to protect the interests of adoptees and their prospective parents. However, do prospective parents usually prefer children of their own race? Or, are adopting parents pleased to have a child—of any race—to love and rear? Do you believe, as suggested in the NO selection, that as respect for all minority cultures and tolerance for diversity continue to pervade our society, the need for "best interest" legislation such as this act may become unnecessary? Will our society ever evolve to the degree that there would never be extenuating circumstances in which children placed for adoption need to be adopted by parents of the same race?

There are many children in need of adoption, and most are minority children. The goal of adoption is to get children out of institutions and orphanages and into loving and caring homes. The vast majority of the literature on transracial adoption finds little to suggest that it harms children when they are adopted by parents of a different race. The National Association of Black Social Workers (NABSW) seems to be the ones who are most vociferous in denouncing transracial adoption. Is this a form of discrimination, to prevent Anglo-Americans from adopting a minority child who is of a different race?

Although the efficacy of transracial adoption has been well established in the research literature, the controversy continues as to whether or not it should be widely practiced. Many feel that the issue should be laid to rest—once and for all—because children thrive more effectively in adoptive homes than in institutions. And, there are simply not enough same-race minority families to adopt children of the given race. Others suggest that although we as a society make overtures to being nondiscriminating, the practice still occurs in adoptions despite the law. Also, in some cases, people believe it is necessary to consider race in placing children. It seems clear that those on either side of the issue would agree, however, on two fundamental goals: (1) to decrease the amount of children in institutions and orphanages and (2) to place children in adoptive homes that will best meet their physical and emotional needs. The problem seems to be in the differing points of view as to how to best achieve these goals.

Additional Resources

Child Welfare Information Gateway. Transracial and Transcultural Adoptions. Retrieved on April 7, 2011, from http://www.childwelfare.gov/pubs/f_trans.cfm.

This Web site defines and discusses reasons for transracial adoptions and expert opinions on their impact on children.

Issues in Transracial Adoption. Retrieved on April 7, 2011, from http://userpages .umbc.edu/~mmcman1/.

This Web site discusses the various issues that must be taken into consideration when considering transracial adoptions.

Morrison, A. (2004) Transracial Adoption: The Pros and Cons and the Parents' Perspective. *Harvard BlackLetter Law Journal*, 20, pp. 163–202. Retrieved on April 7, 2011, from http://www.law.harvard.edu/students/orgs/blj/vol20/morrison.pdf.

This is an article posted online that discusses some of the pros and cons of transracial adoptions, as well as the parents' perspectives on these types of adoptions.

The Adoption History Project. Adoption History. Retrieved on April 7, 2011, from http://pages.uoregon.edu/adoption/topics/transracialadoption.htm.

This Web site describes the history of transracial adoptions in America.

Internet References . . .

Kids Count

This Kids Count section of the Annie E. Casey Foundation Web site posts data on national and state indicators of child well-being, referred to as state report cards. The Annie E. Casey Foundation is an organization that is dedicated to building a better future for disadvantaged children in the United States.

http://www.aecf.org/kidscount/

Children's Defense Fund

The Children's Defense Fund site includes data from every state on issues related to child care.

http://www.cdfactioncouncil.org

National Network for Child Care (NNCC)

This Web site from the National Network for Child Care (NNCC) provides resources for raising children. Included are links to sites designed especially for children, as well as sites that offer activities for children, nutrition information, and information on parent involvement issues.

http://www.nncc.org

Educational Resources Information Center (ERIC)

This Educational Resources Information Center (ERIC) Web site, sponsored by the U.S. Department of Education, leads to numerous documents related to elementary and early childhood education as well as to other curriculum topics and issues.

http://www.ed.gov

Just in Time Parenting Information

The Just in Time Parenting Information Web site includes newsletters that are designed to provide information relating to a child's specific age. These newsletters were developed by the Cooperative Extension Service in several different states. The timely information helps parents to understand how their children are developing.

http://www.parentinginfo.org

Early Childhood

The period of early childhood is sometimes referred to as the preschool years. It generally encompasses ages two or three through four or five. This is a time when children become much more adept at taking part in physical activities, satisfying curiosities, and learning from experience. It is also a time when parents who think they have finally figured their children out realize that they have to adapt what they have been doing and learn new skills to deal with the new skills their children are acquiring. Preschoolers play more frequently with other children, become increasingly skilled in daily tasks, and are much more responsive to people and things in their environment. Many children begin school during their preschool years, an experience that gives them their first extended contacts with a social institution other than the family. Changing attitudes about discipline, family size, divorce, and the mass media all have implications for a child's development. This section examines some of the choices families make in rearing their preschool children.

- Is Spanking Detrimental to Children?
- Are Fathers Really Necessary?
- Does Divorce Create Long-Term Negative Effects for Children?
- Is Viewing Television Violence Harmful for Children?

ISSUE 5

Is Spanking Detrimental to Children?

YES: Elizabeth Thompson Gershoff, from "Corporal Punishment by Parents and Associated Child Behaviors and Experiences: A Meta-Analytic and Theoretical Review," *Psychological Bulletin* (July, 2002)

NO: Diana Baumrind, Philip A. Cowan, and Robert E. Larzelere, from "Ordinary Physical Punishment: Is It Harmful? Comment on Gershoff (2002)," *Psychological Bulletin* (July, 2002)

Learning Outcomes

After reading this issue, you should be able to:

- List some of the arguments in favor of, and opposed to, spanking.
- Describe some of the negative effects that can come from spanking children.
- Identify the difference between mild spanking and physical abuse.

ISSUE SUMMARY

YES: Columbia University researcher Elizabeth Thompson Gershoff analyzed results from 88 studies and concluded that corporal punishment negatively affected children's behavior. Among the 10 negative outcomes were increased child aggression, decreased quality of the parent-child relationship, and increased risk of abusing a child or spouse in adulthood.

NO: Diana Baumrind and Philip Cowan, researchers from the University of California–Berkeley, and Robert Larzelere, from the Nebraska Medical Center, refuted Gershoff's findings by questioning her definition of corporal punishment and analysis techniques of the 88 studies. They feel mild spankings, when appropriately administered, are useful in shaping children's behavior.

The topic of spanking, also known as corporal punishment, provokes highly emotional responses from family practitioners, parents, researchers, and children. There seems to be no one who is neutral about the subject, especially children. It would be interesting to ask children about their feeling toward spanking. Were you spanked as a child? What was used to spank you? Bare hand? Hairbrush? Ruler? Switch? The list could go on and on. Do you think the spankings negatively affected you, or did they teach you how to act appropriately? The following quotes are often used in relationship to spanking: "Spare the rod and spoil the child. I was spanked and I turned out OK. Kids need to be spanked to show them who's boss."

If you were not spanked, what was used to correct your misbehavior? Was the misbehavior explained? Was your correct behavior rewarded and your misbehavior punished? What about children who were not spanked or corrected in any way? Are they considered spoiled or out of control? Perhaps verbal abuse or a slap to the face was used to correct your behavior, or maybe you were ignored altogether. These techniques are considered similar to spanking in that they can become abusive or neglectful.

Ninety-four percent of American parents report spanking their children by the time their children are 3 years old. Although spanking is a popular form of discipline in the United States, several countries have outlawed spanking and the physical punishment of children: Austria, Croatia, Cyprus, Germany, Israel, Italy, Latvia, Norway, Denmark, Sweden, and Finland. Proponents of spanking point out that these countries' rates of child abuse have not declined as a result of banning spanking.

Spanking is associated with family violence and child abuse. These are the stories often found in the media about parents injuring or even killing their children as a result of physical punishment. Although the media exploits these situations and makes the public feel outraged that children are treated this way, one must remember these are extreme cases. Most families feel they use spanking judiciously and do not consider it abusive.

Ultimately, spanking is used as a teaching tool and a way to solve problems. Parents see children misbehave, look for a way to gain the children's attention immediately, and spank them. Parents believe that by inflicting pain, they are changing children's behavior and solving the problem of misbehavior. Opponents of spanking ask the question of how children will change misbehavior if they are not taught what *to do* versus what *not to do*. In addition, the message is sent that I am bigger than you so I can solve this problem by hitting you.

In the YES selection, Elizabeth Thompson Gershoff argues that spanking harms children by decreasing moral internalization, increasing aggression as a child and adult, increasing child delinquency and antisocial behavior, decreasing the quality of the parent–child interaction, decreasing the quality of mental health in childhood and adulthood, increasing the risk of being physically abused in adulthood, and increasing the risk of abusing a child or spouse in adulthood. In the NO selection, Diana Baumrind, Philip Cowan, and Robert Larzelere refute Gershoff's claims by showing flaws in her definition of corporal punishment and her method of analyzing the 88 studies she used for her research study. They feel that Gershoff did not address the real issue of whether or not mild spanking is harmful. Both selections on corporal punishment address the issue of the need to define corporal punishment and to have researchers agree on the definition before they begin research on the subject. Gershoff found a relationship between children being spanked and 10 negative behavioral outcomes in childhood, some of which also extended into adulthood. Although spanking was associated with short-term compliance from the child, the 10 negative outcomes far outweighed the one short-term positive result.

Authors of the opposing selection show that there is no support for a causal relationship between corporal punishment and detrimental child behaviors. The authors concede that no one feels abusive physical punishment is appropriate, but that mild spanking after 18 months of age and before puberty is OK. They feel spanking within the context of other discipline methods is useful.

YES   Elizabeth Thompson Gershoff

Corporal Punishment by Parents and Associated Child Behaviors and Experiences: A Meta-Analytic and Theoretical Review

Corporal punishment has been an integral part of how parents discipline their children throughout the history of the United States and has been a focus of psychological research for decades. Although a growing number of countries have adopted policies or laws that prohibit parents from using corporal punishment as a means of discipline (Austria, Croatia, Cyprus, Denmark, Finland, Germany, Israel, Italy, Latvia, Norway, and Sweden), both support for and use of corporal punishment remain strong in the United States, with 94% of American parents spanking their children by the time they are 3 or 4 years old.

Psychologists and other professionals are divided on the question of whether the benefits of corporal punishment might outweigh any potential hazards; some have concluded that corporal punishment is both effective and desirable, whereas others have concluded that corporal punishment is ineffective at best and harmful at worst. This controversy over corporal punishment has inspired a series of recent debates among psychological, sociological, and legal scholars about what corporal punishment does and does not do for children.

Despite this controversy and the hundreds of scientific studies invoked on either side of the debate, understanding of the child behaviors and experiences associated with parental corporal punishment has been limited to narrative reviews and "vote count" summaries of the number of positive and negative effects that accrue from corporal punishment. Crucial questions remain unanswered, such as what range of child behaviors and experiences are empirically associated with parental corporal punishment, as well as why, how, and for whom corporal punishment might have such effects. This article provides preliminary answers to these questions by synthesizing the current empirical evidence of, and theoretical explanations for, associations between parental corporal punishment and 11 child behaviors and experiences. . . .

From *Psychological Bulletin*, vol. 128, no. 4, July 2002, pp. 539–544 (excerpts, refs. omitted). Copyright © 2002 by American Psychological Association. Reprinted by permission via Rightslink.

Meta-Analyses of Parental Corporal Punishment and Associated Child Behaviors and Experiences

The first step in understanding whether and how parental corporal punishment affects children is to establish to what degree corporal punishment is associated with the child constructs of interest. Toward this end, I present in this section the results of separate meta-analyses of the associations between parental corporal punishment and 11 frequently identified child constructs. Despite the inability of meta-analyses to yield definitive causal conclusions, they do constitute an effective means of establishing whether the associations of interest are present and thus pave the way for further research into causal mechanisms. To underscore the inability of meta-analyses to support causal conclusions, I refer to child "behaviors and experiences" or "constructs" associated with parental corporal punishment rather than to child "outcomes" in the context of the meta-analyses.

Distinguishing Corporal Punishment from Physical Abuse

Before examining the associations between corporal punishment and child constructs, it is important to establish what is meant by the term *corporal punishment*. Regarding legal definitions, 48 states and the District of Columbia specify what constitutes corporal punishment in their legal statutes defining child abuse; 29 states assert that corporal punishment encompasses the use of "reasonable" force with some adding qualifiers that it must also be "appropriate" (AL, AK, AZ, CA, CO), "moderate" (AR, DE, SC, SD), or "necessary" (MT, NH, NY, OR, TX, WI). Three states see the need to clarify that corporal punishment is limited to "nondeadly force" (AK, NY, TX). The present article adopts the definition of corporal punishment offered by Straus. "Corporal punishment is the use of physical force with the intention of causing a child to experience pain but not injury for the purposes of correction or control of the child's behavior."

A frequent criticism of research on corporal punishment is that non-abusive corporal punishment is often confounded with harmful and abusive behaviors, thus preventing conclusions about the effects of everyday spanking. This apparent confound has arisen because the majority of child abuse researchers view corporal punishment and potentially abusive techniques as points on a continuum of physical acts toward children. However, a consensus on where to draw the line between acceptable corporal punishment and dangerous physical abuse is noticeably absent in the United States. State laws defining what constitutes physical abuse often specifically include corporal punishment. Davidson reviewed the state definitions of *child maltreatment* and found that 12 states (DC, FL, IL, MT, NE, NJ, NY, ND, OH, RI, SC, WV) included the phrase "excessive corporal punishment" in their definitions of child maltreatment; an additional 11 states qualified corporal punishment as constituting abuse when characterized as "cruel" (CT, CO, NE, NM, OH, SD), "unlawful" (CA), "excessive or unreasonable" (WY), "severe" (NJ), "cruel and inhuman" (KS), or "extreme" (ME).

For the purposes of this article, I consider physical abuse to be a potential outcome of corporal punishment. Herein, corporal punishment will be operationally distinguished from physical abuse according to the definition of physical abuse provided by the National Clearinghouse on Child Abuse and Neglect Information, namely:

> Physical abuse is characterized by the infliction of physical injury as a result of punching, beating, kicking, biting, burning, shaking or otherwise harming a child. The parent or caretaker may not have intended to hurt the child, rather the injury may have resulted from over-discipline or physical punishment. (What Are the Main Types of Maltreatment? section, para. 2)

Behaviors that do not result in significant physical injury (e.g., spank, slap) are considered corporal punishment, whereas behaviors that risk injury (e.g., punching, kicking, burning) are considered physical abuse. The studies included in the meta-analyses discussed below explicitly targeted parental corporal punishment, rather than parental physical abuse, as potential predictors of child behaviors and experiences. As I describe in detail below, studies that included potentially abusive techniques in their definitions of corporal punishment were excluded from the analyses.

Methodological Concerns in the Measurement of Corporal Punishment

It is important to acknowledge at the outset that the majority of studies examining links between parental corporal punishment and child behaviors and experiences measure both constructs at the same point in time, thus preventing any conclusions about causality. As I discuss below, even measuring parental corporal punishment at one time point and a child behavior at a future time point may not be sufficient to infer causal direction. True detection of causality may require controlling for the child's rate of the behavior of interest at the first time point as well to account for autocontingency of behavior over time. With these points in mind, the meta-analyses described here do not afford causal conclusions but allow understanding only of whether corporal punishment and child constructs are associated.

In addition, because corporal punishment is used primarily with children younger than 5 years of age, because corporal punishment is used rarely by parents (1–2 times per month), and because assigning parents to spank or no-spank experimental conditions is untenable, researchers must rely on parent reports of corporal punishment rather than on observations. Although some methods of having parents report their use of corporal punishment, such as nightly phone calls or detailed daily discipline diaries, do have high validity, the majority of information on corporal punishment comes from parents' or adolescent and adult children's recollections of frequency of corporal punishment.

Child Behaviors and Experiences Associated with Parental Corporal Punishment

The goal of most research on parenting is to identify which practices promote positive and adaptive behaviors in children. However, in the study of parents' use of corporal punishment, much research has been biased toward finding negative child outcomes associated with corporal punishment. The meta-analyses below specifically include a balance of potentially desirable child constructs (immediate compliance, moral internalization, quality of relationship with parent, and mental health) as well as undesirable child constructs (aggression, criminal and antisocial behavior, abuse of own child or spouse, and victim of abuse by own parent). Discussion of why corporal punishment should be associated with such behaviors and experiences is presented briefly here; the hypothesized processes linking the experience of corporal punishment with these constructs are detailed in the process–context model in the second section of the article.

Immediate Compliance

The primary goal most parents have in administering corporal punishment is to stop children from misbehaving immediately. Laboratory research on learning has confirmed that corporal punishment is indeed effective in securing short-term compliance. Although there are many studies that purport to examine relations between corporal punishment and compliance, most of these studies do not involve observations of whether children comply immediately after corporal punishment is administered. Rather, such studies ask parents how often they typically use corporal punishment and correlate this frequency with parents' reports of how compliant their children are to all forms of discipline. To assess corporal punishment's effect on short- and long-term compliance separately, the subsequent meta-analysis of immediate compliance only includes studies that measured children's compliance to corporal punishment. Compliance that occurs at a point in time removed from an instance of corporal punishment is considered evidence of internalization.

Moral Internalization

Although immediate compliance may be a salient goal when parents initiate discipline, promoting the development of children's internal controls is more important to long-term socialization than immediate compliance. *Moral internalization* is defined by Grusec and Goodnow as "taking over the values and attitudes of society as one's own so that socially acceptable behavior is motivated not by anticipation of external consequences but by intrinsic or internal factors," and it is thought to underlie the development of children's social and emotional competence. Children's internalization of morals is thought to be enhanced by parental discipline strategies that use minimal parental power, promote choice and autonomy, and provide explanations for desirable behaviors. Attribution theorists emphasize that power-assertive methods such as corporal punishment promote children's external attributions for their behavior and minimize their attributions to internal motivations. Additionally, corporal punishment may not facilitate moral internalization because it does not teach children the reasons for behaving correctly, does not involve communication of the effects of children's behaviors on others, and may teach children the desirability of not getting caught.

Aggression

The association between corporal punishment and children's aggression is one of the most studied and debated findings in the child-rearing literature. Over the years, several reviews of the literature have concluded that corporal punishment is associated with increases in children's aggressive behaviors. Corporal punishment has been hypothesized to predict increases in children's aggression because it models aggression; promotes hostile attributions, which predict violent behavior; and initiates coercive cycles of aversive behaviors between parent and child. Early experiences with corporal punishment may model and legitimize many types of violence throughout an individual's life, particularly violence in romantic relationships. Indeed, in one longitudinal study, parents' use of corporal punishment in childhood was the strongest predictor of adolescents' aggression 8 years later, whereas permissive parenting was not a significant predictor. It was my expectation that corporal punishment would be associated in the meta-analyses with aggression in childhood as well as in adulthood.

Although aggression is often combined with antisocial behavior to constitute what are typically referred to as externalizing behavior problems, antisocial behaviors such as stealing are nonviolent and may be related to corporal punishment in different ways than aggression. In the present meta-analyses, the extent to which children engage in delinquent or illegal behaviors are separated from the extent of their aggressive behaviors.

Delinquent, Criminal, and Antisocial Behavior

Across decades of research, corporal punishment has been implicated in the etiology of criminal and antisocial behaviors by both children and adults. Attribution theory posits that associations between corporal punishment and child delinquent or antisocial behavior result from an inability of corporal punishment to facilitate children's internalization of morals and values. Social control theory suggests that parental corporal punishment erodes the parent–child relationship and in turn decreases children's motivation to internalize parents' values and those of the society, which in turn results in low self-control. These same processes may explain the relation between corporal punishment and adult criminality. In Glueck and Glueck's longitudinal study of delinquency, whether boys experienced a harsh parental disciplinary style predicted their arrest rates at ages 17 through 45. J. McCord also found in her longitudinal study that the extent to which parents were aggressively punitive predicted their children's criminal behavior as adults. The connection between criminal and antisocial behavior in childhood and adulthood is examined here in separate meta-analyses.

Quality of the Parent–Child Relationship

The potential for parental corporal punishment to disrupt the parent–child relationship is thought to be a main disadvantage of its use. The painful nature of corporal punishment can evoke feelings of fear, anxiety, and anger in children; if these emotions are generalized to the parent, they can interfere with a positive parent–child relationship by inciting children to be fearful of and to avoid the parent. If corporal punishment does lead children to avoid their parents, such avoidance may in turn erode bonds of trust and closeness between parents and children.

Mental Health
Although little theoretical work has been done to identify the processes by which corporal punishment would lead to mental health problems, harsh punishment (including corporal punishment) has been associated significantly with adolescents' depressive symptomatology and distress, even after controlling for age, gender, family socioeconomic status (SES), and history of physical abuse. Coercive techniques have been associated with decreases in children's feelings of confidence and assertiveness and with increases in feelings of humiliation and helplessness. If corporal punishment does have indelible effects on children's mental health, an association between corporal punishment and adult mental health also might be expected. In the meta-analyses I present below, the constructs of child mental health and adult mental health are analyzed separately and include varied indices of poor mental health, including depression, alcoholism, suicidal tendency, and low self-esteem.

Adult Abuse of Own Child or Spouse
If corporal punishment is associated with a general aggressive tendency in adulthood, this aggression also may manifest in relationships with family members, particularly with a child or spouse. The same processes hypothesized to account for an association between corporal punishment and general aggression also are expected to account for a tendency toward violence against family members. Specifically, if parental corporal punishment leads individuals to view aggression or violence as legitimate, make external attributions for their behavior, and attribute hostile intent to the behaviors of others, they may be more likely to resort to aggression and violence during conflicts with their children and spouses. A tendency toward intergenerational transmission of aggression in close relationships is evident in a strong tendency for parents who were corporally punished to continue the practice with their own children. Similarly, experience with both average (e.g., spanking) and extreme (e.g., kicking, biting, burning, and beating up) forms of corporal punishment by parents are associated with increases in an individual's likelihood of acting violently with an adult romantic partner.

Becoming a Victim of Physical Abuse
As stated above, child abuse researchers tend to see corporal punishment and physical abuse on a continuum, such that if corporal punishment is administered too severely or too frequently, the outcome can be physical abuse. The notion of a corporal punishment–physical abuse continuum is corroborated in part by physically abusive parents themselves: Parents who had abused their children revealed that as many as two thirds of their abusive incidents began

as attempts to change children's behavior or to "teach them a lesson." Unfortunately, use of severe and potentially abusive physical techniques may be more common than has been realized. In a recent study, 16% of incidents reported by mothers and 21% of those reported by fathers were rated by independent coders as severe (e.g., use of spoons, sticks, or belts). The potential for the widely used practice of corporal punishment to be associated with a risk for injury to children behooves further research into this connection.

Method

Sample of Studies

I used three main sources to identify all articles that examined the associations between parental corporal punishment and child behaviors and experiences and were available through June 2001. The first source was the reference lists of relevant reviews, namely by Becker, Larzelere, Steinmetz, and Straus. Second, I conducted a computer-based literature search of *Psychological Abstracts* PsycINFO, *Educational Resources Information Center, Social Sciences Index,* and *Dissertation Abstracts International.* Key words used to identify relevant articles were *corporal punishment, physical punishment,* and *spank.* The third and final search involved the "ancestry approach" applied to the reference sections of all retrieved articles, book chapters, and dissertations. In the interest of being exhaustive, qualification for inclusion was not restricted to peer-reviewed journals; I made every attempt to include all relevant and accessible journal articles, book chapters, and dissertations so as to avoid publication biases.

The abstracts and often the full text of over 300 relevant works, including 63 dissertations, were studied for inclusion in the present meta-analyses. Half of these works did not include data, as they were instead focused on the debate about corporal punishment ($n = 69$), the prevalence of corporal punishment in the United States or abroad ($n = 42$), the antecedents to parents' use of corporal punishment ($n = 40$), attitudes about corporal punishment ($n = 21$), or other issues such as the history of corporal punishment and theories about how it affects children ($n = 27$). Of the 189 studies that did present data on potential effects of corporal punishment, 101 were excluded according to the following criteria: (a) 27% combined corporal punishment with abusive techniques or only examined abusive behaviors; (b) 22% predicted dependent variables that have not been considered consistently in the literature on corporal punishment (e.g., intelligence); (c) 22% did not provide sufficient statistics for calculation of an effect size (e.g., only included betas from regression with other variables); (d) 17% combined corporal punishment with other types of discipline (e.g., corporal punishment was grouped with verbal punishment); and (e) 12% did not study corporal punishment administered by parents, used exceptional populations, or were unavailable through interlibrary loan.

A sample of 88 studies, including 8 dissertations, met the above criteria and were included in the analyses. (Multiple articles from the same study were represented in the analyses by the effect size from only one article.) Of the studies included, 67 provided an effect size for a single metaanalysis, 15 provided effect sizes for two meta-analyses, 4 provided three effects sizes, and 2 provided four effect sizes, for a total of 117 effect sizes across the 11 analyses conducted. The total number of participants was 36,309 (studies contributing more than one effect size only counted once), with an average of 413 participants per study and a range of 14 to 4,529 participants per study. The earliest study was from 1938; 5% of the studies were from 1950–1959, 10% from 1960–1969, 10% from 1970–1979, 25% from 1980–1989, 47% from 1990–1999, and 2% from 2000. The range of studies incorporated in the meta-analyses included 26 nonsignificant effect sizes. . . .

Results
Meta-Analyses

. . . All of the composite effect sizes were significant (none of the confidence intervals include zero) and thus parental corporal punishment was associated significantly with each of the 11 child behaviors and experiences. According to J. Cohen's criteria for judging effect sizes, three of the composite mean weighted effect sizes are small (−0.09, 0.13, −0.33), four are small to medium (0.36, 0.42, 0.42, −0.49), two are medium (0.57, −0.58), one is medium to large (0.69), and one is large (1.13, immediate compliance).

Ten of the 11 meta-analyses indicate parental corporal punishment is associated with the following undesirable behaviors and experiences: decreased moral internalization, increased child aggression, increased child delinquent and antisocial behavior, decreased quality of relationship between parent and child, decreased child mental health, increased risk of being a victim of physical abuse, increased adult aggression, increased adult criminal and antisocial behavior, decreased adult mental health, and increased risk of abusing own child or spouse. Corporal punishment was associated with only one desirable behavior, namely, increased immediate compliance. . . .

Diana Baumrind, Philip A. Cowan, and Robert E. Larzelere

 NO

Ordinary Physical Punishment: Is It Harmful? Comment on Gershoff (2002)

In . . . her comprehensive article, Gershoff (2002) used meta-analyses of 88 studies to provide what she offered as a conclusive answer to the question of whether corporal punishment (CP) is significantly associated with 11 frequently identified aspects of children's behavior. She found that except for an association with immediate compliance to parental demands, CP is associated with negative or undesirable behaviors (e.g., aggression, lower levels of moral internalization and mental health). . . .

Measurement Issues: Corporal Punishment, Spanking, and Abuse

Disputes about the potential impact of corporal punishment are occurring in the social context of a vigorous debate about the impact of spanking. There is an international movement by lay organizations such as EPOCH-Worldwide to criminalize corporal punishment or to discourage its use. The advocates of a blanket injunction against spanking have cited associations between physical punishment and detrimental child outcomes, such as those presented in Gershoff's meta-analyses, to support their position. Such direct application of correlational research to social policy decisions presupposes a causal link between physical punishment and the detrimental child behaviors with which it is associated. Before we deal with the issues of causal inference, it is necessary to examine what Gershoff meant by *corporal punishment* to be clear about how it is being defined and measured.

There is a sense in which participants in the current debate about the effects of corporal punishment are talking past each other. One issue to which some attention has been given is the need to make a distinction between legal abuse and corporal punishment. A second issue, which has not been given the attention it deserves, is the distinction between harsh and punitive but not legally designated abusive punishment and the more moderate application of normative spanking within the context of a generally supportive parent–child relationship. Although Gershoff cited Baumrind and Larzelere as concluding

From *Psychological Bulletin*, vol. 128, no. 4, July 2002, pp. 580–584, 586 (refs., notes omitted). Copyright © 2002 by American Psychological Association. Reprinted by permission via Rightslink.

"that corporal punishment is both effective and desirable," it would be more correct to say they concluded only that a blanket injunction against disciplinary spanking is not warranted by the data.

An important scientific consensus conference on corporal punishment defined *spanking* as that subset of the broader category of corporal punishment that is "a) physically non-injurious; b) intended to modify behavior; and c) administered with an opened hand to the extremities or buttocks." Conferees, including Baumrind and Larzelere, agreed that the important debate was not about overly severe forms of corporal punishment but only about parental spanking, which inflicts a minor, temporary level of physical pain, if that. Conferees agreed that abusive corporal punishment should be criminalized and corporal punishment that exceeds mild to moderate spanking or is used with children younger than 18 months or after puberty should be strongly discouraged. Conferees also agreed that a mild spank as a "back-up" to other disciplinary tactics (e.g., reasoning, time-out) could increase the effectiveness of these alternative disciplinary tactics in preschoolers with behavior problems. There was agreement that by itself spanking cannot accomplish the longer term objective of parents—to promote children's competence, moral character, and mental health—and that frequent or severe punishment of any kind signals the presence of a problem in the family dynamics. The issue that was and remains controversial is whether mild to moderate disciplinary spanking (in the years between 18 months and puberty) has been shown to be harmful.

Gershoff's meta-analyses, however, do not address that issue because her conceptual and operational definitions of *corporal punishment* included punishment that was often too severe and was thus a proxy for the harsh, punitive discipline that is acknowledged by all experts to be detrimental to children's well-being and ethically unacceptable. In the fifth moderator variable in the note to her Table 3 (indexing how researchers operationalized corporal punishment), Gershoff included "severity" as Category 2 and "frequency and severity" as Category 3, indicating that severity (as well as frequency) contributed to the CP measure in those studies so categorized. But her other categories, such as "frequency" (Category 1), did not exclude overly severe forms of CP when the specific question asked of the respondent was about their frequency. This meant that slapping in the face or beating with a stick or hitting, pushing, grabbing, or shoving were not coded as severe when the studies asked about their frequency.

Straus claimed that the physical abuse or Severe Violence items in the Conflict Tactics Scale can be used "to partial out physical abuse in a statistical analysis or to remove abused children from the sample in order to avoid confounding corporal punishment with physical abuse." Although Straus's own studies rarely did that, he clearly agreed with us that it is proper to do so. However, Gershoff indicated in her Table 1 that 16% of the 88 studies in her review operationalized CP as "hit with an object," which Straus included in his index of abuse or Severe Violence on the Conflicts Tactics Scale. Thus, some of Gershoff's CP measures included behaviors that are part of Straus's abuse construct.

To determine the influence of overly severe CP on the results of Gershoff's meta-analyses, Larzelere coded the severity of CP for 64 primary studies, including 52 of the 54 studies in the aggression composite (i.e., studies measuring aggression or antisocial behavior in children or aggression, criminal behavior, or physical abuse in adults). Baumrind also coded 41% of the studies for reliability, which yielded good interrater agreement (k = .91) for severe versus not overly severe CP. Almost two thirds (65.4%) of the 52 aggression composite studies used overly severe CP. Variables were categorized as overly severe if there was direct evidence of severity, such as a CP measure based only on hitting with a belt or stick (30.8% of the 52 studies in Gershoff's aggression composite); if severity was part of the definition of the highest CP score (28.8%); or if severity was inferred from the label, such as *punitive discipline* (5.8%). That left only 34.6% of the 52 effect sizes in the aggression composite for which the CP measure was not influenced directly by overly severe CP.

This problem of overly severe (and overly broad) CP can best be illustrated with quotes from Gershoff's primary studies. The following descriptions were used to describe at least part of their definition of CP: "slapped on face, head, and ears" and "shook"; "severity of punishment for aggression to parents"; "throwing something at the child" and "severe, strict, often physical" as contrasted with "nonrestrictive, mostly positive guidance," usage of "switch, belt, razor strap, paddle, buggy whip, boxing ears"; and "hit with belt, stick." In all of these five studies, an effect size could have been based on a CP measure that did not include such overly severe components of CP. For example, Mahoney et al. presented separate data for six tactics included in the revised Conflict Tactics Scale's CP measure. The corresponding effect sizes (*d*) ranged from 0.08 for "spanked bottom with bare hand" to 0.58 for "slapped on face, head, and ears."

In other studies, effect sizes could only be based on CP measures contaminated by overly severe components. Examples include "slaps in the face" and "beating with a stick, a belt, etc."; "slap him in the face" and "wash out his mouth with soap"; "How often were you beaten by your mother (father)?"; "kicked, bit, or hit you with a fist," causing "bruises or cuts," and six more violent items; "rough handling, shaking"; "mom (dad) was a violent or physically abusive person"; and "severe punishment, parents very angry or hostile, beatings, . . . 'Punished him so he wouldn't forget it.'"

In at least one other primary study in the meta-analyses, a large majority of those who were physically punished were also physically abused. In Lester's study of inmate records, 49% of those who had attempted suicide had been physically punished by their fathers, but almost as many (44%) had been physically abused. Therefore, it would appear that only 5% of the inmates were physically punished without being abused.

We thus conclude that the meta-analyses included studies of overly severe CP to a far greater extent than a casual reading of the selection criteria would indicate. To address the current debate about mild to moderate spanking, Gershoff would have had to exclude CP that is excessive, extreme, or cruel. But Gershoff only excluded CP that "knowingly would cause severe injury to the child," although (according to Gershoff) corporal punishment constitutes abuse in definitions of 22 states not merely when it is intended to result in "significant" physical injury but when it is "excessive," "cruel," "extreme," or "severe."

Beyond the question of measurement of CP, there is an important question of meaning. In her review, Gershoff stated that many studies ask parents about their use of CP but do not define what the researchers mean and do not ascertain what the participants mean. The question is whether it makes sense to aggregate all these studies in a meta-analysis when the definition of the key variable measuring CP is so varied and ambiguous.

Threats to the Validity of the Meta-Analyses

With the exception of the links between CP and immediate compliance or physical abuse, Gershoff disavowed causal implications of the meta-analyses she presented. However, it is primarily within a causal context that meta-analysis is judged to be superior to a conventional review for theory development and application to social policy. The very term *effect size* implies a causal relationship. If, for example, an equally plausible argument can be made that child aggression is a contributing cause of CP as can be made that CP is a contributing cause of child aggression, then it is arbitrary to treat CP as though it is the independent variable and child aggression as the dependent variable, and certainly without first establishing temporal order. Yet antispanking advocates frequently draw causal implications from the associations between CP and child behaviors. For example, on the basis of similar associations, Straus projected that a reduction in CP would "result in fewer people who are alienated, depressed or suicidal, and in fewer violent marriages" and "include lower crime rates . . . and less money spent on controlling or treating crime and mental illness."

Methodologists in epidemiology and behavioral science have emphasized the importance of empirically establishing the causal status of a correlate by first showing that it is a risk factor and then that it is a causal risk factor. A *risk factor* (causal or not) must be shown to precede the outcome and to be associated with an increase in the outcome compared with its population baserate. An experimental or prospective longitudinal design is a prerequisite for establishing a temporal sequence by showing that the outcome has not occurred prior to, or simultaneously with, the presumed risk factor. Although, as Greenland stated, "No meta-analysis can compensate for the inherent limits of non-experimental data for making inferences about causal effects," non-experimental studies differ greatly in their research quality and thus in their relevance to a causal argument.

We next consider threats to the validity first of the primary studies in Gershoff's analyses and then of the synthesis itself that may have systematically inflated the effect size estimates or compromised the generalizability of the results.

Threats to the Validity of the Primary Studies

Although experimental studies are the gold standard in separating causal from noncausal explanations, correlational studies can contribute to a causal explanation to the extent that they meet certain criteria, the most important of which are temporality and control of third variables that could plausibly account for an association. Other threats include the use of retrospective reports or shared method variance in assessing parenting behavior and children's outcomes.

Establishing temporal sequences between risks and outcomes. A cross-sectional design cannot show that an association is a risk factor because it cannot establish temporal order. Fifty-eight percent of all the effect size estimates in Gershoff's meta-analyses came from cross-sectional analyses, and only 17% came from either experimental or prospective longitudinal studies. Thus, most of the primary studies did not provide adequate information for identifying a risk factor, much less a causal risk factor. A *causal risk factor* for an outcome is a risk factor believed to be a generative cause of that outcome—that is, to have produced that outcome. Experimental designs or systematic attempts to rule out plausible confounds in quasi-experimental and prospective longitudinal designs are necessary to establish a risk factor as causal.

Prospective longitudinal studies, unlike cross-sectional studies, can establish temporality and have more potential for controlling third variables adequately. They can provide evidence of causal direction from parents' use of CP to subsequent child behaviors by controlling for baseline child behaviors that provoke punishment and for the autocorrelation of behavior over time. We should note that Gershoff cited a paper by Cowan, Powell, and Cowan to the effect that correlational and follow-back studies are not sufficient to establish causality. Although they have some design advantages that we have highlighted in this section, it is still important to note that longitudinal models are necessary but not sufficient to establish the order of events. Parenting behavior assessed at Time 1 may predict child behavior at Time 2, but it is also possible that the parent may be reacting to child behavior that occurred before the study began.

Controlling for third variables. In their seminal discussion of the use of meta-analytic synthesis for theory development, Miller and Pollock stated "Assessing evidence that a relationship exists and that it is nonartifactual is a first step in assessing its validity." In correlational studies this requires controlling for plausible third variables. For a relationship not to be spurious, it must persist in the form of a nonzero partial correlation between the supposed independent variable and the dependent variable with plausible third variables held constant (for example, baseline child misbehavior or parental rejection). Quasi-experimental studies are designed to exclude spurious variables from the group of causal influences affecting the results being observed. However, Gershoff used DSTAT, whose manual explicitly prohibits basing effect sizes on coefficients from multiple regression. If only the zero-order correlations can be used to calculate effect size, the methodological advantage of most quasi-experimental studies is lost, which makes the meta-analytic conclusions less relevant for determining whether CP is a causal risk factor for the detrimental child outcomes with which it is associated.

The use of retrospective recall. As Gershoff pointed out, reliance on retrospective recall in all but three of the studies linking CP in childhood to adult aggression, criminality, mental health, and physical abuse is a severe methodological inadequacy of those studies. Typically, retrospective recall is biased by the current status of the reporter. For example, adult reporters asked to report on their own depression and their parents' disciplinary practices may try to explain their current mental state by their parents' mistreatment.

Shared method variance. Problems associated with the fact that raters are not independent and thus that information about parenting and child outcomes is filtered through the same source constitute a critical limitation of half of the primary studies in the review. Shared method variance results in spuriously high correlations among constructs. The largest proportion of independent data sources occurred in compliance studies (four of five), whereas the smallest proportion of independent data sources were in adulthood studies of abuse (one of five) and aggression (one of four). The bias introduced by shared method variance is well illustrated in the analyses by Yarrow et al. They grouped their results in tables to demonstrate how a "contaminated design" artifactually increases an association. Mothers' reports on "severity of punishment for aggression to parents" correlated at .40 with their reports on the child's aggression toward adults in the home (which the authors refer to as the *contaminated design*), compared with a .13 correlation with teacher-reported aggression. Gershoff chose to base her effect size on the correlation of .40 from the contaminated design rather than the .13 correlation in the uncontaminated design.

Threats to the Validity of the Synthesis

In addition to the problems caused by an overinclusive definition of CP, which could inflate effect sizes, Gershoff also based effect size estimates partly on cross-sectional correlations when longitudinal correlations were available. An alternative strategy would have been to base effect sizes on the most valid associations available in a study or the ones most relevant to the debate about mild or moderate corporal punishment. Gershoff did not state the rules she used to include or exclude effect sizes when several options were available in a study. A rule that seems reasonable in selecting among relevant effect sizes within a study is to choose the one most likely to both exclude severe CP and to minimize shared method variance. To do otherwise would systematically increase the estimate of effect size with contaminated designs and with parents who use CP too severely.

The Yarrow et al. study illustrates the somewhat arbitrary nature of the myriad of decisions the synthesist must make in selecting which statistic should represent a study. Two tables summarized correlations of four punishment measures with three aggression measures. Gershoff based her effect size estimate on the largest of these 12 correlations. Furthermore, that correlation seems to be the poorest choice in terms of CP severity and validity threats. It was a correlation of .40 of "severity of punishment for aggression to parents" and aggression to adults at home, both based on the maternal interview. The most valid correlation was −.19 between maternal-reported physical punishment (overall) and teacher-reported aggression 2 months later. It was more valid because it was based on physical punishment overall, not severity of punishment in general, and because the CP and aggression measures were collected at different occasions from independent sources. Thus, the basis of an effect size between CP and child's aggression varies from −.19 in an uncontaminated design to .40 in a design contaminated by shared method variance, cross-sectional data, and overly severe punishment.

Furthermore, following the DSTAT manual's proscription against basing effect sizes on regression coefficients, even when controlling for third variables thought to be plausible confounds, Gershoff's effect sizes never reflected the most causally relevant statistics in longitudinal designs. Other metaanalytic experts recommend controlling for plausible confounds whenever possible, and some provide equations for calculating effect sizes from regression coefficients.

Reanalysis of the Data to Correct for Flaws in the Included Aggression Composite Studies

There are different views about whether poorly designed studies should be included in a meta-analysis. Mansfield and Busse recommended, and we concur, that all studies with severe methodological inadequacies should be eliminated from consideration and the remainder divided into two categories: those that have significant but not severe methodological limitations (e.g., retrospective longitudinal studies for which the likelihood of biased recall may be small) and those that are well designed in that they do not suffer from shared method variance, do use a prospective longitudinal or experimental design, and explicitly rule out severe corporal punishment. Unfortunately, as we show, that would leave too few studies for a meta-analytic review of the link between CP and most child behaviors (a situation in which one could conclude that a meta-analysis is premature).

Alternatively, methodological qualities of the studies can be coded and then used to see whether effect sizes from poorly designed studies are significantly different from those from the best-designed studies. Gershoff did attempt such analyses with her aggression composite variables, but these analyses were limited in two ways. First, almost all the studies had major methodological problems. More than half of the studies in the aggression composite used overly severe CP measures, more than half used cross-sectional or retrospective designs, and half had shared method variance. These problems were confounded with each other in unknown ways, making it difficult to sort out the differences those problems made by themselves or in combination. Second, Gershoff's analysis of study characteristics used a very conservative criterion for significance, especially considering the large number of categorical predictors (21) and small number of studies (22). This explains the unusual result of accounting for 86% of the variance in effect sizes without any of the categorical predictors being significant according to her conservative Bonferroni correction.

In contrast, we implemented more realistic analyses of whether effect sizes varied by CP severity, research design, or independence of data sources. We analyzed Gershoff's effect sizes in her aggression composite using the chi-square analyses of weighted effect sizes recommended by Hedges. Our analyses differ from Gershoff's analyses in the following ways: We treated each effect size as a separate case rather than combining effect sizes into one per study; we analyzed each methodological issue as a main effect rather than incorporating all predictors into one combined analysis; and finally, we used our codes for overly severe CP and corrected the design code for six cases.

As expected, effect sizes varied significantly by CP severity, by research design, and by independence of data sources. We found significantly higher effect sizes for overly severe than for nonsevere CP measures (mean weighted effect sizes, $d_+ = 0.46$ vs. 0.30, respectively, $\chi^2[1, N = 12,244] = 74.5, p < .001$). Effect sizes were also higher for cross-sectional than for longitudinal studies ($d_+ = 0.46$ vs. 0.37, $\chi^2[1, N = 7,807] = 16.1, p < .001$). Finally, effect sizes were higher for studies based partly or entirely on shared data sources than for independent sources of data ($d_1 = 0.35$ vs. 0.29, $\chi^2[1, N = 13,591] = 8.44, p < .01$). Only 3 of 54 studies in the aggression composite were methodologically sound on all three study characteristics. Their mean weighted effect size was 0.12, significantly less than the other 51 effect sizes in the aggression composite ($d_1 = 0.33, \chi^2[1, N = 13,591] = 5.99, p < .05$). This effect size is smaller than what Cohen labeled as small ($d = 0.20$).

Gershoff's analyses were limited in investigating important substantive distinctions as well. For example, there have been some discussions recently about whether the associations of CP differ by ethnicity. Gershoff could not investigate ethnic differences because none of her primary studies investigated ethnic minorities alone. Nonetheless, two of her primary studies included separate statistics for African American subsamples. In both studies, the mean effect sizes were negative, such that CP predicted less aggression subsequently at school in the African American subsample. Furthermore, Gunnoe and Mariner went beyond a longitudinal correlation by controlling statistically for baseline aggression, which resulted in stronger causal evidence that CP reduces subsequent school aggression in African American children ($\beta = -.30$). At least two other studies have also found that the association of CP with antisocial behavior differs significantly for African American and European American children.

Similarly, it is not clear that mild to moderate CP increases subsequent aggression and antisocial behavior at ages when parents are most likely to use CP (18 months to 6 years of age). Only one effect size in Gershoff's aggression construct was based on longitudinal and independent data on the use of nonsevere CP in this age range, and it was one of the smallest effect sizes ($d = 0.06$). Other primary studies had tiny effect sizes or ones for which CP predicted reductions in aggression for this age range when focusing on a young subsample and using data uncontaminated by the above three methodological problems. Furthermore, Gunnoe and Mariner showed that CP predicted significantly less fighting in 4- to 7-year-olds after controlling for baseline antisocial behavior. . . .

Conclusion

Gershoff acknowledged the necessity to distinguish between the harsh, punitive parental discipline that all experts would regard as both harmful and unethical (including such advocates of spanking as Dobson and Rosemond) and the more normative parental actions that involve the infliction of mild physical pain but not injury. In this response to Gershoff's article, we reana-lyzed portions of Gershoff's meta-analyses to show that this separation was not in fact made in many primary studies. Because her measure included many instances of extreme and excessive physical punishment, her analyses are not relevant to the current political debate about whether normative spanking (a specific form of CP) is harmful for children.

Punishment by definition is aversive and therefore must be used sparingly and efficaciously to be acceptable. As Larzelere stated, "There may be more potential in identifying more vs. less effective ways to use each disciplinary tactic. The effect of any tactic may depend on the overall disciplinary style and the parent–child, family, and cultural contexts." Larzelere suggested a condi-tional sequence model as optimal in which parents begin with the mildest disciplinary tactic they think will be effective, such as reasoning, and resort to firmer tactics only if the child is defiant about a nonnegotiable request. If used efficaciously as a back-up at ages 2 to 6, both physical and nonphysical punishment are less likely to be needed as children learn to attain a reasonable level of behavioral compliance to mild disciplinary tactics such as reasoning.

Larzelere's conditional sequence model and Gershoff's process–context model should be tested with well-designed studies from culturally diverse pop-ulations. Even though randomized clinical trials are probably not practical, intervention studies are possible that would add to the knowledge base. To determine if normative physical punishment has any unique effect on 2- to 6-year-olds over and above that of otherwise optimal parenting, parents could be trained in techniques of authoritative discipline, which would include effi-cacious use of punishments of their choice. Some parents would choose to include spanking in their disciplinary repertoire, providing the opportunity for researchers to assess the child outcomes associated with disciplinary spank-ing when used efficaciously by comparing them with child outcomes associ-ated with the alternative disciplinary tactics used by parents who choose to never spank. With a large and diverse enough sample, it should be possible to evaluate the moderating effects of third variables that would not be control-led, such as child and parent temperament and social stressors, in such quasi-experimental intervention studies. . . .

EXPLORING THE ISSUE

Is Spanking Detrimental to Children?

Critical Thinking and Reflection

1. Explain the effects of corporal punishment on the parent–child relationship. List and explain one positive and one negative reaction to corporal punishment.
2. Did Baumrind, Cowan, and Larzelere feel that Gershoff used valid information to contribute to the debate about whether spanking is harmful to children? Why or why not?

Is There Common Ground?

Although these selections are more concerned with definitions and methodology than with resolving the spanking controversy, there is a real debate over what mild spanking is and how it fits into the overall parenting discipline technique. Child development experts agree that reasoning, talking, and listening to children teaches them how to distinguish right from wrong and preserves their positive self-image. They admit this approach takes more time and effort but that in the long run, it is more effective and leads children to a better adjusted adulthood. What might be some reasons that parents do not report using these techniques as frequently as spanking?

There are authorities in child development who believe spankings, when properly administered and within the context of a loving home, are effective in shaping children's behavior. Most agree to spank from about 2 years of age until puberty and to only use an open hand and never use objects to hit children. They urge parents to explain to their children why they are being spanked. Do you believe that this can make a difference in the outcomes of spanking on children? Why or why not?

Are spankings useful and justified, or is there a fine line between spanking and child abuse? Is it likely that parents who spank will cross that line to abuse in the heat of the moment? Is it really possible to spank with appropriate force and with logical thought? Can studies on the effects of spanking be designed to answer these questions? With all the studies already conducted, methodology and definitions are still being debated. It appears that there are many critical variables that need to be quantified before conducting research on the subject. In the meantime, parents are presented with the dilemma of how best to guide and discipline their children from childhood to becoming responsible adults. If you were advising a parent, what would you suggest?

Additional Resources

Henderson, Tom. (2010). Researcher Says a Little Spanking Is Good for Kids. Retrieved on April 7, 2011, from http://www.parentdish.com/2010/01/05/researcher-says-a-little-spanking-is-good-for-kids/.

This article discusses some reasons why a little bit of spanking can be beneficial for children.

Hunt, J. (1997). The Natural Child Project: Ten Reasons Not to Hit Your Kids. Retrieved on April 7, 2011, from http://www.naturalchild.org/jan_hunt/tenreasons.html.

This website lists reasons that spanking should not be used on children.

Shute, Nancy. (2008). A Good Parent's Dilemma: Is Spanking Bad? Retrieved on April 7, 2011, from http://health.usnews.com/health-news/family-health/articles/2008/06/12/a-good-parents-dilemma-is-spanking-bad.

This article posted online discusses research about the effects of spanking on children.

ISSUE 6

Are Fathers Really Necessary?

YES: Natasha J. Cabrera, Jacqueline D. Shannon, and Catherine Tamis-LeMonda, from "Fathers' Influence on Their Children's Cognitive and Emotional Development from Toddlers to Pre-K," *Applied Developmental Science* (vol. 11, no. 4, 2007)

NO: Peggy Drexler and Linden Gross, from "Good News from the Home Front," *Raising Boys Without Men* (Rodale Books, 2005)

Learning Outcomes

After reading this issue, you should be able to:

- Identify the arguments posed in favor of and in opposition to the importance of a father's involvement in a child's life.
- Critique the type of research that each article reported on, identifying the strengths and weaknesses of the approach.
- List differences that can be found between homes where fathers are present versus those where they are not.

ISSUE SUMMARY

YES: Natasha Cabrera, associate professor of human development, Jacqueline Shannon, assistant professor of early childhood education, and Catherine Tamis-LeMonda, professor of applied psychology, found that young children who experience positive father interaction have increased intellectual, social, emotional, and language development.

NO: Peggy Drexler, assistant professor of psychology in psychiatry and special features editor, and Linden Gross assert that women are capable of raising children without a father figure in the home. Their book is based on Drexler's research that compared boys from female-headed households with boys from traditional mom-and-dad families.

$\mathbf{T}$ here has been a dramatic rise in single-parent homes in the United States in the past 20 years. A more dramatic increase is the number of children being raised by men. Since the 1990 census, households headed by single fathers have risen from 1.3 million homes in 1990 to over 2.1 million in the

2000 census. Because of this increase, an issue that has confronted researchers revolves around the necessity of the two-parent family. Specifically, are both mothers and fathers necessary to raise children effectively?

Children need nurturing, guidance, and economic security. Must they receive these things from both a father and a mother? Some scholars argue that children need active involved fathers throughout their childhood and adolescence. If this does not occur, children may be more prone to involvement in crime, premature sexual activity, out of wedlock childbirth, lower educational achievement, depression, substance abuse, and poverty.

Other scientists question whether the ability to meet children's needs is gender specific. Although few would argue that it is more challenging to raise a child in a single-parent home, well-socialized and successful children have come from single-parent homes that are male as well as female headed. Females head the vast majority of single-parent homes. In fact, there are over 7.5 million single mothers raising children in the United States today.

Another consideration is the increase in adoption by gay and lesbian parents in two-parent homes. Although children may face emotional challenges in dealing with the prejudice associated with being raised in these particular households, one might ask how this arrangement works. Is there evidence that children need both a male and a female parent? Many scientists argue that there is little, if any, scientific evidence that both a female and a male must raise children.

Although there is no consensus on whether or not children need both mothers and fathers to raise them, there is a concern that society makes it difficult for dads to be involved in their children's lives. Philip Cowan and Carolyn Cowan describe six institutional barriers to father involvement in the Family Focus on Fatherhood (National Council on Family Relations, 2009). The six barriers are culturally based gender role stereotypes, government child support programs, social science research, the workplace, family service agencies, and focus on coparents. Overcoming these barriers will not happen from attending a single workshop or reading one memo, but will need the ongoing support of educators and agency personnel.

Philip Cowan and Carolyn Cowan suggest specific ideas to increase father involvement: realize that fathers are motivated to be with their children, but are often prevented from doing so; add emotional support to monetary support in child support mandates; encourage mothers who are the gatekeepers to involve dads with their children; and ask workplaces to implement flex-time schedules for dads. Natasha Cabrera, Jacqueline Shannon, and Catherine Tamis-LeMonda conducted research based on observations verses survey data. They found that fathers with at least a high school education were more supportive than fathers with fewer resources and had a positive effect on children's emotional and cognitive development.

As you read the following selections, consider your family of orientation. Was your upbringing an optimal situation? Did the role that your father played have a positive or negative effect on your life?

YES ↵

**Natasha J. Cabrera,
Jacqueline D. Shannon, and
Catherine Tamis-LeMonda**

Fathers' Influence on Their Children's Cognitive and Emotional Development: From Toddlers to Pre-K

In recent years, scholarship on *resident low-income fathers* has made important contributions to our understanding of how fathers affect children's development. It has shown that men are involved with their young children in multiple ways through their accessibility, responsibility, and engagement; the quality of father engagement, or father–child interactions, can be positive and supportive; positive father–child interactions matter for children's development, with different effects emerging at different points in development; and, that father–child interactions are embedded in a larger ecology that includes mother–father relationship and the family human and financial resources. This article presents an integration of findings across several of our recent studies that have contributed to each of these areas.

First, we present findings that address the question of how resident fathers are engaged with their young children at 2 years, 3 years, and pre-kindergarten (pre-K). These findings are important because they are based on observed rather than survey data and show that the quality of father–child interactions is consistent across time and that fathers, like mothers, can be sensitive and supportive to their children.

Second, we highlight central fathers' personal and contextual characteristics that affect fathers' engagement. In particular, we focus on fathers' human and financial resources and mother–child interactions. These findings shed light onto particular personal and contextual factors that are central to positive parenting over time, which programs and policies can target for effective interventions.

Third, we focus on how fathers' engagements affect their young children's cognitive, language and social, and emotional outcomes over and above mothers' contribution. The extant literature on low-income fathers has focused on the effects of absent fathers and men's lack of resources on children's development. In contrast, our findings show that fathers who engage with their children in positive ways have significant effects on their cognition and language

From *Applied Developmental Science*, vol. 11, no. 4, 2007, pp. 208–213. Copyright © 2007 by Taylor & Francis Journals. Reprinted by permission.

at 2 and 3 years and their social and emotional development at 2 and 3 years and at pre-kindergarten. These findings are important because they show that fathers uniquely contribute to children's cognitive and social and emotional development above the effects on mothers' engagement on children.

These studies are guided by the Dynamics of Paternal Influences on Children over the Life Course Model that stipulates the important contribution of parent characteristics, child, and context to parenting and children's outcomes. These findings add to the literature in several ways: First, they focus on an ethnically/racially diverse, low-income sample of fathers who reside with their young children. Second, they show that low-income fathers can make significant contributions to their children's development. Third, these findings are based on observations of fathers and their children and hence move us beyond methodologies that rely on mothers as proxy respondents for fathers.

Methods

Participants

Participants were drawn from research sites that participated in both the National Early Head Start Research and Evaluation Project (EHS study) and the EHS Father Study's Project. Ten of 17 EHS sites participated in the father component of the main study at 2 and 3 years, and 12 participated at pre-K time point. Families (N = 1,685 at 2/3 years, N = 2,115 at pre-K) were enrolled into the study when they initially applied to have their children receive childcare and parenting services at the local Early Head Start program that is partners in the EHS study. Written consent to participate in the EHS study and family baseline data (e.g., maternal age, race/ethnicity) were obtained from mothers at the start of the research and from fathers at their initial visit.

Because the majority of fathers who participated in the video portion of the study were biological and resident (i.e., 85% at 2 and 3 years, 75% at pre-K), we only include families with a resident biological father at each age point. For the 2 and 3 year time points, we report on a sample of 290, and at pre-K we report on a sample of 313. These samples include families for whom we had father video data on at least one assessment.

Given the design of the study (mothers identified fathers, but not all identified fathers agreed to participate in the study), the fathers who ultimately participated in study 1 (2 and 3 year time point) and study 2 (pre-K time point) of the EHS father study are a select group of men. Compared with those who did not participate in the father study, participating fathers and their children's mothers were more likely to be married and/or cohabiting, White or Latino, completed more years of education, and were more likely to be employed. Additionally, their children had higher scores on cognitive and social and emotional tests than children from nonparticipating families.

The majority of fathers in these reported studies were White (60%, 60%, and 51%, respectively); the remaining fathers were largely African American followed by Latino. Across the three ages, approximately 1/3 to 1/2 of fathers had less than high school degree; remaining fathers had high school degrees or more. Almost all fathers reported working full-time or part-time at the various ages, ranging from 84% to 96%. However, the annual income for families at pre-K was larger ($59,459) than it was at 2 and 3 years ($18,820 and $25,440, respectively). Children averaged 25 months at the time of the 2-year visit, 37 months at the 3-year visit, and 64 months at the time of the pre-kindergarten visit; about half at all three ages were boys.

Procedures

Once fathers had been identified by the child's mother, they were contacted to participate in the study. Participating fathers were administered a father questionnaire and mother–child and father–child dyads were videotaped in separate home visits when children were 2 and 3 years, and about to enter kindergarten. Children's cognitive, language, and social and emotional development were assessed by a trained tester at the mother visit. Fathers were given $20 at the 2- and 3-year visits and $30 at the pre-K visit, and children were given a gift.

Father–child interactions were videotaped during three activities, including 10 or 15 min of semi-structured free play, which was the focus of the investigation. During free play, toys were presented to fathers in three separate bags. Toys were selected to be age appropriate and to offer dyads the opportunity to engage in both concrete and symbolic forms of play (e.g., at 2 years, the father toys included: bag #1—a book, bag #2—a pizza set and telephone, and bag #3—a farm with farm animals). Fathers were asked to sit on a mat with his child, try to ignore the camera, and to do whatever felt most natural. They were instructed to only play with the toys from the three bags and to start with bag #1, move on to bag #2, and finish with bag #3. They were told that they could divide up the 10 min or 15 min as they liked.

Measures

Parent Characteristics

The majority of demographic characteristics were collected from the father interview. Family income was gathered from standards measure of employment. Measures to assess children's development included mental and behavior ratings scales (i.e., emotional regulation and orientation/engagement factors) . . . and children's sociability and emotional regulation.

Parent–Child Interactions

The quality of father–child interactions as well as mother–child interactions were assessed. . . . We assessed three dimensions of positive parenting (i.e., sensitivity, positive regard, and cognitive stimulation) as indicators of fathers' and mothers' *Supportiveness*, which represents parenting that is characterized by emotional support and enthusiasm for the child's autonomous work, responsiveness, and active attempts to expand the child's knowledge and abilities. We included one negative aspect of parenting: *Intrusiveness*, which indicates that the parent is over-controlling and over-involved. All coders were unaware of children's scores on child assessments and father interviews.

Results

Findings from these studies are organized around the three research questions: (1) How do resident fathers engage with their young children? (2) How do human and financial resources and mothers' engagements predict the quality of fathers' engagements with their young children? (3) How do resources and father engagements affect their young children's development, over and above mother engagement?

Fathers' Engagements with Their Young Children

Building on past research that fathers and mothers engage with their children in distinct but also similar ways, our work offers further evidence of the similarities between some parents. Fathers were as sensitive as mothers, and both parents showed low levels of intrusiveness, countering common stereotypes of fathers as aloof. At all child ages studied, fathers and mothers received comparably high scores on their supportiveness . . . and equivalently low scores on their intrusiveness. . . . As observed in the videotaped father–child interaction episodes, children experienced supportive and positive parenting from both their parents.

Financial Resources and Mother–Child Interactions to Father Engagement

Although the samples in our studies represented all resident fathers who were generally higher functioning than nonparticipating fathers, for example, the majority were employed and obtained at least a high school degree, there was variation in the sample that accounted for differences in father engagements.

In terms of human and financial resources, fathers were more supportive at all three ages and less intrusive at 2 years when they had at least a high school education. . . . Income was positively related to fathers' supportiveness at 2 years and pre-K, but not at 3 years . . . , whereas income negatively related to fathers' intrusiveness at these same two ages. . . . At all three ages, mother supportiveness to her child related to father supportiveness. . . . Mother intrusiveness with her child related to father intrusiveness at 2 and 3 years . . . , but not at pre-K. . . .

In summary, fathers' resources and mother supportiveness are significantly related to supportive father engagement at most ages. Also, the finding of covariation between father and mother engagement quality, underscores the need to covary mothers' engagement when considering the unique influence of fathering on children's outcomes.

Human and Financial Resources and Parent Engagement in Relation to Children's Development

Children's scores on the mental scale . . . , language scores . . . and word-recognition and applied problems . . . averaged .5 to 1.0 SD below the national norms. However, children were highly regulated and interactive during the administration of child assessments as indicated by their high scores on the orientation/engagement and emotional regulation factors . . . and on the cognitive-social and emotional regulation composite scales. . . .

Predictors to Children's Cognition and Language

Fathers' education (*more* than high school) was significantly related to children's scores. . . . Family income was significantly related to all child outcomes at pre-K. . . .

After accounting for financial and human resources (and mother engagement), the association between father engagement and child outcomes varied slightly over time depending on type of father engagement. In general, mothers' supportiveness related to children's cognitive outcomes at 2 and 3 years, and at pre-K. . . . Fathers' supportiveness related to children's outcomes at 2 and 3 years, but not at pre-K. . . . Intrusiveness varied in its relation to child outcomes by child age. Neither mother nor father intrusiveness were related to child outcomes at 2 and 3 years. . . .

Predictors to Children's Social and Emotional Behaviors

. . . As with cognitive outcomes, fathers' education (more than high school) consistently predicted children's emotional regulation at 2 and 3 years. . . . Family income, on the other hand, mattered only for children's orientation-engagement at 3 years and emotional regulation at pre-K . . . and approached significance to their cognitive-social behaviors at pre-K. . . .

In terms of parent engagement, surprisingly, maternal supportiveness was unrelated to children's outcomes at all ages . . . , however, father supportiveness, was positively associated with children's emotional regulation at 2 years . . . and marginally related to their orientation-engagement at both 2 and 3 years. . . . Expectedly, maternal intrusiveness was negatively related to children's emotional regulation at 2 years and pre-K as well as their cognitive-social scores at pre-K. At 2 years, father intrusiveness was positively related to orientation-engagement but inversely related to emotional regulation. . . . Father intrusiveness was unrelated to children's social and emotional outcomes at 3 years and pre-K. . . .

Discussion

To date, studies of how fathers matter to their children have produced inconsistent findings. Some studies have reported that father engagement has no direct effect on children's outcomes. First, it is less likely to find an association between father *report* of engagement and child outcomes than when the quality of father engagement is observed. Second, it is possible that fathers have different effects on children's development across time. Findings from this study support both explanations. We also find that fathers' education and income are key predictors of positive father engagement.

It is noteworthy that the quality of fathers' and mothers' parenting is very similar to each other. Insofar as the brief videotape of parent–child interaction provides a window to how children are parented, we find that both parents are more sensitive than intrusive. In line with prior research, we also find that the most consistent predictors of supportive fathering across children's ages are fathers' education and income. It might be that fathers who have more than high school education are more motivated to parent and are more aware of the developmental needs of children than those with less education.

The next question we were interested in was whether parenting has an effect on children's outcomes. Although children in our study scored .5 to 1.0 SD below national norms of cognitive tests, they were highly regulated across ages. As with predictors to father engagement, in general, fathers who have more than high school education have children performing better in all developmental domains—cognition, language, and social and emotional development. Family income, however, matters more at later ages than earlier; presumably as children get older they need more stimulating materials and opportunities to promote learning. This is consistent with resource theories that posit that parents who have more resources are more likely to invest on their children by providing a stimulating environment that promotes growth and learning than fathers with fewer resources.

Once we accounted for the effect of resources on children's development, we examined the unique contribution that parenting had on children's outcomes. For cognitive development, mothers' and fathers' supportiveness were positively related to children's language and cognitive outcomes across ages, although fathers' supportiveness did not matter at pre-K. For social and emotional development, fathers' supportiveness mattered only at earlier ages, while mother supportiveness was not related at any age. It might be that supportive mothering alone might not be enough to teach children to regulate and pay attention. Perhaps supportive parenting coupled with other dimensions of parenting, not measured here, such as discipline, might be more effective, especially with older children. It is also possible parents in our study were not intrusive enough to have a negative effect on children. Our findings are consistent with past research that supportive parenting is important for children's cognitive development across time and it adds to the literature by showing that *supportive fathering* has similar effects on children's cognitive functioning and emotional development especially with younger children, whereas *supportive mothering* only affects cognitive development across ages.

Our results also shed light on the effects of one dimension of negative parenting. We found parent intrusiveness less consistently related to children's development across domains and ages. In contrast to our findings for supportive parenting, intrusive parenting has an expected negative effect on children's cognition and language, but only for older children. Perhaps over controlling parents tend to inhibit older children's autonomy to verbalize and ask questions hence diminishing opportunities for learning. However, parent intrusiveness related to children's emotional regulation differently depending on child's age and gender of parent. At 2 years, both parents' intrusiveness mattered. Parents who are over controlling and over-involved have young children who are less regulated (i.e., less attentive, less able to stay on task) than non-intrusive mothers and fathers. At 3 and pre-K, maternal intrusiveness was almost consistently related to less emotional regulation whereas paternal intrusiveness was not related at all. It is possible that children, especially older children, interpret paternal intrusiveness in a more positive way than they do maternal intrusiveness.

In summary, fathers who have at least a high school education were more supportive and less intrusive than parents with fewer resources. Over and above mother engagements, fathers' supportiveness matters for children's cognitive and language development across ages as well as children's social and emotional behaviors, but less consistently. In contrast, father intrusiveness is not related to older children's social and emotional behaviors; it matters only at 2 years. These findings have important implications for policy and programs. Programs that aim at increasing fathers' education and that promote and encourage father's positive parenting will yield large benefits for children.

Peggy Drexler and
Linden Gross

 NO

Good News from
the New Home Front

"I'm gonna make a club, and my friends can be in my club no matter what they wear."

—4½-year-old Quentin

TWO-AND-A-HALF-YEAR-OLD QUENTIN was kicked in the shins by another little boy on the playground. Crying, he ran over to the yard monitor for comfort, then, of his own volition, approached the little boy who had kicked him. "I do not like what you did, Martin," he told him in a voice full of emotion. "I would not kick you—you should never kick, and that's the truth!" Rather than impulsively kicking back, as many boys his age might have done, Quentin was using his words effectively at an exceptionally young age. A couple of years later, when Quentin found himself excluded from a group of other boys because he was wearing the wrong shoelaces, he announced, "I'm gonna make a club, and my friends can be in my club no matter what they wear."

Eight-year-old Mac was already a talented cartoonist who was into music, sports, math, and language arts. He developed an especially close friendship with his buddy Alec. The two would sit with their arms around each other in the car when one of their parents drove them to soccer games or the playground. Later, after playing rough and tough together, they would read a book side by side and just talk to each other. Then Alec transferred to another school. "It was lonely, like cloud rain," Mac recalled. "You know how a rainy day makes you feel bad? It was like that."

Quentin and Mac are both being raised in households led by women. Quentin is the son of two lesbians, Mac's mother gave birth to him as a single woman, using a anonymous donor, and is parenting him on her own. Like nearly all of the boys I interviewed for my study of sons parented solely by women, both Quentin and Mac exhibited striking levels of stability, independence, creativity, and caring. As I will show in this chapter, these mom-raised sons are avatars of a new social moment, one that is producing boys who promise to become good, even exceptional, men.

Focusing on how these children view themselves, the studies that became this book were the first to investigate lesbian couples and their sons in their own homes and as they lived their lives. To my knowledge, no researchers had previously introduced themselves so intimately into the lives of gay and lesbian families to perform what child psychoanalyst Anna Freud called "direct observation"—establishing a sustained involvement with a person or family that is maintained long enough so that the observer has some basis in experience, in words heard and actions witnessed, for coming to more general conclusions. My similar research of single mothers raising sons (of women who were widowed, divorced, or separated and their sons whose fathers were otherwise to on the scene) is unique in this very new field of study.

I began my work by examining the elementary- and junior-high-school-age sons of lesbians in planned, intact, stable, two-parent relationships in the San Francisco Bay Area—first comparing their moral development with that of boys from two-parent heterosexual families. I also explored how these boys grow up with a sense of their own masculinity with no father around. How do they react to not having a father—indeed, in many cases, having only an anonymous *seed daddy*? Coming from America's newest and fastest-growing sector of minority families, how did they deal with teasing and harassment from other children? Were they developing the kind of moral spine that our culture believes it is up to fathers to provide?

Just to give you a taste of some of those findings: The two groups of boys showed no significant differences in their moral reasoning, and both sets of parents showed no significant difference in their basic beliefs regarding moral behavior. However, when I subjected the parental attitudes data to a sophisticated measure of statistical analysis, I found that lesbian mothers scored higher on the moral attitude scale than their heterosexual counterparts and were more likely to create opportunities for their sons to examine moral and values issues. They were also more likely to talk about morality in terms of broader social implications. The Rasch analysis also suggested that there was a positive correlation between the lesbian-led families' parental attitudes about moral issues and the rate of moral development in their sons.

It turned out, however, that the nonbiological mothers (I call them *social mothers* throughout this book) and the fathers in the heterosexual couples were more likely to teach their sons by talking about principles and what ought to be. The biological mothers, in both groups, tended to teach their sons ethical behavior using emotional and empathic language. The heterosexual fathers and social mothers more readily praised their sons. The biological mothers in both samples were more worried about their sons than the social mothers and heterosexual fathers. But by and large the similarities between the couples outweighed the differences, with a couple of notable exceptions.

My findings revealed that the sons of two-mother families spent less time with an outside caregiver than those of two-parent families. "We don't like the concept of having our children in the care of other people, however lovely, for long periods of time," a lesbian social mom told me. My study showed that not only did these mothers spend more time with their children; they shared parenting responsibilities fairly equally. That didn't go unnoticed by other mothers around them. "In some ways I'm jealous of your relationship," Christine Carson, a 41-year-old married professor and mother of two, told the lesbian mother of one of her son's friends, "because you two tackle this thing [raising children] 50–50."

I did not use questionnaires, but for the first phase of my study, I did rely on objective or standardized measures to ascertain if there were any differences in the moral development of boys from two-mother homes and their counterparts being raised by a mother and father.

A vast majority of studies have concluded that the sons and daughters of gays and lesbians are no more anxious, depressed, insecure, or prone to emotional troubles than the children of heterosexuals.

Michael Lamb, Ph.D., chief of the section on Social and Emotional Development of the National Institute of Child Health and Human Development, has also asserted that being raised by gay parents would not have negative consequences for children. "It's become clear that the absence of a male figure is really not important," Dr. Lamb said. Louise Silverstein, Ph.D., and Carl Auerbach, Ph.D., have agreed with that assessment, concluding that children don't necessarily require an adult male as one of their caregivers.

Still, in the present climate of bias, any differences found in the children of homosexual parents have been equated with deficit.

Charting the moral development of the boys was complicated because it required me to analyze the verbal responses of these children, taking into account developmental-stage issues and levels of sophistication, as well as beliefs about morality. Children share two worlds, one with parents and other adult authorities, and another with peers and friends. The relationships in each world contribute equally, but differently, to children's development. To function successfully in the world, children need to discover why and under what circumstances they have to obey authority figures and how to handle conflict with their peers—including issues of sharing and fairness, such as who gets what when, why, and under what circumstances. By examining how boys from two-parent lesbian families thought about and made use of moral principles with both adults and peers, I was able to ascertain whether these boys were the same as or different from those reared in more conventional families. In addition, in both groups I evaluated the families' parental teaching methods about morality, parental time spent with the boys, and important figures in their lives from birth to their present age.

My original query (and the subject of my dissertation) was intended to establish whether and how the sons of lesbians developed moral character without the presence of a moralizing father figure. Hearing of my proposed work, some of the faculty and my fellow students laughed at me, wondering how I would actually find enough planned, two-parent lesbian families raising sons between the ages of 5 and 9 to perform a direct observation. I admit that I shared their concern. But even as early as 1996, it turned out that these families were everywhere. Word of my study spread, and I ended up with a waiting list of two-mother lesbian families from all over the San Francisco Bay Area, and a few more from across the country, who were raising sons. In a nation still preoccupied with issues of single mothers, lesbian and gay parents were flying under the cultural radar.

Like many straight people of my generation, I had very little firsthand knowledge of gay and lesbian lives. Having lived first in New York and then in San Francisco for 18 years, I knew many gay and lesbian people, but I had never explored their issues and circumstances in any systematic way. I worried about how I would be received by the lesbian-headed families I planned to study. Would they wonder if I was a lesbian, and if they found out I was not, would they accept me? Would they perceive me as violating their hard-won turf, or think me primed to be judgmental of their parenting? But only 1 out of the 32 lesbian mothers I interviewed asked me if I was a lesbian. Most of the lesbian mothers I interviewed—as well as the single mothers by choice that I went on to study—said they felt like pioneers in uncharted territory. They embraced any psychological exploration that would help them raise their sons well. All the lesbian mothers I interviewed welcomed me into their homes, proved extremely cooperative and eager to talk with me, and trusted me. The frank, wide-ranging conversations we shared readily normalized our differences. I learned that I did not have to be concerned about asking honest questions. In fact, the mothers were asking themselves the same questions about their sons' development.

This study centered on two-mother lesbian couples who had given birth to sons they were raising in intact, two-parent households. None of these 16 boys had a father on the premises. Many of them did not even know the names of their fathers—nor did their mothers. Thanks to the technological revolution of anonymous-donor insemination, the identity of a founding father may not even be part of the basic proposition of a two-mother family or a single-mother family.

Once a technology that served mostly married couples, donor insemination is now a practice that assists unmarried women, both straight and gay, and thereby yields many different sorts of families. The fathers of sons I studied were unknown donors, only some of whom wanted their identities to be revealed to their offspring; known donors; or donors who were family friends or relatives of nonbiological mothers. In one situation, a child shared a known donor with a classmate, and in another the father of a classmate was the donor. Whether or not a donor has a social father relationship with his child, he usually has surrendered his legal paternal rights. The relationships vary. In Thomas's case, "I see Chris, like, once every month. I guess he's my dad, but he's mostly my uncle. I don't think he's a parent, exactly, but we have a lot of fun going to the zoo and stuff." Nathan, another boy in the study, saw his own donor father infrequently at best. However, his sister's donor father actively participated in family activities on a weekly and sometimes daily basis.

Because lesbians are constructing families that do not fit standard legal definitions, they cannot usually adopt as couples but must instead undertake single-parent adoptions. Lesbian couples have generated the revolutionary concept of the social mother—the parent who has no genetic connection with the son she helps to raise, who may or may not have a legal relationship with him, but who possesses a vital emotional bond. Talking about his social mother, Nathan said, "It was Stephanie who taught me to play basketball. So when I get to play in the NBA, I'll invite her to the games."

It takes strong women to build a family from scratch. The lesbians I studied were mostly white-collar workers who had succeeded as businesspeople or in their professions. These lesbian moms were "social saboteurs," women who were living and raising children outside the dominant culture in conscious, courageous ways. From coming out as lesbians to deciding to have children, they exhibited the will and temperament to buck prevailing notions and create their own family structures, with very few models from which to work. Moreover, they were very conscious that they were on the cutting edge of a social movement. "Mostly we just have a normal home with Nathan and Beth," said Stephanie Goldman, 10-year-old Nathan's social and adoptive mother and 8-year-old Beth's biological mother. "We go to work, take the kids to ballet lessons and soccer games. But you can't help but realize that beyond your own domestic sphere, you're doing something really new and significant."

I have come to think that this sense of significance informed the parenting style of the mothers I studied. But other factors contributed to their mindfulness. We all know that it's better to be wanted than not, and adoptive parents often repeat that being chosen makes for a very special child. The very nature of parenthood through donor insemination means that children are thought about and brought into the world with care and preparation. Women who are inseminated—and who adopt—must think hard and long before making a family. The children brought into families in these ways are not accidents, and they are not surprises because so much planning has gone into their births. Since many of these women were older, the testing they had undergone had provided information about the sex of the baby (or babies) early, and so they had had more time to begin the mental preparation for having sons or daughters.

In addition to being older, these lesbian mothers tended to be better educated and more financially secure than average moms. They had the wherewithal to develop a parenting style that was both intense and considered. The developmental advantages this offered may help to explain why their sons were so remarkable.

The families who participated in my study turned out to be an extremely stable group. The couples had been together from 8 to 22 years and had lived at the same address for an average of 5½ years. They were predominantly White, middle- to upper-middle-class, and highly educated. I have been asked why there were almost no people of color in my study. Like mine, most research in this area has concerned a primarily White and privileged population. Lesbian identity among socioeconomically subordinate groups is generally less visible or less affirmed than it is among more prosperous, White, educated, urban populations. Ethnographic evidence suggests that closeted lesbian and gay people of color often value racial solidarity over sexual adhesiveness. Racial/ethnic allegiances may deter disproportionate numbers of people of color from coming out.

After my research was completed and analyzed, and my dissertation written, defended, and accepted, I found myself continuing to think about the sons of the two-mother families I had come to know. The boys stayed in my mind, and I wanted to learn more about them. So I went back to the families I had interviewed and did further research on them, using the same methods

I had for my initial study. I wanted to explore the larger issues of the parenting these boys received and how they were forming their identities as boys at home and in the world. Throughout my studies, I was known to these children as a psychologist who came into their homes, talked with them, played games with them, drew with them, and was very interested in what it felt like to be a boy growing up and to come from an alternative family. I also had plenty of questions to ask these boys' mothers.

This time my questions were even more far-reaching. What kind of parents did lesbians make, anyway? What kind of values did they hold up and try to see their sons live out? What were the children of these families like as they grew up? Were the gay and lesbian families representative of families in our society?

I also wanted to look at the major problems and challenges these families faced. Was one mommy more real than the other? In the absence of the standard mom-dad dynamic to divide up the tasks of parenting, which roles did lesbian mothers take on, and how did their sons relate to two female authority figures? What were the fears, worries, and desires of children of gay and lesbian families? Did they look at other, more "normal" families with envy, fear, or even contempt? Was it possible that they felt special having two moms? Might they even have seen benefits accrued as the result of having the extra mom that other children lacked?

My work took me into these families' homes over the course of several years. Spending hour after hour with the boys and their mothers, I encouraged them to talk about the specifics of their lives growing up with two mothers and no "everyday father." When conversation lagged, I played games or had the boys talk about the drawings they made for me. I gathered information through notes, tape-recorded conversations, and summaries of observations.

When I first began visiting the boys, I was on an intellectual journey, seeking to explore a specific psychological and moral issue. But like many journeys, mine was full of twists and turns, and my destination turned out to be different from what I had expected. It became a journey of the heart as well as the mind. It led me beyond the basic questions of my research into the broader and even more compelling issues of maverick mothers of all sorts, women who were raising sons on their own.

After I finished the second stage of research with the sons of lesbians, I happened to be talking to Kamala, a heterosexual single mother by choice who had two sons in their early teens enrolled in my daughter's school. She told me that when she asked one of her sons to define the most important part of being a boy, he replied, "Taking care of others." She was proud of him for that because caregiving is not usually associated with teenage boys. Kamala's comment spurred me to see whether what I had witnessed in the sons of lesbians was also true of boys raised by single mothers. I set out to intensively interview 30 single mothers by choice who were raising sons all across the country, in places like Arkansas, California, Louisiana, New York, North Carolina, and Texas. I also interviewed 30 mothers who were single by circumstance—such as the death of a partner, separation, divorce, or the complete abrogation of a partner's parental responsibilities—who were raising sons without a father present in the home.

Like the lesbian couples who had chosen to have children, the single mothers by choice were highly motivated, successful, self-supporting career women. Though geographic considerations prevented me from meeting many of their sons, their views about raising boys turned out to be very similar to those of the lesbian mothers I interviewed. They were dedicated to their beliefs in non-sexist parenting and said they accepted who their sons were rather than consciously molding them into what they thought their boys should be. They believed in open communication and respect for differences, but they enforced firm limits and sought to instill a high sense of personal, intrafamilial, and social responsibility in their sons. "You are my emissaries," single mom Anna Malicki, 43, would tell her sons. She kept Matthew, 12, and Eddie, 14, in line by making it clear that they represented her best self out in the world.

At home, the sons of both single- and two-mother families were expected to be participatory members of the household, doing chores and fulfilling other age-appropriate responsibilities. By the time he was 6, Quentin was already earning his allowance by pulling the sheets off the beds, helping with the washing on Saturdays, bagging the newspapers for recycling, setting the table at night, and even washing the salad for dinner. "What we say to him is 'Everybody works in this family. We all work. Nobody gets to sit and be waited on,'" his co-mom, Sarah, told me. "He likes having a role in the family and having jobs that are his. I think it's important to a kid to feel like he's got a role and he's part of the team."

These mothers' high expectations stretched past action to interaction. "The guidelines we set up for behavior—treat each other with respect and kindness—extend outward from our family to our neighbors and friends," one social mom told me.

Single mothers and co-moms fostered independence in their sons, encouraging them to do whatever they could by themsleves, from sounding out letters and writing their names to closing the car door and carrying their dishes to the sink. They facilitated this process by providing the tools their sons needed. Single mom Deborah Iverson, for example, made cleanup easier for her three sons by storing little dustpans and whisk brooms under each sink and in the playroom. These mothers also worked to keep their boys connected with their parents and siblings, encouraging free expression of a broad range of feelings. Those sons that I did meet—both grown men and younger boys—reminded me of the sons of lesbians I had come to know so well.

During the time I spent as a gender scholar at Stanford University, I evaluated my clinical data and the sons' and mothers' narratives. Patterns and categories began to jump out at me. To interpret my research, I also drew on my personal experience as both a biological mother and an adoptive mother happily married to a very busy man and a good father. My own experience would serve as a one-woman control group representing married mothers, and as a useful example of a mother who found her maternal role and her relation to fatherhood to be continually evolving.

My study determined, essentially, that boys will be boys. I found sons raised in woman-headed homes to be astonishingly deft at answering questions about—or simply figuring out for themselves—how to be boys. Their mothers were also very good at instilling male confidence in their sons. These boys readily engaged in the task of relating to their parents, siblings, and the men in their lives. Whether they grew up in single-mother families or lesbian-led nuclear families, these boys had an innate and astonishing ability to get what they needed in order to establish a strong and resilient sense of their own masculinity. [I also] tell of my experiences and show how these maverick mothers worked to nurture their sons' development and the various ways in which the boys exhibited their masculinity. You will see that they were acutely aware of the very process of becoming manly and that their mothers fostered this awareness.

The boys in my study were not sissies or mama's boys. Nor did they compensate for the lack of a father figure by becoming overly aggressive. Other studies have shown that sons raised in lesbian households are no more likely to become homosexual than they would if raised in heterosexual families.

But how could they be so boyish without fathers as role models? In the first phase of my study of lesbian and heterosexual families, I found that lesbian mothers reported that their sons had fewer male role models than their heterosexual counterparts did. Yet when I began to meet with the boys biweekly over a 2-year period, I saw that those boys actually had more male figures in their lives than did boys from heterosexual families, where the father was often the sole male in their lives.

Boys raised in mother-only families were remarkably resourceful in securing role models for their masculinity. They searched out teachers, friends of the family, coaches, and neighbors. If the boys were having trouble finding these men, their mothers stepped in to help. Most of the boys were fascinated by sports figures, and they had precocious knowledge of the details of the lives of their heroes. They were especially intrigued by the lives of two-generation athletes, taking special pleasure in following those father-son duos. Since the boys themselves had a big say in the choice of males they admired, they were able to select men whose interests and personalities were in harmony with their own. They gave short shrift to those who were unkind or authoritarian, whether blood relatives or not.

Still, I assumed that the boys I studied must have suffered from the stigma of being raised in unconventional families. Not necessarily. I found that their mothers made serious efforts to help their sons deal constructively with the prejudice they faced, thereby helping them develop significant strengths. Perhaps as a result, maverick mothers' sons seemed to have an easy time thinking independently and standing up for what they believed. They had an advantage when it came to acquiring moral standards and courage.

These boys were remarkably sophisticated about the world and about themselves. They were unusually able to articulate their concerns and their joys. Over the years I spent with them, I learned to expect—and to appreciate—the high degree of emotional savvy they exhibited. I call them *head-and-heart boys,* you will see how they dealt with the vicissitudes of their lives, navigated the shoals of complex family situations, and grew into strong and sensitive young men.

Throughout my work with the boys, it seemed clear to me that their essential boyishness was hardwired (and most biological research into gender substantiates my observations). But I needed to understand the dynamics of the nurturing environment. I listened to many single, widowed, divorced, and lesbian mothers tell me about their ups and downs and their boy-rearing strategies. Almost universally, I found a commitment on their part to talk and talk and talk with their sons. The communication imperative proved to be another big lesson of my research.

We have been raised in a society where mother-son closeness is approached with suspicion. I wanted to find out if this trepidation—especially of maverick mother families and their sons—was warranted. Simply put, it isn't. I found that the combination of closeness and conversation led to a natural intimacy between mother and son that continued throughout their lives. A major factor in this connectedness was the mother's ability to acknowledge mistakes to her son, to let him know what she was feeling, and her determination to treat her son's feelings with respect. By admitting to being only human, these mothers encouraged their sons' humanity. And by taking their sons seriously, they imbued them with self-respect. This clearly constituted a healthy version of mother-son closeness.

I also wanted to know how these single or lesbian mothers went about creating a family setting for their sons. [I also discuss] "Collected Families," [which] tells stories of moms who carved out rich and varied environments for their children from all the parts of their lives: blood relations, friends, colleagues, community organizations, and special groups for single moms. These families reminded me of the Advent calendar, on which each day until Christmas you open another window and see a different scene. It could be soccer with Mom, piano in the afternoon with Grandma, and a tutoring session with a donor dad across town, or perhaps dinner with him, his wife, and their teenage son. A complex summons to adulthood looms for these boys. The challenges they face are also the ones that most preoccupy America's moral arbiters—namely, are sons (even more than daughters) from alternative families equipped to come to terms with their own sexuality? Can they reconcile their sexuality with that of their parents without undue confusion? And most important, can they navigate the larger world without protection from their parents or the communities in which they were raised?

"I admit, sometimes I wonder if Evan would be better equipped for the world if he had an everyday dad around," Vivian told me. "And sure, I worry about what Evan is going to face when he's on his own. When they hear he was raised by two mothers, will they ever vote for him for president?" Vivian shrugged and roled her eyes. For his part, Evan was pretty sure he'd still get to play first base for the San Francisco Giants.

From the evidence offered by their childhoods, I believe these boys will have the social and psychological equipment they need to become steady, inquisitive, well-balanced teenagers able to reconcile the conflicting demands they will face. All of these boys will be strongly supported by their mothers as they venture toward their independent sexuality. "As a young boy and then as a teenager, I did all the same things every normal son does: play sports, have girlfriends, break curfew, have parties when my parents were away," 34-year-old Gene Leighton, son of a lesbian mom and a straight dad, told me. Gene's mom divorced his dad when Gene was 8 and formed a life partnership with another woman. "Like most teenagers, I was confused about a lot of things, but my sexual preference was not one of them," Gene added. "In that sense my growing up was perfectly normal."

Certainly, sons of gay parents will have to establish the terms of their sexuality with more self-consciousness than most other teenage boys will. If my experience with sons in lesbian-led families is any indication about how these boys feel about women, they will probably be able to relate to other females with great respect and openness. In fact, they may grow up to be the strong yet open-hearted men women are purported to want to marry. As lesbian co-mom Sarah confided to me with amused pride about her 12-year-old son, "Quentin is going to make some woman a great husband someday. He'll be a great catch."

EXPLORING THE ISSUE

Are Fathers Really Necessary?

Critical Thinking and Reflection

1. How do lesbian mothers differ from the "average" mother?
2. How has the focus of "strengthening father's effects on families" changed over the years?
3. What do you think is the best way to encourage father involvement? Give three reasons for your answer.
4. What are the three main demographic trends that have increased the likelihood that children will live apart from at least one of their biological parents? Do you think these trends can be reversed? Why or why not?

Is There Common Ground?

What role does the father play in the development of a child? Is it the role of dad and what society says he should be that becomes important to the child rather than how the father treats his child? Or, is it that important? If the former is true, then anyone, regardless of how he or she treats the child, will be important to the child. We often see evidence of this phenomenon in dealing with abused children. No matter what the abuse, most children in this situation want to stay at home with abusive fathers rather than be placed in foster care. When confronted with "telling on" their fathers, children will not say what abuse occurred for fear of losing their father's love and being separated from him.

If it is true that the role of dad and what society says he should be is what is important to the child, the quality of interaction and events that children share with their fathers becomes critical to their development. Then why could women not play that role? Women can interact with children in nearly all the same ways that men can. Women can just as easily accompany children to baseball games, act as the soccer coach, or attend the school play, as can men. Thus, the question might not be "Are fathers really necessary?" but "Are men really necessary for the positive development of children?" To many, this would not only mean an assault on the role of fatherhood, but would also constitute an attack on men in general.

As with most issues, extremes on either side make less sense than the middle ground. Child development experts would probably agree that the more adults, both male and female, involved in a child's life, the better. Having a variety of people in one's life brings a variety of experiences and an extensive social network that can benefit children throughout their lives.

Currently, significant research on fathering is being conducted. Soon, scientists will be able to make more definitive statements about how mothers and fathers influence a child's life. Perhaps, one can conclude that as a society, we are all responsible for fathering and mothering. This is especially true for families that do not have the choice of raising children in a two-parent home due to divorce or the death of a spouse. We must continue to strive to find ways to support all families so that children will experience the optimal growth and development that they all deserve.

Additional Resources

National Organization of Single Mothers, Inc. Retrieved on April 8, 2011, from http://singlemothers.org/cms/index.php.

The National Organization of Single Mothers, Inc., is an organization dedicated to "helping single moms by choice or chance face the daily challenges of life with wisdom, wit, dignity, confidence, and courage."

Parade. Obama's Father's Day Speech. Retrieved on April 8, 2011, from http://www.parade.com/news/2009/06/barack-obama-we-need-fathers-tostep-up.html.

This Web site provides the full text of President Barack Obama's June 21, 2009, Father's Day speech.

The Family Economic Strategies. Retrieved on April 8, 2011, from http://www.sixstrategies.org/.

The Family Economic Self-Sufficiency Project describes six strategies that families, especially women, can follow as they move from welfare to self-sufficiency. See the "Setting the Standard for American Working Families" report.

Work and Family: National Partnership for Women and Families. Retrieved on April 8, 2011, from http://www.nationalpartnership.org.

This public education and advocacy site aims "to promote fairness in the workplace, quality health care, and policies that help women and men meet the dual demands of work and family." This site includes a wealth of information about relevant public policy issues, including the Family Medical Leave Act.

ISSUE 7

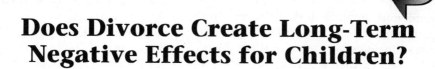

Does Divorce Create Long-Term Negative Effects for Children?

YES: Elizabeth Marquardt, from "The Bad Divorce," *First Things* (February 2005)

NO: Constance Ahrons, from "No Easy Answers: Why the Popular View of Divorce Is Wrong," *We're Still Family: What Grown Children Have to Say About Their Parents' Divorce* (Harper Collins, 2004)

Learning Outcomes

After reading this issue, you should be able to:

- List and discuss some of the problems that children of divorce may face.
- Describe resiliency and the lessons that children learn from divorce.
- Understand some of the complicating factors that make it difficult to determine definitively how divorce affects children.

ISSUE SUMMARY

YES: Elizabeth Marquardt, author and director of the Center for Marriage and Families, states that divorce is a tragedy, which has negative lifelong effects on children. She specifically argues against the data collection method that Constance Ahrons used in her current study.

NO: Constance Ahrons, author, therapist, and co-chair of the Council on Contemporary Families, believes that the idea that children of divorce end up troubled and unable to form adult attachments is a myth. Her research found that children of divorce were strong, wise, and had close family relationships.

How does divorce affect children? Do they perceive it as positive or negative? How would their lives differ if their parents had worked out their problems and stayed together, even if only for the sake of the children? How do children from divorced families differ from those in intact homes—happy or unhappy? Do both groups have similarities, or are they significantly different? These are questions researchers ask when they study the effects of divorce on children.

According to some studies, children from divorced homes are more likely to divorce themselves. Other studies indicate that the quality of the home postdivorce is more likely to affect children's development than the actual divorce event. Is society setting children up for subsequent failed marriages by condoning divorce? Or is divorce simply a solution to the problem of choosing the wrong partner, giving individuals a way of correcting that mistake? Does the divorce spell disaster for children as they grow into adulthood, or are there other explanations for the problems, which children from divorced homes might exhibit?

As the divorce debate evolved from the 1960s to the 1980s, some professionals viewed divorce as an acceptable alternative to living in an unhappy home, while others saw divorce as having devastating effects on children and the family. In the 1990s, a movement to do away with no-fault divorce also spawned a renewed interest in the effects of divorce on children. Family scientists, therapists, and researchers questioned the belief that children eventually adjust to the effects of divorce and that it is better for children to live in a divorced home than in an unhappy, intact home. In the 2000s, longitudinal data on divorce's effects presented conflicting conclusions with more questions than answers to the issue.

There are numerous studies on effects of divorce on children. Some show that children benefit from divorce while others show it is the worst thing that ever happened. On the positive side, children from divorced homes reap benefits as a consequence of their divorce experience, particularly if parents model responsible coping skills. Some children do better in a home without the constant tension and fighting found in an unhappy intact home. These children appear more mature, more realistic about life, and more flexible.

Problems for children in divorced families are well documented. For these children, parents split physically and legally, but not emotionally. These family members might ride an emotional rollercoaster for years after the initial divorce decree. One parent pitted against the other with the child in the middle is all too common for divorced families. Family turmoil may result in children doing poorly in school, beginning to have sex at an early age, and displaying delinquent behavior. Children have no say in the divorce, but must live with the instability and confusion that occurs after the breakup.

If parents decide to divorce, there are things they can do to keep the divorce more healthy according to family life educators. They suggest not putting the other parent down in front of the children. This helps maintain some sense of stability and civility for the children. Seek outside help for the emotional turmoil associated with divorce, rather than using the children as a "sounding board." Make sure any heated discussions with the other parent are held in private where the children cannot hear. Also, try to accept the other parent's new mate so that children do not feel they are betraying the other parent when visiting the new family.

In the following selections, arguments are made about the long-term effects of divorce on children. Based on research and personal experience,

Elizabeth Marquardt feels divorce is "bad" for children. She believes that the types of questions Constance Ahrons asked in her survey led participants to report a positive view of divorce even if they felt differently. Elizabeth Marquardt describes children of divorce as grieving losses following their parents' divorce and negatively affected by the fractured family life that follows divorce. Constance Ahrons interviewed 98 divorced couples in 1992. In the current article, she reports on interviews with the same parents' 173 grown children. Based on the grown children's responses, she believes the divorce was a "good" event and that children learned positive life lessons from it.

According to Elizabeth Marquardt, children of divorce feel a loss of security and confidence when their parents divorce. They are damaged by the event and never recover from the fractured family system they endure. She believes that the conclusions Constance Ahrons drew were inaccurate and based on faulty research methods. Constance Ahrons found that children emerged from divorce wiser, stronger, and with a greater appreciation for strong family relationships.

YES

Elizabeth Marquardt

The Bad Divorce

It is often said that those who are concerned about the social and personal effects of divorce are nostalgic for the 1950s, yearning for a mythical time when men worked, women happily stayed home baking cookies for the kids, and marriages never dissolved. Yet often the same people who make the charge of mythology are caught in a bit of nostalgia of their own, pining for the sexual liberationism of the 1970s, when many experts began to embrace unfettered divorce, confident that children, no less than adults, would thrive once "unhappy" marriages were brought to a speedy end.

Constance Ahrons, who coined the term "the good divorce" in the title of an influential 1992 book that examined ninety-eight divorcing couples, is very much a member of the latter camp. In her new book, *We're Still Family: What Grown Children Have to Say about Their Parents' Divorce,* Ahrons returns to those ninety-eight couples to survey their now-grown children. The result is a study based on telephone interviews with 173 young adults from eighty-nine families that tries to advance the idea it is not divorce itself that burdens children but rather the way in which parents divorce. As in her earlier book, Ahrons argues that the vocabulary we use to discuss divorce and remarriage is negative; she would prefer that we regard divorced families as "changed" or "rearranged" rather than broken, damaged, or destroyed. She claims that upbeat language will, above all, help children feel less stigmatized by divorce. Both of her books offer many new terms, such as "binuclear" and "tribe," to describe divorced families. The specific novelty of the new book is Ahrons' claim that her interviewees view their parents' divorces in a positive light.

It is with delight, then, that Ahrons shares surprising new findings from her on-going study. According to Ahrons, over three-quarters of the young people from divorced families who she interviewed do not wish their parents were still together. A similar proportion feel their parents' decision to divorce was a good one, that their parents are better off today, and that they themselves are either better off or not affected by the divorce. To general readers who have been following the debates about children of divorce in recent years, such findings might sound like big news. But there are problems.

According to Ahrons, over three-quarters of the young people whom she interviewed do not wish that their parents were still together. A similar proportion feel that their parents' decision to divorce was a good one, that their parents are better off today, and that they themselves are either better off because of the divorce or have not been affected by it. Statistically, that sounds overwhelmingly convincing. But an answer to a survey question tells us very little unless we have a context for interpreting it and some grasp of the actual experiences that gave rise to it.

Like those whom Ahrons interviewed, I grew up in a divorced family, my parents having split when I was two years old. Like Ahrons, I am a researcher in the field, having led, with Norval Glenn, a study of young adults from both divorced and intact families that included a nationally representative telephone survey of some 1,500 people. As someone who studies children of divorce and who is herself a grown child of divorce, I have noticed that the kinds of questions that get asked in such studies and the way the answers are interpreted often depend on whether the questioner views divorce from the standpoint of the child or the parent.

Take, for example, Ahrons' finding that the majority of people raised in divorced families do not wish that their parents were together. Ahrons did not ask whether as children these young people had hoped their parents would reunite. Instead, she asked if they wish today their parents were still together. She presents their negative answers as gratifying evidence that divorce is affirmed by children. But is that really the right conclusion to draw?

Imagine the following scenario. One day when you are a child your parents come to you and tell you they are splitting up. Your life suddenly changes in lots of ways. Dad leaves, or maybe Mom does. You may move or change schools or lose friendships, or all of the above. Money is suddenly very tight and stays that way for a long time. You may not see one set of grandparents, aunts, uncles, and cousins nearly as much as you used to. Then, Mom starts dating, or maybe Dad does. A boyfriend or girlfriend moves in, perhaps bringing along his or her own kids. You may see one or both of your parents marry again; you may see one or both of them get divorced a second time. You deal with the losses. You adjust as best you can. You grow up and try to figure out this "relationship" thing for yourself. Then, some interviewer on the telephone asks if you wish your parents were still together today. A lifetime of pain and anger and adjustment flashes before your eyes. Any memory of your parents together as a couple—if you can remember them together at all—is buried deep under all those feelings. Your divorced parents have always seemed like polar opposites to you. No one could be more different from your mother than your father, and vice versa. "No," you reply to the interviewer, "I don't wish my parents were still together." Of course, one cannot automatically attribute such a train of thought to all of Ahrons' interview subjects. Still, it is plausible, and it might explain at least some of the responses. But Ahrons does not even consider it.

Ahrons tells us that the vast majority of young people in her study feel that they are either better off or not affected by their parents' divorce. For a child of divorce there could hardly be a more loaded question than this one. The generation that Ahrons is interviewing grew up in a time of massive changes in family life, with experts assuring parents that if they became happier after divorce, their children would as well. There wasn't a lot of patience for people who felt otherwise—especially when those people were children, with their aggravating preference for conventional married life over the adventures of divorce, and their tendency to look askance at their parents' new love interests.

However, a child soon learns the natural lesson that complaining about a parent's choices is a surefire way to be ignored or worse, and that what parents want above all is praise for those choices. Few things inspire as much admiration among divorced parents and their friends as the words of a child reassuring them that the divorce was no big deal—or even better, that it gave the child something beneficial, like early independence, or a new brother or sister. Parents are proud of a resilient child. They are embarrassed and frustrated by a child who claims to be a victim. And who among us wants to be a victim? Who would not rather be a hero, or at least a well-adjusted and agreeable person? When the interviewer calls on the telephone, what will the young adult be more likely to say? Something like "I'm damaged goods"? Or "Yes, it was tough at times but I survived it, and I'm stronger for it today." It is the second reply that children of divorce have all their lives been encouraged to give; and the fact that they are willing to give it yet again is hardly, as Ahrons would have it, news.

Thus, Ahrons' statistics on their own hardly constitute three cheers for divorce. Far more meaningful and revealing are the extended quotations from interview subjects with which the book is liberally studded. She writes, for instance, that Andy, now thirty-two, sees "value" in his parents' divorce. Why? Because:

> "I learned a lot. I grew up a lot more quickly than a lot of my friends.
> Not that that's a good thing or a bad thing. People were always think-
> ing I was older than I was because of the way I carried myself."

Treating a sad, unfortunate experience (like being forced to grow up more quickly than one's peers) as something neutral or even positive is merely one example of what can happen when a person attempts to conform to a culture that insists that divorce is no big deal. To take such an ambivalent response as clear evidence that divorce does no damage, as Ahrons does is inexcusable.

Ahrons cheerfully reports other "good" results of divorce. Here for example is Brian, whose parents split when he was five:

> "In general, I think [the divorce] has had very positive effects. I see
> what happens in divorces, and I have promised myself that I would do
> anything to not get a divorce. I don't want my kids to go through what
> I went through."

Tracy, whose parents divorced when she was twelve, sees a similar upside to divorce:

> "I saw some of the things my parents did and know not to do that in
> my marriage and see the way they treated each other and know not to
> do that to my spouse and my children. I know [the divorce] has made
> me more committed to my husband and my children."

These are ringing endorsements of divorce as a positive life event? Like the testimony of a child who's learned a painful but useful lesson about the dangers of playing with fire, such accounts indicate that the primary benefit of divorce is to encourage young people to avoid it in their own lives if at all possible.

Then there are the significant problems with the structure of Ahrons' study itself. While the original families were recruited using a randomized method, the study lacks any control group. In other words, Ahrons interviewed plenty of young people from divorced families but spoke to no one of similar ages from intact families. So she really can't tell us anything at all about how these young people might differ from their peers.

Rather than acknowledging that her lack of a control group is a serious limitation, Ahrons sidesteps the issue. In several places she compares her subjects to generalized "social trends" or "their contemporaries" and decides, not surprisingly, that they are not all that different. Thus, Ahrons notes that many of the young people from divorced families told her they frequently struggled with issues of "commitment, trust, and dealing with conflict," but on this finding she comments, "These issues are precisely the ones that most adults in this stage of their development grapple with, whether they grow up in a nuclear family or not." Never mind that she has not interviewed any of those other young people, or cited any studies to back up her contention, or acknowledged the possibility that, while all young people do have to deal with these kinds of interpersonal issues, some have a much harder time doing it than others. Ahrons instead wholly dismisses the pain expressed by the children of divorce and assures us that they are simply passing through a normal development phase.

When it comes to her conclusions, Ahrons claims that "if you had a devitalized or high-conflict marriage, you can take heart that the decision to divorce may have been the very best thing you could have done for your children." While research does show that children, on average, do better after a high-conflict marriage ends (the same research, by Paul Amato and Alan Booth, also shows that only one-third of divorces end high-conflict marriages), no one—Ahrons included—has shown that children do better when an adult ends a marriage he or she perceives as "devitalized." Children don't much care whether their parents have a "vital" marriage. They care whether their mother and father live with them, take care of them, and don't fight a lot. . . .

Ahrons also remains preoccupied with the concept of stigma. She writes, for instance, that we are seeing "progress" because a high divorce rate has the effect of reducing the stigma experienced by children of divorce. That's all well and good, but one wonders why Ahrons gives stigma so much attention while saying nothing about a far more damaging social problem for children of divorce—namely, silence. Consider my own experience. The type of family in which I grew up was radically different from the intact family model. Yet no one around me, not even therapists, ever once acknowledged that fact. Never mind that my beloved father lived hours away, or that the mother I adored was often stressed as she tried to earn a living while also acting as a single parent. I was left to assume, like many children of divorce, that whatever problems I struggled with were no one's fault but my own. The demand that children of divorce keep quiet and get with the program puts them in the position of protecting adults from guilt and further stress—effectively reversing the natural order of family life in which the adults are the protectors of children.

Ahrons is remarkably unsympathetic to the children on whom this burden is laid. What do children of divorce long for? According to Ahrons, they nurture unrealistic hopes for "tidy," "perfect" families. She uses these words so frequently—the first term appears at least six times in the book and the second at least four times—that she sometimes appears to be portraying children of divorce as weird obsessives. Speaking directly to children of divorce, Ahrons offers the following advice: "You may not have the idyllic family you dreamed of . . . [but] often the only thing within our control is how we perceive or interpret an event." "For example, you can choose to see your family as rearranged, or you can choose to see it as broken." Indeed, the curative powers of social constructivism are nothing short of miraculous. Encouraging readers to stop using the descriptive term "adult child of divorce," she asserts that "it's a stigmatizing label that presumes you are deficient or traumatized. . . . If you have fallen prey to using it to explain something about yourself, ask yourself if it is keeping you from making changes that might bring you more satisfaction in your life." Apparently, coming to grips with one's family history and the deepest sources of one's sadness and loneliness is the worst thing a child can do. . . .

Ahrons surely knows more about the tragedies of divorce than her thesis allows her to admit. She has studied divorced families for years. She has worked with them as a clinician. She has been through divorce herself. Yet she inevitably follows up heartbreaking observations of interviewees with the confident assertion that everyone involved would be so much happier if only they talked themselves out of—and even walked away from—their anguish. As she writes in one (unintentionally haunting) passage, "Over the years I have listened to many divorcing parents in my clinical practice talk about how much they look forward to the day when their children will be grown and they won't have to have anything more to do with their exes." Is it possible to image a sadder or more desperate desire than this one—the longing for one's children to grow up faster so that relations with one's ex-spouse can be more effectively severed? In such passages it becomes obvious that all of Ahrons' efforts to explain away the tragedy of divorce and its legacy are in vain. In the end, the theory collapses before reality.

Ahrons' poorly structured study and far too tendentious thesis are of no help to us in thinking through our approach to divorce and its consequences. Children of divorce are real, complex people who are deeply shaped by a new kind of fractured family life—one whose current prevalence is unprecedented in human history. These children are not nostalgic for "tidy," "perfect," "idyllic" families. They grieve the real losses that follow from their parents' divorce. They don't need new words to describe what they've been through. Ordinary words will serve quite well—provided that people are willing to listen to them.

NO

No Easy Answers: Why the Popular View of Divorce Is Wrong

Although it may appear strange, my exhusband's untimely death brought his second and first families closer together. I had mourned at his funeral and spent time with his family and friends for several days afterward. A different level of kinship formed, as we—his first and second families—shared our loss and sadness. Since then, we have chosen to join together at several family celebrations, which has added a deeper dimension to our feelings of family.

You may be thinking, "This is all so rational. There's no way my family could pull this off." Or perhaps, like the many people who have shared their stories with me over the years, you are nodding your head knowingly, remembering similar occasions in your own family. The truth is we are like many extended families rearranged by divorce. My ties to my exhusband's family are not close but we care about one another. We seldom have contact outside of family occasions, but we know we're family. We hear stories of each other's comings and goings, transmitted to us through our mutual ties to my daughters, and now, through grandchildren. But if many families, like my own, continue to have relationships years after divorce, why don't we hear more about them?

Quite simply, it's because this is not the way it's supposed to be. My family, and the many others like mine, don't fit the ideal images we have about families. They appear strange because they're not tidy. There are "extra" people and relationships that don't exist in nuclear families and are awkward to describe because we don't have familiar and socially defined kinship terms to do so. Although families rearranged and expanded by divorce are rapidly growing and increasingly common, our resistance to accepting them as normal makes them appear deviant.

Societal change is painfully slow, which results in the situation wherein the current realities of family life come into conflict with our valued images. Sociologists call this difference "cultural lag," the difference between what is real and what we hold as ideal. This lag occurs because of our powerful resistance to acknowledging changes that challenge our basic beliefs about what's good and what's bad in our society.

From *We're Still Family: What Grown Children Have to Say About Their Parents' Divorce* by Constance Ahrons (HarperCollins, 2004). Copyright © 2004 by Constance Ahrons, Ph.D. Reprinted by permission of the author and Sandra Dijkstra Literary Agency.

Why Good Divorces Are Invisible

Good divorces are those in which the divorce does not destroy meaningful family relationships. Parents maintain a sufficiently cooperative and supportive relationship that allows them to focus on the needs of their children. In good divorces children continue to have ties to both their mothers and their fathers, and each of their extended families, including those acquired when either parent remarries.

Good divorces have been well-kept secrets because to acknowledge them in mainstream life threatens our nostalgic images of family. If the secret got out that indeed many families that don't fit our "mom and pop" household ideal are healthy, we would have to question the basic societal premise that marriage and family are synonymous. And that reality upsets a lot of people, who then respond with familiar outcries that divorce is eroding our basic values and destroying society.

Although we view ourselves as a society in which nuclear families and lifelong monogamous marriages predominate, the reality is that 43 percent of first marriages will end in divorce. Over half of new marriages are actually remarriages for at least one of the partners. Not only have either the bride or groom (or both) been divorced but increasingly one of them also has parents who are divorced.

Families are the way we organize to raise children. Although we hold the ideal image that marriage is a precursor to establishing a family, modern parents are increasingly challenging this traditional ideal. Families today arrange—and rearrange—themselves in many responsible ways that meet the needs of children for nurturance, guidance and economic support. Family historian Stephanie Coontz, in her book *The Way We Never Were,* shows how the "tremendous variety of workable childrearing patterns in history suggests that, with little effort, we should be able to forge new institutions and values."

One way we resist these needed societal changes is by denying that divorce is no longer deviant. We demean divorced families by clinging to the belief that families can't exist outside of marriage. It follows then that stories of healthy families that don't fit the tidy nuclear family package are rare and stories that show how divorce destroys families and harms children are common. In this way, bad divorces appear to represent the American way of divorce and good divorces become invisible.

Messages That Hinder Good Divorces

When the evils of divorce are all that families hear about, it makes coping with the normal transitions and changes that inevitably accompany divorce all the more difficult. Negative messages make children feel different and lesser, leading to feelings of shame and guilt. Parents who feel marginalized in this way are less likely to think about creative solutions to their problems. That all of this unnecessary anxiety is fueled by sensationalized reports of weak findings, half-truths and myths of devastation is deplorable. Only by sorting out the truths about divorce from the fiction can we be empowered to make better decisions, find healthy ways to maintain family relationships, and develop important family rituals after divorce. Let's take a close look at the most common misconceptions about divorce.

Misconception 1: Parents Should Stay Married for the Sake of the Kids

This is message that pervades our culture, and it rests on a false duality: Marriage is good for kids, divorce is bad. Underlying this premise is the belief that parents who divorce are immature and selfish because they put their personal needs ahead of the needs of their children, that because divorce is too easy to get, spouses give up on their marriages too easily and that if you're thinking about divorcing your spouse, you should "stick it out till the kids are grown." A popular joke takes this message to its extreme. A couple in their nineties, married for seventy years, appears before a judge in their petition for a divorce. The judge looks at them quizzically and asks, "Why now, why after all these years?" The couple responds: "We waited until the children were dead."

The research findings are now very clear that reality is nowhere near as simple and tidy. Unresolved, open interparental conflict between married spouses that pervades day-to-day family life has been shown again and again to have negative effects on children. Most experts agree that when this is the case it is better for the children if parents divorce rather than stay married. Ironically, prior to the initiation of no-fault legislation over twenty years ago, in most states this kind of open conflict in the home was considered "cruel and inhumane" treatment and it was one of the few grounds on which a divorce would be granted—if it could be proved.

But the majority of unsatisfying marriages are not such clearcut cases. When most parents ask themselves if they should stay married for the sake of their children, they have clearly reached the point where they are miserable in their marriages but wouldn't necessarily categorize them as "high-conflict." And here is where, in spite of the societal message, there is no agreement in the research findings or among clinical experts. That's because it's extremely complex and each individual situation is too different to allow for a "one-size-fits-all" answer.

A huge list of factors comes into play when assessing whether staying married would be better for your kids. For example,

- Is the unhappiness in your marriage making you so depressed or angry that your children's needs go unmet because you can't parent effectively?
- Do you and your spouse have a cold and distant relationship that makes the atmosphere at home unhealthy for your children?
- Do you and your spouse lack mutual respect, caring or interests, setting a poor model for your children?
- Would the financial hardships be so dire that your children will experience a severely reduced standard of living?

Add to this your child's temperament, resources and degree of resilience, and then the personal and family changes that take place in the years after the divorce, and you can see how the complexities mount.

It is a rare parent who divorces *too easily*. Most parents are responsible adults who spend years struggling with the extremely difficult and complex decision of whether to divorce or stay married "for the sake of the children." The bottom line is that divorce is an adult decision, usually made by one spouse, entered into in the face of many unknowns. Without a crystal ball, no one knows whether their decision will be better for their children. As you read further in this book, however, you may gain some perspective on what will be most helpful in your situation, with your children, by listening carefully to the reactions and feelings of various children of divorce *as they have changed over twenty years*.

Misconception 2: "Adult Children of Divorce" Are Doomed to Have Lifelong Problems

. . . The truth is that, for the great majority of children who experience a parental divorce, the divorce becomes part of their history but it is not a defining factor. Like the rest of us, most of them reach adulthood to lead reasonably happy, successful lives. Although children who grew up with divorced parents certainly share an important common experience, their ability to form healthy relationships, be good parents, build careers, and so on, are far more determined by their individual temperaments, their sibling relationships, the dynamics within their parents' *marriages* and the climate of their *postdivorce* family lives.

Misconception 3: Divorce Means You Are No Longer a Family

There's this myth that as long as you stay married your family is good but as soon as you announce you're separating, your family is thrown into the bad zone. Your family goes from being "intact" to being "dissolved," from two-parent to single parent, from functional to dysfunctional. Even though we all know that people don't jump from happy marriages right into divorce, there is an assumption that the decision to separate is the critical marker. It doesn't seem to matter whether your marital relationship was terrible, whether you were miserable and your children troubled. Just as long as you are married and living together in one household, the sign over the front door clearly states to the world, "We're a normal family."

The inaccurate and misleading message that divorce destroys families is harmful to both parents and children because it hides and denies all the positive ways that families can be rearranged after divorce. It sends the destructive message to children that divorce means they only get to keep one parent and they will no longer be part of a family. Although two-parent first-married households now represent less than 25 percent of all households, and an increasing number of children each year are raised by unmarried adults, many people cling to the belief that healthy families can only be two-parent married families and social change is always bad and threatening to our very foundations. . . .

The truth is that although some divorces result in family breakdown, the vast majority do not. While divorce changes the form of the family from one household to two, from a nuclear family to a binuclear one, it does not need to change the way children think and feel about the significant relationships within their families. This does not mean that divorce is not painful or difficult, but over the years, as postdivorce families change and even expand, most remain capable of meeting children's needs for family.

Misconception 4: Divorce Leaves Children without Fathers

This message is linked closely with the preceding one because when we say that divorce destroys families we really mean that fathers disappear from the family. The myths that accompany this message are that fathers are "deadbeat dads" who abandon their kids and leave their families impoverished. The message strongly implies that fathers don't care and are unwilling or unable to make continuing commitments to their children. While this reflects the reality for a minority of divorced fathers, the majority of fathers continue to have loving relationships with their children and contribute financially to their upbringing. . . .

Misconception 5: Exspouses Are Incapable of Getting Along

. . . Although we have come to realize that parents who divorce still need to have some relationship with one another, the belief that it's not really possible still lingers. In fact, when exspouses remain friends they are viewed as a little strange and their relationship is suspect. Yet, the truth is that many divorced parents *are* cooperative and effective coparents. Like good divorces and involved fathers, they are mostly invisible in the media. . . .

Misconception 6: Divorce Turns Everyone into Exfamily; In-Laws Become Outlaws

When it comes to the semantics of divorce-speak, all of the kinship ties that got established by marriage dissolve abruptly. On the day of the legal divorce, my husband and all of his relatives suddenly became exes. But even though the kinship is *legally* terminated, meaningful relationships often continue. My friend Jan, during her fifteen-year marriage, formed a very close relationship with her mother-in-law. Now, twenty years later, she still calls her eighty-two-year-old exmother-in-law "Mom," talks with her several times a week and has dinner with her weekly. Exmother-in-law is certainly not an adequate description of this ongoing relationship.

As a culture we continue to resist accepting divorce as a normal endpoint to marriage even though it is an option chosen by almost half of those who marry. It is this cultural lag, this denial of current realities that causes the inaccurate language, not only for the family ties that continue but also for the family we inherit when we, our former spouses, our parents or our children remarry. Kinship language is important because it provides a shorthand way for us to identify relationships without wading through tedious explanations. . . .

Misconception 7: Stepparents Aren't Real Parents

. . . Children and their new stepparents start off their relationships with two strikes against them. They have to fight an uphill battle to overcome negative expectations, and they have to do so without much help from society. Since almost 85 percent of the children with divorced parents will have a stepparent at some time in their lives, it is shocking that we know so little about how these relationships work. Clearly, societal resistance to recognizing the broad spectrum of postdivorce families has hindered the development of good role models for stepchildren and their stepparents.

Painting a False Picture

Taken together, these negative messages paint a false picture of divorce, one that assumes family ties are irretrievably broken so that postdivorce family relationships appear to be nonexistent. Despite these destructive messages, many divorced parents meet the needs of their children by creating strong families after divorce. Without a doubt, divorce is painful and creates stress for families, but it is important to remember that most recover, maintaining some of their kinship relationships and adding new ones over time.

By making good divorces invisible we have accepted bad divorces as the norm. In so doing, children and their divorced parents are being given inaccurate messages that conflict with the realities they live and make them feel deviant and stigmatized. It is time we challenge these outdated, ill-founded messages and replace them with new ones that acknowledge and accurately reflect current realities.

The Distortions of Oversimplifying

Just a little over a decade ago, in January 1989, the *New York Times Magazine* ran a cover story called "Children after Divorce," which created a wave of panic in divorced parents and their children. Judith Wallerstein and her coauthor, Sandra Blakeslee, a staff writer for the *New York Times,* noted their newest unexpected finding. Calling it the "sleeper effect," they concluded that only ten years after divorce did it become apparent that girls experience "serious effects of divorce at the time they are entering young adulthood."

When one of the most prestigious newspapers in the world highlights the findings of a study, most readers take it seriously. "That 66 percent of young women in our study between the ages of nineteen and twenty-three will suffer debilitating effects of their parents' divorce years later" immediately became generalized to the millions of female children with divorced parents. The message—just when you think everything may be okay, the doom of divorce will rear its ugly head—is based on a *mere eighteen out of the grand total of twenty-seven women* interviewed in this age group. This detail wasn't mentioned in the fine print of the article but is buried in the appendix of the book that was scheduled for publication a month after the *New York Times* story appeared. And it is on this slim data that the seeds of a myth are planted. We are still living with the fallout.

In sharp contrast to Wallerstein's view that parental divorce has a powerful devastating impact on children well into adulthood, another psychologist made headlines with a completely opposite thesis. In her book, *The Nurture Assumption: Why Children Turn Out the Way They Do*, Judith Rich Harris proposes that what parents do makes little difference in how their children's lives turn out. Half of the variation in children's behavior and personality is due to genes, claims Harris, and the other half to environmental factors, mainly their peer relationships. For this reason, Harris asserts parental divorce is not responsible for all the ills it is blamed for.

These extreme positions—of divorce as disaster and divorce as inconsequential—oversimplify the realities of our complex lives. Genes and contemporary relationships notwithstanding, we have strong evidence that parents still make a significant difference in their children's development. Genetic inheritance and peer relationships are part of the story but certainly not the whole story.

Sorting Out the Research Findings

Drawing conclusions across the large body of research on divorce is difficult. Studies with different paradigms ask different questions that lead to different answers. A classic wisdom story shows the problem. Three blind men bumped into an elephant as they walked through the woods. They didn't know what it was, but each prided himself on his skill at "seeing." So one blind man reached out and carefully explored the elephant's leg. He described in great detail the rough, scratchy surface that was huge and round. "Aha, this is an ancient mighty tree. We're in a new forest." "No, no," said the blind man who had taken hold of the elephant's trunk. "We're in great danger—this is a writhing snake, bigger than any in our hometown. Run!" The third man laughed at them both. He'd been touching the elephant's tusk, noticing the smooth hard surface, the gentle curve, the rounded end. "Nonsense! We have discovered an exquisitely carved horn for announcing the emperor's arrival."

The blind men described what they "saw" accurately. Their mistake was to claim that what they saw was the whole. Much like the three blind men, researchers see different parts of the divorce elephant, which then frames their investigations.

It should come, then, as no surprise that reports of the findings about divorce are often contradictory and confusing. It is impossible for any study to take account of all the complexities of real life, or of the individual differences that allow one family to thrive in a situation that would create enormous stress, and frayed relationships, in another. But it is in these variations that we can begin to make sense of how divorce impacts the lives of individuals and families.

Facing Reality

Hallmark Cards recently launched a line of greeting cards called "Ties That Bind" aimed at various nontraditional unions—from stepfamilies to adopted child households to unmarried partnerships. "Our cards reflect the times," says Marita Wesely-Clough, trend group manager at Hallmark. "Relationships today are so nebulous that they are hard to pin down, but in creating products, we have to be aware that they are there. Companies need to respect and be sensitive to how people are truly living their lives now, and not how they might wish or hope for them to live."

Advertising agencies and marketing services make it their business to assess social realities. To sell their products, they have to evaluate the needs and desires of their potential consumers. They do not share the popular cultural anxiety about the changes in families. Instead they study them and alter their products to suit. Policy makers would do well to take some lessons from them and alter their preconceived notions about families to reflect current realities.

While the political focus today is on saving marriages and preserving traditional family values, Americans in large numbers are dancing to their own drummers. They're cohabiting in increasingly large numbers, having more children "out of wedlock" and engaging in serial marriages. While the rates of divorce have come down from their 1981 highs, they have leveled off at a high rate that is predicted to remain stable. To meet the needs of children and parents, we need to burst the balloon about idealized families and support families as they really live their lives. And that means we have to face the true complexities of *our* families and not search for simple answers.

As you read this book, keep in mind that we can all look back on our childhoods and note something about our mothers or fathers or sisters or brothers that has had lasting effects on our personalities. If you are looking to answer the question of whether a parental divorce results in children having more or less problems than children who grew up in other living situations, you will be disappointed. Nor will you find answers to whether the stresses of divorce are worse for children than other stresses in life. However, you will find answers here to questions about how and why individual children respond in different ways to the variations in their divorced families.

Divorce is a stressful life event that requires increased focus on parenting. The effort and care that parents put into establishing their postdivorce families are crucial and will pay off over the years in their many benefits to the children. But remember, families are complex, and if you find easy answers, they are likely to be wrong.

EXPLORING THE ISSUE

Does Divorce Create Long-Term Negative Effects for Children?

Critical Thinking and Reflection

1. How do you think the media depicts divorce in the United States? Do you think it provides an accurate depiction, a harsher depiction, or a sugar-coated one? Based on what you read in these articles, how accurate do you think the depictions are? Provide examples of movies, television shows, books, and/or magazine articles in making your points.

Is There Common Ground?

When parents find that they are no longer happy in a marriage, which choice is better for their children? Should they stay together to maintain an intact home for their children even though there may be constant conflict? Or should they divorce, creating two households for their children, with the hope that they will find happiness either as a single person or remarried to someone new? How will a remarriage, in addition to a divorce, affect their children? Obviously, there are no easy answers to these questions as the opposing selections clearly indicate. One thing researchers know for sure is that no matter what traumatic event happens to children, whether it is a divorce, death of a parent, or natural disaster, the support and modeling of appropriate behavior by important adults in the child's life is critical. Children who have someone to talk to, who will listen to and guide the child, can make a significant difference in the way children adapt to negative life events.

Perhaps the answer is in making sure parents never have to face trying to end a marriage by divorce. Authors from each selection disagree on the long-term effects of divorce, but would probably agree on society making more of an effort to strengthen marriage to reduce the incidence of divorce. Strengthening marriage by providing marriage education for adolescents would help children learn how intact marriages work. Information on how to deal with current issues of balancing work and family as well as how to deal with conflict could be taught. This education could provide needed support to young adults as they choose marriage partners and help them develop healthy expectations of marriage.

Additional Resources

American Men's Studies Association. Retrieved on April 8, 2011, from http:// mensstudies.org.

The American Men's Studies Association is a not-for-profit professional organization of scholars, therapists, and others interested in the exploration of masculinity in modern society.

Eleoff, Sara. (2003). Divorce Effects on Children. Retrieved on April 7, 2011, from http://www.childadvocate.net/divorce_effects_on_children.htm.

This is an article posted online that discusses some of the ramifications of divorce.

Feminist Majority Foundation. Retrieved on April 8, 2011, from http://www .feminist.org.

The Feminist Majority Foundation Web site provides affirmative action links, resources from women's professional organizations, information for empowering women in business, sexual harassment information, and much more.

Helpguide.org. Children and Divorce: Helping Your Kids Cope with the Outcomes of Divorce. Retrieved on April 7, 2011, from http://www.helpguide .org/mental/children_divorce.htm.

This Web site provides information for parents to help them work with their children during a divorce.

Kid's Health. A Kid's Guide to Divorce. Retrieved on April 7, 2011, from http:// kidshealth.org/kid/feeling/home_family/divorce.html.

This Web site provides information that kids can easily understand about divorce.

ISSUE 8

Is Viewing Television Violence Harmful for Children?

YES: L. Rowell Huesmann, Jessica Moise-Titus, Cheryl-Lynn Podolski, and Leonard D. Eron, from "Longitudinal Relations Between Children's Exposure to TV Violence and Their Aggressive and Violent Behavior in Young Adulthood: 1977–1992," *Developmental Psychology* (March 2003)

NO: Jib Fowles, from "The Whipping Boy: The Hidden Conflicts Underlying the Campaign against Violent TV," *Reason* (March 2001)

Learning Outcomes

After reading this issue, you should be able to:

- Identify some of the effects the television viewing is believed to have on children.
- Discuss the reasons why some researchers believe that violence on television is causing an increase in aggressive behaviors in children.
- Discuss the reasons why some researchers believe that television watching has become a scapegoat for children's behaviors.

ISSUE SUMMARY

YES: L. Rowell Huesmann, Jessica Moise-Titus, Cheryl-Lynn Podolski, and Leonard Eron, from the Research Center for Group Dynamics, Institute for Social Research at the University of Michigan, found that both males and females are more likely to develop violent behavior in adulthood as a result of watching violent TV shows in early childhood.

NO: Jib Fowles, a professor of communication at the University of Houston, asserts that television violence has increased steadily, but the violent crime rate has in fact decreased.

Almost everyone has access to television (TV). There is hardly any other factor so pervasive in our society as television viewing. What is the relationship of TV viewing to violent acts? Those who believe that TV viewing is the root of all evil support unplugging the "boob tube" and going back to the good old days of reading, listening to the radio, and swapping stories while sitting by the fireplace. At the other end of the continuum, those who argue that TV is merely the next evolution of communication technology would promote going with the flow, grinning and bearing TV for it is surely here to stay, and stop worrying about TV.

There are numerous studies on children who watch violent TV shows, as well as on the amount of TV children watch. Some research suggests that children who spend excessive amounts of time watching TV tend to do poorly in school. Other studies show that children who spend moderate amounts of time in front of the set perform better scholastically than those who watch no TV at all. Children are more likely to be overweight when they watch TV versus playing actively. If children are watching TV to excess, they are not communicating with adults in the family and are not learning family values.

The debate over TV violence rages on. Ask any group of people you meet today about violence in contemporary society. The responses will be remarkably similar. "Violence is in epidemic proportions. There is a lot more violence out on the streets now than when I was a kid. It's just not safe to be out anymore. We live in such violent times." The anecdotes and nostalgia about more peaceful times seem to be endless. The unison in which society decries the rise in violence begins to disintegrate, however, when one attempts to discern causes for the increases in crimes like murder, rape, robbery, and assault.

One segment of society that is regularly targeted as a contributing cause to the rise in violence is the media, particularly TV programming. A common argument is that TV is much too violent, especially in children's programming. It has been suggested, for example, that a child will witness in excess of 100,000 acts of simulated violence depicted on TV before graduating from elementary school! Lower socioeconomic status children may view even more hours of violent TV. Many researchers suggest that this TV violence is at least in part responsible for the climbing rates of violent crime, since children tend to imitate what they observe in life.

On the other side, critics argue that it is not what is on TV that bears responsibility for the surge in violence. Programming is merely reflective of the level of violence in contemporary society. The argument is that while TV watching may be associated with violence, it does not mean that it causes violence. As an example, the critics suggest that we have known for some time that aggressive children tend to watch more aggressive TV programming. However, does the aggression predispose an interest in aggressive programming, or does the programming cause the aggression? This is a question that sparks hotly contested debates.

Those who believe TV viewing is at least partly responsible for aggressive behavior in children want the U.S. Congress to more closely regulate the ratings, viewing times, and amount of violence that can be shown on American TV. Those on the other side of the issue point to the infringement on First Amendment rights of freedom of expression if such intense regulation is imposed on the media.

Other factors that contribute to the issue of TV viewing and violence are the types of programs and commercials that children watch. School-aged children are the most targeted when it comes to advertising. There are more commercial breaks per hour for children's programming than for other types of programs. Additionally, with the widespread access to cable TV, children can watch violent adult programming, many times in unsupervised homes.

Several organizations have emerged to address the issue of TV violence and its effects on society. The Center for Media Literacy provides practical information to children and adults by translating media literacy research and theory into easy-to-read resources. They also provide training and educational tools for teachers, youth leaders, parents, and caregivers of children. The National Institute on Media and the Family sponsors "Media Wise," which educates and informs the public, as well as encourages practices and policies that promote positive change in the production and use of mass media. According to their mission statement, they do not advocate censorship of any kind. They are committed to partnering with parents and other caregivers, organizations, and corporations in using the power of the free market to create healthier media choices for families, so that there are healthier, less violent communities. What should be done to effectively address this problem? Is it realistic to revert back to the days prior to the TV era? Or should we just relax and stop worrying about TV? After all, children are resilient; they can eventually understand TV's impact on their lives just as we adults have. Anyone reading this book grew up with the "magic" box and probably turned out OK.

The two articles that follow are typical of the debate centered around violence and TV as it affects children. In the YES article, L. Rowell Huesmann, Jessica Moise-Titus, Cheryl-Lynn Podolski, and Leonard D. Eron studied children at age 6–10 and again 15 years later. They concluded that children are more likely to develop violent behavior in adulthood as a result of watching violent TV shows in early childhood. Children identify with aggressive TV characters and the realism they perceive from TV shows. In the NO article, Jib Fowles believes that TV is used as a whipping boy, blamed for the ills of society including the perceived rise in violent acts. Although there are no champions that rise to TV's defense, Fowles contends that the attack on TV as the source of societal violence is a big lie and is used to cover up society's real problems.

YES

L. Rowell Huesmann et al.

Longitudinal Relations Between Children's Exposure to TV Violence and Their Aggressive and Violent Behavior in Young Adulthood: 1977–1992

Over the past 40 years, a body of literature has emerged that strongly supports the notion that media-violence viewing is one factor contributing to the development of aggression. The majority of empirical studies have focused on the effects of watching dramatic violence on TV and film. Numerous experimental studies, many static observational studies, and a few longitudinal studies all indicate that exposure to dramatic violence on TV and in the movies is related to violent behavior. Furthermore, a substantial body of psychological theory has developed explaining the processes through which exposure to violence in the mass media could cause both short- and long-term increases in a child's aggressive and violent behavior. Long-term effects with children are now generally believed to be primarily due to long-term observational learning of cognitions (schemas, beliefs, and biases) supporting aggression, whereas short-term effects with adults and children are recognized as also due to priming, excitation transfer, or imitation of specific behaviors. Most researchers of aggression agree that severe aggressive and violent behavior seldom occurs unless there is a convergence of multiple predisposing and precipitating factors such as neurophysiological abnormalities, poor child rearing, socioeconomic deprivation, poor peer relations, attitudes and beliefs supporting aggression, drug and alcohol abuse, frustration and provocation, and other factors. The evidence is already substantial that exposure to media violence is one such long-term predisposing and short-term precipitating factor. The current longitudinal study adds important additional empirical evidence that the effects of childhood exposure to media violence last into young adulthood and increase aggressive behavior at that time for both males and females.

Theoretical Background

In discussing the alternative theoretical perspectives that have emerged to explain the obtained relations between exposure to violence (family, community,

From *Developmental Psychology*, March 2003, pp. 201–204, 217–219. Copyright © 2003 by American Psychological Association. Reprinted by permission via Rightslink.

or mass media) and subsequent aggressive behavior in the observer, it is important to distinguish between short-term effects and longer term effects.

In recent theorizing, long-term relations have been ascribed mainly to acquisition through observational learning of three social-cognitive structures: schemas about a hostile world, scripts for social problem solving that focus on aggression, and normative beliefs that aggression is acceptable. Building on the accumulating evidence that human and primate young have an innate tendency to imitate whomever they observe, these theories propose that very young children imitate almost any specific behaviors they see. Observation of specific aggressive behaviors around them increases children's likelihood of behaving in exactly that way. Proactive-instrumental aggressive behaviors in children 2 to 4 years old generally appear spontaneously, as may hostile temper tantrums. However, the observation of specific aggressive behaviors at that age leads to the acquisition of more coordinated aggressive scripts for social problem solving and counteracts environmental forces aimed at conditioning the child out of aggression. As the child grows older, the social scripts acquired through observation of family, peers, community, and the mass media become more complex, abstracted, and automatic in their invocation. In addition, children's social-cognitive schemas about the world around them begin to be elaborated. In particular, extensive observation of violence around them biases children's world schemas toward attributing hostility to others' actions. Such attributions in turn increase children's likelihood of behaving aggressively. As children mature further, normative beliefs about what social behaviors are appropriate become crystallized and begin to act as filters to limit inappropriate social behaviors. Children's own behaviors influence the normative beliefs that develop, but so do the children's observations of the behaviors of those around them, including those observed in the mass media. In summary, social-cognitive observational-learning theory postulates long-term effects of exposure to violence through the influence of exposure on the development of aggressive problem-solving scripts, hostile attributional biases, and normative beliefs approving of aggression.

A major alternative or complementary theory explaining long-term effects is desensitization theory. This theory is based on the empirical fact that most humans seem to have an innate negative emotional response to observing blood, gore, and violence. Increased heart rates, perspiration, and self-reports of discomfort often accompany such exposure. However, with repeated exposure to violence, this negative emotional response habituates, and the observer becomes desensitized. The presumption is that lack of a negative emotional response to observing violence also indicates a flat response to planning violence or thinking about violence. Thus, proactive-instrumental aggressive acts become easier to commit.

There are two other quite different theoretical perspectives that have attempted to explain long-term relations between exposure to violence and aggression without hypothesizing any direct effect of violence viewing on aggression. One theory is that aggressive behavior or a correlate of aggressive behavior stimulates exposure to violence and thus engenders the observed relation between them. Observational studies of aggressive children do show that the aggressive child is likely to provoke others, who then respond aggressively to the child, creating a violent environment that the child "observes." For media violence, however, the usual assumption is that the aggressive child simply "likes" watching media violence more than other children do. Drawing on social comparison theory, Huesmann elaborated on this theme by suggesting that aggressive children feel happier and more justified if they believe they are not alone in their aggression, and viewing media violence makes them feel happier because it convinces them that they are not alone.

The other alternative theory that has been widely discussed is best described as the "third variable" theory. A wide variety of demographic, family, and personal characteristics are known to be correlated both with TV viewing and with aggression, such as social class and IQ. These theories suggest that the observed long-term positive relations between aggression and exposure to media violence are spurious and are derived from their joint association with one or more of these third variables.

These "third variable" explanations should not be confused with the developmental perspectives on the observational learning and desensitization theories, which also assign important roles to parenting, intellectual ability, and social class as contributors to both exposure to violence and acceptability of aggressive behavior. Children of lower socioeconomic status (SES) and lower IQ are known to watch more TV, probably for multiple reasons including social norms, cost of alternative entertainments, and frustration with more intellectually demanding tasks. Parents' TV habits and child-rearing practices also influence the child's TV habits. Of course, early parenting factors such as harsh punishment, rejection of the child, and lack of discipline are also known to influence subsequent aggression by the child. The difference is that these factors are viewed not as explaining away the "effect" of exposure to violence on aggression but as explaining individual differences in exposure to violence and individual differences in the strength of the effect.

Any of these theoretical processes might also contribute to the shorter term relations between exposure to violence and aggressive behavior. However, two other processes have been widely discussed as playing a role in short-term relations: priming and arousal processes. The observation of stimuli that have been paired in the past with observed violence or that inherently suggest violence (e.g., weapons) activates memory traces for aggressive scripts, schemas, and beliefs sufficiently to make their utilization more probable. A provocation that follows a priming stimulus is more likely to stimulate aggression as a result of the priming. Although this effect is short-lived, the primed script, schema, or belief may have been acquired long ago and may have been acquired in a completely different context.

To the extent that observed violence (real world or media) arouses the observer, aggressive behavior may become more likely in the short run for two other possible reasons: excitation transfer and general arousal. First, a subsequent provocation may be perceived as more severe than it is because the emotional response stimulated by the observed violence is misattributed as being due to the provocation. Such excitation transfer could account for a more intense aggressive response in the short run. Alternatively, the increased general arousal stimulated by the observed violence may simply reach such a peak that the ability of inhibiting mechanisms such as normative beliefs to restrain aggression is reduced.

It is important to recognize that these theoretical processes are not mutually exclusive. It is perfectly possible both that observational learning, desensitization, priming, and excitation transfer all contribute to the stimulation of aggression by the observation of violence and that more aggressive children do like to watch more violence. However, there is one theory that is incompatible with all of these processes. Catharsis theory would predict that violence viewing should be followed by reductions in aggression. Because the empirical evidence for any such negative relation is almost nonexistent, catharsis theory seems untenable at this time.

Empirical Background

In contrived experimental studies, children (both boys and girls) exposed to violent behavior on film or TV behave more aggressively immediately afterward. The typical paradigm involves randomly selected children who are shown either a violent or nonviolent short film and are observed afterward as they play with each other. The consistent finding is that children who see the violent film clip behave more aggressively toward each other or toward surrogate objects. In these settings, exposure to violent film scenes clearly causes more aggressive behavior by children immediately afterward.

The demonstration of a relation between the observation of dramatic TV or film violence and the commission of aggressive behavior has not been limited to the laboratory. Evidence from field studies has clearly shown that the amount of TV and film violence a child is regularly watching is positively related to the child's aggressiveness. Children who watch more violence on TV and in the movies behave more violently and express beliefs more accepting of aggressive behavior. Although the correlations are modest by the standards used in the measurement of intellectual abilities (average = .41 for experiments and .19 for field studies), they are highly replicable and are substantial by public health standards. For example, as a comparison, the correlation between cigarette smoking and lung cancer was .34 in Wynder and Graham's classic study. Moreover, the correlation between childhood exposure to media violence and childhood aggression is highly replicable even across researchers who disagree about the reasons and across countries.

Although these one-shot field studies showing a correlation between media-violence viewing and aggression suggest that the causal conclusions of the experimental studies may well generalize to the real world, longitudinal studies with children can test the plausibility of long-term predisposing effects more directly. In perhaps the first longitudinal study on this topic, initiated in 1960 on 856 youth in New York State, Eron, Huesmann, Lefkowitz, and Walder found that boys' early childhood viewing of violence on TV was statistically related to their aggressive and antisocial behavior 10 years later (after graduating from high school) even after initial aggressiveness, social class, education, and other relevant variables were controlled. A 22-year follow-up of these same boys revealed that their early aggression predicted later criminality at age 30 and that early violence viewing also was independently but weakly related to their adult criminality.

A more representative longitudinal study was initiated by Huesmann and his colleagues in 1977. This 3-year longitudinal study of children in five countries also revealed that the TV habits of children as young as first graders also predicted subsequent childhood aggression even after initial levels of aggression were controlled. In contrast to earlier longitudinal studies, this effect was obtained for both boys and girls even in countries without large amounts of violent programming, such as Israel, Finland, and Poland. In most countries, the more aggressive children also watched more TV, preferred more violent programs, identified more with aggressive characters, and perceived TV violence as more like real life than did the less aggressive children. The combination of extensive exposure to violence coupled with identification with aggressive characters was a particularly potent predictor of subsequent aggression for many children. Still, there were differences among the countries. Although the synchronous correlations were positive in all countries, the longitudinal effect of violence viewing on aggression was not significant for girls in Finland or for all children in Australia. In Israel, there were significant effects for children living in a city but not for children raised on a kibbutz.

A few longitudinal studies have seemed to produce results at odds with the thesis that media-violence viewing causes aggression, but closer inspection of most of these studies reveals that their results are not discrepant but simply not strongly supportive of the thesis. For example, although the National Broadcasting Company's longitudinal study of middle-childhood youth conducted in the 1970s reported significant regression coefficients for only 2 out of the 15 critical tests of the causal theory for boys, an additional 10 were in the predicted direction. Furthermore, for girls, 3 out of the 15 critical tests were significant and an additional 7 were in the predicted direction.

The Current Study

As the above review indicates, over the past several decades, the correlation between TV-violence viewing and childhood or adolescent aggression has been unambiguously demonstrated. It has also been clearly confirmed that in the short run, exposure to violence causes an increase in immediate aggressive behavior. These effects have been obtained repeatedly for both boys and girls. The few completed longitudinal studies have also suggested that there is a long-term effect of early childhood exposure on aggression later in childhood, in the teen years, and, less strongly, into adulthood. However, these longer term effects have been found only for boys in the existing studies that were initiated in the 1960s.

The current study is a follow-up of the 1977 longitudinal study of 557 children growing up in the Chicago area that we described above and have reported on elsewhere. Our aim was to investigate the long-term relations between viewing media violence in childhood and young-adult aggressive behavior. The study was designed to provide data that could be used to compare the relative plausibility of the violence effects theories described earlier (observational learning theory or desensitization theory) with the plausibility of the preference-for-violence and "third variable" theories. However, the study was not designed to contrast observational learning theory with desensitization theory. In addition, the examination of the "third variable" hypotheses in this study, as always, is limited by the actual third variables included in the study.

In the follow-up study, we tracked down as many of the original boys and girls in that U.S. study as we could find 15 years later when they were in their early 20s. We interviewed them, interviewed their spouses or friends, and collected data on them from state archives. In this article, we address four major questions with data from this follow-up: (a) To what extent does early childhood exposure to media violence predict young-adult aggression and violence? (b) Are there gender differences in the predictability? (c) Does the extent to which the child viewer identifies with the aggressive character or believes the plot is realistic affect the strength of the prediction? and (d) To what extent does any long-term relation seem to be due to more aggressive children simply liking to watch violence or seem to be due to some environmental, family, or personal "third variable" that stimulates both childhood violence viewing and childhood and adult aggression? . . .

Discussion

In this 15-year longitudinal study of 329 youth, we found that children's TV-violence viewing between ages 6 and 9, children's identification with aggressive same-sex TV characters, and children's perceptions that TV violence is realistic were significantly correlated with their adult aggression. This was true for both male and female participants. It was true for physical aggression for both genders and for indirect aggression for women. Regression analyses that partialed out the effects of early aggression showed that these childhood TV habits were not just correlated with aggression but predicted increases or decreases in aggressive behavior. For both male and female participants, more childhood exposure to TV violence, greater childhood identification with same-sex aggressive TV characters, and a stronger childhood belief that violent shows tell about life "just like it is" predicted more adult aggression regardless of how aggressive participants were as children.

The longitudinal relations primarily reflected the adult behavior of the highest TV-violence viewing children. The upper 20% of boys and girls on any of the three child TV-viewing variables scored significantly higher on aggression as adults than did the rest of the participants. Furthermore, as adults they displayed a higher frequency of very serious antisocial and violent behaviors.

A longitudinal structural modeling analysis of the directionality of the effects suggested that it is more plausible that exposure to TV violence increases aggression than that aggression increases TV-violence viewing. These structural modeling analyses also demonstrated that the effects were not simply a consequence of lower SES children or less intellectually able children both watching more violence and being more at risk for aggressive and violent behavior. The structural models show that for both boys and girls, habitual early exposure to TV violence is predictive of more aggression by them later in life independent of their own initial childhood aggression, their own intellectual capabilities, their social status as measured by their parents' education or their fathers' occupations, their parents' aggressiveness, their parents' mobility orientation, their parents' TV viewing habits (including violence viewing), and their parents' rejection, nurturance, and punishment of them in childhood. Furthermore, the structural models suggest that being aggressive in early childhood has no effect on increasing males' exposure to media violence as adults and only a small effect for females.

Nevertheless, these results should not lead one to conclude that children's aggressiveness plays no role in their TV and film preferences. The paths from childhood aggression to adult TV-violence viewing were not significant, but they were all positive, and adult TV-violence viewing is not predicted much better by almost any childhood variable. Furthermore, in the childhood waves of this study, the comparable paths from aggression in one year to TV-violence viewing in the next were positive and significant. These results certainly are consistent with "justification theory"—that more aggressive children are more likely to watch media violence because it makes their own behavior seem normal. Their subsequent viewing of violence then increases their aggressive scripts, schemas, and beliefs through observational learning and makes subsequent aggression even more likely.

It is particularly interesting that we found longitudinal results that were of about the same magnitude for female as for male participants. In our 1960–1970 and 1960–1982 studies of New York children, longitudinal effects were found only for boys. One possibility is that the change in social norms for appropriate female behavior that occurred with the feminist movement of the late 1960s and 1970s has disinhibited female aggression. In addition, the increase in aggressive female models in movies and TV might have engendered a stronger observational learning effect. The combination of these two factors may have led to an increase in the size of the effect for female participants, making detection easier. It is not that girls were not subject to the observational effect in earlier years. Indeed, they were, as the laboratory experiments showed. Rather, it is that their use of the learned aggressive behaviors or aggressive scripts was inhibited by their existing normative beliefs about appropriate female roles. This explanation is consistent with the information-processing perspectives on learning aggressive behavior that Huesmann and Dodge have offered. According to Huesmann's model, learned scripts for aggressive behavior are not followed if they violate individuals' normative beliefs about what is appropriate for them.

Three notable gender differences in the results were found. First, early TV-violence viewing correlated with adult physical aggression for both male and female participants but correlated with adult indirect aggression only for female participants. Lagerspetz et al. pointed out that indirect aggression is more characteristic of females and more acceptable for them in most societies. The social-cognitive observational learning model suggests that normative beliefs about aggression, hostile biases about the world, and aggressive social scripts are all learned from observing violence. Female participants did not need to have observed indirect aggression to acquire it from observing violence. They only needed to have acquired beliefs more accepting of aggression. This reasoning also suggests that the lack of a finding of a relation between exposure to media violence and female aggression in earlier longitudinal studies may have been due to the failure to measure indirect aggression sufficiently in those studies.

Second, although identification with same-sex aggressive TV characters and the perception that violent TV shows tell about life "like it is" predicted adult aggression for both genders, these factors exacerbated the effect of TV-violence viewing only for male participants. Boys who viewed TV violence *and* identified with male aggressive TV characters or perceived TV violence as true to life were most at risk for adult aggression. The same gender difference had been found earlier for the childhood data relating TV viewing to subsequent aggression—identification was a moderator for boys but not for girls. Why would this exacerbating effect not occur for girls? Theoretically, it is difficult to believe that identification and perception of realism do not enhance observational learning in girls as well as boys. One possibility is that for girls, the relation between early exposure to violence and subsequent aggression is due more to cognitive and emotional desensitization to violence than to observational learning. Desensitization should not depend as much as observational learning on identification or perceptions of realism. Such a hypothesis cannot be tested with the current data but should be examined in future research.

The third notable gender difference was apparent in the structural models. For both male and female participants, there was no significant statistical effect of childhood aggression on adult TV-violence viewing. However, whereas for males the path coefficient from aggression to TV-violence viewing was virtually zero, for females it was a nontrivial positive value. This finding suggests that aggressive females may be more prone than aggressive males to use violent media to make themselves feel better and more justified about their own behavior. In a culture in which female aggressiveness is still less accepted than male aggressiveness, feeling justified about one's aggressive behavior could well be more important for females than for males.

Although longitudinal nonexperimental data do not provide a strong test of causation, they can be used to compare the relative plausibility of alternative causal perspectives. These results are certainly consistent with the observational learning and desensitization theories, which predict long-term statistical effects of early TV-violence viewing on later aggression after the effects of early aggression are statistically controlled. The results are much less consistent with the theoretical perspective that more aggressive children turn to watching more violence because they like it or because it serves as justification for their own aggression. Only for female participants was there a suggestion of such a long-term effect, and the effect estimate was not significant. The hypotheses that these longitudinal effects could be completely explained by "third" variables such as social class, intellectual ability, parent aggression, or parenting differences also did not receive much support. The effects remained even when the variance due to these factors was partialed out in our regression equations and structural models. However, intellectual ability and parents' education did seem to account for some of the effect in female participants. It may be that social norms for female behavior that inhibit the modeling of media violence are related to educational level or intelligence whereas for males this is not true.

Of course, a variety of parenting factors have been shown in the past to be related to both a child's exposure to media violence and that child's later aggression—for example, parents' intellectual ability and social class, parents' viewing habits, and parents' aggression. In the current study, many of these correlations were again found for at least one gender (e.g., for intellectual ability, parental rejection of the child, and parents' frequency of TV viewing). It seems plausible that these factors are indeed influencing both the child's aggressiveness and the child's exposure to media violence. Which children are placed most at risk of being exposed to media violence and of experiencing other learning conditions that reinforce the lessons taught by media violence is undoubtedly influenced by parent factors. However, given the pattern of results obtained, it is not very likely that the relations between early exposure to media violence and subsequent aggression are completely due to these "third" variables.

The effect sizes for media violence on aggression revealed in this longitudinal study are modest; however, there are few other factors that have been shown to have larger effects. That is not surprising considering the large number of factors that must converge before serious adult aggression occurs. Furthermore, as Rosenthal has pointed out, a correlation of .20 can represent a change in the probability of violence from 50/50 to 60/40, which is large enough to generate social concern.

One might also wonder whether the attrition in the sample made it unrepresentative and biased the results. This seems unlikely. Archival data were obtained on 80% of the original sample and interview data on 60%. An analysis of the attrition data showed that those who were not reinterviewed tended to be slightly more aggressive as children. Thus, it seems more plausible that, if anything, the attrition weakened the relations between TV-violence viewing and aggression.

Implications for Prevention of Violence

Overall, these results suggest that both males and females from all social strata and all levels of initial aggressiveness are placed at increased risk for the development of adult aggressive and violent behavior when they view a high and steady diet of violent TV shows in early childhood. The obvious follow-up question is whether society can do anything to prevent or at least moderate this effect.

Several points provide us with guidelines. First, we do not need to be as concerned about adults' or even teenagers' exposure to media violence as much as we do with childrens' exposure. Media violence may have short-term effects on adults, but the real long-term effects seem to occur only with children. This makes some societal controls more palatable in a society that places a high premium on the rights of adults to watch whatever they want.

Second, we need to be aware that media violence can affect any child from any family. The psychological laws of observational learning, habituation/desensitization, priming, and excitation transfer are immutable and universal. It is not, as some have suggested, only the already violence-prone child who is likely to be affected. True, media violence is not going to turn an otherwise fine child into a violent criminal. But just as every cigarette one smokes increases a little bit the likelihood of a lung tumor some day, the theory supported by this research suggests that every violent TV show increases a little bit the likelihood of a child growing up to behave more aggressively in some situation.

Third, the violent films and TV programs that probably have the most deleterious effects on children are not always the ones that adults and critics believe are the most violent. What type of violent scene is the child most likely to use as a model for violent behavior? It is one in which the child identifies with the perpetrator of the violence, the child perceives the scene as telling about life like it is, and the perpetrator is rewarded for the violence. Thus, a violent act by someone like Dirty Harry that results in a criminal being eliminated and brings glory to Harry is of more concern than a bloodier murder by a despicable criminal who is brought to justice. Parents need to be educated about these facts.

Finally, we must recognize the economic realities of media violence. Violence sells. Both children and adults are attracted to violent scenes by the action and intense emotions. Many of the most popular shows and popular films for children have contained violence. Violent TV shows appear to be a little cheaper to produce on the average. Hamilton (1998) reported that from 1991 to 1993, the average production fee per hour for network prime time TV programming was about $1,094,000 for nonviolent shows and $998,000 for violent shows—about 10% cheaper in other words. A more telling statistic may be the finding that among shows with some violence, those with more violence actually cost less. Each additional violent act seems to reduce the cost by about $1,500. Of course, these are only averages for production costs. What really counts are the ability of a TV show to attract enough sponsors to cover its cost or to attract enough syndicated buyers and the ability of a video game to attract enough buyers to cover its cost. Here, a variety of marketing issues become important. For example, foreign markets become very important in these calculations, and generally violent shows and games are easier to sell in foreign markets than are other kinds of games or shows. More specifically, the probability of a TV show being exported successfully increases about 16% if it is violent.

The easiest way to reduce the effects of media violence on children, of course, is to reduce children's exposure to such violence. Prevention programs aimed at reducing exposure could obviously be targeted either at the production sources of the violence or at the child viewing the violence. In a society with strong protections for free speech, it is probably always going to be easier to target prevention efforts at the viewing child than at the producer. However, a more informed legal debate is needed on this subject. Broadcasters and film and program makers cannot avoid all responsibility for what children are exposed to. The argument that "people watch it so we give it to them" is not valid in a modern socially conscious society, and it is unrealistic to expect parents to control completely what children watch in a society with multiple TVs in each household, VCRs everywhere, and both parents working. Furthermore, it is the exposure of the 2- to 14-year-old child that is of the greatest concern here, as described in this article. The social value of reductions in the exposure of adults and even older teenagers is probably small compared to the social value of reducing younger children's exposure.

The ongoing V-chip social experiment is one such attempt to reduce children's exposure by giving parents a mechanism to control what the TV will allow to be broadcast through it. The problem is that the possibilities for this technology were greatly reduced from the start by the producers of violent shows, who managed to scuttle any idea of a content-based rating system that would actually allow parents to make judgments on the basis of violent content. Instead, only age guideline ratings are broadcast for most programs. Why did the producers do this? One can only speculate, but it is certainly likely that income from violent shows would be substantially reduced if violent labels were added—as much because sponsors would withdraw as because parents would actually program them out with the V-chip.

With regard to interventions aimed at the viewing child, there are a number of possibilities. Again, of course, simply reducing children's exposure through parental intervention is an obvious approach. However, the theory and results described in this article suggest a number of approaches aimed at changing the effect of any observed violence on the child as well. Nathanson recently found that parental co-viewing of and commenting on the programs seems to reduce the effects of TV violence on the child, probably because it reduces the child's identification with the perpetrator, reduces the child's perception of the violence as real, and reduces the likelihood that the child will rehearse the observed violent script in fantasy or play immediately after observation. Huesmann, Eron, Klein, Brice, and Fischer showed that the effects of violence on second graders could be reduced by a targeted school-based attitude change intervention that inculcates them with the beliefs that violence on TV does not tell about the world as it is and should not be imitated. A number of interventions based on teaching critical viewing skills in schools are being promoted, though few have yet to undergo rigorous evaluation. One of the problems with many of these interventions may be that they do not focus on those moderating variables that have been shown to be theoretically relevant, such as identification by the child with perpetrators, perception of violent acts as justified, and perception of violent scripts as realistic.

Although some questions remain to be resolved about the exact extent of the effect of observed violence on aggressive and violent behavior and its importance relative to other causal factors, the current study provides compelling additional evidence that habitual exposure of children to violence in the media (or in the real world around them) does have lasting effects on their propensity to behave aggressively and violently. Future research should probably be directed much more at elaborating and testing the kinds of interventions that parents, schools, producers, and the government can promote that will mitigate these long-term effects.

NO

The Whipping Boy

Although television violence has never been shown to cause hostile behavior, its sinister reputation lives on. This is because the issue masks a variety of other struggles. Many of these conflicts are suppressed because they may pose a threat to social order or are considered unseemly topics for public discussion. Hence, we hear only the polite versions of the conflicts between races, genders, and generations, although these struggles roil national life. Because they are denied full expression, such conflicts are transferred into other debates, including and perhaps especially the issue of television violence.

Television violence is a whipping boy, a stand-in for other clashes, real or imagined. As one astute observer put it a few years back during a previous cycle of panic, "The debate about children and media violence is really a debate about other things, many of which have very little to do with the media."

There are several reasons why television violence has become such an exemplary whipping boy. First, it is a large target, present in one form or another in virtually every household in America. Second, if one puts on blinders, there might seem to be some correspondence between the mayhem on the television screen and real-life aggression; both televised entertainment and the real world deal in hostilities. Third and most important, television violence attracts no champions; the very idea of defending it seems silly to most people. Even industry representatives rarely get beyond conciliatory statements when they are compelled to address the matter. In one survey, 78 percent of entertainment industry executives expressed concern about the content of the action dramas they helped produce. In 1993 Ted Turner, perhaps the most conspicuous industry leader at the time, said in congressional testimony that television was "the single most important factor causing violence in America." The object of derision simply stands still and takes all the abuse that can be heaped on it.

What are the real conflicts that are being displaced? Most entail the stronger overwhelming the weaker, but in some conflicts the weaker retaliate through moral exertion. Here is a brief examination of the most important conflicts.

High vs. Low

The attack on television violence is, at least in part, an attack by the upper classes and their partisans on popular culture. In this interpretation, which has been broached repeatedly for a quarter-century, the push to reform television is simply the latest manifestation of the struggle between the high and the low, the dominant and the dominated.

The United States is often regarded as a virtually classless society. Indeed, the overwhelming majority of Americans identify themselves as members of a "middle" class. Everyday experience, however, points in a different direction. Americans constantly make class judgments about one another. They quickly note outward appearances and speech patterns. When necessary, one person learns about the other's occupation and education, where he lives and what car he drives, and locates that person socially. Notions of class rank notoriously crop up in courtship and marriage. Characters in films and television programs radiate class information about themselves to audience members who know precisely how to read such clues.

Perhaps the preeminent living theorist and researcher into matters of class and culture is Pierre Bourdieu. He is best known for his work on the segmentation of society according to preferences in aesthetic taste (for instance, going or not going to art museums). At the center of Bourdieu's work is the concept of habitus, an idea similar to that of the English word, *habit*. Habitus is the system of predispositions ingrained in a particular group or social class. It manifests itself in similar thoughts, behaviors, expressions, and leisure pursuits. The shared habitus unites and defines the social entity. Habitus, however, does not shackle individuals; in Bourdieu's scheme, there is ample room for idiosyncratic action.

Another concept special to Bourdieu is *capital,* approximately equivalent to social power. In addition to conventional economic wealth, there are several other kinds of capital in Bourdieu's system. Cultural capital (preferences gained primarily through education), symbolic capital (prestige and honors), and social capital (whom one knows) work together with financial capital to define a person's location in the overall social structure. Social action then becomes a function of class habitus and personal capitals. A final term from Bourdieu's work is *reproduction,* which is the manner by which social classes reproduce themselves and, in doing so, preserve status differences. For Bourdieu, the reproduction of habitus is the key work of a social class.

Although Bourdieu does not discuss television in his magisterial work, *Distinctions* (1984), it does not take much imagination to extend his analysis. He writes in his opening pages that taste (cultural capital) functions as a marker of social class; therefore, different preferences (such as watching television violence or not) can be used to situate a person hierarchically. According to this system, an attack on the most popular medium, on television and especially its violent content, would also be an attack by the dominant class on the habitus of the dominated. To reconfirm social distinctions and maintain exclusivity, members of the dominant class need only profess an opposition to television violence. (Ironically, Bourdieu, mustering all the trappings of a French intellectual, himself attacked television in a series of lectures published in English in 1998, calling the medium "a threat to political life and to democracy itself.")

In the derisive vocabulary of this dominant class, violent content is delivered via the "mass media." This term is used so much that it seems unremarkable but repetition has concealed its derogatory nature. Programming is not received by an undifferentiated horde; it is received by individuals. In fact, there is no mass, there are no masses. As the cultural critic Raymond Williams wrote in 1958, "The masses are always the others, whom we don't know, and can't know. . . . Masses are other people. There are in fact no masses; there are only ways of seeing people as masses." When dominant Americans chastise the nonexistent phenomena of the "masses" and their "mass medium" of television, with its evil content, what they are really endeavoring is to disparage and suppress the culture of dominated Americans.

The class nature of this conflict is evident in the string of congressional hearings that have addressed television violence. Consider the five such congressional hearings held between 1988 and 1995. Of the 36 non-industry witnesses who testified against television violence, only seven were women. None was black or Hispanic. The 29 white males were identified as presidents, professors, directors, representatives, senators, senior scientists, and other distinguished titles that suggested they were well advanced in their careers. It is this patrician sector of society that for reasons of its own leads the attack on rowdy television violence.

The means by which one enters into society's dominant segment, and in doing so learns to affect reproachful views on television violence, is the academy. The general veneration that greets the academy is a sign of its near-sacred station and of the importance of its role in, as Bourdieu would view it, the reproduction of the dominant class and its habitus. Although the rewards of academics are middling in terms of financial capital, the cultural capital they accrue cannot be surpassed. To have a college degree—only about one-quarter of American adults do—is to have the credential of the dominant; not to have a college degree is to remain forever among the dominated.

Academics strive to regard television with condescension or an affected indifference. "A studied, conspicuous ignorance about television," communication professor Ellen Seiter wrote in 1996, "is a mark of distinction (like all distinctions, it is valued because it is so difficult to maintain)." Professors' general attitude toward television becomes more pointed when the topic of television violence is discussed; they are quick to assert piously that television is dangerously violent. Among college communication teachers, two-thirds of a 1991 sample of 486 instructors agreed that television "increased aggressive behavior." Of 68 scholars who had published papers or reports specifically on television's effects, 80 percent concurred that television violence produced aggressiveness.

Professors researching television's effects, therefore, seem to occupy a doubly honored position. Not only are they, like their colleagues, performing the crucial service of reproducing the dominant classes, but they also are breathing life into a key issue in the struggle between the dominant and the dominated. They may devote their entire careers to demonstrating the dangers of television violence and are bound to receive approbation from the dominant class as a result. No wonder the position of television effects researcher has proven so attractive.

Yet when a given skirmish over violence has exhausted itself and a lull sets in, members of the dominant class revert to their un-self-conscious viewing of televised mayhem. Even college professors watch TV. During one lull in the violence debate, a 1982 study found that media professors did not restrict their children's viewing any more than the rest of the population did.

Us vs. Them

Perhaps the most striking conflict concealed in the debate over television violence involves the fabrication and control of "the Other." The best-known treatment of the concept of the Other is Edward Said's *Orientalism* (1978). The Orient, argued Said, was one of Europe's "deepest and most recurring images of the Other." It was "almost a European invention" that served as "a Western style for dominating, restructuring, and having authority over the Orient." Superiority over the Other was one motive for this phenomenon; another was self-definition. "The Orient," Said wrote, "has helped to define Europe (or the West) as its contrasting image, idea, personality, experience."

Thus the Other, the "not-us," is a fabrication used both to regulate those classified as the Other and to distinguish the culture of those doing the classifying. It is also a mechanism for emphasizing differences and disregarding similarities in order to maintain group solidarity. The Other differs conceptually from the mass in that the mass can be a part of "us," even if a discredited part, whereas the Other remains outside.

In the United States, the Other is often primarily a Dark Other—blacks and, to a lesser extent, Hispanics. The Dark Other is the recipient of an undeniable assault that plays out in racially charged terms. One form of the assault on the Dark Other is the War on Drugs. This "war" promotes definitions of legal and illegal drugs that have favored whites at the expense of the Dark Other; alcohol and prescription tranquilizers (both of whose records of extensive abuse and human damage are well documented) enjoy legal protection, whereas drugs associated with black culture, such as marijuana and cocaine (the health effects of which, on examination of the data, appear to be negligible), are proscribed. Of course, there is nothing inherent in these drugs that allocates them to the legal or illegal categories. These allocations are socially determined.

The anti–television violence crusades are part of this same assault. People do not worry about their own viewing of violent shows, and in fact they are so at peace with it that they are less likely to acknowledge the violence at all. They worry extensively, however, about what the Dark Other is watching. As British media scholar David Buckingham noted in 1997, "Debates about the negative effects of the media are almost always debates about other people."

"People like us" project a scenario onto the Dark Other in which viewing entertainment violence leads to real-life criminal behavior. This scenario is false in every detail—there exists no uniform Dark Other, and symbolic violence does not produce aggression—but it is upheld due to the emotional conviction behind it and the handy availability of rationalizing "scientific proof." Fears of the Dark Other—fears of difference, of being preyed on, of having one's culture overturned, of invalidating one's identity—are denied expression elsewhere but are allowed to sneak into the attack on television violence. In this way, the Dark Other, his culture, his viewing habits, and his behaviors are disparaged.

There is a curious twist to all this, however—a complexity revealing much about the intricacies of social life. Whereas whites push off the Dark Other with vigor, at the same time they subtly beckon him back. Cultural theorists Peter Stallybrass and Allon White observe that whatever is excluded and displaced to the Other then becomes an object of fascination and is summoned back. The desire for cultural homogeneity produces instead a heterogeneous mix. Thus whites are fascinated by the music, dance, clothing styles, and behavior of blacks. Whites study black athletes, seeking to learn about the prowess of the Other. Whites welcome black entertainers, even when (or especially when) black actors are involved in violent scenarios.

Old vs. Young

Adults who enlist in the anti-television crusade always insist that it is "impressionable youths" whom they wish to protect. In the guise of shielding youths, however, adults are trying to contain and control them.

This generational conflict emerges in contemporary polls: A 1997 survey by Steve Farkas and Jean Johnson of 2,000 randomly selected American adults found them ill disposed toward both younger children and adolescents. The majority of respondents used harsh terms to characterize 5-to-12-year-olds, such as "lacking discipline," "rude," and "spoiled." Two-thirds of the respondents were very critical of teenagers, calling them "irresponsible" and "wild." According to the report, "Most Americans look at today's teenagers with misgiving and trepidation, viewing them as undisciplined, disrespectful, and unfriendly." Six hundred teenagers were also surveyed, however; they viewed things differently. Most felt happy in their lives and in their relationships with adults. These discrepant attitudes indicate much about the essential nature of generational strife—of who deprecates whom.

Antagonism toward the young can be especially strong in an adult population configured like that of the United States—one that is aging rapidly due to the baby boom phenomenon. As subculture researcher Dick Hebdige observes, in the consciousness of adult society, "Youth is present only when its presence is a problem, or is regarded as a problem." Overall, adults feel threatened by the next generation.

Social scientist Charles Acland has argued that "youth's complex relationship with popular culture as a live and expressive domain is menacing because the uses of culture cannot be policed completely." With adults able only partially to supervise the "menace" of popular culture, children and adolescents turn to their television shows, their movies, their computer games, and their music as an escape from adult restraint. Passing through a difficult stage in life, indeed perhaps the most strenuous one of all, youths turn to television violence for the vicarious release it can offer.

The consumption of symbolic violent content correlates negatively with age. According to a 1993 study commissioned by the Times Mirror Center for People and the Press, age is the single most significant factor in the viewing of television violence: Younger viewers watch much more than do older viewers. Cultural critic James Twitchell suggests that "if you study the eager consumers of vulgarities, you will soon see that this audience is characterized not so much by class (as we tend to assume, due in part to Marxist interpretations of the culture industry) as by maturity."

Youths do not think it probable that there could be any transfer from television's violence to aggression in the real world; of all age groups, they are the least likely to believe there is a connection. Elizabeth Kolbert, a *New York Times* reporter, interviewed three teenage felons on the subject in 1994 and noted, "The three teenagers . . . all scoffed at the notion that what young people see on the screen bore any relation to the crimes they committed."

Weaker vs. Stronger

There are at least two cases where the anti-television crusade allows a weaker group to mount an attack against a stronger target. The first relates to the struggle between masculinity and femininity. As the male expresses domin-ion and the female resists it, everything in culture becomes gendered, or has reference to gender. This pervasive rivalry would be expected to find its way into the anti-television campaign as another camouflaged conflict between the dominant and the dominated, but in this instance the thrust is completely reversed. That is, when the struggle between genders enters into the debate over television violence, it does so as an act of resistance by the female against the male—as a small counterstrike.

The power of males is most pointedly realized in the violence some of them direct toward women. Alert to the chance of male animosity, women are prone to feeling wary of violence even in its flattened, symbolic form on the television screen. The figment may draw too close to the real thing, whether experienced or imagined, to permit the degree of unimpeded pleasure that male viewers might enjoy. In surveys females are more likely than males to report there is "too much violence in television entertainment" and have been so since the general question was first asked in 1972. When queried about the amount of violence on specific action programs, women viewers will perceive more of it than will men, presum-ably because of their awareness of and uneasiness about the vicious content.

The recurring moral crusade against television violence affords women a choice opportunity for retribution. Seemingly untainted by any overt hostil-ity on its own part, the movement to purify televised entertainment, one that all agree is to be rhetorical only, seems to be shielded from any possibility of retaliatory strikes. How much contention against males is bound up in the 1994 assertion of Barbara Hattemer, president of the National Family Founda-tion, that "as media violence is absorbed into a person's thoughts, it activates related aggressive ideas and emotions that eventually lead to aggressive behav-ior"? How much gender strife is exposed in the hyperbolic 1996 statement of Carole Lieberman, chairperson of the National Coalition Against Television, that "more lives are damaged or destroyed by the effects of on-screen violence than by any other medical problem"? She has forgotten heart disease, cancer, and other maladies, and she has done so for a particular reason.

The second case of a counterstrike against a stronger group involves religion. Many of the groups organized in opposition to television violence have religious ties. Here, neither the contestants nor their motives are camouflaged. The partisans on the attacking side are explicit and vociferous; they stand for religiosity, conservative beliefs, and "family values," and they are against licentiousness, media excesses, and symbolic violence. Those under attack—the entertainment industries and, by extension, all sorts of permissive people—respond first with incomprehension and then with annoyance, wishing the conservative and fundamentalist contingent would disappear. It would be easy for the political left to ignore the religious right if the latter did not comprise a well-defined and adamant voting bloc.

This cultural axis could hardly be more different from class antagonism. Social classes are stacked from bottom to top. Here, the axis and its poles can be understood as horizontal, stretching from the most conservative to the most free-thinking. Those gathered at the conservative and evangelical pole come from a wide range of social strata, although they are frequently depicted by their opponents as occupying lower-status positions exclusively. Seeking certainty in the literal word of the Bible, often believing in creationism and patriarchal traditions, and adhering to longstanding customs and attitudes, those clustered at this pole are often moved to take issue with the novelties of social transitions and the uncertainties of modern life.

Fundamentalists rail against the expanding, heaving tableau of television violence, and in organized fashion they strike out against it. The American Family Association (AFA), headed by the Rev. Donald Wildmon, has objected strenuously to video carnage. In 1993 Randall Murphree, editor of the association's *AFA Journal,* wrote: "Violence on the small screen continues to invade America's homes as television offers more graphic murders, bloodier assaults, and general mayhem. And all the while, the dramatic effects on society grow more and more alarming." In 1997 the AFA announced that, by its count, violent incidents in prime time network programs had increased 31 percent from the previous year—an increase far in excess of those measured by other monitors. As an example of the AFA's activities, in August 1997 its "Action Alert" roused its members to contact CBS and "express your concerns about their dangerous agenda of expanding the limits of violence on television through [the cop drama] *Brooklyn South."*

The issue of television violence affords groups such as the AFA the sanctioned opportunity to carry out a cultural attack—to have at their opponents, to condemn immoral depictions and the entertainment industry that produces and distributes them. Doing so, fundamentalism affirms its presence to others through an issue that is allowed to capture media attention and affirms its role to itself as a guardian of traditional mores. Television violence allows conservative forces the opportunity to carry their standard forward.

As religious conservatives react negatively to social changes of greater and lesser profundity, they may be performing an important service for American civilization. American culture is venturing into areas rarely if ever visited before, and never on such a large scale (for example, in matters of widespread individuality or of social inclusiveness). Some sort of conservative movement may prove useful, much like a sea anchor during turbulence, for steadying the vessel of culture.

The Big Lie

The widely held belief that television fantasy violence stimulates aggression in the real world and should be censured is what propaganda experts might call "a big lie"—a grotesque fabrication to which all unreflectingly subscribe. What makes this particular big lie different from the propagandists' is that it is not bestowed on an acquiescent population by some cabal; rather, this is one that we all repeatedly tell one another, duping ourselves as we dupe others. We do this for reasons of convenience: By repeating this uncontroverted big lie with ever-increasing volume, we can easily vent some of our own hostilities regarding other, truly confounding social conflicts.

While censure is generally directed by the stronger party toward the weaker, in some instances it flows in the opposite direction. Within the gender wars, and in the invectives of the religious right, condemnations are directed by weaker parties toward stronger targets. But whether the chastising energy flows from the stronger toward the weaker or from the weaker toward the stronger has nothing to do with the actualities of television violence.

Whatever its immediate source, the energy that breathes life into the whipping boy of television violence has its ultimate origins in fear—fear of disorder that, in the extreme, could overturn society. As Charles Acland has written, "A society is always concerned with normalization, with the organization of its order, to assure the continuation of its structures and distribution of power." Although social order is a perpetual preoccupation, at this point in history it would seem to be an obsessive one; witness the outsized emphasis on the containment of crime at a time when crime is on the decline and the reckless hysteria of the War on Drugs. Sociologist Graham Murdock refers to the "fear about the precarious balance between anarchy and order in the modern age." Exactly why this fearful fixation on social order should be occurring now is open to question. Its existence, however, should not be doubted. Indeed, the need to strengthen social controls has a correlate in Americans' increasing imposition of self-controls: Per capita alcohol consumption and cigarette smoking have been on the decline and health club memberships on the rise for most of the past 30 years.

Television is new enough that it is not embraced without reservations, and it has not yet accumulated the social equity that would allow it to be shielded by nostalgia. In addition to its relative novelty, it is enormous, filling up the day (television viewing trails only work and sleep in terms of expended time), and can be menacing on this count. Because everyone has access to television, its use cannot be regulated, and thus for those who want to control it, the medium is believed to be out of control and threatening. The rise of television, observes media scholar Richard Sparks, "has been taken to signify the drift of history beyond willed control or direction. The censure of television bears witness to the fear of the future."

General apprehension about the course of history is in several senses the opposite of video violence—the passivity of fear vs. the frenzy of aggression, the amorphous vs. the detailed, and the actual vs. the symbolic. The two find each other as if magnetized, whereupon the flaying of the whipping boy begins.

EXPLORING THE ISSUE

Is Viewing Television Violence Harmful for Children?

Critical Thinking and Reflection

1. Huesmann, Moise-Titus, Podolski, and Eron assert throughout their selection that violent television programming increases aggressive behavior. Do you agree with this assertion? Why, or why not?
2. Because television is in virtually every household in America, is it reasonable to think that television programs could ever be regulated? Explain your answer.
3. Fowles states that the "big lie" is the belief that television fantasy violence stimulates aggression. Do you believe this is true? Why, or why not?

Is There Common Ground?

There are numerous studies on children who watch violent television (TV) shows, as well as on the amount of TV children watch. Some research suggests that children who spend excessive amounts of time watching TV tend to do poorly in school. Other studies show that children who spend moderate amounts of time in front of the set perform better scholastically than those who watch no TV at all. Children are more likely to be overweight when they watch TV versus playing actively. If children are watching TV to excess, they are not communicating with adults in the family and are not learning family values. Logically, there must be middle-ground solutions to the issue of children, TV viewing, and violence.

Ideally, society could move past this dichotomy of thinking TV as simply good or bad. TV viewing could be thought of as an active endeavor rather than a passive one. Parents could become more involved with their children as they watch TV by controlling the amount and type of TV shows their children are watching. Through modeling, parents could teach children to be skeptical about TV advertisements, point out the differences between fantasy and reality, and argue that the moral values being portrayed on the tube are different from values that are important to the parents.

Additional Resources

American Academy of Pediatrics. Smart Guide to Kids Television. Retrieved on April 11, 2011, from http://www.fcctf.org/pdf%20files/Parenting%20 info%20pdfs/Smart%20Guide%20to%20Kids%20TV.pdf.

This Web site provides guidance for parents on how to handle their child(ren)'s television viewing.

KidsHealth. How TV Affects Your Child. Retrieved on April 11, 2011, from http://kidshealth.org/parent/positive/family/tv_affects_child.html.

This Web site discusses the impact that television viewing can have on children.

PBS Parents. Children and Media. Retrieved on April 11, 2011, from http://www.pbs.org/parents/childrenandmedia/article-faq.html.

This Web site addresses the most common questions that parents of children under three have about television viewing.

The University of Maine, Cooperative Extension Publications. Children, Television, and Screen Time. Retrieved on April 11, 2011, from http://umaine.edu/publications/4100e/.

This Web site discusses the impact that television viewing can have on children, in addition to suggestions for what parents can do and alternatives to television viewing.

Internet References . . .

Family: Single Parenting

This Single Parenting page of ParentsPage.com focuses on issues concerning single parents and their children.

http://www.ivillage.com/parenting/search?q=single+parenting

National Institute on Out-of-School Time

Directed by the Wellesley College Center for Research on Women, this National Institute on Out-of-School Time project aims to improve the quality and quantity of school-age child care nationally.

http://www.niost.org

National Black Child Development Institute

At this site, the National Black Child Development Institute provides resources for improving the quality of life for African American children through public education programs.

http://www.nbcdi.org

National Clearinghouse for English Language Acquisition

This National Clearinghouse for English Language Acquisition is funded by the Department of Education and includes information on the latest legislation and conferences, as well as links to bilingual educational materials.

http://www.ncela.gwu.edu/

Action for Healthy Kids

This is a nonprofit organization formed specifically to address the epidemic of overweight, undernourished, and sedentary youth by focusing on changes at school. The organization's goal is to improve children's nutrition and increase physical activity, which will in turn improve their readiness to learn.

http://www.actionforhealthykids.org

Research Center: English-Language Learners

This bilingual education section of Education Week's EPE Research Center Web site provides links and news about bilingual education in K–12 schools.

http://www.edweek.org/rc/issues/english-language-learners/

National Association for Bilingual Education—Bilingual Education

The National Association for Bilingual Education is the only professional organization at the national level wholly devoted to representing both English language learners and bilingual education professionals. Along with their affiliate organizations in 23 states, they represent a combined membership of more than 20,000 bilingual and English-as-a-second-language teachers, administrators, paraprofessionals, university professors and students, researchers, advocates, policymakers, and parents.

www.nabe.org/

Middle Childhood

M*iddle childhood, or school age, is the period from ages five through twelve. The rate of a child's growth that has been relatively steady prior to this point generally declines until the later part of this stage of development. Perhaps the most important experience during middle childhood is schooling. As a child progresses through this stage, new significant others outside the family emerge in the child's life. Children gain a broader understanding of the similarities and differences among them. The peer group (especially same-sex peers), teachers, and media personalities take on increased importance for the child. This section examines issues related to schooling, language development, and self-care.*

- Does Marriage Improve Living Standards for Children?
- Do Children Who Are Homeschooled Have a Limited View of Society?
- Is Television Viewing Responsible for the Rise in Childhood Obesity?
- Do Bilingual Education Programs Help Non-English-Speaking Children Succeed?
- Is Gay Adoption and Foster Parenting Healthy for Children?
- Should the HPV Vaccination Be Mandatory for Girls in Later Childhood?

ISSUE 9

Does Marriage Improve Living Standards for Children?

YES: Wade F. Horn, from "Healthy Marriages Provide Numerous Benefits to Adults, Children, and Society," *Insight* (March 18, 2002)

NO: Stephanie Coontz and Nancy Folbre, from "Marriage, Poverty, and Public Policy," *The American Prospect Online*, http://www.prospect.org/webfeatures/2002/03/coontz-s-03-19.html (March 19, 2002)

Learning Outcomes

After reading this issue, you should be able to:

- List and discuss the benefits to marriage that researchers have identified.
- List some of the ways that living standards for children can be improved.
- Discuss some of the reasons that marriage is considered by some to be detrimental to poor people.

ISSUE SUMMARY

YES: Wade F. Horn, who heads the Marriage Initiative for President George W. Bush, asserts that marriage can remedy the ills of society, including family poverty and poor living standards for children.

NO: Stephanie Coontz, author and family advocate, and Nancy Folbre, professor of economics at the University of Massachusetts, contend that improving the living standards of children is a complicated issue, which needs to be approached from many different angles in order to make improvements.

T here is no doubt that living with two parents who are married and who want to be together, is good for children, psychologically and economically. Having two married parents means that there is a possibility for two incomes, which would provide a higher standard of living for children and would make it more likely that the children will not grow up in poverty. Presently, the majority of children living in poverty live with a single parent, usually their mom.

And yet, is the issue that simple? Should we merely request or require that parents marry? Will that make everything all right? Will children's living standards improve if their parents get married? One-third of poor children live within a two-parent family. If the premise that marriage improves living standards for children is true, what happened to these families?

The complicated issue involving the living standards of children and marriage promotion has become intertwined with the issues of welfare reform fund reauthorization. The whole issue of how marriage influences children's living standards recently emerged in the American political agenda. Key personnel in the George W. Bush administration, led by Wade F. Horn, decided that parents need to be married to each other in order to move families out of poverty and to improve living standards for children. Horn asserts that marriage would solve the problem of children living in poverty. This idea prompted a slew of opposition from some family professionals and public-policy analysts.

As welfare reform has evolved, funding for Temporary Assistance for Needy Families (TANF) has also changed. While improving living standards for children has always been states' prominent goal, by moving families from welfare to work, states have been allowed to choose their own method of using federal dollars to accomplish this goal. The individuation of states has complicated this issue. Some states choose to provide affordable child care, education, and job training as a way to move families from welfare to work, and in so doing, they have managed to improve living standards for children. With the marriage promotion initiative, states that show higher levels of marriage rates receive more federal dollars for the welfare reform initiative. Although there is no empirical evidence that this type of programming works, states are likely to adopt programs that promote marriage, regardless of whether or not these programs are effective in improving living standards for children. Some states do this merely to increase funding levels.

The issue is not merely about living standards for children. It has evolved into the issue of making poor people get married in order to keep children from enduring a lifetime of poverty. In the following selections, the issue is debated within the present political climate. In the YES selection, Wade Horn presents the merits of marriage within the poor population. Horn states that the issue is simple: the government should promote marriage as a way to improve family life in general and more specifically for the children involved. Horn asserts that the U.S. government must take a stand and become pro-marriage. In doing so, the government must remove tax disincentives for marriage and revamp the welfare system so that it does not punish married couples. Horn states that government programs should include premarriage education and teach couples the skills they need to help their marriage succeed. Horn provides specific techniques to encourage marriage among welfare recipients. In the NO selection, Stephanie Coontz and Nancy Folbre describe why marriage within poor families is not always feasible or wise. They contend that this issue is more complicated than Horn suggests. They cite evidence that shows that poor families need job training, increased education, and affordable child care to work their way out of poverty and to provide a higher standard of living for their children. Coontz and Folbre site the number of single parents who have high levels of education, work at well-paying jobs, and live at a middle-class standard of living. For these parents, the lack of marriage has not caused them to live in poverty.

Coontz and Folbre also show how dangerous marriage can be for single mothers and their children. The fathers whom the mothers might marry are twice as likely to abuse alcohol or drugs and are likely to physically abuse them and their children. Marriage would not take these mothers and their children out of poverty and improve their standard of living, but might push them deeper into a desperate way of living, assert Coontz and Folbre.

Does marriage improve children's standard of living? Have we looked for complicated answers to this question and overlooked an obvious way to help children in our society by encouraging their parents to marry? Should the government promote marriage as a healthy lifestyle instead of being afraid to say the "M" word? What is wrong with promoting married parents and children? On the other hand, could this marriage promotion initiative backfire? Instead of helping children, could it actually hurt them? Will the pressure to marry in order to move from welfare to work put additional stress on the family and cause increased child abuse and neglect? Society has a commitment to help children live at a standard of living that encourages positive growth and development. How society can achieve this goal is highly debatable.

YES

Wade F. Horn

Healthy Marriages Provide Numerous Benefits to Adults, Children, and Society

The case for marriage is beyond debate. Marriage is the most stable and healthy environment for raising children. Men and women who are married have been shown to be happier and healthier. And they make more money over time than their single counterparts. Communities with more households headed by married couples are beset by fewer social ills, such as crime and welfare dependency, than communities where marriage is less prevalent.

We really can't argue—or, at least, the data say we shouldn't argue—about the benefits of marriage to children, adults and society. But I do grant that it is reasonable to debate the proper role of government in promoting marriage and that, indeed, reasonable people can disagree on whether government has a place in the marriage debate. I for one, noting that marriage is related directly to child well-being, conclude that government has no choice but to promote healthy marriages.

Let's pose the question this way: Since we know marriage can help adults be happier and healthier, and help children grow up happier and healthier, don't we have a responsibility to figure out ways to help low-income couples who want to be married enjoy a strong, supportive marriage? Of course we do.

Before I lay out my vision for how government can begin to make this happen, allow me a pre-emptive strike against the criticism that descends every time I unequivocally state that government should support and promote healthy marriages. Let me discuss four things that promoting marriage is not about.

First, it is not about government matchmaking or telling anybody to get married. Obviously, government has no business doing that. Choosing to get married is a private decision. Government should [not], and will not get into the business of telling people who, or even whether, to marry. I can state without hesitation that the Bush administration has no plans to create a federal dating service. We have no plans to add an entirely new meaning to the famous phrase, "Uncle Sam Wants You!"

Second, promoting marriage cannot, intentionally or inadvertently, result in policies that trap anyone in an abusive relationship. Seeing more

Americans married is not our goal. Seeing more Americans enjoying healthy marriages is our goal. Healthy marriages are good for children and adults alike. Abusive marriages are not good for anyone.

Abuse of any sort by a spouse cannot be tolerated under any circumstances, and no marriage-promotion effort should provide comfort to spouse or child abusers. The good news is that good marriages are not a matter of luck but, rather, a matter of skill. We can teach couples the skills necessary to have good marriages. We can teach couples how to negotiate conflict and how not to allow unresolved anger to escalate. Marriages that last a lifetime and marriages that dissolve after a short while often face equal amounts of conflict. The difference is that couples who stay married have learned to manage this conflict constructively. We have proven strategies for teaching these skills to couples; standing by and not sharing these skills with low-income couples is irresponsible.

Third, when we talk about promoting marriage we are not talking about withdrawing support and services for single-parent families. As noted, we are for marriage because that's what the data say is best for kids. There is no data suggesting that taking away support from single mothers helps children in any way. Many single parents make heroic efforts to raise their children despite incredible pressures. Promoting marriage and supporting single parents is not, and must not be, mutually exclusive. Together, they are part of an integrated effort to promote child well-being.

Finally, marriage promotion is not the same as cohabitation promotion. For too long, we have treated marriage as if it were a dreaded "M" word. Too afraid to say "marriage," we have instead talked about "committed relationships." But shacking up isn't getting married. Common sense says so. So does research. There is something fundamentally different about the commitment two people make within a marriage relationship versus a cohabiting relationship. In a cohabiting relationship, the commitment of each of the partners primarily is self-serving. By contrast, the marriage commitment is about serving one's spouse. This is a fundamental difference, and one that ought to be reflected in our social policy.

I recommend the following principles for government marriage promotion:

Government must resolve that it will not merely be "neutral" about marriage. For many behaviors government is rightly neutral, for others it is not. For example, the government is not neutral about home ownership because it is good for communities when people own their homes. Furthermore, the government is not neutral about charitable giving because charitable giving is good for society. In the same way, government should not be neutral about healthy marriages because they contribute directly to the general strength of a good and sound society.

First of all, we must remove disincentives for marriage. Under current law if couples (especially low-income couples) marry, our tax code and social welfare system punish them. But striking these disincentives from our laws and policies, while a very important first step, only will bring us to the state of being neutral on marriage. We must go beyond that, into active support of marriage.

More than 90 percent of adults in the United States marry at some point during their lifetimes, and the vast majority enter marriage believing it to be a lifetime commitment. Surveys consistently document that most Americans see marriage as an important life goal. Clearly, providing active support for couples who want to marry and stay married is consistent with the values of the vast majority of Americans.

In doing so, government must not be paralyzed by the unknown. What we don't know about marriage promotion cannot be allowed to stand in the way of what we do know. Some have argued that we don't know enough about marriage promotion and, therefore, we should do nothing. They are partially correct. We have much to learn about promoting and supporting healthy marriages. But there is much we do know.

For example, thanks to a nascent marriage movement in our country, we do know that premarital-education programs work. We know that programs that assign mentoring couples to newlyweds do work. We know that good marriages are a result not of luck or chance but hard work and skill. We know that these skills can be taught. Finally, we know that programs designed to save even the most troubled marriages do work. Yes, there still is much to be learned, but we know enough about what works that standing by and doing nothing would be a tragic mistake.

New research constantly is shedding more light on our path. For example, research is debunking the myth that low-income, inner-city men and women who have children out of wedlock are not linked romantically and have no interest in marriage. A recent study by researchers at Princeton and Columbia universities revealed that 48 percent of unmarried urban couples were living together at the time their child was born. Eighty percent were involved in an exclusive romantic relationship. And half believed their chances of marrying—not at sometime to somebody, but to each other—were "certain" or "near certain." In other words, drive-by pregnancies are an especially insidious urban legend.

Now that we understand the goal for marriage promotion—helping couples who choose marriage develop the skills they need to build healthy marriages—it is time to explore specific actions the government can take. A number of proposals have been put forth. Here are five of my favorites—ideas that have the best chance of improving child well-being by strengthening the institution of marriage:

- Put marriage in the hospital. Hospitals should do more than talk about paternity establishment. They can talk about marriage as well. In most cases, hospital personnel stop at telling a young man that he must establish paternity. Doing so is extremely important. But hospital personnel should also ask the simple question, "Have you considered getting married?" If the answer is "yes," the couple can be referred to helpful services, such as premarital education. If the answer is "no," that's fine. But we can't be afraid to say the "M" word in the labor and delivery ward.
- Develop a referral system for premarital education. Schools, clinics, job-training sites and welfare offices all offer opportunities to provide referrals to premarital education.
- Provide marital-enrichment services through social programs dedicated to strengthening families. Head Start provides a perfect example.

Many children in Head Start live with a married mother and father. While Head Start centers routinely provide parenting-education classes, I don't know of a single Head Start program providing marriage-education classes. Head Start represents a perfect opportunity to teach parents the skills they need to maintain a long-term, healthy marriage. We should seize this and similar opportunities.

- Create public-education campaigns highlighting the benefits of healthy marriages. The government funds numerous public-education campaigns promoting various healthy behaviors. Marriage can and should be added to this list.
- Increase support for intervention services, including mentoring programs, so that troubled marriages can be made whole and strong once again.

It no longer is a question of whether government should do this, but of how. It's time to get started right away, before another generation of children misses out on the benefits of a married mom and dad.

Stephanie Coontz and
Nancy Folbre

 NO

Marriage, Poverty, and Public Policy

One of the stated objectives of welfare legislation passed in 1996 was "to end dependence by promoting marriage." With this legislation coming up for reauthorization, many policymakers want to devote more public resources to this goal, even if it requires cutting spending on cash benefits, child care, or job training. Some states, such as West Virginia, already use their funds to provide a special bonus to couples on public assistance who get married.[1] In December 2001, more than fifty state legislators asked Congress to divert funds from existing programs into marriage education and incentive policies, earmarking dollars to encourage welfare recipients to marry and giving bonus money to states that increase marriage rates. On February 26, 2002, President Bush called for spending up to $300 million a year to promote marriage among poor people.[2]

Such proposals reflect the widespread assumption that failure to marry, rather than unemployment, poor education, and lack of affordable child care, is the primary cause of child poverty. Voices from both sides of the political spectrum urge us to get more women to the altar. Journalist Jonathan Rauch argues that "marriage is displacing both income and race as the great class divide of the new century."[3] Robert Rector of the Heritage Foundation claims that "the sole reason that welfare exists is the collapse of marriage."[4] In this briefing paper, we question both this explanation of poverty and the policy prescriptions that derive from it.

Marriage offers important social and economic benefits. Children who grow up with married parents generally enjoy a higher standard of living than those living in single-parent households. Two parents are usually better than one not only because they can bring home two paychecks, but also because they can share responsibilities for child care. Marriage often leads to higher levels of paternal involvement than divorce, non-marriage, or cohabitation. Long-term commitments to provide love and support to one another are beneficial for adults, as well as children.

Public policies toward marriage could and should be improved.[5] Taxes or benefit reductions that impose a marriage penalty on low-income couples are inappropriate and should be eliminated. Well designed public policies could play a constructive role in helping couples develop the skills they need to develop healthy and sustainable relationships with each other and their children. It does not follow, however, that marriage promotion should be a significant component of anti-poverty policy, or that public policies should provide a "bonus" to couples who marry.

The current pro-marriage agenda in anti-poverty policy is misguided for at least four reasons:

- Non-marriage is often a result of poverty and economic insecurity rather than the other way around.
- The quality and stability of marriages matters. Prodding couples into matrimony without helping them solve problems that make relationships precarious could leave them worse off.
- Two-parent families are not immune from the economic stresses that put children at risk. More than one third of all impoverished young children in the U.S. today live with two parents.

Single parenthood does not inevitably lead to poverty. In countries with a more adequate social safety net than the United States, single parent families are much less likely to live in poverty. Even within the United States, single mothers with high levels of education fare relatively well.

In this briefing paper, we summarize recent empirical evidence concerning the relationship between marriage and poverty, and develop the four points above in more detail. We also emphasize the need to develop a larger anti-poverty program that provides the jobs, education, and child care that poor families need in order to move toward self-sufficiency.

The Economic Context

Children living with married parents generally fare better than others in terms of family income. In 2000, 6 percent of married couple families with children lived in poverty, compared to 33 percent of female householders with children.[6] Mothers who never marry are more vulnerable to poverty than virtually any other group, including those who have been divorced.[7]

But the low income associated with single parenthood reflects many interrelated factors. Income is distributed far more unequally in the United States than in most other developed countries, making it difficult for low-wage workers (male or female) to support a family without a second income. Women who become single mothers are especially likely to have inadequate wages, both because of pre-existing disadvantages such as low educational attainment and work experience and because the shortage of publicly subsidized child care makes it difficult for them to work full time. In 2000, only 1.2 percent of children of single mothers with a college degree who worked full-time year round lived in poverty.[8] For single mothers with some college working full-time, the poverty rate was less than 8 percent.[9]

Whether single or married, working parents face high child care costs that are seldom factored into calculations of poverty and income. Consider the situation of a single mother with two children working full-time, full year round at the minimum wage of $5.15 an hour, for an income of $10,712. If she files for and receives the maximum Earned Income Tax Credit, she can receive as much as $3,816 in public assistance. But the EITC phases out quickly if she earns much more than the minimum wage, and her child care costs are very high. Unless she is lucky enough to have a family member who can provide free child care, or to find a federally subsidized child care slot, more than 20 percent of her income will go to pay for child care.[10] Federally subsidized child care remains quite limited. Most families who made a transition from welfare to employment in the 1990s did not receive a subsidy.[11]

The high cost of child care helps explain why the economic position of single parents has improved little in recent years despite significant increases in their hours of market work.[12] It may also explain why single parents are likely to live in households with other adults who can share expenses with them. About 40 percent of births to single mothers take place among cohabitors, and much of the increase in nonmarital childbearing in recent years reflects this trend rather than an increase among women living without a partner.[13] The economic stress associated with reductions in welfare benefits over the past six years may have increased the pressure on single mothers to cohabit, often with partners who are unwilling or unlikely to marry.[14]

On both a symbolic and a practical level, marriage facilitates the income pooling and task sharing that allows parents to accommodate family needs.[15] Not surprisingly, many low-income families consider marriage the ideal arrangement for child rearing.[16] The Fragile Families and Child Welfare project currently underway in about twenty cities shows that about 50 percent of unmarried parents of newborns live together and hope to marry at some point.[17] Lower expectations among some couples were associated not with disinterest in marriage but with reports of drug or alcohol problems, physical violence, conflict and mistrust.[18]

The advantages of marriage, however, do not derive simply from having two names on a marriage certificate, and they cannot be acquired merely by going through a formality. Rather, they grow out of a long-term and economically sustainable commitment that many people feel is beyond their reach.

Causality Works Both Ways

Liking the abstract idea of marriage and being able to put together a stable marriage in real life are two very different things. Unemployment, low wages, and poverty discourage family formation and erode family stability, making it less likely that individuals will marry in the first place and more likely that their marriages will deteriorate. These economic factors have long-term as well as short-term effects, contributing to changes in social norms regarding marriage and family formation and exacerbating distrust between men and women. These long-term effects help explain why African-Americans marry at much lower rates than other groups within the U.S. population. Poverty is a cause as well as a consequence of non-marriage and of marital disruption.[19]

Dan Lichter of Ohio State University puts it this way: "Marriage can be a pathway from poverty, but only if women are 'marriageable,' stay married, and marry well."[20] Precisely because marriage offers economic advantages, individuals tend to seek potential spouses who have good earnings potential and to avoid marriage when they do not feel they or their potential mates can comfortably support a family. Ethnographic research shows that low-income women see economic stability on the part of a prospective partner as a necessary precondition for marriage.[21] Not surprisingly, men increasingly use the same calculus. Rather than looking for someone they can "rescue" from poverty, employed men are much more likely to marry women who themselves have good employment prospects.[22]

Poor mothers who lack a high school degree and any regular employment history are not likely to fare very well in the so-called "marriage market." Teenage girls who live in areas of high unemployment and inferior schools are five to seven times more likely to become unwed parents than more fortunately situated teens.[23] A study of the National Longitudinal Survey of Youth confirms that poor women, whatever their age, and regardless of whether or not they are or have ever been on welfare, are less likely to marry than women who are not poor. Among poor women, those who do not have jobs are less likely to marry than those who do.[24]

It is easy to spin a hypothetical scenario in which marrying off single mothers to an average male would raise family incomes and reduce poverty. But unmarried males, and especially unmarried males in impoverished neighborhoods, are not average. That is often the reason they are not married. Researchers from the Center for Research on Child Well-Being at Princeton University report results from the Fragile Families Survey showing that unmarried fathers were twice as likely as married ones to have a physical or psychological problem that interfered with their ability to find or keep a job, and several times more likely to abuse drugs or alcohol. More than 25 percent of unmarried fathers were not employed when their child was born, compared to fewer than 10 percent of married fathers.[25]

Poor mothers tend to live in neighborhoods in which their potential marriage partners are also likely to be poorly educated and irregularly employed. Low-earning men are less likely to get married and more likely to divorce than men with higher earnings.[26] Over the past thirty years, labor market opportunities for men with low levels of education have declined substantially.[27] Several studies suggest that the decrease in real wages for low-income men during the 1980s and early 1990s contributed significantly to lower marriage rates in those years.[28]

This trend has been exacerbated by the high incarceration rates for men convicted of non-violent crimes, such as drug use. While in jail, these men are not available for women to marry and their diminished job prospects after release permanently impair their marriageability. High rates of incarceration among black males, combined with high rates of mortality, have led to a decidedly tilted sex ratio within the African-American population, and a resulting scarcity of marriageable men.[29] One study of the marriage market in the 1980s found that at age 25 there were three unmarried black women for every black man who had adequate earnings.[30] As Ron Mincy of Columbia University emphasizes, simple pro-marriage policies are likely to offer less benefit to African-American families than policies encouraging responsible fatherhood and paternal engagement.[31]

In short, the notion that we could end child poverty by marrying off impoverished women does not take into account the realities of life among the population most likely to be poor. It is based on abstract scenarios that ignore the many ways in which poverty diminishes people's ability to build and sustain stable family relationships.

Quality Matters

Happy, healthy, stable marriages offer important benefits to adults and children. But not all marriages fit this description. Marital distress leads to harsh and inconsistent parenting, whether or not parents stay together. Studies show that a marriage marked by conflict, jealousy and anger is often worse for children's well-being than divorce or residence from birth in a stable single-parent family.[32] For instance, research shows that while children born to teenagers who were already married do better than children born to never-married teens, children born to teen parents who married *after* the birth do worse on some measures, probably because of the high conflict that accompanies marriages entered into with ambivalence or under pressure. Some research suggests that, among low-income African-American families, children from single-parent homes show higher educational achievement than their counterparts from two-parent homes.[33]

The idea that marriage can solve the problems of children in impoverished families ignores the complex realities of these families. The Fragile Families study shows that many low-income parents of new born children already have children from previous relationships. Thus, their marriages would not create idealized biological families, but rather blended families in which child support enforcement and negotiation among stepparents would complicate relationships.[34] A recent study of families in poor neighborhoods in Boston, Chicago and San Antonio also reveals complex patterns of cohabitation and coparenting.[35]

Marriage to a stepfather may improve a mother's economic situation, but it does not necessarily improve outcomes for children and in some cases leads to more problems than continued residence in a stable single-parent family. Even if programs succeed in getting first-time parents married, there is no guarantee that the couples will stay married. Research shows that marriages contracted in the 1960s in order to "legitimate" a child were highly likely to end in divorce.[36] Multiple transitions in and out of marriage are worse for children psychologically than residence in the same kind of family, whatever its form, over long periods of time.[37]

Women and children in economically precarious situations are particularly vulnerable to domestic violence.[38] While it may be true that cohabiting couples are more prone to violence than married couples, this is probably because of what social scientists call a "selection effect": People in non-abusive relationships are more likely to get married. Encouraging women in an unstable cohabiting relationship to marry their partners would not necessarily protect them or their children. Indeed, the first serious violent episode in an unstable relationship sometimes occurs only after the couple has made a formal commitment.[39]

Even when it does not take a violent form, bad fathering can be worse than no fathering. For instance, the National Center on Addiction and Substance Abuse at Columbia University found that while teens in two-parent families are, on average, much less likely to abuse drugs or alcohol than teens in one-parent ones, teens in two-parent families who have a poor to fair relationship with their father are *more* likely to do so than teens in the average one-parent family.[40]

Furthermore, even good marriages are vulnerable to dissolution. The current risks of a marriage ending in divorce are quite high, although they have come down from their peak in 1979–81. It is now estimated that approximately 40 percent of marriages will end in divorce, and the risk of divorce is elevated among people with low income and insecure jobs. Sociologist Scott South calculates that every time the unemployment rate rises by 1 percent, approximately 10,000 extra divorces occur.[41] Comparing the income of single-parent families and married-couple families in any particular year leads to an overly optimistic assessment of the benefits of marriage, because it ignores the possibility of marital dissolution.

Marriage may provide a temporary improvement in a woman's economic prospects without conferring any secure, long-term protection for her children. Indeed, if marriage encourages mothers to withdraw time from paid employment, this can lower their future earnings and increase the wage penalty that they incur from motherhood itself.[42]

Two-Parent Families Are Also Under Stress

Poverty among children is not confined to single-parent families. In 2000, about 38 percent of all poor young children lived in two-parent homes.[43] These families have been largely overlooked in the debates over anti-poverty programs and marriage. Indeed, the campaign to increase marriage has overlooked one of the most important public policy issues facing the United States: the growing economic gap between parents, whether married or unmarried, and non-parents.

The costs of raising children have increased in recent years, partly because of the expansion of opportunities for women in the labor market and partly because of the longer time children spend in school. The lack of public support for parenting has also contributed to a worsening of the economic position of parents relative to non-parents.[44] Unlike other advanced industrial countries, the United States fails to provide paid family leaves for parents, and levels of publicly subsidized support for child care remain comparatively low. Most employment practices penalize workers who take time away from paid responsibilities to provide family care.[45] The high cost of parenting in this country helps explain many of the economic disadvantages that women face relative to men.[46] It may also help explain why many men are reluctant to embrace paternal responsibilities.

The Need for a Better Social Safety Net

The association of single parenthood with poverty is not inevitable. In Canada and France, single mothers—and children in general—are far less likely to live in poverty. Sweden and Denmark, with higher rates of out-of-wedlock births, have much lower rates of child poverty and hunger than does the United States. The reason for the difference is simple: These countries devote a greater percentage of their resources to assisting families with children than we do.[47] Similarly, dramatic differences in child poverty rates within our country reflect differences in tax, child care, and income assistance policies across states.[48]

Fans of the 1996 welfare reform law point to a dramatic decline in the welfare rolls since its enactment. Much of this decline is attributable to the economic boom and resulting low unemployment rates of the late 1990s. Despite promises that work requirements and time limits would lead to a more generous package of assistance for those who "followed the rules," cash benefits have declined. Between 1994 and 1999, the real value of maximum benefits fell in most states, with an overall decline in inflation-adjusted value of about 11 percent.[49] Average benefits declined even more, as recipients increased their earnings. Indeed, the declining value of benefits is another reason why caseloads have fallen.[50]

Punitive attitudes, as well as time limits, have discouraged many eligible families from applying for assistance. The Census Bureau estimates that less than 30 percent of children in poverty resided in a family that received cash public assistance in 1998.[51] Take-up rates for Food Stamps and Medicaid have declined in recent years.[52] The implementation of the new Children's Health Insurance program has been quite uneven. As a result, states have saved money, but many children have gone without the food or medical care they needed. Public support for child care increased on both the federal and the state level. Still, most families who made a transition from welfare to work in the late 1990s did not receive a subsidy.[53]

During the economic boom of the late 1990s, increases in earnings among single parents helped make up for declining welfare benefits. As a result, poverty rates among children declined from a high of about 21 percent in 1996 to about 16 percent in 2000.[54] But these figures do not take into account the costs of child care and other work-related expenses, and they offer little hope for the future of children in low-income families as unemployment rates once again begin to climb.[55]

The most important federal policy promoting the welfare of low income families is currently the Earned Income Tax Credit (EITC), a fully refundable tax credit aimed at low-income families with children. Because benefits are closely tied to earnings, and phase out steeply after family income reaches $12,460, the EITC imposes a significant penalty on two-earner married couples, who are less likely to benefit from it than either single-parent families or married couples with a spouse at home. This penalty is unfair and should be eliminated.

Other problems with the EITC, however, should be addressed at the same time. Families with two children receive the maximum benefit, which means that low-income families with three or more children do not receive any additional assistance. More than a third of all children in the country live in families with three or more children. Partly as a result of limited EITC coverage, these families are prone to significantly higher poverty rates.[56] Furthermore, the EITC is phased out in ways that penalize middle income families, who currently enjoy less public support for child rearing than the affluent.[57] An expanded unified tax credit for families with children could address this problem.[58]

Given the pressing need for improvements in basic social safety net programs and the threat of rising unemployment, it is unconscionable to reallocate already inadequate Temporary Assistance to Needy Families (TANF) funds to policies designed to promote marriage or provide a "marriage bonus." There is little evidence that such policies would in fact increase marriage rates or reduce poverty among children. Indeed, the main effect of marriage bonuses would probably be to impose a "non-marriage" penalty that would have a particularly negative impact on African-American children, who are significantly less likely to live with married parents than either whites or Hispanics.[59] As Julianne Malveaux points out in her discussion of the Bush proposal, "a mere $100 million can be considered chump change. But the chump who could have been changed is the unemployed worker who misses out on job training because some folks find those programs—but not marriage-promotion programs—a waste."[60]

Well-designed programs to help individuals develop and improve family relationships may be a good idea. However, they should not be targeted to the poor, but integrated into a larger provision of public health services, or built into existing health insurance programs (mandating, for instance, that both public and private health insurance cover family counseling). Such programs also should not be limited to couples who are married or planning to marry. Fathers and step-fathers who are not living with their biological children also need guidance and encouragement to develop healthy, nurturing relationships. Gay and lesbian families—who are currently legally prohibited from marriage—also merit assistance.

Public policies should not penalize marriage. Neither should they provide an economic bonus or financial incentive to individuals to marry, especially at the cost of lowering the resources available to children living with single mothers. Such a diversion of resources from public assistance programs penalizes the children of unmarried parents without guaranteeing good outcomes for the children of people who are married. A variety of public policies could help strengthen families and reduce poverty among all children, including a broadening of the Earned Income Tax Credit, expansion of publicly subsidized child care, efforts to promote responsible fatherhood, improvements in public education and job training, and efforts to reduce income inequality and pay discrimination. Unlike some of the pro-marriage policies now under consideration, these policies would benefit couples who wish to marry but would not pressure women to enter or remain in intimate relationships they would not otherwise choose.

Notes

1. Alexandra Starr, "Shotgun Wedding by Uncle Sam?" *Business Week,* June 4, 2001.

2. Cheryl Wetzstein, "States Want Pro-Family Funds," *The Washington Times,* December 10, 2001; Robin Toner and Robert Pear, "Bush Urges Work and Marriage Programs in Welfare Plan," *New York Times,* February 27, 2002.

3. Jonathan Rauch, "The Widening Marriage Gap: America's New Class Divide," *National Journal,* Friday, May 18, 2001.

4. Cheryl Weitzstein, "Unwed Mothers Set a Record for Births," *The Washington Times,* April 18, 2001.

5. See Jared Bernstein, Irv Garfinkel, and Sara McLanahan, *A Progressive Marriage Agenda,* forthcoming from the Economic Policy Institute.

6. U.S. Bureau of the Census, "Historical Poverty Statistics—Table 4. Poverty Status of Families, by Type of Family, Presence of Related Children, Race, and Hispanic Origin: 1959–2000." . . . In 1999, 36 percent of single-mother households lived in poverty. *Poverty in the U.S. 1999.* Current Population Reports, P60–210 (Washington, D.C.: Government Printing Office, 2000).

7. Alan Guttmacher Institute, "Married Mothers Fare the Best Economically, Even if They Were Unwed at the Time They Gave Birth," *Family Planning Perspectives* 31, no. 5: pp. 258–60, September, 1999; Ariel Halpern, "Poverty Among Children Born Outside of Marriage: Preliminary Findings From the National Survey of America's Families" (Washington, D.C.: The Urban Institute, 1999).

8. Calculations by Arloc Sherman, Children's Defense Fund, based on the March 2001 Current Population Survey.

9. Ibid. See also Neil G. Bennett, Jiali Li, Younghwan Song, and Keming Yang, "Young Children in Poverty: A Statistical Update," released June 17, 1999. New York: National Center for Children in Poverty. . . .

10. Linda Giannarelli and James Barsimantov, *Child Care Expenses of America's Families,* Occasional Paper Number 40 (Washington, D.C.: Urban Institute, 2000).

11. Rachel Schumacher and Mark Greenberg, *Child Care After Leaving Welfare: Early Evidence From State Studies* (Washington, D.C.: Center for Law and Social Policy, 1999).

12. Kathryn H. Porter and Allen Dupree, "Poverty Trends for Families Headed by Working Single Mothers, 1993–1999," Center on Budget and Policy Priorities, August 16, 2001. . . .

13. Pamela Smock, "Cohabitation in the U.S.: An Appraisal of Research Themes, Findings, and Implications," *American Review of Sociology* 26, no. 1 (2000): pp. 1–20.

14. Gregory Acs and Sandi Nelson, "'Honey, I'm Home.' Changes in Living Arrangements in the Late 1990s," *New Federalism: National Survey of America's Families* (The Urban Institute), June 2001, pp. 1–7. A new study by Johns Hopkins researchers, presented on February 20, 2002 at a welfare forum in Washington D.C., however, shows that these partnerships are unstable and may not be better for children than single-parent

households. See Robin Toner, "Two Parents Not Always Best for Children, Study Finds," *New York Times,* February 20, 2002.

15. Many dual-earner families with preschool age children include a parent who works evenings and nights in order to provide care during the day while their husband or wife is at work. See Harriet Presser, "Employment Schedules Among Dual-Earner Spouses and the Division of Household Labor by Gender," *American Sociological Review* 59, no. 3 (June 1994): pp. 348–364.

16. Kristen Harknett and Sara McLanahan, "Do Perceptions of Marriage Explain Marital Behavior? How Unmarried Parents' Assessments of the Benefits of Marriage Relate to Their Subsequent Marital Decision"; and Marcia Carlson, Sara McLanahan, and Paula England, "Union Formation and Stability in Fragile Families," papers presented at the meetings of the Population Association of America, Washington D.C., April 2001.

17. More details on the Fragile Families study are available at. . . .

18. Maureen Waller, "High Hopes: Unwed Parents' Expectations About Marriage," *Children and Youth Services Review* 23 (2001): pp. 457–84.

19. Sara McLanahan, "Parent Absence or Poverty: Which Matters More?" pp. 35–48 in Greg Duncan and Jeanne Brooks-Gunn, eds., *Consequences of Growing Up Poor* (New York: Russell Sage Foundation, 1997). On the impact of poverty in creating non-marriage and marital disruption, see Aimee Dechter, "The Effect of Women's Economic Independence on Union Dissolution," Working Paper Np. 92–98 (1992).

   Center for Demography and Ecology, University of Wisconsin, Madison, WI; Mark Testa et al., "Employment and Marriage Among Inner-City Fathers," *Annals of the American Academy of Political and Social Science* 501 (1989), pp. 79–91; Karen Holden and Pamela Smock, "The Economic Costs of Marital Dissolution: Why Do Women Bear a Disproportionate Cost?" *Annual Review of Sociology* 17 (1991), pp. 51–58. On the association of low income with domestic violence see Kristin Anderson, "Gender, Status, and Domestic Violence," *Journal of Marriage and the Family* 59 (1997), pp. 655–670; A. M. Moore, "Intimate Violence: Does Socioeconomic Status Matter?" in A. P. Gardarelli, ed., *Violence Between Intimate Partners* (Boston: Allyn and Bacon, 1997), pp. 90–100; A. J. Sedlack and D. D. Broadhurst, *Third National Incidence Study of Child Abuse and Neglect: Final Report* (Washington D.C.: Department of Health and Human Services, 1996).

20. Daniel T. Lichter, *Marriage as Public Policy* (Washington, D.C.: Progressive Policy Institute, September 2001).

21. Kathryn Edin, "A Few Good Men: Why Poor Mothers Don't Marry or Remarry?" *The American Prospect,* January 3, 2000, p. 28; Kathryn Edin and Laura Lein, *Making Ends Meet: How Single Mothers Survive Welfare and Low-Wage Work* (New York: Russell Sage, 1998).

22. Valerie Oppenheimer and Vivian Lew, "American Marriage Formation in the 1980s," in Karen Mason and An-Magritt Jensen, eds., *Gender and Family Change in Industrialized Countries* (Oxford: Oxford University Press, 1994), pp. 105–38; Sharon Sassler and Robert Schoen, "The Effects of Attitudes and Economic Activity on Marriage," *Journal of Marriage and the Family* 61 (1999): pp. 148–49.

23. John Billy and David Moore, "A Multilevel Analysis of Marital and Nonmarital Fertility in the U.S.," *Social Forces* 70 (1992), pp. 977–1011; Sara McLanahan and Irwin Garfinkel, "Welfare Is No Incentive," *The New York Times,* July 29, 1994, p. A13; Elaine McCrate, "Expectations of Adult Wages and Teenage Childbearing," *International Review of Applied Economics* 6 (1992), pp. 309–328; Ellen Coughlin, "Policy Researchers Shift the Terms of the Debate on Women's Issues," *The Chronicle of Higher Education,* May 31, 1989; Marian Wright Edelman, *Families in Peril: An Agenda for Social Change* (Cambridge: Harvard University Press, 1987), p. 55; Lawrence Lynn and Michael McGeary, eds., *Inner-City Poverty in the United States* (Washington, D.C.: National Academy Press, 1990), pp. 163–67; Jonathan Crane, "The Epidemic Theory of Ghetto and Neighborhood Effects on Dropping Out and Teenaged Childbearing," *American Journal of Sociology* 96 (1991), pp. 1226–59; Sara McLanahan and Lynne Casper, "Growing Diversity and Inequality in the American Family," in Reynolds Farley, *State of the Union,* vol. 2, pp. 10–11; Mike Males, "Poverty, Rape, Adult/Teen Sex: Why 'Pregnancy-Prevention' Programs Don't Work," *Phi Delta Kappan,* January 1994, p. 409; Mike Males, "In Defense of Teenaged Mothers," *The Progressive,* August 1994, p. 23.

24. Diane McLaughlin and Daniel Lichter, "Poverty and the Marital Behavior of Young Women," *Journal of Marriage and the Family* 59, no. 3 (1997): pp. 582–94.

25. Wendy Single-Rushton and Sara McLanahan, "For Richer or Poorer?" manuscript, Center for Research on Child Well-Being, Princeton University, July 2001, p. 4; Kathryn Edin, "What Do Low-Income Single Mothers Say About Marriage?" *Social Problems* 47 (2000), pp. 112–33.

26. Robert Nakosteen and Michael Zimmer, "Man, Money, and Marriage: Are High Earners More Prone than Low Earners to Marry?" *Social Science Quarterly* 78 (1997): pp. 66–82.

27. Francine D. Blau, Lawrence W. Kahn, and Jane Waldfogel, "Understanding Young Women's Marriage Decisions: The Role of Labor and Marriage Market Conditions," *Industrial and Labor Relations Review* 53, no. 4 (July 2000): pp. 624–48.

28. Robert Nakosteen and Michael Zimmer, "Men, Money, and Marriage," *Social Science Quarterly* 78 (1997); Frank F. Furstenberg, Jr., "The Future of Marriage," *American Demographics* 18 (June 1996), pp. 39–40; Francine Blau, Lawrence Kahn, and Jane Waldfogel, "Understanding Young Women's Marriage Decisions," *Industrial and Labor Relations Review* 53 (2000): pp. 624–48.

29. William A. Darity, Jr. and Samuel L. Myers, Jr., "Family Structure and the Marginalization of Black Men: Policy Implications," in *The Decline in Marriage Among African Americans: Causes, Consequences, and Policy Implications,* ed. M. Belinda Tucker and Claudia Mitchell-Kernan (New York: Russell Sage Foundation, 1995), pp. 263–308.

30. Daniel T. Lichter, D. McLaughlin, F. LeClere, G. Kephart, and D. Landry, "Race and the Retreat From Marriage: A Shortage of Marriageable Men?" *American Sociological Review* 57 (December 1992): pp. 781–99.

31. Ron Mincy, Columbia University, personal communication, February 18, 2002.

32. Mavis Hetherington, *For Better or for Worse: Divorce Reconsidered* (New York: W. W. Norton, 2001); Paul Amato and Alan Booth, "The Legacy of Parents' Marital Discord," *Journal of Personality and Social Psychology* 81 (2001), pp. 627–638; Andrew Cherlin, "Going to Extremes: Family Structure, Children's Well-Being, and Social Science," *Demography* 36 (November 1999): pp. 421–28.

33. Elizabeth Cooksey, "Consequences of Young Mothers' Marital Histories for Children's Cognitive Development," *Journal of Marriage and the Family* 59 (May 1997), pp. 245–62; Juan Battle, "What Beats Having Two Parents? Educational Outcomes for African American Students in Single- Versus Dual-Parent Families," *Journal of Black Studies* 28 (1998), pp. 783–802.

34. Ron Mincy and Chen-Chung Huang, "'Just Get Me to the Church . . .': Assessing Policies to Promote Marriage Among Fragile Families," manuscript prepared for the MacArthur Foundation Network on the Family and the Economy Meeting, Evanston, Illinois, November 30, 2001. Contact Ron Mincy, School of Social Work, Columbia University.

35. Research by Andrew Cherlin and Paula Fomby at Johns Hopkins University, as reported in Robin Toner, "Two Parents Not Always Best for Children," *New York Times,* February 21, 2002.

36. Frank Furstenberg, Jeanne Brooks-Gunn, and S. Philip Morgan, *Adolescent Mothers in Later Life* (New York: Cambridge University Press, 1987).

37. Frank Furstenberg, "Is the Modern Family a Threat to Children's Health?" *Society* 36 (1999): p. 35.

38. Richard Gelles, "Constraints Against Family Violence," *American Behavioral Scientist* 36 (1993), pp. 575–86; A. J. Sedlack and D. D. Broadhurst, *Third National Incidence Study of Child Abuse and Neglect: Final Report* (Washington, D.C.: Department of Health and Human Services, 1996); Kristin Anderson, "Gender, Status and Domestic Violence," *Journal of Marriage and the Family* 59 (1997), pp. 655–670; Jacqueline Payne and Martha Davis, "Testimony of NOW Legal Defense and Education Fund on Child Support and Fatherhood Initiatives," submitted to the United States House Human Resources Subcommittee of the Ways and Means Committee, June 28, 2001.

39. Catherine Kenney and Sara McLanahan, "Are Cohabiting Relationships More Violent Than Marriages?" manuscript, Princeton University; E. D. Leonard, 1994, "Battered Women and Criminal Justice: A Review," doctoral dissertation cited in Todd Migliaccio, "Abused Husbands: A Narrative Analysis," *Journal of Family Issues* 23 (2002), pp. 26–52; K. D. O'Leary et al., "Prevalence and Stability of Physical Aggression Between Spouses: A Longitudinal Analysis," *Journal of Consulting and Clinical Psychology* 57 (1989), pp. 263–68.

40. National Center on Addiction and Substance Abuse at Columbia University, "Back to School 1999—National Survey of American Attitudes on Substance Abuse V: Teens and Their Parents," August 1999. See also Irvin Molotsky, "Study Links Teenage Substance Abuse and Paternal Ties," *New York Times,* Aug. 31, 1999.

41. "Census Bureau Reports Poor Two-Parent Families Are About Twice as Likely to Break Up as Two-Parent Families Not in Poverty," *New York Times,* January 15, 1993, p. A6; Don Burroughs, "Love and Money," *U.S. News & World Report,* October 19, 1992, p. 58; Scott South, Katherine Trent, and

Yang Shen, "Changing Partners: Toward a Macrostructural-Opportunity Theory of Marital Dissolution," *Journal of Marriage and Family* 63, no. 3 (2001): 743–754. Also see note 17.

42. Michelle Budig and Paula England, "The Wage Penalty for Motherhood," *American Sociological Review* 66 (2001): pp. 204–225; Heather Joshi, Pierella Paci, and Jane Waldfogel, 1999, "The Wages of Motherhood: Better or Worse," *Cambridge Journal of Economics* 23, no. 5 (1999): pp. 543–564. Jane Waldfogel, "The Effect of Children on Women's Wages," *American Sociological Review* 62: 2 (1997): pp. 209–217.

43. "Young Children in Poverty: A Statistical Update," June 1999 Edition. Released June 17, 1999, prepared by Neil G. Bennett, Jiali Li, Younghwan Song, and Keming Yang. New York: National Center for Children in Poverty. . . . Data for 2000 from CPS. . . .

44. Nancy Folbre, *Who Pays for the Kids? Gender and the Structures of Constraint* (New York: Routledge, 1994); Ann Crittenden, *The Price of Motherhood* (New York: Metropolitan Books, 2001); Sylvia Ann Hewlett and Cornell West, *The War Against Parents* (New York: Houghton Mifflin, 1998).

45. Joan Williams, *Unbending Gender: Why Family and Work Conflict and What to Do About It* (New York: Oxford University Press, 2000).

46. Ann Crittenden, *The Price of Motherhood. Why the Most Important Job in the World Is Still the Least Valued* (New York: Henry Holt, 2001).

47. Timothy Smeeding, Barbara Boyle Torrey, and Martin Rein, "Patterns of Income and Poverty: The Economic Status of Children and the Elderly in Eight Countries," in John L Palmer, Timothy Smeeding, and Barbara Boyle Torrey, eds., *The Vulnerable* (Washington, D.C.: Urban Institute Press, 1988); Susan Houseknecht and Jaya Sastry, "Family 'Decline' and Child Well-Being: A Comparative Assessment," *Journal of Marriage and the Family* 58 (1996); Sara McLanahan and Irwin Garfinkel, "Single-Mother Families and Social Policy: Lessons for the United States From Canada, France, and Sweden," pp. 367–83, in K. McFate, R. Lawson, W. J. Wilson eds., *Poverty, Inequality, and the Future of Social Policy: Western States in the New World Order* (New York: Russell Sage Foundation, 1995). Michael J. Graetz and Jerry L. Mashaw, *True Security: Rethinking American Social Insurance* (New Haven: Yale University Press, 1999).

48. Marcia K. Meyers, Janet C. Gornick, and Laura R. Peck, 2001, "Packaging Support for Low-Income Families: Policy Variation Across the U.S. States," *Journal of Policy Analysis and Management* 20, no. 3: pp. 457–483.

49. Table 7–6, *Green Book 2000*. Committee on Ways and Means, U.S. House of Representatives, 106th Congress . . .

50. President's Council of Economic Advisors, *The Effects of Welfare Policy and the Economic Expansion of Welfare Caseloads: An Update* (Washington, D.C.: Council of Economic Advisors, 1999).

51. *2000 Kids Count Data Online.* . . .

52. Jennifer Steinhauer, "States Proved Unpredictable in Aiding Uninsured Children," *New York Times,* September 28, 2000. See also Leighton Ku and Brian Bruen, "The Continuing Decline in Medicaid Coverage," Series A, no. A–37 (Washington, D.C.: Urban Institute, 1999); Sheila Zedlewski and Sarah Brauner, "Are the Steep Declines in Food Stamp Participation Linked

to Falling Welfare Caseloads?" Series B, no. B–3 (Washington, D.C.: Urban Institute, 1999).

53. Rachel Schumacher and Mark Greenberg, *Child Care After Leaving Welfare: Early Evidence From State Studies* (Washington, D.C.: Center for Law and Social Policy, 1999). On the added costs of child care and care-giving activities for low-income families, see Jody Heymann, *The Widening Gap: Why America's Working Families Are in Jeopardy and What Can Be Done About It* (New York: Basic Books, 2000).

54. Bureau of the Census, Current Population Reports, *Money Income and Poverty in the U.S., 1999. . . .*

55. Patricia Ruggles, *Drawing the Line: Alternative Poverty Measures and Their Implications for Public Policy* (Washington, D.C.: The Urban Institute Press, 1990); Constance Citro and Robert Michael, eds., *Measuring Poverty: A New Approach* (Washington, D.C.: National Academy of Science, 1995); Jared Bernstein, Chauna Brocht, Maggie Spade-Aguilar, *How Much Is Enough? Basic Family Budgets for Working Families* (Washington, D.C.: Economic Policy Institute, 2000).

56. Robert Greenstein, "Should EITC Benefits Be Enlarged for Families With Three or More Children?" Washington, D.C.: Center on Budget and Policy Priorities, 2000. . . .

57. David Ellwood and Jeffrey B. Liebman, "The Middle Class Parent Penalty: Child Benefits in the U.S. Tax Code," manuscript, John F. Kennedy School of Government, Harvard University, Boston, MA, 2000.

58. Robert Cherry and Max Sawicky, "Giving Tax Credit Where Credit Is Due," Briefing Paper (Washington, D.C.: Economic Policy Institute, April 2000). . . .

59. Ronald B. Mincy, "Marriage, Child Poverty, and Public Policy," *American Experiment Quarterly*, 4: 2 (Summer 2001): pp. 68–71. See also Wendy Sigle-Rushton and Sara McLanahan, "For Richer or Poorer?" manuscript, Center for Research on Child Well-Being, Princeton University.

60. Julianne Malveaux, "More Jobs, Not More Marriages, Lift Poor," *U.S.A. Today*, February 22, 2002, p. 15A.

EXPLORING THE ISSUE

Does Marriage Improve Living Standards for Children?

Critical Thinking and Reflection

1. According to Coontz and Folbre, how can marriage be a short-term fix for single moms living in poverty but fail in the long term?
2. Discuss two of the realities of the poor population that make marriage difficult to attain. Can you identify any ways that these difficulties could be overcome or even eradicated from society?
3. The research shows conflicting information in regard to the effect of teens marrying before versus after the birth of their children. What is the contradictory information and what do you make of it?

Is There Common Ground?

Horn states that government programs should include premarriage education and teach couples the skills they need to help their marriage succeed. Most people would agree that strengthening marriages would be considered a positive thing. However, it is also understood that the issue is complicated and having a good marriage is not the only important thing necessary for raising living standards. It would seem that a multifaceted approach in dealing with marriage standards but also other components of family living would be the ideal one to take in order to work toward raising the living standards of children in America.

Additional Resources

American College of Pediatricians. Marriage and the Family. Retrieved on April 11, 2011, from http://www.acpeds.org/Marriage-and-the-Family.html.

This Web site discusses some of the benefits of married families on children.

For Your Marriage. Why Married Parents Are Important for Children. Retrieved on April 11, 2011, from http://foryourmarriage.org/married-parents-are-important-for-children/.

This Web site, put out by the Conference of Catholic Bishops, discusses information about how marriage can be important for children.

KidsHealth. Living with a Single Parent. Retrieved on April 11, 2011, from http://kidshealth.org/kid/feeling/home_family/single_parents.html.

This Web site is written for kids who live with single parents. It contains advice and suggestions for this type of living arrangement.

Single Parent Families—The Effects on Children. Retrieved on April 11, 2011, from http://family.jrank.org/pages/1577/Single-Parent-Families-Effects-on-Children.html.

This Web site discusses some of the effects that children can experience when living in a single parent home.

ISSUE 10

Do Children Who Are Homeschooled Have a Limited View of Society?

YES: Rob Reich, from "The Civic Perils of Homeschooling," *Educational Leadership* (April 2002)

NO: Thomas W. Washburne, from The Boundaries of Parental Authority: A Response to Rob Reich of Stanford University, *National Center for Home Education Special Report* (Home School Legal Defense Association, http://nche.hslda.org/docs/nche/000010/200204230.asp, April 22, 2002)

Learning Outcomes

After reading this issue, you should be able to:

- Describe some of the reasons that parents may choose homeschooling for their children.
- Identify challenges that homeschooled children face as a result of their educational situation.
- Identify some of the benefits that children who are homeschooled can experience.

ISSUE SUMMARY

YES: Rob Reich, assistant professor of political science, at Stanford University, states that children who are homeschooled are limited by their teachers, who are usually their parents.

NO: Thomas Washburne, director of the National Center for Home Education, disagrees with Reich and believes his opposition to homeschooling denies parents their unalienable right to educate their children as they choose.

Homeschooling was the accepted method of education in the United States until the 1850s. At that time, it was replaced by public schooling, but home schools made a comeback in the 1970s. Home schools are now legal in every state in the nation and more than two million children are homeschooled every year. There has been a steady rise in homeschooling since 1999. As such, the advantages and disadvantages of homeschooling are becoming an increasingly controversial subject in America. Advocates argue that homeschooling offers an alternative to the growing violence, bullying, and poor academic performance prevalent in schools. Opponents argue that homeschooling eliminates essential social interaction and contact.

According to the National Center for Education Statistics (NCES), students are considered homeschooled if their parents report them as being schooled at home instead of at a public or private school for at least part of their education and if their part-time enrollment in public or private schools does not exceed 25 hours a week. Homeschooling advocates feel that this definition does not accurately account for the true number of homeschooled children. Currently, parents can choose to educate their children at home or send them to public or private school depending on their particular situation. Although one type of setting may look more attractive, parents who look at each child as an individual will choose the type of educational environment that considers the child's unique needs. For example, a child who learns well on his own might do better in a home school, while a child who needs to interact with others in order to learn would perform best in a public or private school setting.

Parents choose to homeschool their children for many reasons. Some parents disagree with the values presented in public as well as private schools. They also site disagreements with specific curricula or teaching methods used by schools. Parents who favor homeschooling believe public schools do not promote self-discipline and self-motivation or provide an environment in which each child's particular talents might flourish.

According to the NCES, in 2003 the most frequently cited factor for homeschooling was parents' concern about the environment of other schools including safety, drugs, or negative peer pressure. Eighty-five percent of homeschooled students were being homeschooled, in part, because of this concern. The other two most often cited reasons for homeschooling were to provide religious or moral instruction (72 percent) and a general dissatisfaction with academic instruction at other schools (68 percent). When asked about the most important reason for the decision to homeschool, parents cited providing moral or religious instruction (33 percent) and concern about the environment of traditional schools (30 percent).

Homeschooling advocates defend their cause by pointing at the better test scores of children schooled at home. They also point to the growing problems of violence, bullying and drug abuse in the public and private school systems. Opponents argue that homeschooled children lose vital social support and contact by being removed from the school environment. They feel that this loss of social interaction outweighs any positive academic effects.

Some educators even fear that homeschooling may be harmful to a child's overall development. Children schooled at home may not have the opportunity to develop and interact with their peer group and miss learning social skills. Another common concern is that homeschool teachers may not have the appropriate skills, training, education, and knowledge to teach children effectively.

Parents who do not want their children shaped by hours of rigid institutional learning may opt for the more flexible home school setting. However, it should be noted that home schooling is challenging and sometimes difficult to implement. Parents must be willing to take the time to learn to teach their children effectively. Homeschooling can be a full time job and may necessitate a separate income source for the parent educator.

Another issue that must be considered in homeschooling is college recognition of high school credits earned via home schools. Although increasing numbers of colleges and universities accept homeschooled students with adequate scores on college entrance tests, parents who are teachers must be mindful of meeting state requirements for certification. Appropriate authorities must sanction class-meeting times and course content so that local boards of education recognize and accept home school credits.

There is a possibility that homeschooling will promote parental enmeshment with children in some families. Abuse and neglect, which are often reported by school personnel, could go unnoticed and unreported if children remain in the home for school. Home educators need to provide their children with social outlets and activities to ensure that their children are able to function effectively in social situations with peers. On the other hand, children who attend public and private schools may model themselves after their peers. They may adopt unacceptable or inappropriate behaviors.

Unfortunately, reliable research on this matter is hard to obtain. Homeschooling advocates point out that those who school their children at home are often resentful of their taxes being used on a school system they do not use. Advocates theorize that homeschooling parents are likely to underreport information about homeschooling.

States have differing definitions and standards of accountability for homeschoolers resulting in a lack of consistent nationwide statistics. In Florida, families can homeschool but must directly report to their school district on an annual basis. One very popular method of avoiding these responsibilities is to enroll the student in a specially established "Cover School." The family has now legally enrolled their child in a private school and has no reporting requirements to the state. In California, there are "homeschool charter schools," which get funds from the state to take responsibility for the children's education. They enroll students and provide distance education that is usually done at home. These are just two examples of different types of homeschooling. With these complexities, it is difficult to gather reliable and accurate data on children schooled at home.

The two selections in this issue question whether the ultimate interest in children's education is the state or the parents. Rob Reich feels that the state needs its citizens to have a certain tolerance in order to make informed judgments. As such, he argues that children need to experience the hassles and rewards of social contact with others of differing viewpoints. On the other hand, Thomas Washburne feels that parents have the ultimate choice in their children's education. He points out that many parents do not feel that increased tolerance is necessarily a good thing and that the Constitution guarantees them the right to make educational decisions for their children.

As you read the following selections, think about the following questions: Do you agree with Reich's argument that children learn important civic lessons in school? Do you believe Washburne's claim that parents have the right to educate their children in whatever way they choose? Who has the greater interest, the state or the parents? Read the following selections and decide for yourself if children who are homeschooled have a limited view of society.

YES

Rob Reich

The Civic Perils of Homeschooling

Just 10 years ago, educating a child at home was illegal in several states. Today, not only is homeschooling legal everywhere, it's booming. Homeschooling is probably the fastest-growing segment of the education market, expanding at a rate of 15 to 20 percent a year (Lines, 2000a). More children are homeschooled than attend charter schools. More children are homeschooled than attend conservative Christian academies.

And it's not just left-wing unschoolers and right-wing religious fundamentalists who are keeping their children at home. Taking advantage of the Internet and other new technologies, more middle-of-the-road suburbanites are homeschooling, too. *Time* and *Newsweek* have featured homeschooling on their covers. The U.S. Congress passed a resolution in 1999 declaring the week of September 19 to be National Home Education Week. Homeschooling has gone mainstream.

In response to the rise of homeschooling, policymakers and public school administrators and teachers need to consider what makes homeschooling so popular. Chief among the many reasons to homeschool is the ability to customize a child's education at home.

Customizing Education at Home

The ability to custom-tailor an education for their children is often the motivation for parents to homeschool. No other education arrangement offers the same freedom to arrange an education designed for an individual student; in homeschools, parents are responsible not only for selecting what their children will learn, but when, how, and with whom they will learn. In this sense, homeschooling represents the apex of customization in education.

But is this customization always a good thing? From the standpoint of the parents who choose to homeschool, it surely is; they wouldn't be doing it otherwise, especially in light of the considerable energy and time it requires of them. But considered from the standpoint of democratic citizenship, the opportunity to customize education through homeschooling isn't an unadulterated good. Customizing education may permit schooling to be tailored for each individual student, but total customization also threatens to insulate students from exposure to diverse ideas and people and thereby to shield them from the vibrancy of a pluralistic democracy. These risks are perhaps greatest for homeschoolers. To understand why we need first to understand more about the current practice of homeschooling.

Homeschooling Today

Homeschooling is more than an education alternative. It is also a social movement (Stevens, 2001; Talbot, 2001). In 1985, approximately 50,000 children were being educated at home. In 2002, at least 1 million children are being homeschooled, with some estimates pegging the number at 2 million, an increase of 20- or 40-fold. (It's symptomatic of the unregulated environment of homeschooling that precise figures on the number of homeschoolers are impossible to establish.) Depending on the estimate you choose (Bielick, Chandler, & Broughman, 2001; Lines, 2000a), homeschoolers account for 2–4 percent of the school-going population.

Homeschooling parents are politically active. Former Pennsylvania Representative Bill Goodling, the former chair of the House Committee on Education and the Workforce, has called homeschoolers "the most effective education lobby on Capitol Hill" (as cited in Golden, 2000). Homeschoolers have established both local and national networks for lobbying purposes and for offering curricular support to one another. Several national organizations, led by the Home School Legal Defense Association, promote homeschooling. Even the former Secretary of Education, William Bennett, is a fan—he has created a for-profit company called K12, the purpose of which is to supply curricular and testing materials to homeschoolers.

But who homeschools, and why? Two main groups of homeschoolers have emerged, both of which raise difficult questions about customization.

The larger of the groups is the Christian right. Although homeschooling has become a much more diverse enterprise in the past 10 years, its strength as a social movement and the majority of its practitioners are conservative Christians. Precise data are scarce, but researchers tend to agree that whereas homeschools of the 1970s "reflected a liberal, humanistic, pedagogical orientation," the majority of homeschools in the 1980s and 1990s "became grounds of and for ideological, conservative, religious expressions of educational matters" (Carper, 2000, p. 16). Today, most parents choose to educate their children at home because they believe that their children's moral and spiritual needs will not be met in campus-based schools.

Those who educate their children at home for religious reasons often object to the secular bias of public schools. By keeping their children at home, they seek to provide a proper religious education free from the damning influences of secularism and pop culture. These homeschoolers wish to avoid the public school at all costs.

The second group practices a different kind of homeschooling. They seek partnerships with public schools to avail themselves of resources, support, guidance, and extracurricular activities that they could not otherwise obtain or provide at home. For these parents, some participation in public schools is desirable.

Various mechanisms have emerged to allow homeschooled students to connect on a partial basis with the public school system. In California, for example, approximately 10 percent of the charter schools serve students whose primary learning is at home (Lines, 2000b). Other districts have set up "virtual" academies online to aid in the enrollment of homeschoolers. Still other school districts permit students to attend some classes but not others and to participate in extracurricular activities (Rothstein, 2002). Finally, a few public school districts have set up homeschooling resource centers, staffed by public school teachers and professional curriculum developers, that home-schooling parents can use at their convenience.

Democratic Citizenship and Customization

Each kind of homeschooler—the family who teaches the child solely at home and the family who seeks some interaction with the public school system—is practicing customization in education. For the first, parents can tailor the education environment to their own convictions and to their beliefs about what their child's needs and interests are. For the second, parents can select the aspects of the public system they and their child want, creating an overall program designed for their child.

What's to worry about either kind of customization? Let me put the matter quite simply. Customizing a child's education through homeschooling represents the victory of a consumer mentality within education, suggesting that the only purpose that education should serve is to please and satisfy the preferences of the consumer. Education, in my view, is not a consumption item in the same sense as the food we select from the grocery store.

Many homeschoolers would surely protest here that their energetic efforts to overcome numerous obstacles to educate their children at home are motivated by a desire to shield their children from rampant consumerism and to offer their children a moral environment in which they learn deeper and more important values. No doubt this is true.

But my point is not that homeschooling parents are inculcating in their children a consumer mentality. My point is that many homeschooling parents view the education of their children as a matter properly under their control and no one else's. They feel entitled to "purchase" the education environment of their children from the marketplace of learning materials, with no intermediary between them and their child. The first kind of homeschooler actually does purchase learning materials for the home. The second kind of homeschooler treats the public school system as a provider of services and activities from which parents choose what they want, as if it were a restaurant with an extensive menu.

And this attitude is the crucial point. Homeschooling is the apogee of parental control over a child's education, where no other institution has a claim to influence the schooling of the child. Parents serve as the only filter for a child's education, the final arbiters of what gets included and what gets excluded.

This potentially compromises citizenship in the following ways:

- In a diverse, democratic society, part of able citizenship is to come to respect the fact that other people will have beliefs and convic-tions, religious and otherwise, that conflict with one's own. Yet from the standpoint of citizenship, these other people are equals. And students must learn not only that such people exist, but how to engage and deliberate with them in the public arena. Thus, students should encounter materials, ideas, and people that they or their parents have not chosen or selected in advance.

- Citizenship is the social glue that binds a diverse people together. To be a citizen is to share something in common with one's fellow citizens. As the legal scholar Sunstein (2001) has argued, a heterogeneous society without some shared experiences and common values has a difficult time addressing common problems and risks social fragmentation. Schooling is one of the few remaining social institutions—or civic intermediaries—in which people from all walks of life have a common interest and in which children might come to learn such common values as decency, civility, and respect.
- Part of being a citizen is exercising one's freedom. Indeed, the freedoms that U.S. citizens enjoy are a democratic inheritance that we too often take for granted. But to be free is not simply to be free from coercion or constraint. Democratic freedom requires the free construction and possible revision of beliefs and preferences. To become free, students must be exposed to the vibrant diversity of a democratic society so that they possess the liberty to live a life of their own design.

Because homeschooled students receive highly customized educations, designed usually to accord with the preferences of parents, they are least likely in principle to be exposed to materials, ideas, and people that have not been chosen in advance; they are least likely to share common education experiences with other children; and they are most likely to have a narrow horizon of experiences, which can curtail their freedom. Although highly customized education for students may produce satisfied parents as consumers, and even offer excellent academic training to the student, it is a loss from a civic perspective.

Civic Perils

I do not argue that homeschooling undermines citizenship in all cases. On the contrary, I have elsewhere defended the practice of homeschooling, when properly regulated (Reich, 2002). Many homeschooling parents are deeply committed to providing their children with an education that introduces them to a great diversity of ideas and people. And for those homeschoolers who seek partnerships with public schools, their children do participate in common institutions with other children. I do not intend to condemn homeschooling wholesale, for I have met many homeschooled students who are better prepared for democratic citizenship than the average public school student.

My claim is about the potential civic perils of a homeschooled education, where schooling is customizable down to the tiniest degree. Customization, and, therefore, homeschooling, seem wonderful if we think about education as a consumption item. But schooling, from the time that public schools were founded until today, has served to cultivate democratic citizenship. And though this may be a largely forgotten aim, as many have argued, we should not allow a new consumer mentality to become the driving metaphor for the education of children.

References

Bielick, S., Chandler, K., & Broughman, S. (2001, July 31). *Home schooling in the United States: 1999* (NCES 2001-033). Washington, DC: U.S. Department of Education.

Carper, J. C. (2000, April). Pluralism to establishment to dissent: The religious and educational context of home schooling. *Peabody Journal of Education, 75*(1,2), 8–19.

Golden, D. (2000, April 24). Homeschoolers learn how to gain clout inside the beltway. *Wall Street Journal,* p. Al.

Lines, P. (2000a, Summer). Home schooling comes of age. *Public Interest, 140,* 74–85.

Lines, P. (2000b, April). When homeschoolers go to school: A partnership between families and schools. *Peabody Journal of Education, 75*(1, 2), 159–186.

Reich, R. (2002). *Bridging liberalism and multiculturalism in American education.* Chicago: University of Chicago Press.

Rothstein, R. (2002, January 2). Augmenting a home-school education. *New York Times,* p. B11.

Stevens, M. (2001). *Kingdom of children: Culture and controversy in the homeschooling movement.* Princeton, NJ: Princeton University Press.

Sunstein, C. (2001). *Republic.com.* Princeton, NJ: Princeton University Press.

Talbot, M. (2001, November). The new counterculture. *Atlantic Monthly, 288*(4), 136–143.

Thomas W. Washburne, J.D.

 NO

The Boundaries of Parental Authority: A Response to Rob Reich of Stanford University

From August 30 to September 2, 2001, the American Political Science Association held its annual meeting in San Francisco, California. Rob Reich, of the Department of Political Science at Stanford University, presented a paper at this meeting which has captured the attention of many home schooling families, including members of the Home School Legal Defense Association (HSLDA). Several members of HSLDA have asked for our opinion of this paper. This report has been prepared to satisfy these inquiries. It is not intended to be a point by point refutation of the paper, but is rather a brief examination of the major themes explored, and some of HSLDA's major criticisms and concerns. Reich's position should not be taken lightly. It is illustrative of many of the challenges home educators are facing as their numbers increase. Moreover, if Reich's views were adopted by the courts, home education as we know it today would simply cease to legally exist.

Mr. Reich's paper was entitled *Testing the Boundaries of Parental Authority Over Education: The Case of Homeschooling*. The paper is a precursor to a book by Reich to be entitled *Bridging Liberalism and Multiculturalism in Education*, which the University of Chicago Press is anticipated to publish in 2002. In his paper, Reich traces the rise of home education, the interests in education held by the government, the parent, and the child, and sets forth his suggestions for balancing these interests. These suggestions lead Reich to conclude that "while the state should not ban homeschooling it must nevertheless regulate its practice with vigilance." He then briefly offers a few suggestions for how a state should regulate home education, and some of the difficulties the state may encounter.

Reich's proposed regulations include "periodic assessments that would measure their success in examining and reflecting upon diverse worldviews." These regulations are in furtherance of Reich's view that:

> Children are owed as a matter of justice the capacity to choose to lead lives—adopt values and beliefs, pursue an occupation, endorse new traditions—that are different from those of their parents. Because the child cannot him or herself ensure the acquisition of such capacities

and the parents may be opposed to such acquisition, the state must ensure it for them. The state must guarantee that children are educated for minimal autonomy.

A brief review of the constitutional basis for home education will lead one to quickly understand the serious implications of Reich's theories. It has long been recognized by Americans, legal scholars, and the Supreme Court that the original intent of the drafters of the Constitution of the United States was to protect many rights which are not expressly set forth in the founding documents. It has also long been held by Americans and the Supreme Court, and rightfully so, that the right of parents to direct the upbringing of their children is a fundamental right. In fact, this basic understanding of the role of parents long predates the founding of the United States.

Nevertheless, no right is absolute. In that regard, the American legal system has created a method by which the limits of fundamental rights are tested. It is said by the Courts examining constitutional challenges to government law and regulation that the fundamental right at issue may not be infringed upon unless the government can show a compelling interest in doing so, and, if there is such an interest, it then infringes in the least restrictive manner. In such cases, the court must balance the "interests" of the state against the "interests" of the individual asserting a right. For example, in the case of the First Amendment right to free speech, the government has a compelling interest to maintain public safety and order and can therefore prohibit the wrongful shouting of "fire" in a crowded theatre, even though this infringes a person's right to free speech.

As noted before, the regulation of home education by the government is limited by the fact that parents have a fundamental right to direct the upbringing of their children which is protected by the Constitution. Accordingly, unless the state can show some compelling interest in regulating the parent's involvement in education, the parent's views are heeded. So, it becomes critical to understand what the state's interest in education is.

Fortunately for home schoolers, this issue was addressed decades ago, and reaffirmed on occasion since. It is well understood from a legal perspective that the government's *compelling* interest in education is limited. It has been held numerous times that the government's interest in education is basically only of two varieties: civic and economic. The first involves the government's interest in seeing that a child is prepared for citizenship. In other words, will he have capability to vote? The economic interest addresses the state's desire to see that citizens will be able to provide for themselves and not become a burden. So, for example, when a state attempts to impose a requirement that all home educators have teaching degrees, the state must show that this requirement is essential in achieving its interest in education—that is, good citizenship, economic success, etc. To rebut the government, the home educator merely needs to show that home educators without teaching degrees are raising children who are competent, functional. Such a showing renders the government's proposed regulation as unnecessary to achieve the government's compelling interest.

There has been considerable debate about whether the government's interest in education should be extended. So far, thankfully, the courts have been reluctant to do so. Not even the most liberal of judges have taken the initiative to override centuries of respect for the institution of the family and the parental interest in raising children.

It is at this point that we can begin to see the implications, indeed danger, of Reich's ideas for home education. For Reich, while recognizing that there can be debate on the topic, essentially concedes that the state's interest in education does not lend itself to regulating home education. It is not Reich's contention that parental rights should be overridden because the state's compelling interest in education is not being fulfilled. Reich rather sets forth the argument that children have their own interests in education, which are different from both the parent's and the state's. It is this interest, the child's, which in Reich's view justifies limiting parental rights.

Reich sees the interest of the child as being twofold. First, "a child has an interest in education because education is necessary to developing into an adult capable of independent functioning." While setting forth this interest, it appears that Reich sees it as largely duplicating what are already addressed by the state and parental interests in education. Reich does "not mean to imply anything potentially controversial about independent functioning." It is in the second interest of children in education, as seen by Reich, that the controversy is made clear.

For Reich, children have a fundamental interest in "becoming autonomous." This refers "to the capacity of the child to develop into an independent adult who can seek and promote his or her own interests, as he or she understands them, and who can participate, if he or she chooses, in political dialog with others." This interest comes from his perception that children should be shielded from "an unquestioning subordination of one's own will to the ethical ideals of another person or persons." In Reich's view, "Neither parents nor the state can justly attempt to imprint indelibly upon a child a set of values and beliefs, as if it were an inheritance one should never be able to question, as if the child must always defer and be obedient. To do so would in effect render the child servile."

The insertion of the supposed interest of children to be autonomous into the balancing of parental and state interests leads to interesting conclusions. Reich provides the following:

> I submit that even in a minimal construal of autonomy, it must be the function of the school setting to expose children to and engage children with values and beliefs other than those of their parents. [citation omitted] To achieve minimal autonomy requires that a child know that there are ways of life other than that into which he or she has been born. Minimal autonomy requires, especially for its civic importance, that a child be able to examine his or her own political values and beliefs, and those of others, with a critical eye. It requires that the child be able to think independently. If this is all true, then, at a bare minimum, the structure of schooling cannot simply replicate in every particularity the values and beliefs of a child's home.

To ensure the children's interest, "[t]he state must therefore ensure that all children, regardless of the environment in which they are schooled, receive an education that exposes them to and engages them with values and beliefs other than those they find at home." Moreover, "[b]ecause children are a politically inert group, regulations in their interest must be defended by other organizations, such as the Children's Defense Fund, which typically have less at stake in home schooling, or by state officials, who are of course responsible for a much broader children's agenda than guarding against home schooling abuses."

At first glance, Reich's arguments appear persuasive. We cannot deny that children have significant rights which the state protects. For instance, children may not be abused, neglected, or abandoned. In fact, the entire juvenile justice system is predicated on the fact that children have unique interests, that children have special concerns. All of this begs the question, "why don't children have an interest in education?" And if they do, could Reich be right? As Reich points out, children are not the property of their parents to do with whatever they desire.

But the subject is more complex than what Reich is setting forth. First and foremost, children are not adults. Children are people, yet children, by their very nature, are in a class of their own. When children are involved, society, and the law, duly note their special status. Accordingly, some human rights are afforded children, and some are not. Generally, this reflects the fact that children cannot fend for themselves and lack the capacity to form certain judgments. In examining what rights children enjoy, and what rights they do not, a helpful distinction may be drawn between rights of children to protection and rights of children to choice.

Rights of protection involve the right to life, freedom from bodily harm, etc. All people, by being people, are entitled to some liberty in their person. Children are no exception. In children, rights of protection take the form of protection from abuse, abandonment, etc.

Rights of choice are legal rights that permit persons to make "affirmative choices of binding consequence. Rights of choice includes such rights as voting, marrying, exercising religious preference, and choosing whether to seek education." These rights, however, are not extended to all. Our law has always recognized that to exercise these rights, a person must have capacity. This is why contracts with children are unenforceable. This is why children may not vote, or marry without permission. These are adult rights and children are not adults. It is in the consideration of rights of choice that Reich's arguments begin to lose their persuasion.

Consider a child's right to autonomy as posited by Reich. Can it really be said that children are owed, "as a matter of justice," the capacity to lead lives different than their parents? Most parents would quickly concur that children do not have, nor should they have, the right to dictate when they go to bed, what they watch on television, what magazines they read, whether they do their chores, or whether they obey their parents. To recognize a child's right to choice would lead to the child's doom. Yes, the law protects children. But the law cannot change children into adults simply by giving them the choices of adults. The law cannot give them something which, being children, they do not have by nature the ability to exercise.

The right to autonomy, to view the world as you want to, is only properly enjoyed by adults. While prudent parenting includes efforts to inform and help children understand the world about them, responsible parenting also demands that children be taught right from wrong, in a word—truth.

A major problem Reich's theory does not directly address is that all teaching has at its base a worldview, a philosophy of life. Even so-called neutrality betrays an underlying worldview of relativism. Accordingly, by definition, reality, or whatever label one puts on it, every child is being taught a worldview by someone. There really is no such thing as neutrality in education. Putting it in Reich's language, even if a child had a right to autonomy in education, it could never be exercised. The state, in enforcing the child's interest, will by necessity become an advocate of some worldview. While there might be some danger in allowing parents to convey worldviews to children, history will attest that having the state indoctrinate children has much larger consequences.

Granting choice rights to children, and having the state enforce them, is especially problematic for worldviews arising out of religion. Many religions, and especially Christianity, necessitate the teaching of truth. Not, "This is my truth," but "True truth." There is no room for relativism. There is no way that the child can be merely exposed to all worldviews. While Christian parenting can involve exposure to other worldviews, Christian parenting cannot allow for a neutral presentation. Christian parents cannot say to the child: "This is true for me, it may not be true for you." The best Christian parents can do is say, "This is true, and you must come to terms with your response to this truth."

In at least one way, Reich anticipates this objection. He notes that:

> [T]he problem arises when the secular state authority is exercised over the rearing of children. Conflict between the state and religious parents on this score may be endemic and inevitable. On my view, even given the deep importance of religious freedom, the state cannot relinquish its regulatory role in education in cases where parents invoke their religious beliefs as a bulwark against secular authority.

One of the reasons why home education has exploded as a movement is that the public schools no longer teach truth as truth. The court has so hemmed in the role of public education that secular humanism and relativism have become the only underlying philosophies that survive constitutional scrutiny. To a certain degree, Reich's ideas have met with success, as evidenced by the number of children in public education. While this is acceptable to many Americans, and in particular the so-called intellectual elite, it is simply unacceptable to many others.

We must ask ourselves at this point, "why is Reich so afraid of home education?" We are a small segment of society. If we are really afraid that children are suffering from a lack of autonomy in education, why not focus upon the much larger populations of children who really will suffer a lack of autonomy, even as adults. By any definition, children who grow up illiterate, unable to do basic math, and lack even the capacity as adults to exercise choice rights are far less autonomous than home educated children who have received an education based on the world view of their parents. Home schoolers represent little more than 2% of school aged students. Why focus on them? If it is children we care about, we should focus on those kids who are not being given even the most rudimentary of education in America's failing public schools. If Reich really cares, perhaps he should initially focus on those children trapped in educational failure.

The real root of the problem home education presents to Reich is that home educators have removed themselves from America's educational system and its underlying values. Their children are beyond the reach of the elite and the predominate worldview of relativism or secular humanism. As home schooling continues to grow and prosper, this will become increasingly troublesome to the educational establishment. But more than being beyond the intellectual elite, the children of home educators are largely beyond the reach of the state. It will take novel legal theories to break this constitutional protection. And it is here that Reich's theories are most concerning, indeed dangerous.

What Reich is doing, intentional or not, is setting an academic framework by which an activist judge might rule in favor of heavy restrictions on home education, while at the same time avoiding the obvious assault on precedent and the Constitution. By extending what are in essence adult rights of choice to children, and declaring children to have an interest in education separate from the state's and separate from their parent's, Reich provides the opportunity to take away freedoms which Americans, indeed humans in general, have deemed fundamental for thousands of years.

EXPLORING THE ISSUE

Do Children Who Are Homeschooled Have a Limited View of Society?

Critical Thinking and Reflection

1. What does Reich claim are the potential civic perils of education? Do you believe these are as great a threat as he proposes? Why or why not?
2. Do you believe homeschooling is a good idea or a bad one? Give three reasons for your answer from the readings.
3. What are the limits on regulation of education by the government? Do you think these are a good thing? Why or why not?
4. Explain the difference between the government's civic and economic interests in education.

Is There Common Ground?

Do children who are homeschooled have a limited view of society? Who has the greater claim on education, the state or the parents? Is a tolerant population the best thing for the state? Do you agree that it is a good thing for children to be exposed to a range of ideas? Do you agree that parents have the right and the duty to educate their children as they see fit? With an ever-increasing homeschooling population, society will continue to face this issue. The challenge is answering these questions while taking the best interest of students into consideration. It is obvious that a one-size-fits-all approach to education is not the best way to go; therefore, finding some middle ground is very important in this debate.

Additional Resources

About.com Homeschooling. Retrieved on April 13, 2011, from http://homeschooling.about.com/cs/supportgroups/a/hsingusa.htm.

This Web site provides legal information, organizations, support groups, community events, and online resources about homeschooling for each state.

A to Z Homeschool Curriculum, Laws, Programs, Social Networks. Retrieved on April 13, 2011, from http://homeschooling.gomilpitas.com/.

This Web site is a comprehensive guide to curriculum, laws, and so forth for homeschooling.

Homeschool Central. Retrieved on April 13, 2011, from http://www.homeschoolcentral.com/.

This Web site provides resources for families who homeschool their children.

Public Schools vs. Home Schools. Retrieved on April 13, 2011, from http://www.allaboutparenting.org/public-schools-vs-home-school-faq.htm.

This Web site discusses the pros and cons of homeschooling versus public school.

ISSUE 11

Is Television Viewing Responsible for the Rise in Childhood Obesity?

YES: The Henry J. Kaiser Family Foundation, from "The Role of Media in Childhood Obesity," *Issue Brief—The Henry J. Kaiser Foundation* (February 2004)

NO: Center for Science in the Public Interest, from "Dispensing Junk: How School Vending Undermines Efforts to Feed Children Well," *Report from Center for Science in the Public Interest* (May 2004)

Learning Outcomes

After reading this issue, you should be able to:

- Summarize each author's stance on the reasons for the increase in childhood obesity.
- Decide which of the author's positions you feel is the largest contributor to the increase in childhood obesity and give supporting reasons for your answer.
- Demonstrate an understanding of food items that are identified as unhealthy and contributing to obesity in children as well as the types of ads that are believed to influence unhealthy eating habits.

ISSUE SUMMARY

YES: The Henry J. Kaiser Family Foundation, a private nonprofit foundation focusing on major health care issues facing the nation, cites research studies that show that the more children watch television, the more likely they will be overweight. They also contend that the rise in childhood obesity can be traced to the increased use of media.

NO: The Center for Science in the Public Interest, a consumer advocacy organization on nutrition and health, views the high-calorie, non-nutritious foods found in school vending machines as the culprit in the rise in childhood obesity rates.

The rise in childhood obesity is considered an epidemic because the rates of childhood overweight have grown so rapidly in such a short amount of time. According to the Centers for Disease Control and Prevention, National Center for Health Statistics, since 1980 the proportion of overweight children has more than doubled. The rate for teens has tripled since 1980. Currently, 10 percent of 2- to 5-year-olds are overweight, and 15 percent of 6- to 19-year-olds are overweight. The numbers go up to 20 percent for 2- to 5-year-old children, and 30 percent for 6- to 19-year-old children when you add in those at risk for being overweight. Children of color are at greater risk with 4 out of 10 Mexican-American and African-American children being overweight. Recently, the problem has gained renewed interest as Michelle Obama has become an advocate for prevention strategies to curb the rates of obesity in children.

Childhood obesity is the term used to describe the problem in the population while individual children are generally referred to as being overweight. Overweight and at risk for being overweight are terms used to define children whose height and weight fall within a certain range on a chart referred to as the BMI (body mass index). The BMI measures the ratio of weight to height. BMI measures for children are age- and gender-specific because children's body fat varies with age and gender. A child's BMI is plotted on a growth curve that reflects that child's age and gender. This plotting yields a value, BMI for age, that provides a consistent measure across age groups. Percentile scores indicate how a particular child compares with other children of the same age and gender. The Centers for Disease Control classifies children above the 95th percentile for their age and gender as overweight. Children are considered at risk for being overweight if they fall between the 85th and 95th percentile for age and gender. Healthy children have a BMI of 6 to 85 percent, and underweight children have a BMI of less than 5 percent.

Why is the rise in childhood obesity considered such a problem? Along with being overweight comes a host of physical and mental health problems such as diabetes, high blood pressure, depression, and poor body image. The health care costs for these medical conditions are exorbitant, not to mention the reduced quality of life for the children. The probability that overweight children will become overweight adults is 50 percent; thus, these health care issues may follow the child into adulthood. The subsequent reduced productivity levels of adults, whose overweight condition follows them into adulthood, have economic and social implications. Instead of contributing to society and the economy, individuals may be relying on these institutions to take care of them.

A review of the extensive literature that has been emerging on childhood obesity shows there are a multitude of reasons cited for the epidemic. Almost every American institution has been blamed as being responsible for the increase in children's weight. Grocery stores, schools, communities, families, restaurants, fast food, media, and the economy have had a role in making children overweight. Specifically, grocery stores are accused of stocking high-fat, high-calorie foods; the cost of healthy foods such as fruits and milk are more than processed snack foods and sodas. Schools house vending machines full of foods with little nutritive value and loads of calories; often school officials hesitate to get rid of the offending machines because they depend on them for revenue to purchase needed school supplies. There has been a reduction in the amount of hours and level of intensity of physical education classes in the schools, thus children do not get a chance to burn off calories in school the way they have in the past.

Other institutions have encouraged overeating while discouraging physical activity. Communities and neighborhoods do not lend themselves to exercise with few sidewalks for walking and few parks in which to play. Children do not feel safe enough in their neighborhoods to go out and play after school. Full-service restaurants and fast food venues have super sized their portions and encourage people to overeat. Buffets lure people to overeat by offering "all you can eat" for a lower price than a nutritious meal with vegetables and reasonable portions.

The work/family dilemma of too little time shows up in family schedules that are hectic and leave little time for family meals together. Eating together as a family has been associated with reducing child weight. Parents may be contributing to childhood obesity by providing too much and the wrong type of food as well as not encouraging more physical activity of their children or themselves.

There is an overwhelming amount of media available to encourage sedentary behavior. Watching television, surfing the Web, and playing video games create an environment that discourages physical activity. Interestingly enough, research studies show that when children reduce time watching TV, physical exercise time does not necessarily increase; the children may replace this TV time with other sedentary activities like reading, talking on the phone, or playing board games.

Although there are many factors that contribute to childhood obesity, will the concern for reducing childhood weight turn into an obsession with weight and lead to other types of problems? Already, there is a concern among educators that more eating disorders such as anorexia or bulimia will emerge. In addition, there may be more of a tendency for overweight children to be discriminated against and develop a poor body image, which can ultimately lead to mental illness and depression. In the YES selection, personnel from The Henry J. Kaiser Family Foundation propose that the rise in childhood obesity is due to the influence of the media, specifically the huge numbers of hours of television that children watch. In the NO selection, personnel from the Center for Science in the Public Interest assert that the high-calorie, low-nutrient food found in school vending machines encourages children to develop poor eating habits and leads to their being overweight.

YES

The Henry J. Kaiser
Family Foundation

The Role of Media in Childhood Obesity

Introduction

In recent years, health officials have become increasingly alarmed by the rapid increase in obesity among American children. According to the Centers for Disease Control and Prevention (CDC), since 1980 the proportion of over-weight children ages 6–11 has more than doubled, and the rate for adolescents has tripled. Today about 10% of 2- to 5-year-olds and 15% of 6- to 19-year-olds are overweight. Taking into consideration the proportion who are "at risk" of being overweight, the current percentages double to 20% for children ages 2–5 and 30% for kids ages 6–19. Among children of color, the rates are even higher: 4 in 10 Mexican American and African American youth ages 6–19 are considered overweight or at risk of being overweight.

According to the American Academy of Pediatrics, the increase in child-hood obesity represents an "unprecedented burden" on children's health. Medical complications common in overweight children include hypertension, type 2 diabetes, respiratory ailments, orthopedic problems, trouble sleeping, and depression. The Surgeon General has predicted that preventable morbidity and mortality associated with obesity may exceed those associated with cigarette smoking. Given that an estimated 80% of overweight adolescents continue to be obese in adulthood, the implications of childhood obesity on the nation's health—and on health care costs—are huge. Indeed, the American Academy of Pediatrics has called the potential costs associated with childhood obesity "staggering."

In an effort to seek the causes of this disturbing trend, experts have pointed to a range of important potential contributors to the rise in childhood obesity that are unrelated to media: a reduction in physical education classes and after-school athletic programs, an increase in the availability of sodas and snacks in public schools, the growth in the number of fast-food outlets across the country, the trend toward "super-sizing" food portions in restaurants, and the increasing number of highly processed high-calorie and high-fat grocery products.

The purpose of this issue brief is to explore one other potential contributor to the rising rates of childhood obesity: children's use of media.

During the same period in which childhood obesity has increased so dramatically, there has also been an explosion in media targeted to children: TV shows and videos, specialized cable networks, video games, computer activities and Internet Web sites. Children today spend an average of five-and-a-half hours a day using media, the equivalent of a full time job, and more time than they spend doing anything else besides sleeping. Even the very youngest children, preschoolers ages six and under, spend as much time with screen media (TV, videos, video games and computers) as they do playing outside. Much of the media targeted to children is laden with elaborate advertising campaigns, many of which promote foods such as candy, soda, and snacks. Indeed, it is estimated that the typical child sees about 40,000 ads a year on TV alone.

For the first time, this report pulls together the best available research, going behind the headlines to explore the realities of what researchers do and do not know about the role media plays in childhood obesity. In addition, the report lays out media-related policy options that have been proposed to help address childhood obesity, and outlines ways media could play a positive role in helping to address this important public health problem.

Pediatricians, child development experts, and media researchers have theorized that media may contribute to childhood obesity in one or more of the following ways:

- The time children spend using media displaces time they could spend in physical activities;
- The food advertisements children are exposed to on TV influence them to make unhealthy food choices;
- The cross-promotions between food products and popular TV and movie characters are encouraging children to buy and eat more high-calorie foods;
- Children snack excessively while using media, and they eat less healthy meals when eating in front of the TV;
- Watching TV and videos lowers children's metabolic rates below what they would be even if they were sleeping;
- Depictions of nutrition and body weight in entertainment media encourage children to develop less healthy diets.

The research to date has examined these issues from a variety of perspectives ranging from health sciences and public health, to child development and family relations, to advertising and mass communications. These investigations have been methodologically diverse, and the results have often been mixed. As with any research, caution must be used when comparing the outcomes of studies because of variations in the methods and measures used. For example, some studies are regional, while others use large, nationally representative samples. Some focus on specific demographic subsets, such as 6th-grade girls, while others are broader. Some studies rely on detailed data sets, others on fairly simplistic measures. For example, television use may be measured through self-reports, parental reports, or detailed diaries. Likewise, body fat may be assessed through multiple clinical measures or by self-reports of height and weight.

DEFINING CHILDHOOD OBESITY

The phrases "obese," "overweight," and "at risk for being overweight" are commonly used in the public health community. With regard to children, the terms "obese" and "overweight" are generally used interchangeably in the medical literature. The Body Mass Index (BMI), which measures the ratio of weight to height, is a standard tool used to define these terms. BMI definitions for children and adolescents are age- and gender-specific in order to accommodate growth patterns. The Centers for Disease Control and Prevention (CDC) classify children as "overweight" if they are above the 95th percentile for their age and sex, and "at risk of being overweight" if they are between the 85th and 95th percentile.

The following section of this report reviews the major research that has been conducted on the key issues concerning media and childhood obesity, and summarizes the major findings.

Research on Media and Childhood Obesity

Do major studies find a relationship between childhood obesity and the time children spend using media?   The first major evidence that children's media consumption may be related to their body weight came in a 1985 article by William Dietz and Stephen Gortmaker in the journal *Pediatrics,* and it was dramatic. An analysis of data from a large national study of more than 13,000 children, the National Health Examination Survey (NHES), found significant associations between the amount of time children spent watching television and the prevalence of obesity. The authors concluded that, among 12- to 17-year-olds, the prevalence of obesity increased by 2% for each additional hour of television viewed, even after controlling for other variables such as prior obesity, race, and socio-economic status. Indeed, according to the authors, "only prior obesity had a larger independent effect than television on the prevalence of obesity." In a commentary published in 1993, the authors went on to note that another interpretation of their findings is that "29% of the cases of obesity could be prevented by reducing television viewing to 0 to 1 hours per week."

Since then, several more studies have found a statistically significant relationship between media use and rates of obesity, while others have found either a weak relationship or no relationship at all. In addition to the Dietz and Gortmaker study, other large-scale national studies have found a correlation between media use and body weight:

- Analysis of data from a nationally representative survey of more than 700 kids ages 10–15, conducted in the late 1980s, concluded that "the odds of being overweight were 4.6 times greater for youth watching more than 5 hours of television per day compared with those watching for 0–1 hours," even when controlling for prior overweight, maternal overweight, race, and socio-economic status. The authors concluded, "Estimates of attributable risk indicate that more [than] 60% of overweight incidence in this population can be linked to excess television viewing time."

- Data from the 1988–1994 waves of the National Health and Nutrition Examination Surveys (NHANES) were analyzed to explore the relationship between TV watching and obesity among 8- to 16-year-olds. The study concluded that "television watching was positively associated with obesity among girls, even after controlling for age, race/ethnicity, family income, weekly physical activity, and energy intake." The study did not find a correlation for boys.

- Another analysis of the 1988–1994 NHANES data found that among 8- to 16-year-olds, both boys and girls "who watched the most television had more body fat and greater BMIs than those who watched less than 2 hours a day."

- A study based on the CDC's 1999 Youth Risk Behavior Survey which sampled more than 12,000 high school students nationwide, found that watching television more than 2 hours a day was related to being overweight; these findings were consistent for the entire student population, controlling for race, ethnicity, and gender.

- A later study found a link between television viewing and obesity using a different methodology. The Framingham Children's Study was a longitudinal study in which slightly more than 100 children were enrolled as preschoolers and followed into early adolescence. In this study, published in 2003, the authors found that "television watching was an independent predictor of the change in the child's BMI" and other measures of body fatness. They noted that the effect of TV viewing was "only slightly attenuated" by controlling for factors such as the child's body-fat measures at the time they were enrolled in the study, and their parents' BMI or education. The authors concluded that "television watching is a risk factor for change in body fat, not simply reflective of more obese children tending to watch more television as a consequence of their obesity making it difficult to exercise."

Other studies—one from a nationally representative cross-sectional sample and the others from specific regions or communities—have not found a relationship between television viewing and childhood obesity:

- A recent analysis of data from a national study of more than 2,800 children ages 12 and under, which relied on detailed time-use diaries, found a "striking" lack of relationship between time spent watching television and children's weight status. On the other hand, this study did find a relationship between obesity and time spent playing video games, although that relationship was not linear: Children with higher weight played moderate amounts of games, while those with low weight played electronic games either very little or a lot.

- A 1993 study of 6th- and 7th-grade girls in Northern California found that over a two-year period "baseline hours of after-school television viewing was not significantly associated with either baseline or longitudinal change in BMI." The authors argued that their study "refutes previous suggestions that . . . television viewing is causally related to obesity."
- A study of nearly 200 preschoolers in Texas observed the children for several hours on each of four different days a year, over the course of three years, recording the amount of TV the children watched and their physical activities. This study found that although television watching was weakly negatively correlated with physical activity levels, it was not associated with body composition.

In evaluating this research, it is important to note that some of these studies are cross-sectional rather than longitudinal—that is, they take a specific point in time and look at whether TV viewing is associated with obesity. One problem with this approach is that while a study may indicate a relationship between TV viewing and being overweight, it does not prove that the TV viewing *caused* the increased weight. Controlling for other risk factors such as socio-economic status and parental body weight (as many studies do) can help clarify the results. Another problem with the cross-sectional approach is that the causal relationship could run in the opposite direction: that is, being obese may cause children to engage in more sedentary (and isolated) activities, including watching more television.

Longitudinal studies can help address the causality issue; however, the results of these studies have varied. As noted above, the two-year longitudinal study of adolescent girls in Northern California did not find a causal relationship between children's weight and the time they spent with media. On the other hand, the Framingham Children's Study, which tracked preschoolers through early adolescence, did find such a relationship. The authors of the latter study have theorized that the effects of media use on body weight may emerge slowly over time, and hence were not revealed in the two-year study in Northern California. It has also been argued that the lack of effect in that study may be due to factors specific to the sample of 6th- and 7th-grade girls in Northern California. Additionally, the study of 700 10- to 15-year-olds referenced above used height and weight data from 1986 and compared it to TV viewing and BMI measures in 1990. These authors concluded that "no evidence was found for a selective effect of overweight; i.e., children who were overweight in 1986 were unlikely to watch more television in 1990 than were children who were not overweight."

Others argue that the only way to truly demonstrate a causal relationship is through an experimental trial; for example, reduce TV viewing and see whether that affects children's weight when compared to a control group. Several interventions of this nature have been found to have a positive impact in reducing children's body weight.

Do experimental interventions that reduce children's media time result in weight loss? Experimental trials are considered the best way of determining whether there is a causal relationship between television viewing and childhood obesity. Some experiments have incorporated reductions in media time as part of a more comprehensive program involving diet and increased physical activity as well. Another experiment used reduced media time as the only intervention, yet still found an impact on children's weight and body fatness.

- During the 1996–97 school year, Stanford University researchers conducted a randomized controlled trial in which they reduced the amount of time a group of about 100 3rd- and 4th-graders in Northern California spent with TV, videos, and video games. Two matched elementary schools were selected to participate, one of which served as the control group. The intervention involved a "turnoff" period of no screen time for 10 days followed by limiting TV time to 7 hours per week, as well as learning media literacy skills to teach selective viewing. At the end of a 6-month, 18-lesson classroom curriculum, students who received the intervention achieved statistically significant reductions in their television viewing and meals eaten in front of the TV set, as well as decreases in BMI, triceps skinfold thickness, waist circumference, and waist-to-hip ratio. While these changes were not accompanied by reduced high-fat food intake or increased physical activity, the findings do appear to demonstrate the feasibility of decreasing body weight by reducing time spent with screen media.
- Another school based intervention found improved diet, increased physical activity, and decreased television time to be effective. The study, which measured prevalence, incidence, and remission of obesity among ethnically diverse middle-school boys and girls, involved a randomized controlled field trial with five intervention and five control schools. Classroom teachers in math, science, language arts, social studies, and physical education incorporated lessons within the existing curricula over two years. The lessons focused on decreasing television viewing to 2 hours per day, increasing physical activity, reducing consumption of high-fat food, and increasing servings of fruits and vegetables. For each hour television viewing was reduced, the prevalence of obesity was reduced among girls in the intervention schools compared with the control schools; no similar effect was found for boys. The program also resulted in an increase in girls' consumption of fruits and vegetables.
- A family-based weight-control program found that decreasing sedentary behaviors (such as screen media use) is a viable alternative to increasing physical activity in treating childhood obesity. Families with obese children ages 8–12 were randomly assigned to one of four groups that included dietary and behavior-change information, but differed in whether they tried to decrease sedentary activities or increase physical activity. Results indicated that significant decreases in percent of overweight and body fat were associated with decreasing sedentary behaviors such as watching TV or videos, or playing video or computer games.

These interventions indicate that reducing the time children spend with media may indeed be an effective way to address childhood obesity. Researchers, health professionals, and advocates have theorized several ways media may contribute to childhood obesity. The following sections summarize some of the major scientific studies in order to provide an understanding of media's potential influence on the incidence of overweight among children and adolescents in the United States.

Does the time children spend using media displace time spent in more physical activities?   From toddlers to teens, American youth are spending a substantial part of every day of their lives using media. But the time children spend using media does not necessarily mean a decrease in time spent in physical activities. Surprisingly, few studies have examined this relationship, and results have been mixed. Some studies have found a weak but statistically significant relationship between hours of television viewing and levels of physical activity, while others have found no relationship between the two.

- A study of 6th- and 7th-grade adolescent girls in four Northern California middle schools found that the number of hours they spent watching TV after school was negatively associated with their level of physical activity; however, the relationship accounted for less than 1% of the variance and there was no connection with body weight.
- A study of a small sample of preschool children in Texas, conducted in a naturalistic setting, found a weak but statistically significant relationship between TV viewing and physical activity, although it did not find a relationship between viewing and body weight.
- A recent national telephone survey of parents of children ages 4–6 found that children who spent more than two hours watching TV the previous day spent an average of a half-hour less playing outside that day than did other children their age.
- A review of data from the 1999 National Youth Risk Behavior Study, which includes a nationally representative sample of more than 15,000 high school students, found that among white female students only, time spent watching TV was associated with being sedentary.
- A survey of close to 2,000 9th-graders in Northern California found a weak but statistically significant relationship between TV viewing and physical activity for white males only.
- A study of national data from the 1988–1994 NHANES found no relationship between TV viewing and the number of bouts of vigorous physical activity, although it did find a statistically significant relationship between TV viewing and body weight.

While logic suggests that extensive television viewing is part of a more sedentary lifestyle, the evidence for this relationship has been surprisingly weak to date. In order for this relationship to be true, as one study noted, children who watch less TV would have to be choosing physically vigorous activities instead of TV, rather than some other relatively sedentary pastime such as reading books, talking on the phone, or playing board games.

Another possibility is that the act of watching TV itself actually reduces children's metabolic rate, contributing to weight gain. One study of 8- to 12-year-olds found that TV viewing decreased metabolic rates even more than resting or sleeping, but several other studies found no such effect.

The fact that most studies have failed to find a substantial relationship between the time children spend watching TV and the time they spend in physical activity may suggest that the *nature* of television viewing—that is, how children watch and what they watch—may be as or more important than the number of hours they watch.

Do the food ads children are exposed to on TV influence them to make unhealthy food choices?   Many researchers suspect that the food advertising children are exposed to through the media may contribute to unhealthy food choices and weight gain. Over the same period in which childhood obesity has increased so dramatically, research indicates that the number of ads children view has increased as well. In the late 1970s, researchers estimated that children viewed an average of about 20,000 TV commercials a year; in the late 80s, that estimate grew to more than 30,000 a year. As the number of cable channels exploded in the 1990s, opportunities to advertise directly to children expanded as well. The most recent estimates are that children now see an average of more than 40,000 TV ads a year.

The majority of ads targeted to children are for food: primarily candy (32% of all children's ads), cereal (31%), and fast food (9%). One study documented approximately 11 food commercials per hour during children's Saturday morning television programming, estimating that the average child viewer may be exposed to one food commercial every 5 minutes. According to another study, even the two minutes of daily advertising targeted to students in their classrooms through Channel One expose them to fast foods, candy, soft drinks, and snack chips in 7 out of 10 commercial breaks.

A review of the foods targeted to children in commercials on Saturday morning television indicates that the nutritional value has remained consistently low over the past quarter-century. Over the years, the most prevalent foods advertised have been breakfast cereals. Up until the 1990s, the next most-advertised products were foods high in sugar, such as cookies, candy, and other snacks. By the mid-1990s, canned desserts, frozen dinners, and fast foods overtook ads for snack foods. The data indicate that ads for these high-fat and high-sodium convenience foods have more than doubled since the 1980s. While studies vary as to the exact percentages, the same pattern emerges: a predominance of ads for high-sugar cereals, fast food restaurants, and candy, and an absence of ads for fruit or vegetables.

The effect of food advertising on children   The vast majority of the studies about children's consumer behavior have been conducted by marketing research firms and have not been made publicly available. Clearly, the conclusion advertisers have drawn is that TV ads can influence children's purchases—and those of their families. Fast food outlets alone spend $3 billion in television ads targeted to children. Recent years have seen the development of marketing firms, newsletters, and ad agencies specializing in the children's market. The New York Times has noted that "the courtship of children is no surprise, since increasingly that is where the money is," and added that marketing executives anticipate that children under 12 will spend $35 billion of their own money and influence $200 billion in household spending in 2004. The enthusiasm of marketers can be felt in the Februray 2004 edition of Harris Interactive's "Trends and Tudes" newsletter, which notes that "This generation has become a huge consumer group that is worthy of attention from many businesses seeking to maximize their potential. Kids, teens and young adults spend significant amounts of their own money, and they influence the shopping behavior of their parents, their siblings, their relatives, and other adults in their lives."

Scientific studies that are available in the public realm back up these marketing industry assessments of the effectiveness of advertising directed at children. Studies have demonstrated that from a very young age, children influence their parents' consumer behavior. As many parents can attest after a trip down the grocery aisle with their children, television viewing has also been found to impact children's attempts to influence their parents' purchases at the supermarket. For example, several studies have found that the amount of time children had spent watching TV was a significant predictor of how often they requested products at the grocery store, and that as many as three out of four requests were for products seen in TV ads. These studies have also found that children's supermarket requests do indeed have a fairly high rate of success.

One study found that among children as young as 3, the amount of weekly television viewing was significantly related to their caloric intake as well as their requests and parent purchases of specific foods they saw advertised on television. Another study manipulated advertising shown to 5- to 8-year-olds at summer camp, with some viewing ads for fruit and juice, and others ads for candy and Kool-Aid. This study found that children's food choices were significantly impacted by which ads they saw.

Experimental studies have demonstrated that even a brief exposure to food commercials can influence children's preferences. In one study, researchers designed a randomized controlled trial in which one group of 2- to 6-year-olds from a Head Start program saw a popular children's cartoon with embedded commercials, and the other group saw the same cartoon without commercials. Asked to identify their preferences from pairs of similar products, children who saw the commercials were significantly more likely to choose the advertised products. Preference differences between the treatment and control group were greatest for products that were advertised twice during the cartoon rather than only once.

Researchers are beginning to document a link between viewing television and children's consumption of fast foods and soda, a possible result of exposure to food advertising. A recent study found that students in grades 7–12 who frequently ate fast food tended to watch more television than other students. Another study found that middle-school children who watched more television tended to consume more soft drinks.

Other evidence of television's potential impact on children's dietary habits indicates a negative relationship between viewing television and consuming fruits and vegetables. The USDA's Dietary Guidelines recommend that youth eat three to five daily servings of fruits and vegetables, yet only 1 in 5 children meet the guideline, and one-quarter of the vegetables consumed reportedly are french fries. In a recent study, more than 500 middle school students from ethnically diverse backgrounds were studied over a 19-month period to determine whether daily television and video viewing predicted fruit and vegetable consumption. Using a linear regression analysis, researchers found that for each additional hour of television viewed per day, daily servings of fruits and vegetables decreased among adolescents. The researchers who conducted the study conclude that this relationship may be a result of television advertising.

Some researchers believe that TV ads may also contribute to children's misconceptions about the relative health benefits of certain foods. One of the earlier studies found that 70% of 6- to 8-year-olds believed that fast foods were more nutritious than home-cooked foods. Another study showed a group of 4th- and 5th-graders a series of paired food items and asked them to choose the healthier item from each pair (for example, corn flakes or frosted flakes). Children who watched more television were more likely to indicate that the less healthy food choice was the healthier one. These results replicated the results of an earlier study conducted with children of the same age.

Do cross-promotions between food products and popular TV and movie characters encourage children to buy and eat more high-calorie foods? Recent years have seen what appears to be a tremendous increase in the number of food products being marketed to children through cross-promotions with popular TV and movie characters. From SpongeBob Cheez-Its to Hulk pizzas and Scooby-Doo marshmallow cereals, today's grocery aisles are filled with scores of products using kids' favorite characters to sell them food. Fast food outlets also make frequent use of cross-promotions with children's media characters.

A recent article in the New York Times business section noted that "aiming at children through licensing is hardly new. What has changed is the scope and intensity of the blitz as today's youth become unwitting marketing targets at ever younger ages through more exposure to television, movies, videos and the Internet." One food industry executive was quoted as saying that licensing "is a way to . . . infuse the emotion and popularity of a current kids' hit into a product."

Some promotions involve toys based on media characters that are included in the food packages or offered in conjunction with fast food meals. McDonald's and Disney have an exclusive agreement under which Happy Meals include toys from top Disney movies. In the past, Happy Meals have reportedly also included toys based on the Teletubbies TV series, which is aimed at pre-verbal babies. Burger King has also featured Teletubbies tie-ins, along with Rugrats, Shrek, Pokemon and SpongeBob. More than a decade ago, researchers were finding that the typical "kid's meal" advertised to children consisted of a cheeseburger, french fries, soda, and a toy. One study found that about 1 in 6 (16.9%) food commercials aimed at children promise a free toy. In addition to the use of toys as an incentive in marketing food to children, many commercials use cartoon characters to sell products, which research has shown to be particularly effective in aiding children's slogan recall and ability to identify the product.

A recent example of the effectiveness of this technique is the growth in the dried fruit snack market. Almost half (45%) of fruit snacks had licensing agreements in 2003 compared to 10% in 1996. Sales have increased substantially every year since 1999: 5.6% in 2000, 8.7% in 2001, 3.2% in 2002, and 5.5% in 2003. Marketing experts attribute the sales growth to children's influence on their parents' purchasing decisions and parental beliefs that dried fruit snacks are healthier than other sweets.

Do depictions of nutrition and body type in entertainment media encourage children to develop less healthy diets and eating habits? Over the years, some critics have argued that TV, movies, and magazines have promoted unrealistically thin body types as the ideal, possibly encouraging teen girls to engage in unhealthy dieting or eating disorders. But after years of an imbalance toward depictions of thin characters, the true weight-related health emergency among young people is, paradoxically, obesity. This paradox has yet to be explained.

Some advocates note that television gives children and teens contradictory messages about dietary habits and ideal body type: be thin but eat fatty foods, sugary sweets, and salty snacks. They point out that on the one hand, the stories media tell are about thin people who are popular and successful, while on the other hand, thin and average-size people on TV can eat whatever they want and almost never gain weight.

Some advocates and researchers also have criticized TV producers for not including more depictions of obese characters, and for negatively portraying the obese characters that do make it onto the screen. On the other hand, it could be argued that portraying obesity as an unhealthy and undesirable characteristic—and associating it with overeating—sends an *appropriate* message to youth. And while some critics fault the media for leaving obese characters off the screen, adding to stigmatization and isolation, other critics complain that too many minority characters are overweight.

**Center for Science in
the Public Interest**

 NO

Dispensing Junk: How School Vending Undermines Efforts to Feed Children Well

Executive Summary

In September and October 2003, 120 volunteers in 24 states (including the District of Columbia) surveyed the contents of 1,420 vending machines in 251 schools, including 105 middle and junior high schools, 121 high schools, and 25 schools with other combinations of these grade levels (e.g., 7th–12th grades).

The results suggest that the overwhelming majority of options available to children in school vending machines are high in calories and/or low in nutrition. **In both middle and high schools, 75% of beverage options and 85% of snacks were of poor nutritional quality.** The most prevalent options are soda, imitation fruit juices, candy, chips, cookies, and snack cakes. The high prevalence of junk food in school vending machines does not support students' ability to make healthy food choices or parents' ability to feed their children well.

This is of concern because 1) 74% of middle/junior high schools and 98% of senior high schools have vending machines, school stores, or snack bars, 2) children are in school for a substantial portion of the week, and 3) obesity rates are rising rapidly in children and teens.

Given the rising obesity rates and children's poor eating habits, the time has come to ensure that school environments support healthy eating and parents' efforts to feed their children well. A number of policies and programs should be put in place or strengthened to address childhood obesity. **One important strategy is for federal, state, and/or local governments, schools, and school districts to enact policies to ensure that foods sold out of vending machines, school stores, fundraisers, a la carte, and other venues outside of the school meal programs are healthful and make a positive contribution to children's diets.**

At the federal level, Congress should give the U.S Department of Agriculture (USDA) authority to establish and enforce regulations for all food sales anywhere on school campuses throughout the school day as a condition for participating in the National School Lunch Program or School Breakfast Program. USDA has strong nutrition policies for school meals. It also should set nutrition standards for foods and beverages sold outside those meals.

States, cities, school districts, and schools also could implement strong nutrition standards for foods and beverages sold out of vending machines, school stores, a la carte (snack lines), fundraisers, and other venues outside of the school meal programs. We recognize that school budgets are tight and that the sale of foods in schools provides much-needed revenue. However, a number of schools around the country have replaced soda in school vending machines with healthier beverages and have not lost money.

Introduction

Vending machines are prevalent in schools, yet quantitative data regarding their contents are lacking. Such data would be important to have because most children eat diets of poor nutritional quality, with too much saturated fat, sodium, and refined sugars and too few nutrient-rich fruits, vegetables, and whole grains. Those nutrient imbalances can lead to heart disease, high blood pressure, cancer, dental cavities, and other health problems. In addition, children's calorie intake has increased (and they are insufficiently active) and, as a result, rates of overweight in children have increased. While obesity is a complex, multi-factorial problem, over-consumption of soft drinks and snack foods plays a key role.

Junk food in school vending machines undermines parents' efforts to feed their children well. (This is especially problematic when children have diet-related health problems, such as high cholesterol or diabetes.) When parents send their child to school with lunch money, they do not know whether the child will buy a balanced school lunch or a candy bar and a soda. Long cafeteria lines, short lunch periods, and activities during the lunch period mean that some students rely on foods from vending machines rather than buy lunch from the cafeteria line.

The food industry is taking advantage of schools' financial problems by offering them incentives to sell low-nutrition foods in schools. But bridging school budget gaps by selling junk food to students is a shortsighted approach. In the long run, society is sure to spend more money treating the resulting obesity and diet-related diseases, such as diabetes, heart disease, cancer, and osteoporosis, than schools can raise by selling soda and snack foods to students.

There are ways schools can raise money without jeopardizing children's health. A number of schools in Maine, California, Minnesota, Pennsylvania, and elsewhere have replaced soda with healthy beverages and not lost revenue. In addition to selling healthy foods, schools can sell gift wrap or candles, sponsor fun runs, host car washes, or conduct other profitable fundraisers that do not undermine children's health.

Methods

In late September and early October 2003, 120 individuals in 24 states (including Arkansas, California, Connecticut, the District of Columbia, Illinois, Iowa, Maine, Maryland, Michigan, Mississippi, Missouri, Montana, New Mexico, New York, North Carolina, North Dakota, Ohio, Oregon, Pennsylvania, South Carolina, South Dakota, Vermont, Washington, and Wisconsin) surveyed the contents of vending machines in their local middle and high schools. The individuals collecting the data were primarily health professionals, employees of health organizations, and school employees. Volunteers surveyed a total of 1,420 vending machines in 251 schools, including 105 middle and junior high schools, 121 high schools, and 25 schools with other combinations of these grade levels.

School sites included both urban and rural schools, schools in a range of socioeconomic areas, and schools ranging in size from 110 to 2,600 students. Vending machines in areas accessible only to teachers and staff were not included.

The average number of vending machines per high school was eight. Some high schools had only one vending machine, while others had as many as 22 vending machines. The average number of vending machines per middle or junior high school was four. Some middle and junior high schools had only one vending machine, while others had up to 10 vending machines.

Vending machines were assessed by counting the number of slots per machine for each beverage or snack category and totaling the number of slots in all machines. Study participants were given a standardized survey form . . . and protocol. Participants had the opportunity to participate in a pre-survey conference call to discuss the protocol and methods for the survey. Participants sent their completed surveys to the Center for Science in the Public Interest (CSPI) for data aggregation and analysis.

The categorization of foods and beverages as "healthier" and "less healthful" was based on and generally in accordance with the nutrition standards for school foods developed by a national panel of experts convened by the California Center for Public Health Advocacy. The following types of beverages were categorized as "healthier" options: water, fruit juice containing at least 50% real juice, low-fat (1%) or fat-free milk (regular or flavored), and diet drinks. The following types of beverages were categorized as "less healthful" options: soda pop (regular), fruit drinks containing less than 50% real juice, whole or 2% milk, sports drinks, iced tea, and lemonade. Only 1% of the options in beverage vending machines ended up being categorized into the "other" category.

The following types of snacks were categorized as "healthier" options (which includes healthy foods and nutritionally-improved versions of unhealthy vending snacks): low-fat chips, pretzels, crackers, Chex Mix, fruits, vegetables, granola bars, cereal bars, nuts, trail mix, low-fat cookies, and other low-fat baked goods. While some of the options are not the healthiest products—high in sodium or made with refined flour—they are considered healthier alternatives to common vending options. The following types of snacks were categorized as being of "poor nutritional quality": regular chips, crackers with cheese, candy, cookies, snack cakes, and pastries. Foods that did not fit into these categories were categorized as "other." Just 2% of the options in snack vending machines ended up being categorized into the "other" category.

Table 1

Beverages Available in Middle and High School Vending Machines

Beverage Type	Middle Schools Percent of Total (Number of Slots)	High Schools Percent of Total (Number of Slots)	Middle Schools, High Schools, & Other Secondary Schools Combined Percent of Total (Number of Slots)
Soda (regular)	28 (1110)	39 (3489)	36 (4860)
Fruit drinks (less than 50% real juice)	17 (664)	12 (1079)	13 (1801)
Sports drinks	17 (671)	11 (994)	13 (1826)
Iced tea, lemonade, or other sweetened drink	9 (362)	8 (752)	9 (1167)
Whole or 2% milk (including flavored)	1 (46)	3 (268)	3 (367)
Water	13 (515)	11 (1001)	12 (1611)
Fruit juices (at least 50% real juice)	8 (295)	6 (563)	7 (896)
Diet soda	4 (149)	6 (555)	6 (769)
Low-fat/1% or fat-free milk (including flavored)	1 (47)	2 (177)	2 (276)
Other drinks	2 (64)	< 0.5 (13)	1 (77)
TOTAL	100 (3,923)	98 (8,891)	102 (13,650)

Results

The vending machine options in middle and high schools were markedly similar. In middle-school vending machines, 73% of beverage options and 83% of snack options were of poor nutritional quality. In high-school vending machines, 74% of beverage options and 85% of snack options were nutritionally-poor options.

The types of beverages available in middle and high school vending machines are listed in Table 1. **Seventy percent of those beverages were sugary drinks such as soda pop, juice drinks, iced tea, and sports drinks.** Of the sodas available in vending machines for both high schools and middle schools, 86% of soda slots were regular sugary sodas and 14% were diet. 12% of the beverages available were water. Of the "juices" offered, two-thirds (67%) were juice drinks that contained less than 50% juice. Only 5% of beverage options were milk. The majority (57%) of milks offered in school vending machines were the fattier types (either whole or 2%), with 43% of the milk either low-fat (1%) or fat-free.

The types of snacks available in middle and high school vending machines are listed in Table 2. The snack items most commonly available were: candy (42%), chips (25%), and sweet baked goods (13%), which together accounted for 80% of snacks available in school vending machines.

Table 2

Snacks Available in Middle and High School Vending Machines

Snack Type	Middle Schools Percent of Total (Number of Slots)	High Schools Percent of Total (Number of Slots)	Middle Schools, High Schools, & Other Secondary Schools Combined Percent of Total (Number of Slots)
Candy	38 (882)	43 (3028)	42 (4062)
Chips (regular)	24 (555)	25 (1787)	25 (2391)
Cookies, snack cakes, and pastries	14 (310)	13 (928)	13 (1270)
Crackers with cheese or peanut butter	7 (154)	4 (306)	5 (484)
Chips (low-fat) or pretzels	7 (152)	5 (332)	5 (489)
Crackers or Chex Mix	2 (52)	3 (235)	3 (303)
Granola/cereal bars	2 (56)	1 (103)	2 (171)
Low-fat cookies and baked goods	2 (44)	1 (106)	2 (155)
Nuts/trail mix	2 (41)	1 (89)	1 (141)
Fruit or vegetable	< 0.5 (8)	< 0.5 (18)	< 0.5 (26)
Other snacks	2 (39)	3 (178)	2 (231)
TOTAL	100 (2,293)	100 (7,110)	100 (9,723)

Children need fruits and vegetables to provide key nutrients and reduce future risk of heart disease and cancer. Yet of 9,723 total snack slots, only 26 slots contained a fruit or vegetable. Only 7% of the beverage options were fruit juice (i.e., contained greater than 50% real juice). This finding highlights the potential value of increasing the number of refrigerated snack vending machines in schools to provide more fruits and vegetables to children.

Rationale for Improving School Foods

I. Schools Should Practice What They Teach

This study found that most choices available in school vending machines are of poor nutritional quality. Current school vending practices are not supportive of healthy eating.

Schools should practice what they teach. Selling low-nutrition foods in schools contradicts nutrition education and sends children the message that good nutrition is not important. The school environment should reinforce nutrition education in the classroom to support and model healthy behaviors.

II. The Sale of Low-Nutrition Foods in Schools Undermines Parents' Ability to Feed Their Children Well

Parents entrust schools with the care of their children during the school day. The sale of low-nutrition foods in schools makes it difficult for parents to ensure that their children are eating well. This is especially problematic when children have diet-related conditions, such as diabetes, high cholesterol, or overweight.

Without their parents' knowledge, some children spend their lunch money on the low-nutrition foods from vending machines rather than on balanced school meals. Long cafeteria lines, short lunch periods, or activities during the lunch period lead some students to purchase foods from a vending machine rather than a lunch from the cafeteria line.

III. Children's Eating Habits and Health

Obesity rates have doubled in children and tripled in adolescents over the last two decades. As a result, diabetes rates among children also have increased and type 2 diabetes can no longer be called "adult onset" diabetes. Also, 60% of obese children have high cholesterol, high blood pressure, or other risk factors for cardiovascular disease. While obesity is a complex, multi-factorial problem, over-consumption of soft drinks and snack foods plays a key role.

While low levels of physical activity are an important part of the problem, children are clearly eating more calories now than in the past. Between 1989 and 1996, children's calorie intake increased by approximately 80 to 230 extra calories per day (depending on the child's age and activity level). Soft drinks and low-nutrition snack foods are key contributors to those extra calories. Children who consume more soft drinks consume more calories and are more likely to be overweight than kids who drink fewer soft drinks. A recent study found that a school-based nutrition education program that encouraged children to limit their soda consumption reduced obesity among the children.

Consumption of soft drinks also can displace from children's diets healthier foods like low-fat milk, which can help prevent osteoporosis, and juice, which can help prevent cancer. In the late 1970s, teens drank almost twice as much milk as soda pop. Twenty years later, they are drinking twice as much soda pop as milk. The number of calories children consume from snacks increased by 30% (from 460 to 610 calories) between 1977 and 1996.

The health benefits of eating fruits and vegetables are well-documented; eating enough fruits and vegetables is important for preventing cancer, heart disease, high blood pressure, and other diseases. People who eat five or more servings of fruits and vegetables each day have half the cancer risk of those who eat fewer than two servings per day. However, children are not consuming enough fruits and vegetables to receive maximum health benefits. The average 6 to 11 year old eats only 3.5 servings of fruits and vegetables a day, achieving only half the recommended seven servings per day for this age group. Fewer than 15% of elementary-school-aged children eat the recommended five or more servings of fruits and vegetables daily. While fruit juices can have as many calories as soda, they provide important nutrients and health benefits that soda does not.

Milk is an important source in children's diets of essential vitamins and minerals, such as calcium and vitamins A and D. Since 98% of maximum bone density is reached by age 20, it is especially important that children get enough calcium. However, milk is also the largest source of saturated fat in children's diets. While low-fat and fat-free milk make important contributions to children's diets, whole and 2% milk contribute to children's risk of heart disease.

IV. Short-Term Profits from Selling Junk Food in Schools Pale in Comparison with the Long-Term Costs for Diet-Related Diseases

While schools are facing serious budget gaps, it is shortsighted to fund schools at the expense of our children's health. Diet- and obesity-related diseases, such as diabetes, heart disease, and cancer, cause disabilities and affect quality of life. The financial costs also are staggering. Annual medical spending attributed to obesity is estimated to be $75 billion per year, and half of that amount is financed by federal taxpayers through Medicare and Medicaid. From 1979 to 1999, annual hospital costs for treating obesity-related diseases in children rose threefold (from $35 million to $127 million).

The federal government also spends large amounts of money treating other diet-related diseases such as heart disease, cancer, diabetes, stroke, and osteoporosis through the Medicaid and Medicare programs and federal employee health insurance. Those diseases have their roots in childhood. According to the USDA, healthier diets could save at least $71 billion per year in medical and related costs.

V. Schools That Stop Selling Soda and Junk Food Are Not Losing Money

Even in the short-term, schools are finding that they can raise funds without undermining children's diets and health. A number of schools and school districts including Aptos Middle School (CA), Folsom Cardova Unified School District (CA), Monroe High School (CA), Venice High School (CA), Vista High School (CA), Fayette County Public Schools (KY), Old Orchard Beach Schools (ME), School Union 106 (ME), Shrewsbury School District (MA), North Community High School (MN), McComb School District (MS), Whitefish Middle School (MT), Sayre Middle School (PA), and South Philadelphia High School (PA) have improved the nutritional quality of school foods and beverages and not lost money.

Venice High School in Los Angeles eliminated unhealthy snack and beverage sales on campus. The school vending machines now offer a variety of waters, 100% juices and soy milk as well as a variety of healthy snacks including granola and cereal bars. After one year, snack sales in the student store were up by over $1,000 per month compared to the same time the previous year. Two years after the changes, snack sales per month had roughly doubled ($6,100 in May 2002 compared with $12,000 in March 2004). The students also raise significant funds with fundraisers that do not undermine children's health, such as a celebrity basketball game, car washes, and holiday gift wrapping.

Old Orchard Beach Schools in Maine wrote school vending policies that led to the removal of sodas and junk foods, and replaced them with water, 100% fruit juices, and healthier snack options. The vending machine signage was changed to advertise water instead of soda pop. Vending revenues have remained the same as they were prior to the changes.

North Community High School in Minneapolis replaced most of its soda vending machines with machines stocked with 100% fruit and vegetable juices and water and slightly reduced the prices of those healthier options. As a result, the sale of healthier items increased and the school has not lost money.

Though school vending is lucrative, it often represents only a small percentage of total school budgets. Soft drink contracts generate between $3 and $30 per student **per year;** even the most profitable contracts provide less than 0.5% of a school district's annual budget. In addition, the money raised from vending machines in schools is not a donation from the soft drink and snack food industries—it comes from the pockets of children and their parents.

VI. School Foods Can Be Improved at the Federal, State, or Local Level

States and localities have historically left the development of nutritional guidance to the federal government. The federal government has developed the [Food Guide Pyramid], *Dietary Guidelines for Americans*, and nutrition facts labeling standards for packaged foods.

In addition, unlike other aspects of education that are primarily regulated at the state and local level, school foods have historically been regulated at the federal level—by Congress and the U.S. Department of Agriculture (USDA). The National School Lunch Program was created in 1946 under the Truman administration, "as a measure of national security, to safeguard the heath and well-being of the Nation's children and to encourage the domestic consumption of nutritious agricultural commodities and other food."

The federal government invests enormous resources in the school meal programs ($8.8 billion in FY 2003, including cash payments and commodities) and has strong nutrition standards for those meals, as well as provides technical assistance and support for states and local food service authorities to meet those standards. Selling junk foods in school vending machines undermines that investment.

USDA sets detailed standards and requirements for the foods provided through the school meal programs, including which foods are served, the portion sizes of those foods, and the amounts of specific nutrients that school meals must provide over the course of a week. In contrast, foods sold in vending machines, a la carte lines, fund-raisers, and other venues outside the school meal programs are not required by the USDA to meet comparable nutrition standards. The USDA currently has limited authority to regulate those foods.

For foods sold outside of school meals, USDA restricts only the sale of "Foods of Minimal Nutritional Value" (FMNV). A FMNV provides less than 5% of the Reference Daily Intake (RDI) for eight specified nutrients per serving. During meal periods, the sale of FMNV is prohibited by federal regulations in areas of the school where USDA school meals are sold or eaten. However, FMNV can be sold anywhere else on-campus—including just outside the cafeteria—at any time. In addition, many nutritionally poor foods are not considered FMNV despite their high contents of saturated or trans fat, salt, or refined sugars, including chocolate candy bars, chips, and fruitades (containing little fruit juice), and thus can be sold anywhere on school campus anytime during the school day.

In order for USDA to set nutrition standards for all foods sold on school campuses throughout the school day, Congress needs to grant USDA additional authority. Implementation of those nutrition standards could be required as a condition for participating in the school meal programs.

States and cities have express authority to set nutrition standards in addition to the federal standards for foods sold out of school vending machines, a la carte lines, and other venues outside of the meal programs. A number of states have set or are working to set stronger nutrition standards for such foods (for examples, see http://cspinet.org/schoolfood/school_foods_kit_part3.pdf). Such state and local actions are needed given the limitations of current federal regulations.

Modest improvements in vending machine offerings can significantly reduce the calorie content of items purchased by students. . . .

Conclusions

This study found that the overwhelming majority of beverage and snack options in school vending machines are of poor nutritional quality. While foods and beverages sold in school vending machines are not the sole cause of childhood obesity, improving school nutrition environments is a key step toward ensuring that children have access to foods that promote their health and well-being. (For more information and model policies regarding other approaches to addressing nutrition, physical activity, and obesity, visit www.cspinet.org/nutritionpolicy.)

With skyrocketing childhood obesity rates, it is urgent that schools, school districts, and local, state, and federal governments enact policies to ensure that all foods and beverages available in schools make a positive contribution to children's diets and health. . . .

EXPLORING THE ISSUE

Is Television Viewing Responsible for the Rise in Childhood Obesity?

Critical Thinking and Reflection

1. Briefly describe each side of the issue of childhood obesity according to the authors. Give examples of supporting research provided in the readings for each perspective.
2. What is your opinion of each side of the childhood obesity issue? Do you think television viewing is the primary contributing factor or is it the vending machines in schools? Or, do you think it is another factor altogether? Why?
3. What types of foods do the authors identify as contributors to childhood obesity?
4. In the introduction to this issue, it is stated that Mexican American and African American children are at a higher risk of being overweight. However, the two papers addressing the topic of childhood obesity focus on television viewing and vending machines in schools. Is it possible that these two ethnic groups engage in viewing more television and eating more unhealthy snacks from vending machines more than other ethnic groups? If so, what might be a reason for this? What else might explain the higher risk that these ethic groups have for childhood obesity?

Is There Common Ground?

The Henry J. Kaiser Family Foundation points out that since 1980 the rates of childhood obesity doubled in 6- to 11-year-olds and tripled in adolescents. It later pointed out that kids are not choosing to play outside but instead turn to video games, reading, board games, and so forth, when television was not available in the studies they examined. Television viewing and technology are probably not the only contributors to reduced physical activity outside. Other factors, such as safety concerns for the outside environment/neighborhood must be considered. Researcher and practitioners need to take a comprehensive approach to address the issue of childhood obesity.

Authors of numerous research reports and surveys, which have appeared in the popular press as well as professional journal articles, agree that there is an increase in the rate of childhood obesity in the United States, where the debate begins is over the reasons for this obesity epidemic. The Kaiser Foundation believes media is the culprit, while the Center for Science in the Public Interest feels vending machines in the schools are the cause of the problem. A balanced perspective would include both of these variables in explaining childhood overweight in addition to other factors such as parental influence, community access to exercise and nutritious food, economic cost of nutritious food, neighborhood safety, and education.

The Center for Science in the public interest argues that vending machines contribute to childhood obesity. One of their arguments is that due to kids not wanting to stand in long lines and other factors such as short lunch periods, kids use their lunch money to purchase snacks from vending machines rather than the healthy lunch provided by the school, thus undermining the parents' attempt to feed their child a well-balanced diet. Would removing the vending machines solve the other problems related to why the adolescents do not purchase their lunches? Would not having the vending machine option mean that they would buy their lunch from the school? If the parents are sending their children to school with lunch money, how many snacks are they able to purchase given the high cost of vending machines? Is this enough to significantly impact the child's weight?

Additional Resources

Kids Health: How TV Affects Your Child. (2008). Retrieved on May 27, 2011, from http://kidshealth.org/parent/positive/family/tv_affects_child.html#.

This Web site provides information regarding television viewing and how it affects children. It addresses different factors associated with television viewing such as the amount of time spent watching television, negative exposures such as violence, sexual content and drugs that may be viewed, the effects of commercials and how too much television is associated with obesity in children. The Web site also provides pointers for encouraging healthy television viewing with your child.

Medical Advices: The Greatest Wealth Is Health. (2010). Retrieved on May 24, 2011, from http://www.medicaladvices.net/Child_Health/rising-childhood-obesity-and-vending-machines-a14.html.

This Web page addresses nutritional factors regarding vending machine food choices and how it is difficult for the schools to turn down the unhealthy food and drink choices with the financial gains they are offered from the companies. The Web page also addresses encouraging healthy eating at home.

National Center for Chronic Disease Prevention and Health: Promotion Division of Adolescent and School Health. (2010). Retrieved on May 24, 2011, from http://www.cdc.gov/heatlhyyouth/obesity/.

This Web site provides some basic facts regarding childhood obesity and addresses school involvement. An article on the Web site explains body mass index (BMI) and national and local school-based programs that are intended to monitor BMI.

Pros and Cons of In-School Vending Machines. (2010). Retrieved on May 24, 2011, from http://www.ehow.com/list_6778100_pros-cons-in_school-vending-machines.html.

This Web site addresses pros and cons of having vending machines in schools. It also provides a list of articles and references for more information on this topic.

ISSUE 12

Do Bilingual Education Programs Help Non-English-Speaking Children Succeed?

YES: **Jill Wu**, from "A View from the Classroom," *Educational Leadership* (December 2004/January 2005)

NO: **Christine Rossell**, from "Teaching English Through English," *Educational Leadership* (December 2004/January 2005)

Learning Outcomes

After reading this issue, you should be able to:

- Understand and describe different bilingual education programs that are offered in the public school system.
- Describe each author's perspective and justification for the issue of bilingual education.
- Decide where you stand on the issue of whether to teach non-English-speaking students in English or first teach them in their native language and transition them into English instruction.

ISSUE SUMMARY

YES: Jill Wu, a former graduate student at the University of Colorado, shares her experiences in helping students develop literacy skills in their native languages first, as a more effective means of transferring those skills to learning English.

NO: Christine Rossell, a professor of political science at Boston University, suggests that English immersion programs tend to be more effective for students learning English because they actually learn in the second language (i.e., English).

Since bilingual education first became a political issue in the 1960s, it has been hotly debated. A child who does not speak English has as much of a right to an education as a child who does speak English. However, parents, politicians, researchers, and educators cannot seem to agree on the best way to educate non-English-speaking children. When children are taught in their native language only, opponents argue that they may lack sufficient immersion into the culture and appropriate fluency in the dominant language (i.e, English), which are necessary to succeed in our society. When children are taught in an English-only classroom, opponents argue, this leads to the students (especially ones who are of middle-school age or older) disliking school. These students do not understand what is being said. This, in turn, leads to disenchantment with the educational system and an alarmingly high number of non-English-speaking students becoming dropouts.

There is little consistency among bilingual programs throughout schools in the United States. Numerous types of bilingual programs are being implemented. Each program is different, and each comes with its own set of advocates and opponents. For example, one school may have a program in which every subject is taught in the child's native tongue, with a small amount of class time reserved for English instruction. In another school, the child may start out being taught in Spanish, for example, and within 3–5 years be transitioned into an English-only classroom. In yet another school, a child may be immersed into English-only classes with a small amount of time reserved for tutoring in his or her native language.

Even in more successful bilingual education programs, in which students are oriented to the language before being immersed in English, there are problems. These types of programs may take much longer in integrating the students into English-only classrooms. This, in turn, leaves the non-English-speaking students in danger of falling behind the other students academically, which could require them to be in school for more years than their English-speaking counterparts. If research were consistent enough to determine the best way to provide services to English-as-a-second-language learners, we would still be left with the dilemma of dealing with bilingual education when more languages need to be taught. Although the majority of children in bilingual classrooms speak Spanish as their native tongue, there are students who speak Portuguese, Korean, Chinese, and any number of other languages. Is it possible to implement bilingual programs in every school for every language needed?

In the selections that follow, you will read two points of view about the argument over what types of bilingual education programs best help non-English-speaking children to succeed. In the YES selection, Jill Wu details what her experiences were in successfully teaching students in their native language first and then in English. In the NO selection, Christine Rossell believes that immersion is the most efficient and effective way to teach English as a second language. The controversy over the efficacy of bilingual education continues in states, provinces, counties, school districts, and even in individual schools and homes. Arguments ensue over the statistics and how to interpret the existing body or research literature in the field. However, one must not lose sight of the most important thing in this battle—the children. What approaches provide the best possible education for the non-English-speaking students involved? As debates spiral round and round, we need to be mindful of why we are debating in the first place. Both sides want the same thing—an education for these students.

As you read the following sections, put yourself in the positions of decision makers—teachers, school administrators, politicians, parents. Which approach do you believe is most effective? Which teaching methods are most feasible in terms of time and money? Which methods lead to integration into English-speaking society and guard best against school drop-out?

YES

Jill Wu

A View from the Classroom

As the number of English language learners in U.S. schools increases, experts continue to seek ways to effectively educate these students. Those who argue for English immersion and for other practices emphasizing English-only instruction believe that this approach avoids segregating language learners, promotes assimilation of immigrants, and helps students learn English as quickly as possible. Bilingual education, they feel, divides society and limits Latinos' opportunities. These supporters cite evidence of ineffective bilingual programs and stories of immigrant children who have succeeded in immersion programs (Chavez, 2000; Duignan, n.d.).

Many second-language acquisition experts and others counter that immersion programs have not been proven effective. They believe that bilingual education programs, which provide initial instruction in students' first language, are more successful in helping students acquire English (Krashen, 2000; Mora, 2002; Slavin & Cheung, 2004). For example, Crawford (1998) found that students in programs that stressed native language instruction had much larger increases in English reading and math skills than did students in English immersion programs or programs that stressed early transition to English.

My experiences teaching English language learners in three different settings help to explain why bilingual education programs sometimes work and sometimes do not. These experiences demonstrate what advocates on both sides of the issue often fail to realize: that not all bilingual programs are the same; that no program will guarantee success for all students in all settings; and that English language learners often receive confusing and inconsistent instruction whether their program is called bilingual or immersion.

A Dual Language Classroom

My first experience with bilingual education was in a dual language immersion school in Wisconsin. In this setting, native English speakers and native Spanish speakers learned together in the same classroom. Instruction began in Spanish for both English and Spanish speakers. As students acquired a good reading base in Spanish, we gradually incorporated English. By 5th grade, students received half of their instruction in each language.

From *Educational Leadership*, December 2004/January 2005, pp. 40–44. Copyright © 2005 by ASCD. Reprinted by permission. The Association for Supervision and Curriculum Development is a worldwide community of educators advocating sound policies and sharing best practices to achieve the success of each learner. To learn more, visit ASCD at www.ascd.org.

Unlike transitional bilingual education, which views native language instruction as a means to learn English, dual language programs aim to produce students who are fluent in both languages. According to speech-language experts Roseberry-McKibbin and Brice (2004), studies have shown that English language learners in dual immersion programs have higher academic achievement than do those taught in English immersion programs. By taking an enrichment approach rather than a remedial approach, dual language immersion produces bilingual and biliterate students who can switch effortlessly from one language to the other.

As I worked in this school, I realized why the dual language immersion approach was successful. No one group had the dominant language— the language of power. The native Spanish speakers felt empowered, not only because they acquired literacy and found success in their own language, but also because they were models for the English-speaking students. The English-speaking students also benefited by acquiring a second language at an early age.

In 1st grade, these students were exciting to teach. They spurred one another on. Classroom discourse naturally alternated between English and Spanish, unlike the conversation in many bilingual classrooms where students never speak English except when talking to the teacher.

Socially, this approach had powerful implications. At the beginning of the year, I saw many shy Spanish speakers who congregated together. As I taught these students to read in Spanish, they became more confident in their Spanish literacy skills, but they were still reluctant to use English. Slowly, however, the native Spanish speakers and the native English speakers began to communicate with one another. As students interacted, they learned English and Spanish in meaningful ways, communicating with their peers on the playground and in the classroom. When one of the English speakers had a birthday party at her house, I had the opportunity to see the children interact outside the classroom. I was surprised when Leah, a native Spanish speaker whom I had never heard use English, spoke in fluent English as she communicated with her English-speaking friends at the party.

Bilingual Education Inconsistently Applied

When I left Wisconsin, I was enthusiastic about dual immersion bilingual education and all that it could accomplish. My next school district, in Colorado, had recently adopted a transitional bilingual model in which Spanish-speaking students would acquire literacy in their primary language and then gradually achieve literacy in English.

I took a job as a 1st grade bilingual teacher. Most of my students were Spanish speakers who did not know any English. I was surprised to discover that they had no letter-recognition skills—in fact, no literacy skills at all. I soon figured out that the problem stemmed from their kindergarten experience the year before.

The district-adopted transitional bilingual policy had not yet filtered down from the central office to the school level, so my 1st grade students had not received reading readiness instruction in their primary language. Instead, the school had placed all of the native Spanish speakers in one kindergarten class with an English-speaking teacher who made little effort to make English comprehensible to them. These students spoke Spanish in almost all settings of their lives. But for a few hours each day, they came to school and listened to a lady speak English. The input they received was similar to what we might hear from Charlie Brown's teacher—"wa, wa, wa, wa." Although some of my students had learned their colors and how to say words like *bathroom,* they had no phonemic awareness or letter-recognition skills in either language.

When I tested the students' knowledge of letter-sound correlation, I got another shock. I asked students which words started with the *A* sound and gave them some examples of Spanish words from alphabet posters with corresponding pictures. The students insisted that *manzana* started with an *A* sound, *abeja* started with a *B* sound, *belado* started with an *I* sound, and so on. I was confused. Why couldn't the students hear the beginning sounds of these words?

Then I realized what had happened. *Manzana* means *apple* in English; *abeja* means *bee;* and *belado* means *ice cream.* In kindergarten, the students had memorized the pictures that go with the letters in the English alphabet. They had never learned how to say *apple, bee,* or *ice cream* in English; they had translated the words into Spanish. They had never learned to hear the sounds; they had merely learned that the picture of a *manzana* somehow matches the symbol *A.*

Although the students' kindergarten instruction had given them almost no prereading skills, I was eager to teach them to read in Spanish, as directed by the district's new bilingual policy. We spent hours every day working on letter sounds. Simultaneously, I taught other core subjects (math, social studies, and science) in Spanish, gradually incorporating more English and developing the students' oral English skills as we discussed concepts from these subjects.

As the students and I struggled through the first four months, I began to wonder when they would make progress learning to read in any language. Many of them still struggled with blending letters. Eventually, however, it all seemed to click. A few students started to read, and the rest soon followed.

Because Spanish is a completely phonetic language, when students know how to decipher syllables they can decode almost anything. Learning how to read in Spanish empowered my students. After their Spanish literacy skills became more solid and their oral English skills improved, many of them began to read in English. This time, the goal seemed easily attainable because all their reading skills from Spanish transferred to English. This experience confirmed the views of language experts who have found that once we can read in one language, we do not need to learn how to read all over again (August, Calderon, & Carlo, 2001; Krashen, 2000). In addition, my students had the English vocabulary to comprehend what they read; they were delighted when they could sound out *C-O-W* and know what the word meant.

Although this method of teaching was not quite as natural or easy as teaching in the dual language school in Wisconsin, it still worked and gave me many reasons to support transitional bilingual education. If I had taught the students to read in English initially, it would have taken much longer for them to acquire literacy. Because I taught core subjects in Spanish, students could keep up with grade-level content because they could understand what they were learning. Their success learning in one language motivated them to succeed in the second.

Another 1st grade class of English language learners in the school that year had a different experience. After their bilingual teacher left early in the year, they received instruction from a full-time substitute who spoke no Spanish. When my students went on to 2nd grade, their teachers told me that they were much better prepared and spoke and wrote better English than the students who had been taught in an English-only class. My students had acquired English in a natural way, and they had transferred their Spanish reading skills smoothly to English.

Incoherent Programs

Later, I moved to 4th grade at a different school in the same district. I was excited by the change; I wanted to see firsthand how older students were gaining English literacy skills.

To meet the needs of the bilingual students, the school had decided to group the 4th and 5th grade English language learners for reading. Two teachers would teach a group of 4th and 5th graders who were performing on or near grade level, which included many native Spanish speakers who had transitioned to English. Another teacher would teach a group of Spanish-speaking students who had just moved to the United States and were not ready to transition. I would teach the group of students who were just beginning to transition to English literacy. I was excited about teaching these students, assuming that like my 1st graders, they would just need a little push to master learning and reading in English.

Unfortunately, the reality soon became clear. All the students in my reading group were performing far below grade level and lacked many reading skills. They did not have the same motivation that the 1st graders had displayed. How had the bilingual program failed them? Why, by the time they reached 4th grade, were these 30 kids still reading at the 1st grade level or below?

Ineffective Grouping

At first, I thought that the practice of grouping our students by language level for reading instruction sounded wonderful; the students' needs would be similar and I would be able to teach them more effectively. Unfortunately, my group included not just the bilingual students, but all students who came into 4th or 5th grade reading at the 1st grade level or below. This meant that the class contained struggling English readers who spoke Spanish, the school's few Vietnamese and Cambodian students, and many of the special education and emotionally disturbed students.

A class that could have helped students transition into reading in English became the class to dump all the students with "needs." But just because these students struggled to read did not mean that they struggled to read for the same reasons. Effective instruction for the class's English language learners would not necessarily address the needs of other struggling students with different needs.

Even the English language learners in the group had experienced many different instructional environments. Some had attended the same school since kindergarten and had received Spanish language reading instruction through 1st grade, with a transition to English in 2nd grade. Others were new immigrants to the United States. Some had recently moved from other districts or from other schools in the same district that were unable to staff bilingual classes. Because of high mobility rates, some students had switched several times between Spanish language and English language instruction.

Reading Skills and Background Knowledge

Reading involves many complex processes, and learning to read presents extra challenges for second-language learners. August and colleagues (2001, 2003) discovered that English language learners acquire decoding skills easily, but they struggle more than native English speakers in their reading comprehension. By the time these students read to the end of a sentence or a book, they may have no idea what either means. They have a hard time monitoring their comprehension.

My 4th and 5th graders' struggles confirmed August's observations. My students' biggest challenge was their lack of background knowledge and vocabulary. They had no frame of reference to understand the books we studied. I often heard such questions as "What is the ocean?", "What is a zoo?", and "Do we really have mountains near here?" Because many of the students had never left their neighborhoods, a book about life under the sea posed difficulties for them. They not only had to work on their decoding, fluency, and vocabulary, but they also had to comprehend content that was outside their realm of experience.

Second-language acquisition experts say that developing students' first language gives them subject-matter knowledge that enables them to comprehend what they read and hear in English (Krashen, 2000). I found that many of my students had not been given the opportunity to develop skills in any language. Perhaps the students had been transitioned too quickly, before they developed solid reading skills and background knowledge in Spanish, and thus they did not have fully formed skills to transfer over to English. Consequently, they had not experienced success that would motivate them. Instead of creating bilingual students, we had created students who could speak two languages to some degree but who could not read or comprehend academic material in either.

Success in Spite of Frustration

In spite of the barriers that the system had put in their way, many of my students learned and progressed. Hard work and belief in students can accomplish a lot. And a few students far exceeded expectations. What accounted for their success?

Maria and Marcos, two 5th graders in my reading class, had only been in the United States a little more than a year, but they were ready to transition to reading in English. Both progressed to near grade-level proficiency in one year, surpassing other students who had been in the country longer.

One of the reasons Maria and Marcos succeeded was that they had a solid education in their native language. They were fluent readers in Spanish and had strong background knowledge. Researchers have found that the amount of formal schooling a student receives in the first language is the strongest predictor of how that student will perform academically in the second (Thomas & Collier, 2002) and that the most successful English language learners are those who have maintained bilingualism and a strong connection with their family's culture (Rumbaut & Portes, 2001). Marcos and Maria could connect whatever they read about in English with knowledge and concepts that they had learned in Spanish. Thus, they felt successful and motivated.

Experience Supports Research

For English language learners, becoming fluent in English is a challenging process that cannot be accomplished in a single year. Because of accountability pressures, the debate that surrounds bilingual education, and the panic to get students on grade level, schools often push students rapidly into English-only instruction, where they flounder or get labeled as needing special education.

My experience suggests that students acquire a second language most easily when they develop literacy skills and content knowledge in their native language, have opportunities to interact with English-speaking peers, and learn with students of different ability levels. We need to remember that the fastest way is not necessarily the most effective way. When advocates push for English fluency at any cost, they fail to realize that the cost may be students' literacy and academic development.

Christine Rossell **NO**

Teaching English Through English

During the last 25 years, U.S. public schools have developed six different instructional approaches to support students learning English as a second language:

- *Structured immersion—or sheltered English immersion—*provides instruction almost entirely in English, but in a self-contained classroom consisting only of English language learners (ELLs).
- *ESL pullout* programs supplement regular, mainstream classroom instruction with instruction in a small-group setting outside the mainstream classroom aimed at developing English language skills.
- The *sink-or-swim* approach provides mainstream classroom instruction with no special help or scaffolding.
- *Transitional bilingual education* initially delivers instruction and develops students' literacy in the students' native language but puts a priority on developing students' English language skills.
- *Two-way bilingual education* (also known as *two-way immersion*) is designed to develop fluency in both the students' first language and a second language; teachers deliver instruction in both languages to classes consisting of both native English speakers and speakers of another language (most commonly Spanish).
- *Bilingual maintenance* programs generally consist of non-English speakers and, like two-way bilingual education programs, place equal emphasis on maintaining students' primary language and developing their English proficiency.

Notice the order in which I have listed these programs. According to my own research and my reading of others' research, this list proceeds from the most effective to the least effective approaches in terms of helping students become proficient at speaking, writing, and learning in English. This research indicates that in general, the most effective way for students to learn a second language and to learn subject matter in that second language is to learn *in* the second language—as in the first three programs—rather than learn in the students' native language, as in the last three programs (see Baker & de Kanter, 1981, 1983; Genesee, 1976, 1987; Gersten, Baker, & Otterstedt, 1998; Lambert & Tucker, 1972; Rossell, 2002, 2003, 2004; Rossell & Baker, 1996a, 1996b).

From *Educational Leadership*, December 2004/January 2005, pp. 32–36. Copyright © 2005 by ASCD. Reprinted by permission. The Association for Supervision and Curriculum Development is a worldwide community of educators advocating sound policies and sharing best practices to achieve the success of each learner. To learn more, visit ASCD at www.ascd.org.

I am aware that this conclusion is highly controversial. In the past, bilingual education has enjoyed enormous support among many researchers and educators. But the apparently successful implementation of sheltered English immersion in California, Arizona, and Massachusetts may change the common perception.

When Is "Bilingual" Not Bilingual?

Despite the common belief in the effectiveness of bilingual education, my observations and my analyses of data from state department of education Web sites indicate that only a minority of immigrant children in the United States are enrolled in bilingual programs in any form. In California, only about 29 percent of English language learners were enrolled in bilingual education in 1998, the year in which this approach was voted out as the default assignment for such students. Approximately 71 percent of California's English language learners participated in programs that used English as the dominant language of instruction—most of them in sink-or-swim or near-sink-or-swim situations (Rossell, 2002). Similarly, in Arizona in 2000 and in Massachusetts in 2002—the years in which these states mandated a switch to structured immersion—only 40 percent of English language learners at most were enrolled in bilingual education (Arizona Department of Education, 2004; Massachusetts Department of Education, personal communications, 2004).

Indeed, despite the lack of intellectual support for the sink-or-swim method, it seems to be the dominant approach to educating English language learners throughout the United States—perhaps because educators believe that the benefits of integration and language role modeling by fluent English speakers outweigh the disadvantages of students' initial noncomprehension of the curriculum, or perhaps because it is simply easier.

Another approach, sheltered English immersion (also called structured immersion), similarly predominates in more schools than one would assume from looking at statistical reports. A sheltered English immersion classroom differs from a mainstream, sink-or-swim classroom because the class is composed entirely of English language learners and is taught by a teacher trained in second-language acquisition techniques. The teacher conducts instruction almost exclusively in English, but at a pace students can keep up with.

Many programs throughout the United States identified as "bilingual education" can be more accurately described as sheltered English immersion because they are actually taught completely or almost completely in English. For example, during the two decades I have spent observing bilingual classrooms across the country, I have observed many Chinese "bilingual education" programs—but have never seen one taught in Chinese. Teachers in these classes believe that Chinese reading and writing skills are not transferable to English because the two written languages are so different. Teachers seldom even teach orally in Chinese because spoken Chinese encompasses many dialects, and it is rare that all students in a classroom speak the same one.

In fact, after observing numerous Russian, Vietnamese, Chinese, Khmer, Haitian, Cape Verdean, Spanish, Japanese, Hebrew, and Portuguese "bilingual education" classrooms and talking with their teachers, I have concluded that schools almost never offer bilingual education that fits the theoretical model, in which students learn to read and write initially as well as learn subject matter in their native language. The sole exception is in languages that use a Roman alphabet. If the primary language doesn't use the Roman alphabet, teachers perceive the transferability of reading skills as too small to justify the effort.

These practical reasons—ignored in the theoretical literature—account for the fact that in the United States, non-Spanish "bilingual education" programs are actually sheltered English immersion programs. This also means that statistics on bilingual education enrollment consistently overestimate the number of students who actually receive native language instruction.

Sheltered English immersion also travels under other labels, such as *content ESL* and, at the secondary level, *sheltered subjects*. I once visited a school in New York City that, according to the board of education Web site, had a Bengali bilingual program. When I arrived at the classroom door, however, I found a sign that said *Content ESL*. In this classroom, Bengali-speaking English language learners were taught by a teacher who was fluent in Bengali. Students who had little English fluency spent most of the day in this class learning English and learning subjects through English. The teacher taught no Bengali at all; he claimed that he did not even use it orally to clarify or explain. These students were actually in a sheltered English immersion class that tailored instruction to their needs.

At the secondary level, many students receive sheltered English immersion in the form of sheltered subject classes (such as sheltered algebra and sheltered U.S. history). *Sheltered subject* classes have been around for decades, but they often go unnoticed because the language of instruction is English and the curriculum is similar to that of a mainstream classroom. In a sheltered algebra class, for example, the teacher would teach algebra in English to a class composed solely of English language learners.

Although the literature specifies a number of ways in which sheltered English immersion classes differ from mainstream classes (Echevarria & Graves, 2002; Haver, 2002), I have observed many of these classrooms and have seen little difference between the two. Teachers in sheltered English immersion classes seem to speak no more slowly than those in mainstream classes do, and they do not use more visual props. The teachers tell me that the major difference is that they cover less material and use more repetition. Some of these sheltered classes are called "bilingual" if all the students have the same country of origin, but only Spanish speakers in secondary bilingual classes ever hear more than a minimal amount of their native language used in instruction.

Lessons from California

Although sheltered English immersion has been around for decades under various labels, it became the default assignment for English language learners by state mandate in California in 1998, in Arizona in 2000, and in Massachusetts in 2002. Research and observation in California yield some valuable insights about the ways in which teachers implement instruction for their English language learners and the relative effects of the bilingual education and sheltered immersion approaches.

Responding to the Research

In response to the California law (Proposition 227), schools developed two structured immersion models that differ by the ethnic composition of the classrooms and by the amount of sheltering provided. Programs serving English language learners from a variety of linguistic backgrounds provide instruction and conversation in English only. Programs serving exclusively Spanish-speaking students, however, often use Spanish to explain or clarify concepts.

Because the school districts do not reliably distinguish between these different models, evaluating the academic impact of sheltered English immersion is difficult, if not impossible. We can, however, compare with some confidence the academic outcomes of keeping or dismantling transitional bilingual education because the California, Arizona, and Massachusetts laws all allow a school to offer bilingual education to students if the students' parents sign a waiver and if the school can justify using this approach on pedagogical or psychological grounds.

Approximately 10 percent of English language learners in California are still enrolled in bilingual education. My analyses (Rossell, 2002, 2003) show that after controlling for student and school characteristics, the average score increased by six points in reading and by three points in mathematics in schools that eliminated bilingual education. This is a .56 standard deviation gain in reading (a large effect) and a .21 standard deviation gain in math (a small effect). Bali (2001) found that taking Pasadena students out of bilingual education increased their reading scores by two points (.18 standard deviation) and their math scores by one-half point (.03 standard deviation) compared with ELLs who had always been in English immersion classes.

Testing rates are another measure of the effectiveness of alternative programs because a lower testing rate means that the school considers more students unready to take the test. My research (Rossell, 2002) found that schools with more than 240 ELLs enrolled in bilingual education had lower testing rates in reading and math than did those with no ELLs enrolled in bilingual education, after controlling for student and school characteristics. Bali (2000) found that prior to 1998, the rate of testing for English language learners enrolled in bilingual education was 50 percent, compared with 89 percent for those enrolled in English language classrooms. Los Angeles Unified School District found that after five years of participating in the program, only 61 percent of ELLs enrolled in bilingual education were tested, compared with 97 percent of those in English language classrooms (1998).

Unfortunately, there is no scientific research that directly compares the success rates of English language learners in a sheltered English immersion classroom with the success rates of ELLs in a mainstream classroom with

ESL pullout. Nevertheless, I believe that at least for the first year, a sheltered classroom is a better environment for most English language learners than a mainstream classroom. My interviews in California indicated that teachers who formerly taught bilingual education but who now teach in sheltered English immersion programs believe the same.

After the first year, however, most English language learners are probably better off in a mainstream classroom with some extra help. Most of them will know English well enough that a sheltered English immersion classroom would slow them down unnecessarily, particularly when new students without any English skills enter the class. The one-year time limit ("not normally intended to exceed one year") is part of the sheltered English immersion laws in California, Arizona, and Massachusetts and is a provision my fellow researcher and I recommended in our writing (Rossell & Baker, 1996a, 1996b).

Teacher Implementation

My observations of almost 200 classrooms in California from spring 1999 through fall 2004 identified several themes that provide insight into the effectiveness of sheltered English immersion in the state.

Former Spanish bilingual education teachers were impressed by how quickly and eagerly their Spanish-speaking English language learners in kindergarten and 1st grade learned to speak and read in English and how proud the students were of this accomplishment. The teachers were also surprised at how much they themselves liked teaching in sheltered English immersion classrooms, although they had never worked harder (see Haager, Gersten, Baker, & Graves, 2001).

When I asked the teachers in 2001 whether they would ever want to return to teaching in a bilingual education classroom, all of them said no (Rossell, 2002). Bilingual education was a good theory, they claimed, but in practice it had too many problems. They attributed these problems to a lack of materials, teachers, and support.

Interestingly, Chinese bilingual teachers saw Proposition 227 as a nonevent. Because they had already been teaching in English, nothing had changed for them except that Proposition 227 justified their practices.

Besides moving most English language learners into sheltered immersion programs, Proposition 227 also changed the way Spanish bilingual education programs operated. The teachers with whom I spoke in the remaining Spanish bilingual education classes in spring 1999 said that they were using more English for instruction than they had in the past. They gave two reasons. First, the Proposition 227 vote expressed California's citizens' preference for a greater emphasis on English, and teachers believed that they should respond to the wishes of the people they served. Second, because the law greatly reduced the demand for bilingual classes, there was no guarantee in any specific school that a bilingual class could be assembled for the next grade in the following year. Accordingly, teachers felt the need to prepare their students for the possibility that they could soon be in an English language classroom. Thus, the task of comparing the effectiveness of bilingual education with that of sheltered immersion is further complicated by the fact that the former is less bilingual than it has been in the past.

Instruction in the Target Language Is Key

Despite the strong support for sheltered English immersion that now exists among educators, policymakers, and the public in California, only about half of all English language learners are actually enrolled in such programs. Most of the other half are in mainstream classrooms, and about 10 percent are still in bilingual education, albeit with more use of English than before.

My classroom observations in California indicate that most educators base decisions about how to teach not just on state mandates but also on their assessment of what their English language learners need, the numbers of English language learners in their classes, and their own philosophy. Most teachers with whom I have talked believe that teaching students in English is more important than ensuring that the students are in a sheltered environment (although the state law requires both).

In general, a mainstream classroom that provides extra help seems to be more practical for many schools, and any academic harm caused by such classrooms is apparently not significant enough to be noticeable to most educators or to offset the relative ease with which schools can form such classrooms. After all, most immigrant children in the United States and throughout the world are in mainstream classrooms, and most of them seem to swim, not sink.

EXPLORING THE ISSUE

Do Bilingual Education Programs Help Non-English-Speaking Children Succeed?

Critical Thinking and Reflection

1. What bilingual education programs were identified by the authors? In your opinion, which program is best and why?
2. What does each author say about bilingual education programs? Do you see any problems with either author's perspective regarding how non-English speaking children should be integrated into the education system?
3. After reading both articles, what is your opinion of bilingual education programs? What about the children who speak languages that are not offered in schools?

Is There Common Ground?

Christine Rossell argues that in order for students to learn English they must be taught in English. She gives an example of a teacher who only spoke English to his students in spite of the fact that he was fluent in the students' native language of Bengali. Rossell did not go on to clarify whether this method was effective with the students in this class; however, if it were, is it possible that it was effective because the teacher could effectively communicate with the parents versus a teacher who only speaks English? What role do the parents play in the education of their child and how important do you feel it is for parents to feel a sense of empowerment with regard to their child's education and assisting them in succeeding?

Jill Wu discusses how inconsistent bilingual instruction is and Christine Rossell makes the same point in her paper. Rossell goes on to address scores of students in California who switched into mainstream classrooms actually scoring a few points higher on reading and math tests. Does this evidence point to mainstream classrooms being more effective? Is it possible that the California programs are not providing consistent instruction and/or poor instruction due to grouping many students with different needs together such as in the example that Jill Wu gave? Does this example of higher scores justify the need to do away with bilingual education programs or does this mean that the programs need to be reevaluated and restructured?

Additional Resources

National Association for Bilingual Education. (2009). Retrieved on April 3, 2011, from http://www.nabe.org/.

This document
The NABE Web site, which provides information on becoming a member, NABE's mission statement, and information on their work to better bilingual education.

Rethinking Schools: Bilingual Education Resources. (2011). Retrieved on April 3, 2011, from http://www.rethinkingschools.org/special_reports/bilingual/resources.shtml.

This Web site provides a list of articles on bilingual education that have been published by Rethinking Schools.

Teaching Indigenous Languages: Bilingual Education Links. (2011). Retrieved on April 3, 2011, from http://www2.nau.edu/~jar/BME.html.

This site provides a list of general resources, articles, organizations, and government offices that can be utilized as resources regarding bilingual education.

ISSUE 13

Is Gay Adoption and Foster Parenting Healthy for Children?

YES: National Adoption Information Clearinghouse, from "Gay and Lesbian Adoptive Parents: Resources for Professionals and Parents," *Adoption Information Clearinghouse* (April 2000)

NO: Paul Cameron, from "Gay Foster Parents More Apt to Molest," *Journal of the Family Research Institute* (November 2002)

Learning Outcomes

After reading this issue, you should be able to:

- Describe the issues that surround homosexual adoption and foster parenting.
- Identify and discuss the main points addressed by each article concerning this issue.
- Decide where you stand on the issue of homosexual adoption and foster parenting.

ISSUE SUMMARY

YES: The National Adoption Information Clearinghouse (NAIC) presents facts regarding gay and lesbian adoptive parents. The NAIC gives current information on the background and laws regarding homosexual parenting, and confronts the issues and concerns many people have regarding homosexual adoption, including the idea that children are molested by homosexual parents.

NO: Dr. Paul Cameron, of the Family Research Institute, presents his case against allowing homosexuals to become parents—foster parents in particular. He mainly discusses case study information regarding the proclivity for homosexual parents to molest foster children.

A current topic being hotly debated in our society is gay and lesbian marriage. On the heels of this topic comes a closely related one regarding the fitness of homosexuals to raise children. Does sexual orientation affect parenting skills? Are gay and lesbian parents likely to promote homosexual behavior in their children? Will children "learn" to become homosexual from their gay parents? Are children at greater risk of molestation if they are raised in a homosexual household? These are just a sampling of the multitude of questions that some segments of our society have raised as we embrace this highly controversial and volatile issue. Although there are segments of the heterosexual population that do not disfavor homosexual parenting, there are many concerns and fears that others have about homosexual parents. The question is whether or not any of those concerns have merit.

Those opposed to homosexual parenting, foster parenting, and adoption fear for the effects it may have on the children. Will children in these homes experience ridicule by their peers when a child tells a friend that they have two moms and no dad? Are young boys who are being raised by gay men being exposed to a lifestyle that is morally wrong? Will this exposure cause these boys to "turn gay"? Those opposed also worry about the safety of the children. In particular, they fear that children living in these environments could be molested by a parent or family friend. Furthermore, some groups have claimed that the children themselves will become gay because they are learning the lifestyle from their parents. The teasing children may endure from their friends because of having homosexual parents is a haunting concern. Those opposed to homosexual parenting also point to the need for children to have both a father and mother figure in order to grow up "normally." Some also contend that the vast majority of religions are vehemently against children being raised in a homosexual family because this is an "unnatural lifestyle."

There are not only homosexual, but heterosexual, segments of society that support the right of gays and lesbians to bear or adopt children and parent them. These groups contend that most of the concerns mentioned above are founded in the deep-seated homophobia that exists throughout the world. They point to research on homosexuality, which suggests that while homosexual parenting is challenging, especially with respect to children's relations with peers, most of the concerns of the opposition group are not based upon any scientific evidence and therefore are unfounded and without merit. They contend that homosexual parents face the same challenges as any other parent in raising their children. Gays and lesbians can be just as appropriately loving and nurturing as anyone else, and have the right to raise children and experience family life to the same degree that heterosexuals enjoy this right.

In the YES article, which supports gay and lesbian parenting, the National Adoption Information Clearinghouse presents information about adoption in general and how gays and lesbians can initiate the adoption process as well. The article addresses many of the concerns that segments of society have regarding homosexual parenting. Current laws regarding adoption, by homosexual parents, are also presented. Dr. Paul Cameron, from the Family Research Institute, in the NO article, which opposes homosexual parenting, argues that one of the most worrisome concerns that people have regarding homosexual parenting—children being molested—is occurring, yet social workers and placement agencies are choosing to overlook it.

There are increasing types of unique family forms that are coming to light as we move more deeply into the twenty-first century. Gay- and lesbian-headed families are perhaps the most prominent of these forms. As a consequence, these new family forms challenge the traditional notions of who should be a parent and how families should look. Gay and lesbian families force us as a society to examine the relation between gender and parenting, the role of society in family life, and biological relations as prerequisite to the formation of a family. Is, for example, a lesbian mother, who is the biological parent of her seven-year-old daughter, and the mother's partner, who is committed to loving and caring for the seven-year-old, a family in the legal sense? Is it necessary for a family to be a "legal" family for the children within the family to develop into well-adjusted adults? Are these nontraditional homosexual families significantly different than common law–type heterosexual families?

The intensity of the beliefs and feelings behind the arguments for each side of the issue of homosexual parenting is immense. This is, however, but one issue in the ongoing dialogue of what is moral and what is immoral in our society. Some factions believe that it is immoral to raise a child without exposing that child to a religion. Atheists, however, are allowed to adopt and raise children and be foster parents. Others feel that adulterers, chronic gamblers, and those who abuse drugs and alcohol are immoral. Clearly, there are countless families where children are raised as parents grapple with these issues. Who decides where we draw the line as to who is moral and who is not when it comes to raising children? With such powerful feelings and emotions coming from the adults involved in this argument, it is most important to remember that we, as a community, should be working toward what is best for the children, rather than satisfying the urge to be right in our beliefs.

As you read the following articles, realize that your personal beliefs and value system will heavily influence how you respond to each article. The issue of homosexuality and homosexual rights is one of the more divisive controversies in our society. As a personal challenge, read each article with the intent of not supporting one side or the other. Instead, try your best to understand the points made in the article that is more opposite of your views on homosexual parenting. Remember, to understand a point of view different than yours does not necessarily mean that you condone such a view. It merely aids you in seeing things from a different perspective.

Gay and Lesbian Adoptive Parents: Resources for Professionals and Parents

Introduction

Gay men and lesbians have always adopted, though in the past they usually hid their sexual orientation. Today, just as they are becoming visible in all other aspects of U.S. society, they are being considered more seriously as potential adoptive parents. This change has been aided by the increase in the number of gay and lesbian biological parents in the United States.

In 1976, there were an estimated 300,000 to 500,000 gay and lesbian biological parents; as of 1990, an estimated 6 to 14 million children *have* a gay or lesbian parent.[1] And, between 8 and 10 million children are being *raised* in gay and lesbian households.[2] The US Department of Health and Human Services, Adoption and Foster Care Analysis Reporting System (AFCARS), estimated in 1999 there were approximately 547,000 children in foster care in the United States, of which 117,000 are legally free and therefore eligible for adoption. But, in 1997, there were qualified adoptive families (including single parents) available for only twenty percent of these children. It is also estimated that approximately ten percent of the U.S. population—or 25 million individuals—are homosexual.[3]

Based on these increasing numbers, can gay and lesbian individuals be realistically and automatically excluded from consideration as potential adoptive parents?

Despite this increase in gay and lesbian parenting, social workers may have reservations when considering gay adoptive parents for a child. They might wonder how the children will be raised and how they will feel about themselves and their parents. Will they be embarrassed because they have two mothers or two fathers, or because their single mother dates women or their unmarried father has a boyfriend? Will their friends tease them? Will they be more likely to be homosexual than will children raised by heterosexual parents? And most important, how will having been raised by gay or lesbian parents affect them as they grow into adulthood?

This fact sheet addresses the issues faced both by social workers evaluating prospective gay or lesbian adoptive parents and by gays and lesbians considering adoption. An extensive list of sources of support and information that may be

From Adoption Information Clearinghouse, April 2000.

helpful to gay and lesbian adoptive parents and adoption professionals is available online . . . , or by contacting the Clearinghouse at . . . (888) 251–0075.

The Status of Gay and Lesbian Parenting

Defining the family structure of gay and lesbian parents can be a challenging task. The most common type of homosexual household is step or blended families. These are gay and lesbian parents who had their biological children in a former heterosexual relationship, then "came out," and created a new family with another partner. Other types of family structures include single gay or lesbian parents and couples having children together. Both of these family types may be created through adoption, but more frequently reproductive technology is being utilized.[4]

There has been some research on biological families with gay and lesbian parents. This research focuses mainly on children born to donor-inseminated lesbians or those raised by a parent, once married, who is now living a gay lifestyle. While research on these situations has not addressed all the issues relevant to adoptive parenting, this information is invaluable for social workers struggling with difficult decisions, for gay men and lesbians who want to be parents, for their families and friends, and for anyone seeking information on this nontraditional type of family.

Unfortunately, the effects on children of being raised by lesbian and gay adoptive parents cannot be predicted. The number of homosexuals who have adopted is unknown, and because of the controversial nature of the issue, their children are often reluctant to speak out. Testimony of children who have grown up in gay households may turn out to provide the best information about the results of gay parenting.

Research studies, often conducted by individuals or organizations with a vested interest in the outcome, are contradictory. Studies linked to conservative political and religious groups show negative effects on children of gay and lesbian parents; while studies which support homosexual parenting are said to reflect the bias of those who are themselves gay or who support gay rights. Clearly, what are needed are definitive studies that would follow larger numbers of children over a long period of time. That research, when completed, will provide more definitive information for the debate.

In the meantime, it is critical to address the issues and concerns so that social workers can examine their own personal biases to make informed decisions and gay and lesbian adoptive families can receive the support they need to thrive.

Issues and Concerns

"What Is Sexual Orientation?"

The American Psychological Association defines sexual orientation as "one of four components of sexuality and is distinguished by an enduring emotional, romantic, sexual or affectionate attraction to individuals of a particular gender. The three other components of sexuality are biological sex, gender identity (the psychological sense of being male or female) and social sex role (the adherence to cultural norms for feminine or masculine behaviors)."[5]

For most people sexual orientation emerges in early adolescence without any prior sexual experience. Sexual orientation is different from sexual behavior because it refers to innate feelings and self-concept and may not be expressed in behavior. Understanding the source of sexual orientation depends on which side of the nature versus nurture debate you fall. Some theories point to genetic or inborn hormonal factors; others to early childhood life experiences. Many believe sexual orientation is shaped at an early age through a combination of biological, psychological and social factors.[6]

"Children Will Be Molested by Homosexual Parents"

There is no legitimate scientific research connecting homosexuality and pedophilia. Sexual orientation (homosexual or heterosexual) is defined as an adult attraction to other adults. Pedophilia is defined as an adult sexual attraction or perversion to children.[7] In a study of 269 cases of child sex abuse, only two offenders where found to be gay or lesbian. More relevant was the finding that of the cases involving molestation of a boy by a man, seventy-four percent of the men were or had been in a heterosexual relationship with the boy's mother or another female relative. The conclusion was found that "a child's risk of being molested by his or her relative's heterosexual partner is over one hundred times greater than by someone who might be identifiable as being homosexual."[8]

"Children Will Be Teased and Harassed"

Children of gay men and lesbians are vulnerable to teasing and harassment, particularly as they approach adolescence, when any sign of difference is grounds for exclusion. How much of a problem is it? Is it likely to cause lasting psychological damage?

Gay and lesbian parents are well aware of the difficulties that a child may face—many have dealt with prejudice all of their lives. Most see it as an opportunity for ongoing discussion that will help their children grow as people.

Abby Ruder, a therapist, lesbian, and adoptive mother, acknowledges that children will be teased, and takes great pains to prepare her gay and lesbian clients for some of the problems that their children will face. She feels that families should have a plan for dealing with society's attitude toward them. "Children with gay or lesbian parents need to be taught when it's okay to tell people and when not to. A family doesn't have to be 'out' all of the time. My 9-year-old . . . has become very adept at knowing when to tell people that she has two mommies."

Wendell Ricketts and Roberta Achtenberg, in the article "Adoption and Foster Parenting for Lesbians and Gay Men: Creating New Traditions in Family" from *Homosexuality and Family Relations*, address social workers grappling with the issue by asking, ". . . should children be sheltered from every experience in which their difference might challenge prejudice, ignorance, or the status quo (or in which they would be 'exposed' to the difference of others)? Agencies conforming to such a standard must ask themselves whether it is their function to honor the system that generates stigma by upholding its constraints." They continue, "Teasing is what children do. Does this mean that child welfare policy must be set at a level no higher than the social interactions of children?"

In custody cases involving a gay or lesbian parent, courts have considered the fact that a child might be teased as contrary to the best interests of the child. They argue that the stigma attached to having a gay or lesbian parent will damage a child's self-esteem. This has been refuted in many studies. Research has found that although children of gays and lesbians do report experiencing teasing because of their parent(s), their self-esteem levels are no lower than those of children of heterosexual parents.[9]

In 1984 the Supreme Court heard a case, *Palmore v Sidoti*, in which a Florida man sought custody of his daughter on the grounds that his white ex-wife was now married to a black man and that this would expose his daughter to the stigma of living in an interracial family. The Court ruled that the girl should stay with her mother, saying that under the Equal Protection Clause of the Fourteenth Amendment, "private biases may be outside the reach of the law, but the law cannot, directly or indirectly, give them effect." Although the Court's ruling dealt specifically with racial prejudices, several researchers have mentioned the case as a rebuttal to the argument that placing a child in a family subject to social stigma is automatically contrary to the child's best interests.[10]

Nonetheless, social workers and even some gay men and lesbians considering adoption wonder if it is in the best interest of a child to be raised by homosexual parents. "It can be too hard a transition for some children, especially those who are older and have already formed preconceived notions about homosexuality," explains therapist Ruder. "Younger children usually have an easier time adjusting to a gay and lesbian parented home. They haven't learned the societal biases against gays and lesbians yet." When a gay person is being considered as a potential adoptive parent for an older child, the child should be told about the person's sexual orientation and asked his feelings about it. If the child is comfortable with the information, the caseworker can proceed to the next step.

Gay and lesbian adoptive parents must also think about how they will explain to younger children, in age-appropriate language, not only how and why the child was adopted but also about the parents' sexual orientation. Both are complex subjects that should be addressed a number of times as the child grows and matures, each time adding new information as the child asks and is able to absorb and understand more. Then both topics become accepted facts of family life.

"Children Raised in Homosexual Households Will Become Gay"

The bulk of evidence to date indicates that children raised by gay and lesbian parents are no more likely to become homosexual than children raised by heterosexuals. As one researcher put it, "If heterosexual parenting is insufficient to ensure that children will also be heterosexual, then there is no reason to conclude that children of homosexuals also will be gay."[11]

Studies asking the children of gay fathers to express their sexual orientation showed the majority of children to be heterosexual, with the proportion of gay offspring similar to that of a random sample of the population. An assessment of more than 300 children born to gay or lesbian parents in 12 different samples shows no evidence of "significant disturbances of any kind in the development of sexual identity among these individuals."[12]

"Children Will Develop Problems Growing Up in an 'Unnatural' Lifestyle"

Courts have expressed concern that children raised by gay and lesbian parents may have difficulties with their personal and psychological development, self-esteem, and social and peer relationships. Because of this concern, researchers have focused on children's development in gay and lesbian families.

The studies conclude that children of gay or lesbian parents are no different than their counterparts raised by heterosexual parents. In "Children of Lesbian and Gay Parents," a 1992 article in *Child Development,* Charlotte Patterson states, "Despite dire predictions about children based on well-known theories of psychosocial development, and despite the accumulation of a substantial body of research investigating these issues, not a single study has found children of gay or lesbian parents to be disadvantaged in any significant respect relative to children of heterosexual parents."

Psychiatrist Laurintine Fromm, of the Institute of Pennsylvania Hospital, agrees with that finding. "[The] literature . . . does not indicate that these children fare any worse [than those of heterosexual parents] in any area of psychological development or sexual identity formation. A parent's capacity to be respectful and supportive of the child's autonomy and to maintain her own intimate attachments, far outweighs the influence of the parent's sexual orientation alone."

What the Law Says

Only one state, Florida, specifically bars the adoption of children by gay and lesbian adults. Similar legislation was introduced in Utah prohibiting unmarried couples, including same-sex couples, from adopting children. The bill claims it is not in a child's best interest to be adopted by persons "cohabiting in a relationship that is not a legally valid (binding) marriage." The bill passed the State of Utah's House and Senate in February 2000 and is waiting the Governor's signature. The Governor has pledged to sign it. [Editorial note: The Governor signed the bill in 2000. In 2011, a Utah Senate Committee voted to table a bill that would have allowed second-parent adoptions for unmarried couples, including gay and lesbian couples. The Salt Lake Tribune reports [http://www.sltrib.com/sltrib/home/51205267-76/bill-committee-couples-lake.html.csp]: By a 5-1 vote, the Senate Health and Human Services committee voted to table SB62, which would have allowed a legal parent of a child to designate a second, adoptive co-parent. Utah law prohibits anyone who is living in an unmarried, cohabiting relationship from adopting or fostering children. Married couples and single individuals may adopt.

http://www.connexion.org/gay-news/news?id=966175
Utah Rejects Second-Parent Adoption Bill That Included Gay Couples

Gay News From Towleroad News
2/7/2011 11:49 AM - 302 views]

Yet, in April 2000, Vermont lawmakers approved legislation that makes the State the first in the nation to recognize same-sex couples' right to form "civil unions." Partners in a civil union would be given the same benefits of married couples—the ability to transfer property, to make medical decisions for each other, to be eligible for inheritance, and the necessity to dissolve the union in Family Court (equivalent to a divorce). More than 30 other states have tried to avoid such unions through the passage of the Defense of Marriage Act. The act defines marriage as a union between a man and a woman and denies recognition of same-sex marriages performed elsewhere.

Legislation has also been introduced in Mississippi that would ban gay and lesbian couples from adoption and forbid the State of Mississippi from recognizing gay and lesbian adoptions that have previously been granted by other state courts—an unprecedented provision. Anti-sodomy statutes in 19 states and the lack of legal recognition of homosexual couples complicate adoption in the states that don't specifically prohibit gay and lesbian adoption.

Professor William Adams Jr., co-counsel in a case challenging Florida's ban on adoptions by gays and lesbians, has noted courts are increasingly turning to expert testimony to resolve questions in gay rights cases. He theorizes that there are several factors contributing to this trend, among them the courts' desire to justify their decisions in light of the controversy surrounding the issue and the efforts of gay litigants and civil rights organizations to provide the court with information. Although Adams sees this as a positive step, he comments, "citation to social science data should not be mistaken for a court's full understanding of it, however, because courts sometimes struggle to make sense of the research, or strain to ignore it."[13]

Nine states—California, Massachusetts, New Jersey, New Mexico, New York, Ohio, Vermont, Washington and Wisconsin—and the District of Columbia have allowed openly gay or lesbian individuals or couples to adopt. Although some joint adoptions have been successful, the most common practice is for a single person to apply as the legal adoptive parent of the child. Couples who both want custody then apply for a second parent, or coparent, adoption.

Second parent adoption or the adoption by non-marital partners, leaves the parental rights of one legally recognized parent intact and creates a second legally recognized parent for the adoptive children. Second parent adoption, which has become routine for children of heterosexual stepparents, is the only way for gay couples to both become legal parents of their children.[14] Although state statutes generally provide a "stepparent exception," these exceptions emphasize the existence of a legal marriage between the biological parent and the stepparent.[15]

This growing practice was tested in a landmark case in Vermont in 1993. Jane Van Buren had given birth to two boys through anonymous donor insemination. According to the law, only Ms. Van Buren was considered their parent—her partner, Deborah Lashman, had no legal standing. The couple filed a petition for a second parent adoption, asking the probate court to allow Ms. Lashman to adopt the children while leaving Ms. Van Buren's parental rights intact. The court denied the adoptions because Ms. Lashman was not married to the biological parent. On June 18, 1993, the Vermont Supreme Court unanimously reversed the decision of the lower court and awarded joint custody to the couple.[16] With this decision, the Vermont Supreme Court became the first State Supreme Court to recognize lesbian co-parent adoptions. As a result of this finding, other couples are likely to find second parent adoptions easier to accomplish in Vermont and other areas of the country.

Second parent adoptions (by unmarried couples) have been granted by the courts (the approvals were generally from the lower level courts) in 21 states and the District of Columbia: Alabama, Alaska, California, Illinois, Indiana, Iowa, Maryland, Massachusetts, Michigan, Minnesota, Nevada, New Jersey, New Mexico, New York, Ohio, Oregon, Pennsylvania, Rhode Island, Texas, Vermont and Washington.[17]

Types of Adoption

Depending on the type of adoption gay and lesbian parents are interested in—public, private, independent, open or international—there may be different considerations involved in disclosing sexual orientation. How open prospective adoptive parents are about their homosexuality depends upon the couples' personal feelings on disclosure, whether direct questions are asked and what the laws in the State of residency are.

One important point for all prospective adoptive parents to be aware of is the difference between not sharing private information and deliberately lying at any time in the adoption process. Although it is completely legal to omit information regarding homosexuality, it is illegal to lie about it when confronted directly.[18] Let it be clear that failing to tell the truth is considered fraud and raises the opportunity for either an adoption not being finalized or a possible disruption.

Public Agency Adoption

Success in adopting from the public child welfare system depends on the State adoption law and the attitude of the agency. For example, in New York and California, gay and lesbian prospective adoptive parents are protected against discrimination. It is illegal for public agencies in those states to reject adoptive parents on the basis of sexual orientation. However, that is not a guarantee that prejudices don't exist. Social workers who are uncomfortable with homosexuality may find the prospective adoptive parents unsuitable for other reasons.[19]

Each state decides independently who can adopt. Since, the final decision is made by judges at the county level, the availability of adoption as an option to openly gay and lesbian couples is influenced by the political and social community in which the family lives. The court's decision hinges on the "best interest" of the child, a concept interpreted differently by different judges.

Private Agency Placements

Private agencies establish their own criteria for the prospective adoptive parents. Age, religion, fertility status, marital status and sexual orientation all may be agency considerations. Some private agencies may disregard sexual orientation, and present the prospective parent as a single adopter who lives with another adult who will share the responsibilities of raising the child. This omission of sexual orientation is based on the agency's judgement and relevancy to the applicant's parenting qualifications.

Independent and Open Adoption

An independent adoption is an adoption facilitated by those other than caseworkers associated with an agency. They may be a physician, an attorney, or an intermediary and are illegal in some states. In an independent adoption the placement decision (within the provisions of the state statute) is completely up to the families involved. However, independent adoption does not necessarily mean an open adoption. An open adoption involves some amount of initial and/or ongoing contact of birth and adoptive families. The adoptive and birth parents agree upon the birth parents' role, future communication and the degree of openness prior to adoption. Being honest with the birth parents from the first contact allows gay and lesbian adoptive parents the opportunity to have a relationship without the possibility of a disrupting secret.

International Adoption

Adopting a child from a foreign country may involve finding an agency willing to accept the adoptive parents' sexual orientation, disclosing the information to the contacts in the sending country, and presenting the information to the foreign government. However, conservative, or religious and often developing countries may not be as receptive to gay and lesbian couples. Adoptive parents need to be aware that foreign governments and courts are making placement decisions based on their cultural standards and what they feel is in the best interest of the child.

The Social Worker's Dilemma

Placement Decisions

The debate goes on and will continue as long as there are conflicting views about homosexuality. Considering these different views, should social workers place children with gay men or lesbians? To make the best placement decision for children, social workers need to answer the following questions:

- Is this person or couple caring, nurturing, and sensitive to others?
- Do they have the qualities needed to parent a child?

- What are their individual strengths and weaknesses?
- How do their strengths/weaknesses complement the needs of the child?
- Do they have the capacity to nurture a child not born to them?

In addition, for prospective homosexual adoptive parents, Denise Goodman, Ph.D., a consultant and trainer in Ohio, firmly believes that workers need to have a holistic understanding that includes finding out answers to questions about their homosexuality:

> "I counsel workers to ask homosexual applicants where they are in their individual development. Have they recently come out? Are they comfortable with their self-image and with being gay? Having a positive self-image will provide a model for an adopted child. I want to know about family support and how those who are important in their lives view them and their idea of adopting. I ask questions about the stability of their relationship and try to see how committed they are to each other. Do they have wills? Have they bought a home? Do they share finances? Once you know more about their situation, you can help them access appropriate resources and connect them with other gay or lesbian adoptive parents."

Goodman, who has trained thousands of social workers in Ohio, sees the opportunity for change, but has a few concerns:

> "While it is gratifying to see social workers become more open, if agency administrators are not fully behind the workers, little will change. Families will be approved and never hear about an available child; those who aren't open about their sexuality will receive a child, while "honest" applicants will wait, or other issues will surface so that a family is not accepted."

If a sense of trust and openness is established between a social worker and applicant, the worker can help to decide when privacy is the best route or when an applicant can be more outspoken. It ultimately depends on state laws and the views of presiding judges.

Professional Prejudices and Policy Decisions

Adoption professionals need to be aware of their own personal prejudices and prejudgments when working with gay and lesbian prospective adoptive parents. Experiences and beliefs come from family background and values, religious beliefs, and community views on homosexuality and will affect social workers' and agency staff's ability to assess the couple.[20] Ann Sullivan, of the Child Welfare League of America, suggests in her article "Policy Issues in Gay and Lesbian Adoption," that professionals consider several key issues:

- The client is the child in need of an adoptive family. All families should be given equal consideration and the potential resources available weighed for the placement of the child.
- No single factor should be the determining factor in assessing suitability for adoption.

- In considering gay and lesbian prospective adoptive parents, sexual orientation and the capacity to nurture a child are separate issues and should not be confused in the decision making process.
- Each placement decision should be based on the strengths and needs of the individual child and the perceived ability of the prospective adoptive family to meet those needs and develop additional strengths.

Coping with the Agency Preference Hierarchy

Many gay and lesbian prospective adoptive parents are troubled by the feeling that adoption agencies offer them the children who are the most difficult to place: those with physical, mental, or emotional disabilities; those who are older; children of color; and members of sibling groups.

"Often gay parents will get harder children because it's the last resort," Bob Diamond, the former Executive Director of AASK Northern California in Oakland, admits. "A lot of social workers will say, 'Well, no one is going to take this kid except gay people.' Being homosexual is not usually seen as a positive factor," he adds, noting that single people in general are usually treated as "second-class citizens" by most adoption agencies.[21]

Roberta Achtenberg, Executive Director of the National Center for Lesbian Rights in San Francisco, bluntly confirms that there is an unspoken ranking within the adoption network. "The hierarchy prefers white, married, middle or upper middle class couples, and these couples don't want the special needs kids. The less preferred children then go to unmarried couples of all kinds, single individuals, and gay people. The children are less preferred, and the recipients are less preferred."

What strikes psychologist April Martin, author of *The Lesbian and Gay Parenting Handbook*, as ironic is that the same bureaucracies that believe that lesbians and gay men are not suitable parents will place children who require the most highly skilled parenting with them. She and others have pointed out that nontraditional families have unique strengths that make them excellent, and in some cases, the best homes for certain children. Among them is an ability to accept differences, to understand what it is like to be in the minority, to demonstrate flexible gender roles, to be open about sexuality with children who have been sexually abused, and to understand the special needs of homosexual children.

April Martin suggests that gays and lesbians who want to adopt younger, healthier children can find them by working with private agencies or by working directly with birthparents. Some birthparents have specifically chosen openly gay households for their children.

Life after Adoption

Explaining Sexuality to Children

All families at one time or another will have "the" discussion on sexuality. For gay and lesbian families this can be an even more sensitive subject. However, a healthy family, regardless of sexual orientation, shares the same core values—love and respect, commitment and understanding. It is especially important when talking with children to stress what these values mean to the family and to recognize that there are many different cultures, communities and families around the world.

The Family Pride Coalition, a national advocacy and support organization, offers several suggestions for parents discussing sexuality with their children:[22]

- Be honest about your own identity and comfort level.
- If you are uncomfortable, let your children know you find this hard to talk about, but that you feel it is important for families to talk about difficult things.
- Listen closely to your child and when possible, let your children take the lead. Let them ask questions. Take cues about their level of understanding from the questions they ask and interact at that level.
- Be as clear as you can be about your own feelings connected to sexuality, coming out, privacy, and family values.
- Consider your child's age and how much information they need.

Getting Support

Once an adoption is completed, the business of family life begins. Like all adoptive parents, gay men and lesbians are seeking ways to incorporate their children into their lives and to help them make a smooth transition. They also want to meet other homosexuals who have taken on the challenge of parenting. There are a growing number of support groups to meet these needs.

Len and Fernando, a multiethnic gay couple who adopted 3-year-old Isabel as a toddler, are members of an active group in the Philadelphia area. "Speaking to the parents of older children gives us ideas of how to cope with issues as they come up. Most of the members are women. We could use a few more men!"

Isabel, who is African-American, has the chance to meet other African-American adopted children and enjoys the many activities planned for families. Their group is part of a larger support network, Philadelphia Family Pride, that serves more than 250 gay and lesbian families in the Delaware Valley. In addition to giving its members a chance to socialize, the group's advocacy and educational projects encourage parents to work with teachers on adoption, race, and alternative family issues that affect their children. Members participate in conferences, receive local and national newsletters, and learn about books and articles for themselves and their children. Older children of gay parents have formed their own network, Colage—Children of Lesbians and Gays Everywhere.

A vital support network of family and friends is important for any family— adoptive, biological, one with heterosexual parents, or one with homosexual parents. Some gay and lesbian adoptive parents have found that even if their parents had a difficult time accepting their homosexuality, the parents readily accept their new role as grandparents. It is almost as if having children makes them more like mainstream families. "Our parents reacted to our desire to parent pretty much the same way they reacted to our coming out," says Tim

Fisher, father of two and former Executive Director of the Family Pride Coalition (formerly Gay and Lesbian Parents Coalition International). "They said, 'We love you . . . but let's not talk about it.' With the kids, they have softened their tone a little. They are grandparents who adore their grandchildren."

Conclusion

The increasing number of gay men and lesbians choosing to adopt has brought the issue of gay and lesbian parenting to the forefront. Social workers are being asked to look carefully at their own feelings and to make reasonable judgments about what is in the best interest of children who need families. And, the increasing number of children needing adoptive families puts pressure on workers to find appropriate families.

The questions linger—should stable, nurturing, mature applicants be turned away on the basis of sexual orientation? What if a substantial number of children face the possibility of never achieving permanency, when they could have been adopted by a gay or lesbian family?

Endnotes

1. Sullivan, A., (1995). Issues In *Gay and Lesbian Adoption: Proceedings of the Fourth Annual Peirce-Warwick Adoption Symposium*, Washington, DC: Child Welfare League of America.

2. Editors of the *Harvard Law Review*. (1990). *Sexual Orientation and the Law*. Cambridge, MA: Harvard University Press.

3. Sullivan, A.

4. Rohrbaugh, J.B. Lesbian Families: Clinical Issues and Theoretical Implications. (1992). *Professional Psychology: Research and Practice,* 23: 467–473.

5. Blommer, S.J. (undated). Answers to Your Questions About Sexual Orientation and Homosexuality: A Fact Sheet. Washington, DC. American Psychological Association.

6. Blommer, S.J.

7. Lesbian and Gay Rights Project—ACLU. (1999). ACLU Fact Sheet—Overview of Lesbian and Gay Parenting, Adoption and Foster Care. New York, NY: American Civil Liberties Union.

8. Carole, J. Are Children at Risk for Sexual Abuse by Homosexuals? (1994). *Pediatrics,* 94 (1)

9. Huggins, S.L. A Comparative Study of Self-Esteem of Adolescent Children of Divorced Lesbian Mothers and Divorced Heterosexual Mothers. (1989). *Journal of Homosexuality,* 18 (1/2): 123–135.

10. Adams, W. E. Whose Family Is It Anyway? The Continuing Struggle for Lesbians and Gay Men Seeking to Adopt Children. (1996). *New England Law Review,* 30 (3): 579–621.

11. Bigner, J. J., Bozett, F. W. 1990. Parenting by Gay Fathers. In: *Homosexuality and Family Relations.* Bozett, F. W., Sussman, M. B. New York, NY: Haworth Press, Inc.

12. Patterson, C. J. Children of Lesbian and Gay Parents. (1992). *Child Development:* 1025–1039.

13. Adams, W. E.

14. Lambda Legal Defense and Education Fund. (1997). Lesbian and Gay Parenting: A Fact Sheet. New York: NY: Lambda Legal Defense and Education Fund.

15. Mishra, D. The Road to Concord: Resolving the Conflict of Law Over Adoption by Gays and Lesbians. (1996). *Columbia Journal of Law and Social Problems*, 30 (1): 91–136.

16. Patterson, C. J.

17. Lambda Legal Defense and Education Fund.

18. Martin, A. (1993). *The Lesbian and Gay Parenting Handbook.* New York, NY: HarperCollins Publishers, Inc.

19. Martin, A.

20. Sullivan, A. Policy Issues in Gay and Lesbian Adoption. (1995). *Adoption and Fostering*, 19 (4): 21–25.

21. Perry, D. Homes of Last Resort. (1993). *The Advocate*: 46.

22. Cronin, M. E. (1999). Guide to Talking with Your Child About California's Knight Initiative. San Diego, CA: Family Pride Coalition.

Paul Cameron **NO**

Gay Foster Parents More Apt to Molest

No matter how professionals in our society extol the virtues of 'science,' if empirical evidence goes against their beliefs, they often ignore it or avoid it. The employment of homosexuals as foster parents is a perfect case in point.

When a 16-year-old foster son was molested and raped by two gay foster parents in Vermont, Tom Moore, Deputy of the State's Social and Rehabilitation Services, told me on June 25, 2002 that neither he nor the Commissioner knew of any evidence about the molestation rates of children by homosexual foster parents. He was apparently echoing his boss, Commissioner William Young, who the papers quoted as saying "I don't know of any screening instrument for [sexual molestation]. Certainly, sexual preference doesn't have anything to do with it, or religious beliefs or socioeconomic status. It's so frustrating because there isn't a predictor." (*Rutland Herald* 6/21/02)

Really? Traditional common sense holds that married parents are likely to be the best foster placement, and homosexuals among the worst, in part because of the risks of sexual molestation. But tradition holds almost no weight for these bureaucrats. How can this be? Can the traditions that worked to build arguably the world's most successful culture be ignored without injuring society? What kind of belief-system is so much better that it should be followed instead?

When I interviewed the reporter who wrote the story for the *Rutland Herald*, he refused to specify whether what he had called the "male couple" in the newspaper story was in fact a homosexual couple. He said that the *Rutland Herald* never released the sexual orientations of those accused of crimes. When I spoke with his editor, she repeated the policy. The "male couple" certainly acted as though they were gay, but the newspaper staff wasn't about to say or print it.

Fortunately, those at the District Court of Vermont were not so protective of 'sexual orientation privacy.' They provided the entire record. The rest of the story about the 16-year-old fit traditional common sense perfectly.

It turns out that the natural parents of the boy who was victimized strenuously objected to the placement of their hard-to-control son with these two gays. Yet, following a policy laid down 15 years ago, their objections were ignored. Additionally, when the boy complained to the Department that his new foster parents had asked him whether he had engaged in anal intercourse

From *Journal of the Family Research Institute,* vol. 17, no. 7, November 2002. Copyright © 2002 by Dr. Paul Cameron. Reprinted by permission of the author.

with his brother, the Department, through David Stanley, its Case Worker, concluded that the boy had been 'coached' to say this by his natural parents. Stanley said the gay foster parents denied saying such a thing and he believed them. So as far as the case worker was concerned, the boy had lied, so he was forced to stay with the 'male couple.'

Soon thereafter, the men gave the boy a magazine containing depictions of scantily clad men. They told the boy to 'masturbate to these pictures.' The boy complied, and hid the magazine under his bed.

Here, another factor of the case supported traditional common sense. Traditional thought holds that homosexuals have difficulty containing their sexual desires for youth. And sure enough, even in the face of all this investigation and conflict about possible molestation, the boy was with these homosexuals only two more weeks before they began to rape him!

Think of it. The investigation had already put these two gays 'on notice,' and yet this warning kept them from acting upon their temptation for only two weeks. Then, both men, who were in a 'committed relationship' with one another, had their way sexually with the boy. Sometimes, just one of them raped the boy alone, sometimes it happened when they were together. The boy managed to escape only by pretending that the sex was OK, and then fleeing to a hospital when the 'family' went to town to shop.

As it turned out, the men's magazine was the 'clincher' when the boy fingered his foster 'parents.' Because the magazine was where the boy said it was, the police were able to get the men to confess.

Notice what happened here. Vermont's child protective agency, without evidence of any sort, adopted a new policy 15 years ago that discarded tradition. Why? Because traditional common sense relegated homosexuals as 'not suitable for foster-placement' status. The child protective agency thought it had a 'better way.'

What was this 'better way?' What is this belief system that is so much better than traditional thought?

I filed a Freedom of Information request regarding this case and the policy changes that had been instituted by the agency, asking 17 specific questions. Some of these included: how many foster parents or foster parent pairs who have been involved in foster parenting a child or children were homosexual? Did your department conclude that the 16-year-old boy's claim was false that his foster parents had asked him whether he performed anal intercourse with his brother?

Less than a month later, Jody Racht, the Assistant Attorney General for Vermont, informed me that asking specific questions rather than "access to identified public records" fell outside of "any provision of state law."

So while certain policies had apparently been established to protect homosexuals—both in the child protective agency and at the *Rutland Herald*—neither institution would explain their basis. They just followed 'the policy.'

So what was this 'better way'?

Deputy Commissioner Moore said that, because of privacy and confidentiality concerns, no follow-up of placements with homosexuals had been conducted, nor were any contemplated. This strategy of 'deliberate ignorance' is not unique to Vermont. Over the past 10 years, I have talked with representatives of the District of Columbia, El Paso County (Colorado Springs, CO), and Seattle, WA—jurisdictions which place foster children with homosexuals—and gotten the same replies. In Colorado Springs, the wishes of the family regarding the placement of a 6-year-old boy—whose lesbian mother was judged unsuitable to parent—were overridden by child protective services in favor of the 'right of homosexuals to keep their children.' The little boy was given to a lesbian couple instead of his married aunt—an aunt who had been chosen by the extended family as the 'best fit' for the boy.

The social work representatives in the other three jurisdictions with whom I had contact said that since the National Association of Social Workers (NASW) declared homosexuals to be foster parents 'as fit' as heterosexuals, they believed that they were as unlikely to sexually abuse their charges as non-homosexuals. Indeed, the 1987 NASW resolution decrying "resistance to using single parents, . . . including lesbian and gay parents, as potential foster care and adoption resources" was passed, in substantial part, to counter the traditional belief that children placed with homosexual foster parents would be at higher risk of sexual exploitation.

NASW Influence

This NASW resolution and the new 'theory' behind it has informed social workers for the past 15 years. In one high profile case in 1992, the faculty of the Saint Cloud State University Social Work Department told potential students that this new 'theory' trumped not only traditional common sense, but also any religious beliefs. These faculty decreed that 'social homophobia' is a form of "human oppression." And citing the NASW code of ethics (Sec. 2.3), they noted that "accepting gay and lesbian people does not mean accepting them as individuals while simultaneously abhorring their behavior. . . . The only legitimate position of the social work profession is to abhor the oppression that is perpetrated in gay and lesbian people and to act personally and professionally to end the degradation in its many forms." That is, this 'new faith statement' must trump any other belief—including traditional religious beliefs like Christianity.

Is the NASW claim that homosexual and unmarried foster parents are 'as fit' as married heterosexuals warranted? No empirical literature concerning the issue appears to exist—although the evidence regarding the general parenting of homosexuals suggests that it is inferior to that of the married. Under the current system for placing foster children, putting the NASW claim to an empirical test cannot be done. The bureaucrats who could track the success of homosexual foster parents refuse to do so, and—citing privacy and confidentiality concerns—also prevent outsiders from doing it.

The 'faith' of the social worker profession, consisting of resolutions passed by a tiny committee within the NASW, is sufficient. No evidence is required! What a maddening mess! Fortunately, I found a way to bypass the current bureaucratic strategy of 'deliberate ignorance' regarding foster placements with homosexuals. My strategy exploited recent changes in the technology of newspaper publishing.

Here Is What I Did

While a successful foster-parenting outcome does not make the news, a highly unsuccessful outcome does. If homosexual foster parents do not differ from non-homosexuals, gross failure at foster parenting—such as the sexual molestation of foster kids—ought to occur at rates approximately proportionate to the frequencies of homosexual and heterosexual foster parents. Lexis-Nexis Academic Universe, an internet search service, scans the whole text of over 50 regional and national newspapers, largely in the U.S., but also including major papers in Australia, England, Canada, and New Zealand (e.g., *Baltimore Sun, Boston Globe, Independent* [England], *Ottawa Citizen* [Canada]).

This past summer, I examined every news story from 1989 through 2001 that included "child molestation"—a total of 5,492 stories. The findings were double-checked by also running "foster" against this database in early September, 2002. Only news stories or first-person accounts were tallied, not editorials nor opinion pieces, so the stories basically covered recent events, not reflections on older items.

This technique is obviously different from a comparison study where matched parents—homosexual and heterosexual—are randomly drawn from the total set of foster parents to see how they stack up. News stories are limited in the content they cover, nor are they necessarily consistent from reporter to reporter or paper to paper. Nonetheless, this method has its advantages. News stories are reports about 'the real world,' and not just responses to questionnaires from people who know they are being questioned or scrutinized.

Only a few of the news stories listed the sexual preferences of the perpetrators. Nevertheless, following the classification of method of infection for AIDS by the U.S. Centers for Disease Control, I was able to classify the perpetrators by the kinds of sex they engaged in (e.g., 'male with male' was considered homosexual, 'male with female' heterosexual). Since marital status is generally provided in stories about child molestation, where it was not reported, the perpetrator was assumed to be unmarried.

What I Found

Thirty stories about molestation of foster kids were located. They were numbered by date of the first newspaper story about the molestation, from 1 to 30. The location and date are given below. In 22 stories foster children were sexually abused. Five stories bore upon the character of the foster parent or guardian, though no foster child was reported as having been sexually molested. In three stories, foster caregivers molested their charges as they were held in group quarters.

Result #1. In 22 stories, the perpetrator(s) molested foster children:

1. Arlington, VA (3/2/89): An unmarried man, who had had boys placed in his home for 10 years, was charged with having sex with one of the foster boys (this was counted as one homosexual male perpetrator, one victim).

2. San Diego (3/1/89): A mother (who was married to an oft-absent husband in the military) and son lost their foster day care license when charges of possible molestation of two children were filed against her (counted as a female perpetrator and two victims of unknown sex).

4. Los Angeles (6/6/90): A man and wife lost their license when the man was accused of molesting two foster daughters (counted as a heterosexual male perpetrator and two girl victims).

7. St. Louis (10/21/90): An unmarried man, both a foster parent to one boy and the supervisor of a unit at a children's home, was convicted of molesting his foster son as well as 4 other boys at the home (counted as a homosexual male perpetrator and one boy victim).

8. British Columbia, Canada (3/26/92): A man (marital status not provided) was released from prison for molesting a 14-year-old foster daughter (counted as a male heterosexual perpetrator and one girl victim).

10. Los Angeles (7/8/93): A man and wife lost their foster care license when the man was charged with molesting 2 of his foster daughters (counted as a male heterosexual perpetrator and 2 girl victims).

11. St. Petersburg, FL (1/11/94): An unmarried man was convicted of molesting his 12-year-old foster son (counted as a homosexual male perpetrator and one boy victim).

12. Maryland (4/16/94): An unmarried judge was charged with molesting his 17-year-old foster son (counted as a homosexual male perpetrator and one boy victim).

13. San Francisco (12/13/94): A married man was convicted of molesting boys and girls, including 3 foster children (counted as one homosexual male perpetrator and 3 victims of unknown sex).

15. Atlanta (1/30/97): A married man molested his 12-year-old foster son (counted as a homosexual male perpetrator and one boy victim).

17. Connecticut (3/22/97): A man and wife lost their foster-care license when he was accused of molesting his foster son (counted as a homosexual male perpetrator and a boy victim).

18. New York (6/29/97): An apparently unmarried foster mother sexually molested her foster daughter from the time she was age 5 until she was 17 (counted as a homosexual female perpetrator and a female victim).

19. Seattle (12/3/97): An unmarried couple molested an 8-year-old foster daughter (counted as a homosexual female perpetrator and a male heterosexual perpetrator and a female victim).

21. England (12/5/98): An unmarried foster parent was convicted of molesting his 12-year-old foster son (counted as a homosexual male perpetrator and a boy victim).

22. Atlanta (2/27/99): An unmarried foster parent was convicted of molesting his 3 foster children, a girl and two boys (counted as a homosexual male perpetrator and a girl and two boy victims).

23. Boston (11/3/99): A married foster parent was convicted of molesting "foster children" (counted as a male perpetrator with 2 victims of unknown sex).

24. Toronto (4/3/00): A married foster parent was convicted of molesting a foster daughter (counted as a heterosexual male perpetrator and a girl victim).
25. San Diego (4/25/00): An married foster parent was convicted of molesting two twin 9-year-old foster daughters (counted as a heterosexual male perpetrator and two girl victims).
26. San Diego (6/23/00): An unmarried foster father was charged with sexual improprieties with his foster son, 11, and hiring him out for sex with other men (counted as a homosexual male perpetrator and a boy victim).
28. San Diego (9/24/00): An unmarried openly homosexual male, living with a partner who was a convicted homosexual child molester (the partner had sexually abused his own son and daughter), was given custody of an 11-year-old foster son. He then raped him. Over the years the foster father also offered his foster son to others who were sexually interested in the boy. At least three individuals accepted the foster-father's offer (counted as a homosexual male perpetrator and a boy victim).
29. Los Angeles (7/10/01): An unmarried woman pled no contest to the accusation of sexually abusing her 12-year-old foster daughter, and then lost her foster-care license (counted as a homosexual female perpetrator and a female victim).
30. St. Louis (12/31/01): An unmarried foster father was charged with molesting 2 foster sons, both 13 years old (counted as a homosexual male perpetrator and two boy victims).

Comment: It is noteworthy that in two of the 12 stories involving gays, the homosexual not only molested his foster son, but prostituted him as well. Something seems to be morally 'wrong' with homosexuals.

Result #2. Five stories concerned the character of the foster parent:

3. Boston (5/18/89): An unmarried man had illicit pictures of boys. Although he had been convicted of child molestation on a boy in 1967 (and given a suspended sentence), starting in 1977 the Massachusetts Probation Department used him as a placement for "24 adolescent males during the past 12 years."
5. Seattle (8/28/90): An unmarried man, with whom 5 foster children were currently living, admitted to molesting two boys, 14 and 15, in his Scout troop. He had been dishonorably discharged from the Navy for "similar incidents involving young boys."
6. St. Louis (8/31/90): An unmarried child molester had a 14-year-old boy placed in his home by the Missouri Division of Family Services. The boy's older brother also lived with the man. The child molester had been convicted of attempted rape of and then stabbing a 12-year-old boy. It is not clear whether he had had sex with the foster boys.
9. Los Angeles (12/29/92): A man and wife lost their foster care license when the man was charged with molesting 2 of his daughters from a previous marriage.

20. Seattle (11/3/98): An unmarried foster parent of a boy was accused of molesting 5 boys. The boys were apparently from a church youth group he assisted.

Comment: Is it a statistical fluke that 3 of the 4 gay foster parents above already had 'a record of child molestation' and yet were given boys to foster parent? Perhaps. But the bias that child protective services seem to exhibit in favor of homosexuals offers a more chilling possibility. While the 'fox' is not running the henhouse, there appear to be a considerable number of 'foxes' in these agencies—and in the current climate of ceding victimhood status to gays, even the non-foxes are inclined to 'give homosexuals a second chance.'

Result #3. In three stories, children in a group home were molested:

14. Los Angeles (5/2/96): For the second time in the year, the state initiated action to revoke the foster home license of Gay and Lesbian Adolescent Social Services because an additional number of boys reported having been molested by male staff members (counted as 3 homosexual male perpetrators and 6 boy victims).
16. Wales, Great Britain (2/4/97): Dozens of staff members at 30 children's homes sexually abused 180 victims, "most . . . were boys, some as young as 8."
27. Los Angeles (8/30/00): At least 3 male counselors raped at least 3 boys and a girl at group homes. One of the perpetrators was single, and at least one boy he raped obtained a judgment against him. There were no follow-up stories about the other perpetrators.

Comment: These stories suggest character flaws inherent to the homosexual lifestyle—flaws that put children under the care of homosexuals at considerable hazard. Note that although there are a lot of girls in children's homes, the boys appear to be at special risk. And why was a homosexual social service allowed to run group homes?

What Do These Stories Suggest?

A pattern of disproportionate molestation of foster children by those who engage in homosexuality is evident in each of the three sets of stories above. The 22 stories involving molestation of foster children, in particular, bear directly upon whether homosexual or unmarried foster parents commit more sexual offenses against their charges. Of the 22 stories, 15 (68%) involved homosexual molestation. Of the 23 perpetrators, 19 (83%) were men, and 4 (17%) were women. Of the 19 men, 12 (63%) engaged in homosexuality. Three (25%) of these 12 were married, while 9 were single. Seven (37%) of the 19 male perpetrators practiced heterosexuality. Of these 7, at least 5 (71%) were married and at least one was single.

Of the 4 women, 3 engaged in homosexuality and were unmarried. The other was married but her sexual proclivities were not revealed. Overall, of the 22 perpetrators whose marital status was known, 13 (59%) were single.

In the 22 stories, among the 32 foster children who were victimized, at least 12 (38%) were girls and at least 13 (41%) were boys. Since 2.5 of the girls were victimized by females (counting the girl who was victimized by the unmarried man and woman as being 0.5 homosexually and 0.5 heterosexually victimized), altogether, out of the 28 victims of perpetrators where a sexual preference could be determined, 8.5 (30%) were victimized by heterosexuals and 19.5 (70%) by homosexuals. Also, of the 32 children, at least 15 (43%) were victimized by the unmarried.

So What Does This Evidence Indicate about Gay Foster Parents?

Undoubtedly, only a fraction of child molestation by foster parents over the 13 years I examined was included in any news stories. If they did 'make the paper,' many—like the molestation of the boy in Vermont in 2002 that led me to conduct this study—only made the local newspaper, not the newspapers covered by Academic Universe. But there is no reason to believe that this sample was biased against those who engage in homosexuality. Indeed, a number of the newspapers included in Academic Universe have editorialized in favor of special social protections for those who engage in homosexuality (e.g., *Los Angeles Times*, *New York Times*, *Boston Globe*). And these same newspapers have also expressed support for 'marital status nondiscrimination.' So they would have seemingly little reason to 'pick on' gay foster parents.

That at least 15 of the 22 instances of molestation of a foster child by a foster parent involved those who engaged in homosexuality is sharply at odds with the National Association of Social Workers' (NASW) 1987 resolution decrying "resistance to using single parents, . . . including lesbian and gay parents, as potential foster care and adoption resources." It also flies in the face of the NASW's appeal to its members to 'correct' this 'injustice.'

The empirical evidence is lined up against the NASW—of the 21 stories where the sexual proclivities of the perpetrator could be determined, 71% implicated homosexuals! Likewise, at least 57% of the 22 perpetrators were unmarried, and they accounted for at least 47% of the 32 child victims.

Homosexuality was also a disproportionate problem in the other 8 stories. When they are around or 'in charge' of kids, homosexuals are far more apt to seek to have sex with them. Nevertheless, we hear a lot from talk show hosts that homosexuals are no more apt to molest kids—tell that to the children who were victimized in these stories!

These news stories suggest that homosexuals and unmarried individuals are more apt to molest their foster charges. Because of this, they would not seem to be 'as fit' foster parents as married heterosexuals. The boy in story number 28, despite being raped, desired to return to live with the perpetrator. So he was apparently willing to 'live with molestations,' perhaps because there were other compensatory benefits in the arrangement. However, no matter how 'great' a parent they might be otherwise, there is no way someone can be a 'fit' foster parent if they sexually abuse their placements.

In a study FRI published earlier this year, interviews with 57 children with gay parents revealed that living in a homosexual home was a trying experience for children. In addition, the largest comparison study done to date—58 kids with married parents, 58 kids with cohabiting heterosexual parents, and 58 kids with homosexual parents—reported that the children with homosexual parents did less well at school, less well socially, and often gave evidence of personal distress. Thus, there is no particular reason to believe that either homosexuals or the unmarried generally compensate for their sexual weaknesses by offering exceptional foster-service in 'other areas.'

If the welfare of children is regarded as the most important consideration in foster-placement, these findings that the unmarried and those who engage in homosexuality are more likely to sexually molest their foster children suggest that the traditional aversion to their use as foster parents is rational and reasonable. Our society makes a lot of noise about 'protecting the children' and 'for the sake of the children.' But our foster system—which may process almost half a million kids every year—is being run throughout the country according to an alien, anti-child social philosophy.

Organizations like the NASW and many child protective service agencies across the land should lose their federal and state funding, until and unless they quit using kids' lives as bricks to reinforce unproven assertions that 'homosexuals are just as good' or that 'the unmarried are just as good.' Kids who need foster care are usually already under considerable stress—they don't need social revolutionaries putting them in highly sexually-charged environments.

EXPLORING THE ISSUE

Is Gay Adoption and Foster Parenting Healthy for Children?

Critical Thinking and Reflection

1. What are some of the main concerns that social workers tend to have with regard to allowing a child to be adopted or fostered by a homosexual person or couple?
2. With the issue of molestation, what does each article say about the likelihood that a homosexual person will molest? Do you agree with Paul Cameron's perspective that homosexuals are more likely molest? Why or why not?
3. What is your perspective of gay adoption or fostering? Did any of the information in the articles help you see valid arguments for the opposite perspective and if so, which information?

Is There Common Ground?

The National Adoption Information Clearinghouse includes a statement given by Abby Ruder, a therapist and lesbian adoptive mother, where she stated that children with homosexual parents may need to be taught when it is okay to tell people about their parents and when it is not. What is your opinion of this statement? Should a child be put into a situation where they feel that they have to conceal their home/family life? Is this sending the child mixed messages about whether their family is immoral or not?

Paul Cameron argues that homosexuals are more apt to molest their foster and adoptive children. However, the basis for his argument comes from 22 news stories where he assumes that the perpetrators were homosexual because they molested a child of the same gender. Do you agree with Cameron's assumption or is it possible that the adults were in fact heterosexual? Cameron only found 22 articles of the total 5492 stories listed that possibly implicated homosexual perpetrators as the molesters to their foster or adoptive children. What about the rest? Is this small number evidence enough to prove that homosexuals are at a higher risk of molesting? What could be some problems with basing your evidence for something simply off of news stories?

Cameron ends his article by stating the findings in a study, which he fails to reference, that compared 58 kids from married homes, cohabiting heterosexual homes, and homes where there were homosexual parents. He then goes on to state that the study found that the children with homosexual parents did less well in school, less well socially, and often gave evidence of personal distress. What is your opinion of these findings and this study? Do you feel that this is a credible source?

With the need for qualified foster parents and adoptive parents for older children rising, should society automatically disqualify foster and adoptive parents because of their sexual orientation? It is true that there are many heterosexual married couples ready and waiting to adopt newborns in this country, but the need for reliable foster parents and adoptive parents for older children is great. Would it be better for a child to be raised in a loving home, rather than moved from placement to placement, regardless of the sexual orientation of the parents? Some advocates for homosexual parenting rights suggest that children raised in gay and lesbian families will develop a greater capacity for empathy, tolerance for others, and a healthy respect for differences among people than those children raised in traditional, heterosexual families because these children are forced to embrace these issues more overtly. Is teaching tolerance and respect for differences not a significant goal for *all* parents in the twenty-first century?

Additional Resources

Gates, G., Badgett, L., Macomber, J., & Chambers, K. (2010). Adoption and Foster Care by Lesbian and Gay Parents in the United States. Retrieved on April 4, 2011, from http://www.urban.org/publications/411437.html.

This Web site lists an article with full text available regarding information provided by government data sources regarding gay, lesbian, and bisexual parents who are fostering or adopting children.

Jones, E. (2009). Adoption of Children by Same Sex Couples. Retrieved on April 4, 2011, from http://www.idebate.org/debatabase/topic_details.php?topicID=51.

This article lists the pros and cons associated with the debate of allowing gays and lesbians to adopt and foster children.

Soulforce Inc.: Relentless Nonviolent Resistance. (2011). Discrimination in Adoption and Foster Care for Children. Retrieved on April 4, 2011, from http://www.soulforce.org.article/647.

This site lists current policies and issues surrounding the gay/lesbian foster and adopted parenting debate in five states where the policies may discriminate against gays and lesbians.

ISSUE 14

Should the HPV Vaccination Be Mandatory for Girls in Later Childhood?

YES: Cynthia Dailard, from "Achieving Universal Vaccination Against Cervical Cancer in the United States: The Need and the Means," *Guttmacher Policy Review* (Fall 2006)

NO: Roni Rabin, from "A New Vaccine for Girls, but Should It Be Compulsory?" *The New York Times* (July 18, 2006)

Learning Outcomes

After reading this issue, you should be able to:

- Describe what the HPV vaccine is and what purpose vaccinating all young girls would serve.
- Understand each perspective regarding this issue.
- Decide where you stand on this issue and give supporting evidence.

ISSUE SUMMARY

YES: Cynthia Dailard, a senior public policy associate for the Alan Guttmacher Institute, suggests that the HPV vaccine be administered to females as a school entry requirement. She believes the vaccine is safe and effective and therefore should be universally administered to young girls. The best way to ensure the vaccine is available to these girls is by enacting state laws or policies requiring children to be vaccinated before school or day care enrollment.

NO: Roni Rabin, a columnist for *The New York Times*, objects to making the HPV vaccine mandatory for girls. She agrees that the vaccine is a significant development for the health and safety of our children. However, she does not believe every girl should be required to be vaccinated because the vaccine is costly and HPV can be managed through current, less costly procedures such as Pap smears.

Human papillomavirus (HPV) is a common sexually transmitted disease that most infected individuals do not realize they have. It usually clears up within a few years on its own. The problem with HPV is that some strains (e.g., HPV-16 and HPV-18) cause most of the genital warts and the vast majority of cancers of the cervix, anus, and even the throat. People who contract the various strains of HPV do not always develop cancer or genital warts, but the risk of contracting the strains that cause these problems is ever present. Gardasil is the brand name for an HPV vaccine that was approved by the Food and Drug Administration in 2006 to prevent cervical cancer and genital warts.

The HPV vaccination may be one of the greatest health advances for women in the past several decades. In two studies by the Centers for Disease Control and Prevention (CDC), the vaccine was 100 percent effective in preventing precancerous lesions and genital warts. In the second study, it was 98 percent effective in protecting against precancerous cervical lesions. Because Gardasil prevents the human papillomavirus from infecting sexually active women, the CDC recommends that females obtain the vaccination prior to becoming sexually active. They suggest being inoculated at ages 11 to 12. However, girls as young as 9 can get the vaccination, and those aged 13 to 26 are still advised to receive the vaccine even though it is not as effective if sexual activity has already begun. Since the CDC has added Gardasil to the recommended childhood vaccination schedule, several states are currently considering whether to make the vaccine mandatory for public school attendance.

Advocates for the vaccine promote universal vaccination and support laws to mandate vaccination as a prerequisite to attending school. A recent CDC study found that nearly 25 percent of women aged 14 to 59 and 49 percent of women aged 20 to 24 currently have HPV. HPV is very prevalent not only in the United States but in less industrialized countries as well. In places where Pap tests are not as readily available, there is greater prevalence of cervical cancer. In order to minimize the spread of HPV, advocates for the vaccination believe young girls across the globe should be inoculated prior to any sexual activity. To prevent deaths from measles and Polio, vaccinations for these diseases had to reach the universal level. Advocates for the HPV vaccine hope the same should happen for Gardasil.

Opponents believe vaccination should be a personal choice for parents to make for their children. Mandating inoculation would further erode parents' rights to raise their children as they see fit. Other opponents are fearful that having the vaccination may actually encourage girls to engage in premarital sex because they would not be fearful of contracting HPV. Still others prefer having regular Pap screenings, which they believe are preferable in detecting HPV, because the long-term effects of the vaccine are still unknown. They argue that the virus is not transmitted through casual contact. Consequently, the vaccination should not be universally mandated. They do not believe all girls need to be vaccinated that young. Another argument states most cases of cervical cancer in the United States come from women who do not regularly receive Pap tests. Opponents also say the vaccine is expensive and contend that the women who can afford the HPV vaccine are not the women who need it because they are annually getting Pap tests, which detect the HPV virus.

The following selections convey points for and against universal use of the HPV vaccine. Are viruses that are transmitted through casual contact more easily approved and subsequently mandated by federal law? Is sexual contact such a controversial issue that it affects the judgment of policymakers and parents? Think about these questions as you read the next two articles arguing for and against making the vaccination for HPV mandatory for young girls.

Cynthia Dailard

Achieving Universal Vaccination Against Cervical Cancer in the United States: The Need and the Means

The advent of a vaccine against the types of human papillomavirus (HPV) linked to most cases of cervical cancer is widely considered one of the greatest health care advances for women in recent years. Experts believe that vaccination against HPV has the potential to dramatically reduce cervical cancer incidence and mortality, particularly in resource-poor developing countries where cervical cancer is most common and deadly. In the United States, the vaccine's potential is likely to be felt most acutely within low-income communities and communities of color, which disproportionately bear the burden of cervical cancer.

Because HPV is easily transmitted through sexual contact, the vaccine's full promise may only be realized through near-universal vaccination of girls and young women prior to sexual activity—a notion reflected in recently proposed federal guidelines. And history, as supported by a large body of scientific evidence, suggests that the most effective way to achieve universal vaccination is by requiring children to be inoculated prior to attending school. Yet the link between HPV and sexual activity—and the notion that HPV is different than other infectious diseases targeted by vaccine school entry requirements—tests the prevailing justification for such efforts. Meanwhile, any serious effort to achieve universal vaccination among young people with this relatively expensive vaccine will expose holes in the public health safety net that, if left unaddressed, have the potential to exacerbate long-standing disparities in cervical cancer rates among American women.

The Case for Universal Vaccination

Virtually all cases of cervical cancer are linked to HPV, an extremely common sexually transmitted infection (STI) that is typically asymptomatic and harmless; most people never know they are infected, and most cases resolve on their own. It is estimated that approximately three in four Americans contract HPV at some point in their lives, with most cases acquired relatively soon

Dailard C., Achieving Universal Vaccination Against Cervical Cancer in the United States: The Need and the Means, *Guttmacher Policy Review*, 2006, 9(4):12–16.

after individuals have sex for the first time. Of the approximately 30 known types of HPV that are sexually transmitted, more than 13 are associated with cervical cancer. Yet despite the prevalence of HPV, cervical cancer is relatively rare in the United States; it generally occurs only in the small proportion of cases where a persistent HPV infection goes undetected over many years. This is largely due to the widespread availability of Pap tests, which can detect precancerous changes of the cervix that can be treated before cancer sets in, as well as cervical cancer in its earliest stage, when it is easily treatable.

Still, the American Cancer Society estimates that in 2006, almost 10,000 cases of invasive cervical cancer will occur to American women, resulting in 3,700 deaths. Significantly, more than half of all U.S. women diagnosed with cervical cancer have not had a Pap test in the last three years. These women are disproportionately low income and women of color who lack access to affordable and culturally competent health services. As a result, the incidence of cervical cancer is approximately 1.5 times higher among African American and Latina women than among white women; women of color are considerably more likely than whites to die of the disease as well. Two new HPV vaccines— Gardasil, manufactured by Merck & Company, and Cervarix, manufactured by GlaxoSmithKline—promise to transform this landscape. Both are virtually 100% effective in preventing the two types of HPV responsible for 70% of all cases of cervical cancer; Gardasil also protects against two other HPV types associated with 90% of all cases of genital warts. Gardasil was approved by the federal Food and Drug Administration (FDA) in June; GlaxoSmithKline is expected to apply for FDA approval of Cervarix by year's end.

Following FDA approval, Gardasil was endorsed by the Centers for Disease Control and Prevention's Advisory Committee on Immunization Practices (ACIP), which is responsible for maintaining the nation's schedule of recommended vaccines. ACIP recommended that the vaccine be routinely administered to all girls ages 11–12, and as early as age nine at a doctor's discretion. Also, it recommended vaccination of all adolescents and young women ages 13–26 as part of a national "catch-up" campaign for those who have not already been vaccinated.

The ACIP recommendations, which are closely followed by health care professionals, reflect the notion that to eradicate cervical cancer, it will be necessary to achieve near-universal vaccination of girls and young women prior to sexual activity, when the vaccine is most effective. Experts believe that such an approach has the potential to significantly reduce cervical cancer deaths in this country and around the world. Also, high vaccination rates will significantly reduce the approximately 3.5 million abnormal Pap results experienced by American women each year, many of which are caused by transient or persistent HPV infections. These abnormal Pap results require millions of women to seek follow-up care, ranging from additional Pap tests to more invasive procedures such as colposcopies and biopsies. This additional care exacts a substantial emotional and even physical toll on women, and costs an estimated $6 billion in annual health care expenditures. Finally, widespread vaccination fosters "herd immunity," which is achieved when a sufficiently high proportion of individuals within a population are vaccinated that those who go unvaccinated—because the vaccine is contraindicated for them or because they are medically underserved, for example—are essentially protected.

The Role of School Entry Requirements

Achieving high vaccination levels among adolescents, however, can be a difficult proposition. Unlike infants and toddlers, who have frequent contact with health care providers in the context of well-child visits, adolescents often go for long stretches without contact with a health care professional. In addition, the HPV vaccine is likely to pose particular challenges, given that it must be administered three times over a six-month period to achieve maximum effectiveness.

A large body of evidence suggests that the most effective means to ensure rapid and widespread use of childhood or adolescent vaccines is through state laws or policies that require children to be vaccinated prior to enrollment in day care or school. These school-based immunization requirements, which exist in some form in all 50 states, are widely credited for the success of immunization programs in the United States. They have also played a key role in helping to close racial, ethnic and socioeconomic gaps in immunization rates, and have proven to be far more effective than guidelines recommending the vaccine for certain age-groups or high-risk populations. Although each state decides for itself whether a particular vaccine will be required for children to enroll in school, they typically rely on ACIP recommendations in making their decision.

In recent months, some commentators have noted that as a sexually transmitted infection, HPV is "different" from other infectious diseases such as measles, mumps or whooping cough, which are easily transmitted in a school setting or threaten school attendance when an outbreak occurs. Some socially conservative advocacy groups accordingly argue that the HPV vaccine does not meet the historical criteria necessary for it to be required for children attending school; many of them also contend that abstinence outside of marriage is the real answer to HPV. They welcome the advent of the vaccine, they say, but will oppose strenuously any effort to require it for school enrollment.

This position reflects only a limited understanding of school-based vaccination requirements. These requirements do not exist solely to prevent the transmission of disease in school or during childhood. Instead, they further society's strong interest in ensuring that people are protected from disease throughout their lives and are a highly efficient means of eradicating disease in the larger community. For example, states routinely require school-age children to be vaccinated against rubella (commonly known as German measles), a typically mild illness in children, to protect pregnant women in the community from the devastating effects the disease can have on a developing fetus. Similarly, states currently require vaccination against certain diseases, such as tetanus, that are not "contagious" at all, but have very serious consequences for those affected. And almost all states require vaccination against Hepatitis B, a blood born disease which can be sexually transmitted.

Moreover, according to the National Conference of State Legislatures (NCSL), all 50 states allow parents to refuse to vaccinate their children on medical grounds, such as when a vaccine is contraindicated for a particular child due to allergy, compromised immunity or significant illness. All states except Mississippi and West Virginia allow parents to refuse to vaccinate their children on religious grounds. Additionally, 20 states go so far as to allow parents to refuse to vaccinate their children because of a personal, moral or other belief. Unlike a medical exemption, which requires a parent to provide documentation from a physician, the process for obtaining nonmedical exemptions can vary widely by state.

NCSL notes that, in recent years, almost a dozen states considered expanding their exemption policy. Even absent any significant policy change, the rate of parents seeking exemptions for nonmedical reasons is on the rise. This concerns public health experts. Research shows that in states where exemptions are easier to obtain, a higher proportion of parents refuse to vaccinate their children; research further shows that these states, in turn, are more likely to experience outbreaks of vaccine-preventable diseases, such as measles and whooping cough. Some vaccine program administrators fear that because of the social sensitivities surrounding the HPV vaccine, any effort to require the vaccine for school entry may prompt legislators to amend their laws to create nonmedical exemptions where they do not currently exist or to make existing exemptions easier to obtain. This has the potential not only to thwart the effort to stem the tide of cervical cancer, but to foster the spread of other vaccine-preventable diseases as well.

Financing Challenges Laid Bare

Another barrier to achieving universal vaccination of girls and young women will be the high price of the vaccine. Gardasil is expensive by vaccine standards, costing approximately $360 for the three-part series of injections. Despite this high cost, ACIP's endorsement means that Gardasil will be covered by most private insurers; in fact, a number of large insurers have already announced they will cover the vaccine for girls and young women within the ACIP-recommended age range. Still, the Institute of Medicine estimates that approximately 11% of all American children have private insurance that does not cover immunization, and even those with insurance coverage may have to pay deductibles and copayments that create a barrier to care.

Those who do not have private insurance or who cannot afford the out-of-pocket costs associated with Gardasil will need to rely on a patchwork system of programs that exist to support the delivery of subsidized vaccines to low-income and uninsured individuals. In June, ACIP voted to include Gardasil in the federal Vaccines for Children program (VFC), which provides free vaccines largely to children and teenagers through age 18 who are uninsured or receive Medicaid. The program's reach is significant: In 2003, 43% of all childhood vaccine doses were distributed by the VFC program.

THE POTENTIAL ROLE OF FAMILY PLANNING CLINICS IN AN HPV VACCINE 'CATCH-UP' CAMPAIGN

Family planning clinics, including those funded under Title X of the Public Health Service Act, have an important role to play in a national "catch-up" campaign to vaccinate young women against HPV. This is particularly true for women ages 19–26, who are too old to receive free vaccines through the federal Vaccines for Children program but still fall within the ACIP-recommended age range for the HPV vaccine.

Almost 4,600 Title X—funded family planning clinics provide subsidized family planning and related preventive health care to just over five million women nationwide. In theory, Title X clinics are well poised to offer the HPV vaccine, because they already are a major provider of STI services and cervical cancer screening, providing approximately six million STI (including HIV) tests and 2.7 million Pap tests in 2004 alone. Because Title X clients are disproportionately low income and women of color, they are at particular risk of developing cervical cancer later in life. Moreover, most Title X clients fall within the ACIP age recommendations of 26 and under for the HPV vaccine (59% are age 24 or younger, and 18% are ages 25–29); many of these women are uninsured and may not have an alternative source of health care.

Title X funds may be used to pay for vaccines linked to improved reproductive health outcomes, and some Title X clinics offer the Hepatitis B vaccine (which can be sexually transmitted). Although many family planning providers are expressing interest in incorporating the HPV vaccine into their package of services, its high cost—even at a discounted government purchase price—is likely to stand in the way. Clinics that receive Title X funds are required by law to charge women based on their ability to pay, with women under 100% of the federal poverty level (representing 68% of Title X clients) receiving services completely free of charge and those with incomes between 100–250% of poverty charged on a sliding scale. While Merck has expressed an interest in extending its patient assistance program to publicly funded family planning clinics, it makes no promises. In fact, a statement on the company's Web site says that "Due to the complexities associated with vaccine funding and distribution in the public sector, as well as the resource constraints that typically exist in public health settings, Merck is currently evaluating whether and how a vaccine assistance program could be implemented in the public sector."

The HPV vaccine, however, is not just recommended for children and teenagers; it is also recommended for young adult women up through age 26. Vaccines are considered an "optional" benefit for adults under Medicaid, meaning that it is up to each individual state to decide whether or not to cover a given vaccine. Also, states can use their own funds and federal grants to support the delivery of subsidized vaccines to low-income or uninsured adults.

Many states, however, have opted instead to channel these funds toward childhood-vaccination efforts, particularly as vaccine prices have grown in recent years. As a result, adult vaccination rates remain low and disparities exist across racial, ethnic and socioeconomic groups—mirroring the disparities that exist for cervical cancer.

In response to all this, Merck in May announced it would create a new "patient assistance program," designed to provide all its vaccines free to adults who are uninsured, unable to afford the vaccines and have an annual household income below 200% of the federal poverty level ($19,600 for individuals and $26,400 for couples). To receive free vaccines, patients will need to complete and fax forms from participating doctors' offices for processing by Merck during the patients' visits. Many young uninsured women, however, do not seek their care in private doctors' offices, but instead rely on publicly funded family planning clinics for their care, suggesting the impact of this program may be limited. . . .

Thinking Ahead

Solutions to the various challenges presented by the HPV vaccine are likely to have relevance far beyond cervical cancer. In the coming years, scientific breakthroughs in the areas of immunology, molecular biology and genetics will eventually permit vaccination against a broader range of acute illnesses as well as chronic diseases. Currently, vaccines for other STIs such as chlamydia, herpes and HIV are in various stages of development. Also under study are vaccines for Alzheimer's disease, diabetes and a range of cancers. Vaccines for use among adolescents will also be increasingly common. A key question is, in the future, will individuals across the economic spectrum have access to these breakthrough medical advances or will disadvantaged individuals be left behind?

When viewed in this broader context, the debate over whether the HPV vaccine should be required for school enrollment may prove to be a healthy one. If the HPV vaccine is indeed "the first of its kind," as some have characterized it, it has the potential to prompt communities across the nation to reconsider and perhaps reconceive the philosophical justification for school entry requirements. Because the U.S. health care system is fragmented, people have no guarantee of health insurance coverage or access to affordable care. School entry requirements might therefore provide an important opportunity to deliver public health interventions that, like the HPV vaccine, offer protections to individuals who have the potential to become disconnected from health care services later in life. Similar to the HPV vaccine's promise of cervical cancer prevention, these benefits may not be felt for many years, but nonetheless may be compelling from a societal standpoint. And bearing in mind that school dropout rates begin to climb as early as age 13, middle school might be appropriately viewed as the last public health gate that an entire age-group of individuals pass through together—regardless of race, ethnicity or socio-economic status.

Meanwhile, the cost and affordability issues raised by the HPV vaccine may help draw attention to the need to reform the vaccine-financing system in this country. In 2003, the Institute of Medicine proposed a series of reforms designed to improve the way vaccines are financed and distributed. They included a national insurance benefit mandate that would apply to all public and private health care plans and vouchers for uninsured children and adults to receive immunizations through the provider of their choice. Legislation introduced by Rep. Henry Waxman (D-CA) and Sen. Edward Kennedy (D-MA), called the Vaccine Access and Supply Act, adopts a different approach. The bill would expand the Vaccines for Children program, create a comparable Vaccines for Adults program, strengthen the vaccine grant program to the states and prohibit Medicaid cost-sharing requirements for ACIP-recommended vaccines for adults.

Whether the HPV vaccine will in fact hasten reforms of any kind remains to be seen. But one thing is clear: If the benefits of this groundbreaking vaccine cannot be enjoyed by girls and women who are disadvantaged by poverty or insurance status, then it will only serve to perpetuate the disparities in cervical cancer rates that have persisted in this country for far too long.

Roni Rabin **NO**

A New Vaccine for Girls, but Should It Be Compulsory?

Around the time report cards came home this spring, federal health officials approved another new vaccine to add to the ever-growing list of recommended childhood shots—this one for girls and women only, from 9 to 26, to protect them from genital warts and cervical cancer.

One of my own daughters, who just turned 9, would be a candidate for this vaccine, so I've been mulling this over. A shot that protects against cancer sounds like a great idea, at first. States may choose to make it mandatory, though the cost for them to do so would be prohibitive.

But let's think carefully before requiring young girls to get this vaccine, which protects against a sexually transmitted virus, in order to go to school. This isn't polio or measles, diseases that are easily transmitted through casual contact. Infection with this virus requires intimate contact, of the kind that doesn't occur in classrooms.

Besides, we already know how to prevent cervical cancer in this country, and we've done a darn good job of it. In the war against cancer, the battle against cervical cancer has been a success story.

Why, then, did federal health officials recommend the inoculation of about 30 million American girls and young women against the human papillomavirus, a sexually transmitted disease that in rare cases leads to cervical cancer?

Vaccine supporters say that some 3,700 American women die of cervical cancer each year, and close to 10,000 cases are diagnosed. Cervical cancer has a relatively high survival rate, but every death is tragic and treatment can rob women of their fertility.

Still, you have to see the numbers in context. Cervical cancer deaths have been dropping consistently in the United States—and have been for decades.

Cervical cancer has gone from being one of the top killers of American women to not even being on the top 10 list. This year cervical cancer will represent just 1 percent of the 679,510 new cancer cases and 1 percent of the 273,560 anticipated cancer deaths among American women. By contrast, some 40,970 women will die of breast cancer and 72,130 will die of lung cancer.

According to the American Cancer Society Web site, "Between 1955 and 1992, the number of cervical cancer deaths in the United States dropped by 74 percent." Think about it: 74 percent.

The number of cases diagnosed each year and the number of deaths per year have continued to drop, even though the population is growing.

From 1997 to 2003, the number of cervical cancers in the United States dropped by 4.5 percent each year, while the number of deaths dropped by 3.8 percent each year, according to a government Web site that tracks cancer trends, called SEER or Surveillance, Epidemiology and End Results. . . . This, while many other cancers are on the rise.

If current trends continue, by the time my 9-year-old daughter is 48, the median age when cervical cancer is diagnosed, there will be only a few thousand cases of the cancer in women, and about 1,000 deaths or fewer each year, even without the vaccine.

The secret weapon? Not so secret. It's the Pap smear. A simple, quick, relatively noninvasive test that's part and parcel of routine preventive health care for women. It provides early warnings of cellular changes in the cervix that are precursors for cancer and can be treated.

An American Cancer Society spokeswoman said that most American women who get cervical cancer these days are women who either had never had a Pap smear or had not followed the follow-up and frequency guidelines. So perhaps we could redirect the public money that would be spent on this vaccine—one of the most expensive ever, priced at $360 for the series of three shots—to make sure all women in the United States get preventive health care.

Because even if you have the new vaccine, which protects against only some of the viral strains that may bring on cervical cancer, you still need to continue getting Pap smears.

To be clear, I'm talking only about American women. Sadly, hundreds of thousands of women worldwide die of cervical cancer each year because they don't have access to Pap smears and the follow-up care required. For them, and for American women at high risk, the vaccine should be an option.

Black, Hispanic and some foreign-born women are at higher risk, though rates have dropped precipitously among blacks. Certain behavior—smoking, eating poorly, having multiple sexual partners and long-term use of the pill, for example—are also associated with an increased risk. But most people infected with the human papillomavirus clear it on their own.

Vaccine supporters, including the American Cancer Society, say the immunization will reduce abnormal Pap test results, and the stress, discomfort and cost of follow-up procedures and painful treatments. That's a strong argument for the vaccine.

But vaccines carry risks. In recent years, children have been bombarded with new immunizations, and we still don't know the full long-term implications. One vaccine, RotaShield, was removed from the market in 1999, just a year after being approved for infants.

Merck has tested the cervical cancer vaccine in clinical trials of more than 20,000 women (about half of them got the shot). The health of the subjects was followed for about three and a half years on average. But fewer than 1,200 girls under 16 got the shots, among them only about 100 9-year-olds, Merck officials said, and the younger girls have been followed for only 18 months.

Public health officials want to vaccinate girls early, before they become sexually active, even though it is not known how long the immunity will last.

But girls can also protect themselves from the human papillomavirus by using condoms; a recent study found that condoms cut infections by more than half. Condoms also protect against a far more insidious sexually transmitted virus, H.I.V.

So yes, by all means, let's keep stamping out cervical cancer. Let's make sure women and girls get Pap smears.

EXPLORING THE ISSUE

Should the HPV Vaccination Be Mandatory for Girls in Later Childhood?

Critical Thinking and Reflection

1. What population receives the HPV vaccine? What is the purpose of this vaccine and what does it protect against?
2. Briefly describe each author's perspective about making the HPV vaccine mandatory for young and adolescent girls.
3. What is your opinion about this issue? Should the government be able to make a vaccination that is so relatively new mandatory without knowing the long-term effects?

Is There Common Ground?

Roni Rabin makes a point in her article that cervical cancer has dramatically decreased over the years due to Pap testing. However, Dailard points out that cervical cancer is not the only consequence of HPV. Dailard argues that females who contract HPV must still seek follow-up care due to genital warts and abnormal Pap results leading to a physical and emotional toll as well as possible infertility. Although the Pap test detects the HPV virus, women still go through biopsies and colposcopies, which can be invasive. Given this information, would you want to vaccinate your daughter?

Rabin argues that Pap tests are effective in preventing cervical cancer. However, she makes the point that women of color are less likely to receive routine Pap tests, which she attributes to cost. She then makes the suggestion that instead of government funding going to provide vaccines, they should offer free Pap tests to women who otherwise could not receive one due to no insurance. Can you think of any other reasons why women of color may not be receiving regular Pap tests? Would offering free Pap tests ensure that all women would receive annual Pap tests?

Dailard points out that some who oppose the HPV vaccine for young girls fear that they would be sending the wrong message encouraging premarital sex. What is your opinion of this fear? Do you think it is good cause not to vaccinate?

Neither of the articles mentioned males getting vaccinated for HPV although males can be vaccinated. How might the opinions change if we were talking about making it mandatory for males and females to be vaccinated or just males? Why do you think this is not mentioned?

Additional Resources

Centers for Disease Control and Prevention. (2011). Human Papillomavirus. Retrieved on April 24, 2011, from http://www.cdc.gov/hpv/.

This Web site provides information about HPV regarding prevention, treatment, signs and symptoms, and so forth. The Web site also gives information regarding being vaccinated.

Health Information and Education. (2011). Helping Parents Understand the HPV Vaccine. Retrieved on April 24, 2011, from http://www.healthed.org/consulting/Articles/20081216ParentsUnderstandHPVVaccine.htm.

This Web site addresses questions that parents may have regarding the HPV vaccine. It provides information about the safety of the vaccine as well as other issues that parents may have with deciding whether or not to have their daughters vaccinated.

The American Congress of Obstetricians and Gynecologists. (2010). Ob-Gyns Recommend HPV Vaccination for Young Girls: Adolescents and Young Women May Also Benefit. Retrieved April 24, 2011, from http://www.acog.org/from_home/publications/press_releases/nr08-23-10-3.cfm.

This article gives supporting evidence for vaccinating girls as young as 11 or 12 for HPV as well as some guidelines that parents should know with regard to the vaccine.

Internet References . . .

Positive Parenting

This site contains information and articles related to how parents and educators can communicate more effectively with children and adolescents.

http://www.positiveparenting.com

CYFERNet

The Children, Youth, and Families Education and Research Network (CYFER-Net), sponsored by the U.S. Department of Agriculture's Cooperative Extension Service, provides practical research-based information in health, child care, family strengths, science, and technology.

http://www.cyfernet.org

The American Academy of Child and Adolescent Psychiatry

Here the American Academy of Child and Adolescent Psychiatry provides information as a public service to assist families and educators in socializing children and adolescents.

http://www.aacap.org

Adolescent Health Online

This online site of the American Medical Association (AMA) provides extensive information on adolescent health issues and the AMA's Guidelines for Adolescent Preventive Services (GAPS) program.

http://www.ama-assn.org/ama/pub/physician-resources/public-health/ promoting-healthy-lifestyles/adolescent-health.shtml

CDC: Youth Violence Prevention

This Web site from the Center for Disease Control and Prevention provides resources for preventing youth violence and aggression.

http://www.cdc.gov/ViolencePrevention/youthviolence/index.html

National Youth Violence Prevention Center

The mission of the NYVPRC is to provide key leaders in with dynamic resources to help support their efforts to plan, develop, implement, and evaluate effective youth violence prevention efforts.

http://www.safeyouth.org

Bullying and Harassment Information for Teens

Crisis Connection's section on Teen Bullying contains up-to-date links, resources, and information about teenage aggression.

http://www.crisisconnectioninc.org/teens/bullying.htm

320

Adolescence

Many people use the term teenage years to describe adolescence. This is the period of time from ages 13 through 19. During this period of development the child typically begins puberty, and there are dramatic physical changes that occur as the child becomes a young adult. Much less obvious than the physical changes are the cognitive and emotional changes in children at this stage of development. In early adolescence the child is increasingly able to think on an abstract level. Adolescents also undertake the daunting process of identity development, defining who they are. This final section considers some of the key issues related to decisions about values and sexuality that teens make as they move through adolescence.

- Are Male Teens More Aggressive Than Female Teens?
- Is Abstinence-Only Sex Education the Best Way to Teach About Sex?
- Is the Internet a Safe Place for Teens to Explore?

ISSUE 15

Are Male Teens More Aggressive Than Female Teens?

YES: Christina Salmivalli, and Ari Kaukiainen, from "Female Aggression Revisited: Variable and Person-Centered Approaches to Studying Gender Differences in Different Types of Aggression," *Aggressive Behavior* (March/April 2004)

NO: Melanie J. Zimmer-Gembeck, Tasha C. Geiger, and Nicki R. Crick, from "Relational and Physical Aggression, Prosocial Behavior, and Peer Relations: Gender Moderation and Bidirectional Associations," *Journal of Early Adolescence* (November 2005)

Learning Outcomes

After reading this issue, you should be able to:

- Describe the overall findings from each article that either support or do not support gender differences with regard to aggression in teens.
- Identify limitations in each article that may question the generalizability of the findings.
- Decide for yourself if the research presented is compelling enough to help you decide which side of the issue you are on.

ISSUE SUMMARY

YES: Christina Salmivalli and Ari Kaukiainen, both professors of psychology at the University of Turku, argue that on the whole male teens are more relationally and physically aggressive than female teens. However, there is a small subset of girls who when in a group are more aggressive than males.

NO: Malanie Zimmer-Gembeck, Tasha Geiger, and Nicki Crick, researchers at Griffith University, University of Rochester, and the University of Minnesota, argue that once they attain the age of 10 years, girls are actually more relationally aggressive than boys.

Research on aggression and adolescents suggests that aggressive acts are neither uncommon nor restricted to a certain demographic. School bullying and aggression cut across all economic, cultural, ethnic, and gender boundaries. The reported rates of bullying and aggression for the United States suggest that a significant number of adolescents have either been a victim of school aggression or have bullied others themselves. This is a concern because aggression is associated with a host of behavioral, social, and emotional adjustment difficulties.

In order to answer the question "Are male teens more aggressive than female teens?" it is important to understand what we mean by "aggression." Social scientists define aggression as behavior intended to hurt, harm, or injure another person. However, research has demonstrated that children engage in a variety of forms of aggressive behavior. The most important distinction for classification purposes is whether aggression is physical or relational in form.

Physical, or direct, aggression consists of behaviors that harm another through damage to one's physical well-being. Physical aggression among adolescents has received considerable attention from researchers. Some have argued that there is a general tendency for physical violence to worsen over time, with behaviors like minor aggression giving way to more serious behaviors, including assault and robbery. Other research has shown that, among boys, early physical aggression predicts an elevated risk of physical violence in adolescence as well as nonviolent forms of delinquency.

Relational, or indirect, aggression includes behaviors that harm others through damage to relationships or feelings of friendship, acceptance, or social inclusion. Existing evidence suggests that relational aggression, like physical aggression, can result in emotional harm to victims. Outcomes include a range of psychosocial problems including lower social and emotional adjustment, poorer relationships with peers, and more loneliness. An added concern among some researchers who study relational aggression is the potential for retaliatory violence by those who have been victimized. Research has shown that a majority of females use relational aggression to secure their social status and maintain social harmony.

In general, males tend to employ more physical aggression, while females are more likely to use relational aggression. However, recent research suggests that it is not always appropriate to categorize aggression types by gender. Several studies have found that male and female teens appear to use a complex combination of both physical and relational aggression.

In addition to the aggression issue, be mindful of the age group on which these selections focus. Adolescence is a time of physical, developmental, social, and emotional change. Adolescents often feel out of control and overwhelmed by daily living. Remember when you were a teenager? Were you ever a victim or perpetrator of physical or relational aggression? Who were more aggressive, males or females? Which one of these views best reflects your experiences?

The question remains: Are male teens more aggressive than female teens? As you read the following two selections, keep in mind the different types of aggression. Salmivalli and Kaukiainen argue that male teens are both more physically and more relationally aggressive than females. On the opposite side, Zimmer-Gembeck, Geiger, and Crick argue that there is no difference between the genders, only the types of aggression used.

YES

Christina Salmivalli and
Ari Kaukiainen

"Female Aggression" Revisited: Variable- and Person-Centered Approaches to Studying Gender Differences in Different Types of Aggression

Introduction

During recent decades, increasing attention has been drawn to subtle forms of aggression, in which the perpetrator harms the target person by damaging or manipulating his/her relationships or status in the peer group rather than by making any overt (physical or verbal) attacks. Such forms of aggression have been referred to as indirect, [Lagerspetz et al., 1988], relational, [Crick and Grotpeter, 1995], or social aggression [Cairns et al., 1989; Galen and Underwood, 1997]. Each of these concepts emphasizes slightly different aspects of, or strategies by which, the harm is delivered [for a debate on their shared and unique features, see Archer, 2001; Björkqvist, 2001; Underwood et al., 2001]. In the present paper, we refer to the above forms of aggression as *indirect*.

When studies on indirect forms of aggression started to emerge, it was a common argument that while boys are more directly (i.e., physically and/or verbally) aggressive than girls, girls in turn use more indirect forms of aggression than boys [also supported by empirical evidence, see Björkqvist et al., 1992a; Crick et al., 1997; Crick and Grotpeter, 1995, Lagerspetz et al., 1988; Salmivalli et al., 2000]. Since then, this statement has been taken more or less as a universal truth, even if the evidence seems to be far from conclusive.

What seems quite clear now is that females use more indirect than direct, at least physical, aggression [Lagerspetz and Bjorkqvist, 1994], and in proportional terms, i.e., when expressed as proportions of the total aggression scores, girls may even use more indirect aggression than boys. For instance, Osterman et al. [1998] found that 55 per cent of all aggression used by 8–year-old girls was indirect, while the corresponding proportion for boys was 26 per cent (among the 11– and 15–year-old adolescents, the proportions were 41 per cent and 52 per cent for girls vs. 23 per cent and 20 per cent for boys, respectively).

It might, however, be premature to say that 'the claim that human males are more aggressive than females appears to be false' [Björkqvist et al., 1994],

From *Aggressive Behavior*, March/April, 2004, pp. 158–163. Copyright © 2004 by International Society for Research on Agression (ISRA). Reprinted by permission of John Wiley & Sons, Inc.

or that indirect aggression would be an exclusively 'female' type of aggression [for an excellent discussion on this, see Underwood et al., 2001].

Already among the early studies, there were some that found few or no gender differences in indirect aggression [e.g., Galen and Underwood, 1997; Rys and Bear, 1997; Österman et al., 1998], while some even found that boys used more indirect aggression than girls [Tomada and Schneider, 1997]. These findings were, however, generally ignored in the ongoing academic debate, which was dominated by the view of females being more indirectly aggressive than males. There are, again, some recent studies showing very mixed patterns of findings regarding the use of indirect aggression. Underwood [2002], studying different subtypes of gender exclusivity and social aggression in children (10 to 14 years old), found no gender difference in verbal social aggression towards a provoking playmate in a laboratory setting, while girls showed more nonverbal, i.e., facial and gestural social aggression, than boys. On the other hand, there was a trend for boys to report using more relational aggression toward others than girls. Preliminary results from a meta-analysis by Scheithauer and Petermann [2002] showed no gender difference in the use of indirect, or what they call 'unprototypical' aggression across 70 studies. However, the effect sizes found varied according to age: adolescent girls, for instance, showed more this type of aggression than boys.

The aim of the present report is to participate in the ongoing discussion about gender differences in aggression by presenting results based on questionnaire data from three age groups in middle childhood and adolescence. In addition to comparing the mean scores of boys and girls on different types of aggression, we took a person-oriented approach and formed clusters with different 'aggression profiles.' In the latter approach, individuals' value profiles rather than their scores on single variables are taken into consideration, and the person (with his/her unique combination of values on the relevant variables) is the central unit of analysis [Bergman, 1998].

We were looking for two kinds of manifestations of 'female aggression.' If indirect aggression is typical of females, this would become apparent, first, in girls scoring higher than boys on indirect (while not on physical and verbal) aggression. Another manifestation of female indirect aggression would be the identification of a group of highly aggressive girls employing indirect, rather than direct aggressive strategies.

Method

The participants were 526 children (274 girls, 252 boys) from 22 school classes in two towns in Finland. They were from three grade levels, aged 10, 12, and 14 years. Aggression was measured by the DIAS [Björkqvist et al., 1992b], administered as a peer- and self-report procedure in which children evaluated all their same-sex classmates, as well as themselves, in terms of their use of direct physical (e.g. hits, kicks), direct verbal (e.g. yells, insults), and indirect aggression (e.g. says bad things behind the other's back, tries to get the others to dislike the person), on a five-point scale ranging from 0 = 'never' to 4 = 'very often'.

Results

Multivariate analyses of variance (with both self- and peer-reports of physical, verbal, and indirect aggression as dependent variables) were conducted across all age groups and in each age group separately. Multivariate F's were significant at the p = .000 level in all cases. Across age groups, *boys used all three types of aggression more than girls . . .*, with only one exception: in self-reported indirect aggression, the difference between boys and girls was not significant. Looking at the three age groups separately, boys were again, in most cases, significantly more aggressive than girls. In indirect aggression, however, a significant gender difference was found only among the 10-year-old children, and only in peer reports.

SPSS K-means cluster analysis was performed with the standardized peer-reported scores on the three aggression scales as criterion variables for forming the clusters. Five clusters with different aggression profiles were identified. According to oneway analyses of variance, the members of these clusters differed significantly from each other in self-, as well as peer-reported physical, verbal, and indirect aggression. . . .

Girls and boys were not evenly distributed in the clusters (chi-square (4) = 169.04, p < .001). There were more boys than would have been expected by chance in clusters two and three, which were characterized by extremely high scores on all kinds of aggression (cluster two) or high scores on direct aggression (cluster three). Girls, on the other hand, were overrepresented in clusters four and five. The former cluster was a group of nonaggressive children. The latter consisted of children with very high scores on indirect, above-average scores on verbal, and average scores on physical aggression. *All 36 children in this cluster were girls*. This suggests that even if girls are not—when comparing the average scores of all girls and all boys—more indirectly aggressive than boys are, there is a group of girls who are very aggressive, and predominantly indirectly so.

Discussion

While there seems to be clear evidence of boys being more physically (and perhaps verbally) aggressive than girls, a debate is going on regarding the gender difference—or lack of it—in indirect/social/relational aggression [Crick and Grotpeter, 1995; Lagerspetz and Bjorkqvist, 1994; Österman, 2001; Underwood et al., 2001]. In the present study, boys and girls in middle childhood and adolescence were compared with respect to 1) their average scores on direct, verbal, and indirect aggression, and 2) their 'aggression profiles', i.e., their combinations of values on the three aggression scales [Bergman, 1998]. Comparing the mean scores of boys and girls on the different types of aggression used (direct physical, direct verbal, and indirect), all the differences found showed boys being more aggressive than girls. The differences were largest in physical aggression, somewhat smaller in verbal aggression, and smallest, or in many cases non-existent in indirect aggression.

The person-oriented approach, however, revealed two cluster groups in which girls were overrepresented: the nonaggressive group, and the indirectly aggressive group. This suggests that, first, girls are nonaggressive as compared with boys, and second, highly aggressive girls rarely use all types of aggression to any great extent. There is a group of highly aggressive girls whose use of aggression was *predominantly indirect*. When boys were aggressive, on the other hand, they either tended to prefer direct (physical and verbal) strategies or to use quite high levels of *all kinds of aggression*. The latter is in line with Scheithauer and Petermann's [2002] finding that boys showed a combination of direct and indirect aggression more often than girls.

Should indirect aggression be called 'female aggression' at all? In the light of our data [as well as several other studies, see Galen and Underwood, 1997; Tomada and Schneider, 1997; Österman et al., 1998] we argue that it should not, at least in the sense of girls being, on average, more indirectly aggressive than males. But, perhaps in the sense that for a group of highly aggressive girls, it is the predominant way of being aggressive, we can talk about 'female aggression'.

From the methodological point of view, we suggest that studies of psychosocial adjustment and direct and indirect aggression might benefit from a person-oriented approach. Although direct and indirect aggression are highly intercorrelated, their common variance is often neglected when studying associations between indirect aggression and adjustment. For instance, direct aggression is rarely controlled for, when predicting concurrent or longitudinal adjustment from indirect aggression [e.g. Crick et al., 1997; Werner and Crick, 1999]. It would be enlightening to see whether students in our cluster five, for instance, (i.e., the 'indirectly aggressive' ones) suffer from adjustment difficulties, or whether they are in fact relatively well-adjusted. Unfortunately, our data do not allow such observations.

Melanie J. Zimmer-Gembeck,
Tasha C. Geiger, and Nicki R. Crick

Relational and Physical Aggression, Prosocial Behavior, and Peer Relations: Gender Moderation and Bidirectional Associations

Relationships among children, and children's reputation and status in the peer group, are important for social and emotional development. Being held in positive regard by peers has been associated with future social competence and relatively fewer behavioral problems (Hymel, Rubin, Rowden, & LeMare, 1990). Furthermore, in numerous studies, peer rejection has been consistently associated with later individual maladjustment, such as learning difficulties, poor academic achievement, loneliness and depressive symptoms in childhood, and mental health problems and criminality in adolescence and adulthood (see Coie, Dodge, & Kupersmidt, 1990 and Parker & Asher, 1987 for reviews).

Because children's status with their peers is one of the most robust indicators of maladjustment, both cross-sectional and prospective studies have been conducted to investigate why some children and adolescents are more preferred by peers than other children (e.g., Cillessen, Bukowski, & Haselager, 2000; Coie & Dodge, 1983). In particular, researchers have focused on whether children's own behaviors predict acceptance and rejection by peers (e.g., Coie, Dodge, & Coppotelli, 1982; Coie, Lochman, Terry, & Hyman, 1992; Parke et al., 1997). Convincing evidence has emerged showing that children's physically aggressive behaviors are predictive of rejection by the peer group (Newcomb, Bukowski, & Pattee, 1993).

It is not yet clear whether earlier children's behaviors influence their relationships with peers after the transition from childhood to adolescence and the transition to a new school environment. Few longitudinal studies of behavior and peer relationships have followed children as they make these transitions. This is an important question to address as the progression from childhood into early adolescence is a time marked by significant change in the nature and form of peer groups (B. B. Brown, 1990) and friendships (Berndt & Keefe, 1995). Concurrent changes in the biological, cognitive, and social domains characteristic of entry into adolescence can mark a time when

From *Journal of Early Adolescence*, vol. 25, no. 4, November 2005, pp. 421–452 (excerpts). Copyright © 2005 by Sage Publications. Reprinted by permission via Rightslink.

peer relations become increasingly important for support and when a variety of problem behaviors can emerge or escalate (Caspi, Lynam, Moffitt, & Silva, 1993; Lerner & Galambos, 1998; Zimmer-Gembeck, Siebenbruner, & Collins, 2001). Similarly, the transition to middle school has been reported as difficult for some children; there have been reports of declining self-conceptions, confidence, and school achievement (see Eccles, Wigfield, & Schiefele, 1998, for a review; Skinner, Zimmer-Gembeck, & Connell, 1998) as well as increases in depression, especially among girls (Nolen-Hoeksema, 2001; Hankin & Abramson, 2001; Prinstein & Aikins, 2004; Rudolph & Asher, 2000).

Peer Status and Children's Behaviors

. . . Certain behaviors often place children at risk for poor relations with peers, and in turn, these problems or successes with peers may exacerbate problem behavior or undermine the development of prosocial behaviors. For example, physically aggressive behavior among young boys has been associated with maintaining rejected peer status during a 1-year period, and peer rejection in kindergarten has been associated with physically aggressive behavior in Grade 2 after accounting for the boys' earlier aggressive behavior (Cillessen, van Ijzendoorn, van Lieshout, & Hartup, 1992; Dodge, 1993). . . . We estimated the influence of children's earlier behaviors on their middle school standing in the peer group and, simultaneously, examined converse associations to determine if children's earlier peer status influenced behaviors in middle school.

. . . Cillessen and colleagues (Cillessen et al., 2000) reviewed the individual and group mechanisms by which social experiences can exert influence on behavior over time and across a school transition. They emphasized the different learning opportunities for accepted versus rejected peers in terms of the ongoing information they receive about their social skills and the ability to practice and benefit from the modeling of these social skills by peers with whom they affiliate (see also Hartup, 1983). Others (Crick & Ladd, 1993; Rudolph & Clark, 2001) have also described how views of the self in peer relationships may develop from experiences of peer rejection or acceptance. Compared to children, adolescents' self-views in the domains of social appeal and skills are very important and may be overemphasized (Harter, 1999). By early adolescence, interactions with peers are likely to become consistent with the positive (Rabiner & Coie, 1989) or negative (Coie, 1990) views of self and peers that have developed in earlier years. For example, in a 3-year longitudinal study of adolescents, there was evidence that withdrawal (measured as social disengagement) had an influence on later self-views, and reciprocally, negative relational self-views were associated with later withdrawal from peers (Caldwell, Rudolph, Troop-Gordon, & Kim, 2004).

Peer Status, Children's Behaviors, and Gender

. . . *Children's behaviors and gender.* Most studies of peer status and children's behavior have identified low peer status with classmates, such as rejection, as a correlate of physical forms of aggression, especially among males (e.g.,

Bierman & Wargo, 1995; Cillessen et al., 1992). However, beginning at about age 4, physical aggression has been found to be more common among males than females (Hood, 1996; Parke & Slaby, 1983), so studies have often included only boys (e.g., Bierman & Wargo, 1995; Cillessen et al., 1992). This focus on physical forms of aggression and exclusion of girls has resulted in less knowledge about behaviors that may lead to girls' social difficulties or success with peers. Furthermore, approximately one half of boys who are rejected are not physically aggressive (Bierman & Wargo, 1995; French, 1988), and the association between peer rejection and physical aggression declines as children get older (Franzoi, Davis, & Vasquez-Suson, 1994). . . .

Relational aggression. Relational aggression involves "behaviors that harm others through damage (or threat of damage) to relationships or feelings of acceptance, friendship, or group inclusion" (Crick, 1996b, p. 77). For example, relational aggression includes the use of social exclusion to harm others (Crick, 1996b; Crick & Grotpeter, 1995). Although physical aggression tends to be stable or decline during late childhood and adolescence (Loeber & Hay, 1997), relational aggression and related behaviors have been found to increase around early adolescence (about age 11 through 12; Cairns, Cairns, Neckerman, Ferguson, & Gariépy, 1989). As desires for intimacy and exclusivity in relationships increase from late childhood to early adolescence (B. B. Brown, 1990; Furman & Buhrmester, 1992; Parker & Asher, 1993), some young people may increasingly use relationally aggressive strategies rather than physical aggression to harm others or influence their relationships. In past studies of early adolescents, relational aggression has been more common than physical aggression, and relational aggression has been associated with poorer peer relationships (Crick, 1996b; Rys & Bear, 1997). For example, in a 6-month longitudinal investigation of children in Grades 3 to 6 (Crick, 1996b), relational aggression was associated with increases in peer rejection, especially for girls, even after accounting for the influence of physical aggression.

Prosocial behavior. There have been recent appeals to expand the study of peer interactions by placing more emphasis on positive behaviors during the transition into adolescence (Carlo, Fabes, Laible, & Kupanoff, 1999; Fabes, Carlo, Kupanoff, & Laible, 1999). A link has been established between prosocial behavior and peer acceptance, with prosocial children being more accepted by their peers (Asher & Coie, 1990). Given this association and the age-related increases in prosocial behaviors that have been found, particularly for females in early adolescence (Fabes et al., 1999), longitudinal associations between peer relationships and positive social behaviors also were examined in the current study.

Social preference and social impact. . . . Social preference has been referred to as a measure of likability and peer acceptance, whereas social impact has been referred to as a measure of prominence and visibility in the peer group (Schneider, 2000). Recent qualitative (Adler & Adler, 1995) and quantitative (Bukowski, Sippola, & Newcomb, 2000; Pellegrini, 1995) investigations have shown likability, dominance, and prominence in the peer group becoming increasingly salient in adolescence after a transition to middle school. . . .

Gender moderation hypotheses.   Based on empirical findings, we expected that gender would moderate associations between peer status and children's behaviors. First, the association between physical aggression and social preference was expected to be greater among males than females. Multiple studies, especially studies of boys, have reported negative associations between physical aggression and peer social preference (see Newcomb et al., 1993, for a review).

Second, associations between relational aggression and social preference and between relational aggression and social impact were expected to be stronger for girls than for boys. With regards to peer preference, we expected that engagement in relational aggression in Grade 3 will be associated with lower peer preference in early adolescence because these behaviors can violate the emphasis on trust that is becoming more salient and characteristic of peer relationships during this transitional period (Bigelow & La Gaipa, 1975). Yet previous research findings have shown that relational aggression is associated with lower peer preference for girls (but not for boys), after physical aggression was taken into account (Crick, 1996b; Rys & Bear, 1997). Earlier relational aggression was also expected to be associated with greater social impact in early adolescence as there is evidence that one motivation for relational aggression may be to increase dominance and prominence in the peer group (Werner & Hill, 2003). . . . It appears that relationally aggressive girls can have more social impact in the peer group but be less preferred when compared to girls who are less relationally aggressive (Crick & Grotpeter, 1995; Geiger, Zimmer-Gembeck, & Crick, 2004). However, overall, we did anticipate that relational as well as physical aggression would have independent effects on later social preference and impact for both genders. It was unclear whether the converse associations (i.e., earlier peer status associated with later aggression) would be found during this age period.

Finally, we expected bidirectional associations between peer status and prosocial behavior; earlier prosocial behavior would predict later peer status, and earlier social preference and impact would be associated with prosocial behavior by early adolescence. We expected these associations to be stronger among females as compared to males. These hypotheses are consistent with theory regarding the importance of children's social experience with peers for the development of positive social behaviors (Hartup, 1983). Prosocial behavior has been noted to increase in adolescence, particularly among females and may be more important for the developing peer status of girls as compared to boys (Fabes et al., 1999).

Three-Year Stability of Peer Status and Children's Behaviors

In addition to examining the associations between peer status and children's behaviors and the moderation of these associations by gender, a final aim of the current study was to examine the stability of social preference, social impact, and children's behaviors across a 3-year interval spanning entry into adolescence and a middle school environment. A particular interest was in the 3-year stability of relationally aggressive behavior. Stability and change in peer status have been examined in previous studies, but it is uncommon for studies to span a school transition. Prior to the school transition in childhood, 1- and 2-year stabilities of social preference and social impact have ranged from .46 to .52 and .29 to .41, respectively (Terry & Coie, 1991). Many studies of physical aggression (see Coie & Dodge, 1998, for a review) report high stability regardless of the time span, but there is less information on the stability of relational aggression and prosocial behavior. To our knowledge, only one previous longitudinal study of 6-month duration included relational aggression and prosocial behavior (Crick, 1996b), and this study did not span the transition into adolescence and a new school environment.

Method

Procedure

Peer nominations were collected in Grades 3 and 6. All students who returned parent consent forms participated. The parental consent rate was just more than 70%. Students were given candy and small school-related gifts prior to and after participation. Two research assistants were present for assessments. One assistant was responsible for highlighting portions of instructions such as confidentiality, discouraging students from discussing items with their classmates, telling students that talking to their parents about the research was not discouraged, and reading survey items to the students. The second assistant was available to help individual students. Children were supplied with alphabetized rosters of their classmates and nomination forms. Each child on a roster was assigned an identification number. Students used identification numbers to nominate three classmates (male or female) for each item. . . .

Discussion

Researchers have identified some of the correlates of peer status, and this work has revealed the significant role of peer reputation in the social development of children. However, few empirical investigations have had the opportunity to examine the independent effects of boys' and girls' physical aggression, relational aggression, and prosocial behavior on social preference and impact from childhood to early adolescence. Evidence exists concerning the negative influence of physical aggression on peer status, but the present investigation illustrated the additional importance of relational aggression and prosocial behavior as well as the gender of the child when explaining children's concurrent and future status with peers. Despite the stringent tests of cross-lag associations conducted in the current study, bidirectional influences between children's behaviors and peer relations were found. Not only do children's aggressive and prosocial behaviors predict future peer relations, but the balance of being liked and disliked by classmates is important for shaping future aggressive and prosocial behaviors when interacting with peers.

Bidirectional Cross-lag Associations Between Children's Behavior and Peer Relations

. . . Social preference.   Peer social preference, where high scores indicate being highly liked and rarely disliked by others and low scores indicate the opposite, seemed to have a greater influence on children's later physical aggression, relational aggression, and prosocial behaviors rather than vice versa among both boys and girls. Preference scores in Grade 3 predicted all later behaviors among boys and all behaviors with the exception of relational aggression among girls. These results concur with other evidence (Coie et al., 1990; Crick, 1996b; Farmer & Rodkin, 1996) that positive peer experiences are important for learning appropriate social skills such as negotiating conflict and helping others (e.g., Hartup, 1983) as well as indicating that the lack of these opportunities may be detrimental to interactions with schoolmates (Parker & Asher, 1987).

Although developmental theorists have discussed how children's status with their peers potentially influence their future behaviors, such as aggression and prosocial behavior (Hartup, 1983; Parker & Asher, 1987), with a few exceptions (e.g., Dishion, Patterson, Stoolmiller, & Skinner, 1991; Kupersmidt, Burchinal, & Patterson, 1995), fewer empirical studies have focused on children's behaviors as influences on later peer status. When these converse longitudinal links between children's behavior and later social preference were investigated in the current study, there was limited influence of earlier behaviors on later social preference scores after accounting for stabilities and concurrent associations between all constructs. Only relational aggression in Grade 3 was linked to later social preference, and this association was significant only among girls. However, although some path coefficients were significant among boys only or girls only, gender did not moderate any cross-lag paths in this model indicating no significant gender differences in the magnitude of these path coefficients.

. . . In general, findings of gender moderation supported a gender normative hypothesis with behaviors more commonly associated with boys (physical aggression) linked to later social impact for boys and behaviors more commonly associated with girls (relational aggression) linked more strongly to later social impact for girls. Gender normative aggressive behaviors appear to be having an affect on status with other children at the transition from childhood to early adolescence. Gender did not moderate the path from earlier prosocial behavior to later social impact. Prosocial behavior had a positive and similar influence on later social impact for both boys and girls.

Conversely, social impact in Grade 3 also predicts children's aggressive behaviors in Grade 6. Earlier social impact is associated with increasing physical aggression for all children and relational aggression among boys only. Yet the association between earlier social impact and later physical aggression is stronger among boys compared to girls. Peers are increasingly noticing children with relatively more negative or positive behaviors, and this recognition seems to play a role in maintaining and escalating children's, especially boys', aggressive behaviors.

Aggression, peer status and gender.   Although previous research has consistently found negative associations between physical aggression and rejection and acceptance by peers (see Newcomb et al., 1993, for a review), when both physical and relational aggression are considered, the current findings show that it is girls' relational aggression, and not physical aggression, that predicts both social preference and impact 3 years later. . . . Findings suggest that aggression may partly escalate among boys between Grades 3 and 6 as a reaction to their peer experiences rather than vice versa. Girls may use relational aggression for reasons other than as a response to their peer status, such as gender socialization or arising from their greater focus on dyadic friendship interactions (L. M. Brown, Way, & Duff, 1999; Crick, 1996a; Crick, Bigbee, & Howes, 1996). In other words, girls' relational aggression emerges and, in turn, affects their peer status; boys' aggression may be more of an outcome of their peer status and associated peer experiences. However, this interpretation of the findings is speculative as some model paths differed in magnitude between boys and girls but were not significantly moderated by gender.

Concurrent Associations and Gender Moderation

We should also briefly note that gender moderated many concurrent (within Grade 3 or within Grade 6) associations between children's behaviors and peer relations in the current study. It was these concurrent correlations that primarily resulted in the need for models with different path coefficients for boys and girls. For example, relational aggression and physical aggression co-occurred among boys and girls, but this was more likely among boys than girls. Thus, boys who have the highest physical aggression scores are often the same boys who have the highest relational aggression scores. However, the correlation between relational and physical aggression was not as strong for girls, indicating that these two forms of aggression do not as strongly covary among girls. These findings indicate that it continues to be important for researchers interested in aggression and gender to include separate assessments of relational and physical aggression.

In general, the behaviors of boys and girls and their social preference and impact scores were intercorrelated in both Grade 3 and Grade 6. . . . This is consistent with previous research that has found that prosocial behavior is more important to girls' acceptance by peers than boys' acceptance (Crick, 1996b). It is still unclear why this occurs. However, children may simply attend to and expect prosocial behavior from girls, as it is consistent with gender stereotypes. On the other hand, other social behaviors may be more salient when considering the likability of boys, but these factors are yet to be clearly identified.

As anticipated, gender moderation was also found when examining aggression. Yet these findings were more age related and complex than we had hypothesized. Among males, aggression (physical and relational) was consistently associated with social preference and impact in both Grade 3 and Grade 6. Among females, the impact of physically and relationally aggressive behaviors on their peer status changed with age. Aggressive behaviors were increasingly reflected in girls' peer social impact scores (like and dislike scores combined) rather than only in lower peer social preference scores (like scores net of dislike scores). These findings are supportive of other evidence that aggression can be associated with social dominance and liking by some peers, and dislike by other peers, especially in early adolescence. . . .

Stability of Children's Behaviors and Peer Relations

A final objective of this investigation was to examine the 3-year stability of all constructs with particular focus on relational aggression and girls. It was clear that children's early social behavior, including relational aggression, and reputations established with classmates tend to accompany children into early adolescence even after they change schools and classrooms. In fact, stabilities of physical aggression and peer status were similar to those reported in studies that did not include a school transition (see Coie & Dodge, 1998; Schneider, 2000, for reviews). In the current study, social preference scores were somewhat more stable than impact scores, but there was moderate 3-year stability in physical aggression, relational aggression, and prosocial behavior. Yet physical aggression was more stable among boys than girls.

Peer status is generally stable over time and across settings (Coie & Dodge, 1983), even with direct efforts to change peer status through social interventions (Bierman, Miller, & Stabb, 1987; La Greca, 1993). Our findings are consistent with evidence suggesting that individual factors (e.g., aggressive behavior) and group processes may be at work that maintain the effects of social experiences across a transition to a new setting and new peer group (e.g., Cillessen et al., 2000; Parker & Asher, 1987).

Gender Differences and Relational Aggression

There have recently been questions regarding whether relational aggression is more prevalent among females or males (for reviews on this topic see Geiger et al., 2004; Underwood, Galen, & Paquette, 2001). The current study findings regarding relational aggression by gender and age are important to consider in conjunction with these questions. We found that gender differences in levels of relational aggression differed depending on children's age. There was no gender difference in relational aggression among third grade children (about age 9); however, by sixth grade (about age 12), girls were more relationally aggressive than their male peers. Findings are consistent with that of Bjoerkqvist and colleagues (Bjoerkqvist, Lagerspetz, & Kaukiainen, 1992) who reported that gender differences in indirect aggression did not occur until about age 10. However, because girls have been found to be more relationally aggressive than boys as early as preschool (Crick & Grotpeter, 1995; see Geiger et al., 2004, for a review; Lagerspetz, Bjoerkqvist, & Peltonen, 1988), firm conclusions await further research. . . .

Summary and Conclusion

In sum, there are bidirectional longitudinal links between children's positive and negative social behaviors and their status in the peer group even when the moderate stabilities of children's behaviors and peer status, and concurrent associations, were taken into account. Gender was a moderator of concurrent associations between children's behavior and peer relations in childhood (Grade 3) and early adolescence (Grade 6) and also moderated a few longitudinal associations between children's behaviors and social impact in the peer group. These findings suggest that analyses should be done separately for males and females (or interactions should be examined) to provide the most accurate accounts of associations between aggressive and prosocial behaviors and peer status. It is important to consider gender, relational aggression, and prosocial behavior in addition to the more commonly studied behavior of physical aggression when investigating stability and change in peer status during childhood and adolescence. Furthermore, differential results across the two gender-moderation models presented here indicate the importance of examining both social preference and social impact as distinct constructs. Doing so allowed a more complete understanding of the age-related and gendered interface between children's positive and negative behaviors when interacting with peers and schoolmates' perceptions of others as liked or disliked members of the group.

EXPLORING THE ISSUE

Are Male Teens More Aggressive Than Female Teens?

Critical Thinking and Reflection

1. What evidence did each article present for whether the authors believe there are gender differences in aggressive behavior among teens?
2. Identify some limitations in each article regarding the participants, methods, and overall generalizability to the entire teen population. Given these limitations, can you think of ways to improve these studies and build on the research?

Is Their Common Ground?

Both articles examined gender differences in aggression among teenage males and females. However, neither of the articles mentioned the ethnic or cultural background, other than Salmivalli and Kaukiainen's article where they mentioned that their study was carried out in two different towns in Finland. Whether this was omitted for the purposes of condensing the articles or it was just left out, could this information explain some of the findings? How might ethnic or cultural background influence aggression in each gender? What about teens in rural versus urban areas?

Both sets of researchers utilized children from elementary school as part of their study, partly to examine patterns of aggression based on earlier experiences and behavior patterns at a younger age into adolescence. How might the results of their findings be different if only adolescents had been used? Although information regarding the behaviors from childhood to adolescents is important, is it possible that these behaviors my change as the adolescents move further away from their preadolescent years?

Can you think of ways in which the research presented and other research like it will contribute to school-age children (elementary through high school)? What is the significance of knowing whether gender differences exist with regards to these possible contributions of the research?

Additional Resources

Karriker-Jaffe, K. J., Foshee, V. A., Ennett, S. T., & Suchindran, C. (2008). The Development of Aggression During Adolescence: Sex Differences in Trajectories of Physical and Social Aggression Among Youth in Rural Areas. *Journal of Abnormal Child Psychology*, 36(8), pp. 1227–1236.

doi: 10.1007/s10802-008-9245-5. Retrieved on April 24, 2011, from http://www.ncbi.nlm.nih.gov/pmc/articles/PMC2773662/.

The authors report findings in the study that support that male teens tend to be more physically aggressive than female teens.

National Youth Violence Prevention Resource Center. (2002). Facts for Teens: Aggression. Retrieved on April 24, 2011, from http://herkimer county.org/content/departments/View/11:field=services;/content/Department Services/View/68:field=documents;/content/Documents/File/123.PDF.

This Web site offers information about different types of aggression and explains some of the contributing factors to aggression in adolescents and how this might relate to earlier childhood.

Nichols, T. R., Graber, J. A., Brooks-Gunn, J., & Botvin, G. J. (2006). Sex Differences in Overt Aggression and Delinquency Among Urban Minority Middle School Students. *Applied Developmental Psychology,* 27, pp. 78–91. doi: 10.1016/j.appdev.2005.12.006. Retrieved on April 24, 2011, from http://www.med.cornell.edu/ipr/PDF/Nichols-et-al-2006-JADP.pdf.

This article describes a longitudinal study that examined minority male and female adolescents' aggressive behavior with relation to precursors such as family disruption, anger, and self-control.

ISSUE 16

Is Abstinence-Only Sex Education the Best Way to Teach About Sex?

YES: Robert E. Rector, Melissa G. Pardue, and Shannan Martin, from "What Do Parents Want Taught in Sex Education Programs?" *The Heritage Foundation Backgrounder* (January 28, 2004)

NO: Debra Hauser, from *Five Years of Abstinence-Only-Until-Marriage Education: Assessing the Impact* (Advocates for Youth, 2008)

Learning Outcomes

After reading this issue, you should be able to:

- Define both abstinence-only and comprehensive sex education.
- Discuss the major tenets of the abstinence-only sex education movement.
- Discuss the major tenets of a comprehensive sex education program.
- Describe the arguments for and against abstinence-only and comprehensive sex education programs.

ISSUE SUMMARY

YES: Robert Rector, who is a research fellow for the Heritage Foundation, and Melissa Pardue and Shannan Martin, policy analysts for the Heritage Foundation, argue that comprehensive sex education approaches are misleading because they do little to promote abstinence. Under the auspices of the Heritage Foundation, a conservative organization based in Washington, D.C., they present the results of a poll they conducted that sought to measure parental support for ideas taught in "abstinence-only" and "comprehensive sex education" programs.

NO: Debra Hauser, vice president of Advocates for Youth, argues that the assertions made by proponents of *abstinence-only sex education* are unfounded. In reviewing the efficacy of abstinence-only programs, she found that although these programs may show changes in attitudes about abstinence, they also discourage safe sexual practices and actually increase the risks of premarital pregnancy and the spread of sexually transmitted infections.

In our culture, it is impossible to avoid the constant presence of sexual references. Sex is the number one marketing tool to sell a product in our society. Sex is pervasive on television, on the Internet, and in the movies. The media oftentimes gives a false image of what sex really is, so that teens may see sex in unrealistic contexts, with no responsibility associated with sex-related decisions. Sex education in schools may be the only sound information sources available to adolescents. Most people agree about the need for some type of sex education for our children in our schools. There is little argument that abstinence is the safest choice an adolescent can make regarding sexual activity. It is the only 100 percent effective way to avoid pregnancy and the hundreds of sexually transmitted diseases that are epidemic in our society. However, the reality is that adolescents do engage in premarital sexual behaviors. The problem is that parents and educators cannot agree on the best way to teach children and adolescents about the implications of premarital sex. One group believes that the best approach is comprehensive sex education, which encourages abstinence but also provides information on birth control, protection against sexually transmitted diseases, and the emotional aspects of engaging in sex. Other groups promote abstinence-only sex education, which provides information on the hazards of sex (i.e., pregnancy, STDs, broken hearts, etc.) and sometimes includes information on self-esteem and dealing with peer pressure to have premarital sex.

Advocates for comprehensive sex education argue that many adolescents will have premarital sex; as a consequence, adolescents need to be taught about birth control methods and STD prevention techniques. Those supporting abstinence-only sex education believe that teaching about birth control methods and STD prevention sends mixed messages about premarital sex. It could give teens the impression that teachers and parents accept that adolescents cannot help themselves from having sex, which is contrary to the pro-abstinence movement's goals.

To intensify the debate, the government has established a federal entitlement program for "abstinence-only-until-marriage" education. When schools and other agencies accept these grants, they must adhere to the program's rules, which include requiring schools to teach little about sexuality but instead to send a strong message that sexual activity outside of marriage is psychologically and physiologically harmful. Therefore, teaching about or discussing premarital sex should be avoided. This is worrisome for comprehensive sex education advocates because they believe that education about sexuality is the best way to empower adolescents to make sound decisions regarding premarital sex.

In the YES selection, Robert Rector, Melissa Pardue, and Shannan Martin argue against comprehensive sex education on the grounds that this approach does not do enough to promote abstinence and that according to their poll, parents overwhelmingly prefer their children to be taught abstinence-only programs in sex education. In the NO selection, Debra Hauser counters with the argument that abstinence-only programs, when closely examined, do not show much evidence of having a long-term impact on attitudes and behaviors regarding premarital sex. She goes on to say that these programs discourage the use of contraception, such as condoms, to prevent premarital pregnancy and sexually transmitted infections among adolescents.

Many questions should be considered when deciding on a sex education curriculum. Should parents or professionals have the sole decision-making power to decide what type of sex education a student receives? Should students have a voice in this decision? Should religion and moral values be a factor when deciding which type of sex education is best? Will comprehensive sex education encourage teens to have more casual sex as long as they use protection? Will comprehensive sex education encourage teens to start having sex sooner? Is abstinence-only sex education very realistic? Are we as a society being realistic if we believe that most teens will abstain from premarital sex? As you read both selections, think back to your days in high school and the sources and types of education about sexuality you received. Was the education sufficient? Should it have been different? If so, in what ways? Also, put yourself in the place of a parent of an adolescent. Consider what approach to sex education this parent would support and why.

YES ⬅ Robert E. Rector, Melissa G. Pardue, and Shannan Martin

What Do Parents Want Taught in Sex Education Programs?

Debates about sex education have focused on two different approaches: "safe sex" courses, which encourage teens to use contraceptives, especially condoms, when having sex, and abstinence education, which encourages teens to delay sexual activity.

In recent years, advocacy groups such as SIECUS (the Sex Information and Education Council of the United States) and Advocates for Youth have promoted another apparent alternative, entitled "comprehensive sexuality education" or "abstinence plus." These curricula allegedly take a middle position, providing a strong abstinence message while also teaching about contraception. In reality, this claim is misleading. Comprehensive sexuality education curricula contain little or no meaningful abstinence material; they are simply safe-sex programs repackaged under a new, deceptive label.

Abstinence programs teach that:

- Human sexuality is primarily emotional and psychological, not physical, in nature;
- In proper circumstances, sexual activity leads to long term emotional bonding between two individuals; and
- Sexual happiness is inherently linked to intimacy, love, and commitment—qualities found primarily within marriage.

Abstinence programs strongly encourage abstinence during the teen years, and preferably until marriage. They teach that casual sex at an early age not only poses serious threats of pregnancy and infection by sexually transmitted diseases, but also can undermine an individual's capacity to build loving, intimate relationships as an adult. These programs therefore encourage teen abstinence as a preparation and pathway to healthy adult marriage.

By contrast, comprehensive sex-ed curricula focus almost exclusively on teaching about contraception and encouraging teens to use it. These curricula neither discourage nor criticize teen sexual activity as long as "protection" is used. In general, they exhibit an acceptance of casual teen sex and do not encourage teens to wait until they are older to initiate sexual activity. For example, the curricula do not encourage teens to abstain until they have finished high school. "Protected" sex at an early age and sex with many different partners are not treated as problems. Sexuality is treated primarily as a physical phenomenon; the main message is to use condoms to prevent the physical problems of sexually transmitted diseases and pregnancy. Comprehensive sex-ed curricula ignore the vital linkages between sexuality, love, intimacy, and commitment. There is no discussion of the idea that sex is best within marriage.

Determining Parental Attitudes toward Sex-ed Curricula

This paper presents the results of a recent poll on basic issues concerning sex education. The poll questions seek to measure parental support for the themes and values contained in abstinence curricula as well as support for the values embodied in comprehensive sex education.

The data presented are drawn from a survey of parents conducted by Zogby International in December 2003. Zogby conducted telephone interviews with a nationally representative sample of 1,004 parents with children under age 18. Parents were asked 14 questions concerning messages and priorities in sex education; the questions used were designed by Focus on the Family. The margin of error on each question is plus or minus 3.2 percent points. The responses to the questions showed only modest variation based on region, gender of the parent, or race.[1] The poll questions were designed to reflect the major themes of abstinence education. The descriptions of the messages contained in abstinence and comprehensive sex-ed curricula in the following text are based on a forthcoming content analysis of major sex-ed curricula conducted by The Heritage Foundation. . . .

"Sex Should Be Linked to Marriage; Delaying Sex Until Marriage Is Best"

Abstinence education curricula stress a strong linkage between sex, love, and marriage. The Zogby poll shows strong parental support for this message.

Parents want teens to be taught that sexual activity should be linked to marriage.

Parents Want Teens to Be Taught to Delay Sexual Activity until They Are Married or Close to Marriage

Some 47 percent of parents want teens to be taught that "young people should not engage in sexual activity until they are married." Another 32 percent of parents want teens to be taught that "young people should not engage in sexual intercourse until they have, at least, finished high school and are in a relationship with someone they feel they would like to marry."

When these two categories are combined, we see that 79 percent of parents want young people taught that sex should be reserved for marriage or for an adult relationship leading to marriage. Another 12 percent of parents believe that teens should be taught to delay sexual activity until "they have, at least, finished high school." Only 7 percent of parents want teens to be taught that sexual activity in high school is okay as long as teens use contraception.

These parental values are strongly reinforced by abstinence education programs, which teach that sex should be linked to marriage and that it is best to delay sexual activity until marriage. By contrast, comprehensive sex-ed programs send the message that teen sex is okay as long as contraception is used; the underlying permissive values of these programs have virtually no support among parents.

Parents Want Teens to Be Taught That Sex Should Be Linked to Love, Intimacy, and Commitment and That These Qualities Are Most Likely to Occur in Marriage

Some 91 percent of parents want teens to be taught this message about sexuality.

This is a predominant theme of all abstinence curricula. By contrast, comprehensive sex-ed programs do not discuss love, intimacy, or commitment and seldom mention marriage. Casual sex is not criticized; sex is presented largely as a physical process; and the main lesson is to avoid the physical threats of pregnancy and disease through proper use of contraception. Comprehensive sex-ed programs do not present sexuality in a way that is acceptable to most parents.

Parents Want Teens to Be Taught That It Is Best to Delay Sex until Marriage

Some 68 percent of parents want schools to teach teens that "individuals who are not sexually active until marriage have the best chances of marital stability and happiness."

This theme is strongly supported by abstinence programs, all of which urge teens to delay sexual activity until marriage. It is ignored completely by comprehensive sex-ed courses, which do not criticize casual sex and seldom mention marriage.

General Support for Abstinence

The poll shows overwhelming parental support for other abstinence themes as well.

Parents Want Teens to Be Taught to Abstain from Sexual Activity during High School Years

Some 91 percent of parents support this message. However, for most parents, this is a minimum standard; 79 percent want a higher standard taught: abstinence until you are married or near marriage.

All abstinence curricula strongly encourage abstinence at least through high school, and preferably until marriage. By contrast, comprehensive sex-ed curricula do not encourage teens to delay sex until they have finished high school; most do not even encourage young people to wait until they are older.

Parents Want Teens to Be Taught That Abstinence Is Best

Some 96 percent of parents support this message.

Abstinence curricula obviously support this theme. Comprehensive sex-ed programs may claim to support this message, but in reality they do not. They teach mainly that abstinence is the "safest" choice, but that teen sex with protection is safe. Their overall message is that abstinence is marginally safer than safe sex. Beyond this, they have little positive to say about abstinence.

"Sex at an Early Age, Sex with Many Partners, and Casual Sex Have Harmful Consequences"

Parents believe that sex at an early age, casual sex, and sex with many partners are likely to have harmful consequences. They want teens to be taught to avoid these behaviors.

Parents Want Teens to Be Taught That the Younger the Age an Individual Begins Sexual Activity, the Greater the Probability of Harm

Some 93 percent of parents want teens taught that "the younger the age an individual begins sexual activity, the more likely he or she is to be infected by sexually transmitted diseases, to have an abortion, and to give birth out-of-wedlock."

Abstinence programs strongly support this message; they teach teens to delay sex until they are older, preferably until they are married. Comprehensive sex-ed programs teach about the threat of unprotected sex, not about the harm caused by sex at an early age. They do not urge young people to delay sex until they are older; voluntary sex at any age is depicted as okay as long as "protection" is used.

Parents Want Teens Taught That Teen Sexual Activity Is Likely to Have Psychological and Physical Effects

Some 79 percent of parents want teens to be taught this message.

Abstinence curricula clearly teach this message; comprehensive sex-ed curricula do not. Comprehensive sex-ed curricula focus on encouraging condom use; they do not criticize or discourage teen sex as long as "protection" is used.

Parents Want Schools to Teach That Teens Who Are Sexually Active Are More Likely to Be Depressed

Some 67 percent of teens who have had sexual intercourse regret it and say they wish that they had waited until they were older. (The figure for teen girls is 77 percent.)[2] Sexually active teens are far more likely to be depressed and to attempt suicide than are teens who are not sexually active.[3] Nearly two-thirds of parents support the message that sexually active teens are more likely to be depressed; a quarter of parents oppose it.

Abstinence curricula inform teens about the basic facts of regret and depression; comprehensive sex-ed curricula ignore this topic.

Parents Want Sex Education to Teach That the More Sexual Partners a Teen Has, the Greater the Likelihood of Physical and Psychological Harm

Some 90 percent of parents want this message taught to teens.

Abstinence curricula emphasize the harmful effects of casual teen sex; comprehensive sex-ed curricula do not.

Parents Want Teens Taught That Having Many Sexual Partners at an Early Age May Undermine One's Ability to Develop and Sustain Loving and Committed Relationships as an Adult

Some 85 percent of parents want teens to be taught that "having many sexual partners at an early age may undermine an individual's ability to develop love, intimacy and commitment." Another 78 percent of parents want teens to be taught that "having many different sexual partners at an early age may undermine an individual's ability to form a healthy marriage as adult."

These are major themes of abstinence programs. They teach that teen sexual relationships are inherently short-term and unstable and that repeated fractured relationships can lead to difficulties in bonding and commitment in later years. This perspective is accurate; women who begin sexual activity at an early age will have far more sexual partners and are less likely to have stable marriages as adults.[4] Comprehensive sex-ed curricula ignore this topic completely.

"What's More Important, Abstinence or Contraception?"

Parents believe that abstinence should be given emphasis that is more than, or equal to, that given to contraception. Some 44 percent of parents believe that teaching about abstinence is more important than teaching about contraception; another large group (41 percent) believe that abstinence and contraception should be given equal emphasis. Only 8 percent believe that teaching about contraception is more important than teaching about abstinence.

Regrettably, government spending priorities directly contradict parental priorities. Currently, the government spends at least $4.50 promoting teen contraceptive use for every $1.00 spent to promote teen abstinence.[5]

Parents Overwhelmingly Reject Main Values and Messages of Comprehensive Sex Education

Despite the claims of advocacy groups such as SIECUS and Advocates for Youth, comprehensive sex education curricula contain weak to non-existent messages about abstinence. These programs focus almost exclusively on (1) explaining the threat of teen pregnancy and sexually transmitted diseases and (2) encouraging young people to use contraception, especially condoms, to combat these threats. Many of these curricula appear to be written from a limited health perspective. Sexuality is treated as a physical process (like nutrition), and the goal is to reduce immediate health risks.

While comprehensive sex-ed curricula do not explicitly and directly encourage teen sexual activity, they do not discourage it either. As long as "protection" is used, teen sexual activity is represented as being rewarding, normal, healthy, and nearly ubiquitous. While "unprotected" sex is strongly criticized and discouraged, "protected" teen sex is presented as being fully acceptable. There is little or no effort to encourage young people to wait until they are older before becoming sexually active. By presenting "protected" teen sex activity as commonplace, fulfilling, healthy, and unproblematic, comprehensive sex-ed courses send a strong implicit anti-abstinence message to teens.

The new poll of parental attitudes shows that less than 10 percent of parents support the main values and messages of comprehensive sex education programs. Specifically:

Parents Oppose Teaching That Teen Sex Is Okay If Condoms Are Used

In comprehensive sex-ed curricula, "protected" teen sex is neither criticized nor discouraged. These courses explicitly or implicitly send the strong message that "it's okay for teens in school to engage in sexual intercourse as long as they use condoms." Only 7 percent of parents support this message; 91 percent reject it.

At a Minimum, Parents Want Teens to Be Taught to Abstain from Sexual Activity until They Have Finished High School

Some 91 percent of parents want teens to be taught this minimum standard; most want a far higher standard. But comprehensive sex-ed curricula do not teach that teens should abstain until they have finished high school; in fact, these courses do not provide any clear standards concerning when sexual activity should begin. For the most part, they do not even encourage young people to wait until they are vaguely "older"; they are simply silent on the issue.

Comprehensive Sex-Ed Courses Are Silent on Vital Issues Such as Casual Sex, Intimacy, Commitment, Love, and Marriage

. . . Parents overwhelmingly support the main themes of abstinence education and want these topics to be taught to their children. These themes are conspicuously absent from comprehensive sex-ed. These courses therefore fail to meet the needs and desires of most parents.

Should Abstinence Programs Teach about "Safe Sex" or Contraception?

The poll shows an apparent divergence between abstinence education and parental attitudes on only one issue: Some 75 percent of parents want teens to be taught about both abstinence and contraception. Except for describing the likely failure rates of various types of birth control, abstinence curricula do not teach about contraception.

However, the fact that abstinence programs, per se, do not include contraceptive information does not mean that teens will not be taught this material. Abstinence and sex education are seldom taught as stand-alone subjects in school; they are usually offered as a brief part of a larger course, most typically a health course.[6]

In addition, sex education is usually taught not once, but in multiple doses at different grade levels as the student matures. When students are taught about abstinence, in most cases, they will also receive biological information about reproduction and contraception in another part of their course work. By 11th or 12th grade, some 91 percent of students have been taught about birth control in school.[7]

There is no logical reason why contraceptive information should be presented as part of an abstinence curriculum. Not only would this reduce the limited time allocated to the abstinence message, but nearly all abstinence educators assert that it would substantially undermine the effectiveness of the abstinence message.

In general, parents tend to agree that abstinence and contraceptive instruction should not be directly mixed. . . . Some 56 percent of parents believe either that contraception should not be taught at all or that, if both abstinence and contraception are taught, they should be taught separately. (Some 22 percent believe that contraception should not be taught, while 35 percent want the two subjects taught separately.)

Although most parents want teens to be taught about both abstinence and contraception, there is no strong sentiment that these topics must be combined into one curriculum. The stronger a parent's support for abstinence, the less likely he or she is to want abstinence and contraception merged into a single curriculum.

The fact that 75 percent of parents want both abstinence and contraception taught to teens should not, in any way, be interpreted to mean support for comprehensive sex-education. Comprehensive sex-ed curricula are focused almost exclusively on promoting contraceptive use and contain little or no mention of abstinence, yet only 8 percent of parents believe that schools should give greater emphasis to contraception than to abstinence.

Moreover, parents have reservations concerning the type of contraceptive education these curricula contain. While 52 percent of parents want schools to provide "basic biological and health information about contraception," only 23 percent want schools "to encourage teens to use condoms when having sex, teach teens where to obtain condoms, and have teens practice how to put on condoms." The latter aggressive type of contraceptive promotion is typical of comprehensive sex-ed curricula, though it lacks wide support among parents.

In general, parents want teens to be taught a strong abstinence message as well as being given basic biological information about contraception. The polls suggest that most parents would be satisfied if young people were given a vigorous abstinence course and were taught about the basics of contraception separately. This is probably the typical situation in most schools where authentic abstinence is taught. On the other hand, extremely few parents (7 percent to 8 percent) would be happy if abstinence education were to be replaced by comprehensive sex-ed.

Conclusion

The newly released poll shows strong (in many cases, nearly unanimous) support for the major themes of abstinence education. Abstinence programs provide young people with the strong, uplifting moral messages desired by nearly all parents.

Multiple evaluations show that abstinence programs are effective in encouraging young people to delay sexual activity.[8] The effectiveness of these programs is quite remarkable, given that they typically provide no more than a few hours of instruction per year. In those few hours, abstinence instructors seek to counteract thousands of hours of annual exposure to sex-saturated teen media, which strongly push teens in the opposite direction.

Most parents not only want vigorous instruction in abstinence, but also want teens to be taught basic biological information about contraception. Such information is not contained in abstinence curricula themselves but is frequently provided in a separate setting such as a health class. Overall, the values and objectives of the overwhelming majority of parents can be met by providing teens with a strong abstinence program while teaching basic biological information about contraception in a separate health or biology class. This arrangement appears common in schools where abstinence is taught.

In recent years, groups such as Advocates for Youth and SIECUS have sought to eliminate funding for abstinence or to replace abstinence education with comprehensive sex-ed. This is always done under the pretext that comprehensive sex-ed contains a strong abstinence message and, thereby, renders traditional abstinence superfluous. In reality, comprehensive sex-ed curricula have weak to nonexistent abstinence content. Replacing abstinence education with these programs would mean eliminating the abstinence message in most U.S. schools; nearly all parents would object to this change.

Only a tiny minority (less than 10 percent) of parents support the values and messages taught in comprehensive sex education curricula. Since the themes of these courses (such as "It's okay for teens to have sex as long as they use condoms") contradict and undermine the basic values parents want their children to be taught, these courses would be unacceptable even if combined with other materials.

The popular culture bombards teens with messages encouraging casual sexual activity at an early age. To counteract this, parents want teens to be taught a strong abstinence message. Parents overwhelmingly support abstinence curricula that link sexuality to love, intimacy, and commitment and that urge teens to delay sexual activity until maturity and marriage.

Regrettably, this sort of clear abstinence education is not taught in most schools. As a result, the sexual messages that parents deem to be most important are not getting through to today's teens.

Notes

1. Responses to individual questions categorized by region, gender, and race are available upon request.
2. National Campaign to Prevent Teen Pregnancy, *America's Adults and Teens Sound Off About Teen Pregnancy*, December 2003, p. 17.
3. Robert E. Rector, Kirk A. Johnson, Ph.D., and Lauren R. Noyes, "Sexually Active Teenagers Are More Likely to Be Depressed and to Attempt Suicide," Heritage Foundation Center for Data Analysis Report No. 03–04, June 3, 2003.
4. Robert E. Rector, Kirk A. Johnson, Lauren Noyes, and Shannan Martin, *The Harmful Effects of Sexual Activity and Multiple Sexual Partners Among Women: A Book of Charts*, The Heritage Foundation, June 23, 2003, pp. 4, 10.
5. Melissa G. Pardue, Robert E. Rector, and Shannan Martin, "Government Spends $12 on Safe Sex and Contraceptives for Every $1 Spent on Abstinence," Heritage Foundation Backgrounder No. 1718, January 14, 2004.
6. Some 85 percent of the sex education taught in the United States is part of a larger course on a broader subject, most typically a health or biology class. See *Sex Education in America* (Menlo Park, Cal.: Kaiser Family Foundation, 2000), p. 90.
7. Ibid., p. 18.
8. Robert E. Rector, "The Effectiveness of Abstinence Education Programs in Reducing Sexual Activity Among Youth," Heritage Foundation Backgrounder No. 1533, April 8, 2002.

Debra Hauser

Five Years of Abstinence-Only-Until-Marriage Education: Assessing the Impact

Introduction

Since 1991, rates of teenage pregnancy and birth have declined significantly in the United States. These are welcome trends. Yet, teens in the United States continue to suffer from the highest birth rate and one of the highest rates of sexually transmitted infections (STIs) in the industrialized world. Debate over the best way to help teens avoid, or reduce, their sexual risk-taking behavior has polarized many youth-serving professionals. On one side are those that support comprehensive sex education—education that promotes abstinence but includes information about contraception and condoms to build young people's knowledge, attitudes, and skills for when they do become sexually active. On the other side are those that favor abstinence-only-until-marriage—programs that promote "abstinence from sexual activity outside marriage as the expected standard" of behavior. Proponents of abstinence-only programs believe that providing information about the health benefits of condoms or contraception contradicts their message of abstinence-only and undermines its impact. As such, abstinence-only programs provide no information about contraception beyond failure rates.

In 1996, Congress signed into law the Personal Responsibility & Work Opportunities Reconciliation Act, or "welfare reform." Attached was the provision, later set out in Section 510(b) of Title V of the Social Security Act, appropriating $250 million dollars over five years for state initiatives promoting sexual abstinence outside of marriage as the only acceptable standard of behavior for young people.

For the first five years of the initiative, every state but California participated in the program. (California had experimented with its own abstinence-only initiative in the early 1990s. The program was terminated in February 1996, when evaluation results found the program to be ineffective.) From 1998 to 2003, almost a half a billion dollars in state and federal funds were appropriated to support the Title V initiative. A report, detailing the results from the federally funded evaluation of select Title V programs, was due to be released more than a year ago. Last year, Congress extended "welfare reform" and, with it, the Title V abstinence-only-until-marriage funding without benefit of this, as yet unreleased, report.

As the first five-year funding cycle of Title V came to a close, a few state-funded evaluations became public. Others were completed with little or no fanfare. This document reviews the findings from the 10 evaluations that Advocates for Youth was able to identify. Advocates for Youth also includes evaluation results from California's earlier attempt at a statewide abstinence-only initiative.

Available Evaluations

Ten states made some form of evaluation results available for review. For Arizona, Florida, Iowa, Maryland, Minnesota, Oregon, Pennsylvania, and Washington, Advocates was able to locate evaluation results from state Title V programs. For Missouri and Nebraska, Advocates located evaluation findings from at least one program among those funded through the state's Title V initiative. Finally, the evaluation of California's abstinence-only program was published in a peer-reviewed journal and readily available.

Funding*

During the first five years of abstinence-only-until-marriage Title V programming, the 10 states received about $45.5 million in federal funds. To further support the initiatives and to cover their required funding match, these states appropriated about $34 million in additional funds over the five years. In addition, California spent $15 million in state funds between 1991 and 1994 to support its abstinence-only initiative. In sum, the program efforts discussed in this paper cost an estimated $94.5 million in federal and state dollars.

Program Components

For the most part, Title V funds were administered through states' departments of health and then sub-granted to abstinence-only contractors within each state. Program components varied from state to state and from contractor to contractor within each state. However, all programs discussed in this document included an abstinence-only curriculum, delivered to young people in schools or through community-based agencies. Popular curricula included: *Education Now Babies Later (ENABL), Why Am I Tempted? (WAIT), Family Accountability Communicating Teen Sexuality (FACTS), Choosing the Best Life, Managing Pressures before Marriage,* and AC Green's *Game Plan,* among others. Some programs

---

* In federal fiscal year 2003, the 10 states discussed here with evaluations of Title V programs received $8,810,281 in federal funds. Under the law, states are required to provide matching funds of three state-raised dollars for every four federal dollars received. Thus in 2003, the 10 states supplied $7,268,060 in state dollars, bringing the total of public monies to Title V funded abstinence-only-until-marriage programs to $16,078,341.

included peer education, health fairs, parent outreach, and/or *Baby Think it Over* simulators. Some states supplemented their educational programs with media campaigns, also funded through Title V.

Evaluation Designs

The 11 evaluations summarized in this document represent those Advocates for Youth could uncover through extensive research. The quality of the evaluation designs varied greatly. Most evaluations employed a simple pretest/ posttest survey design. Slightly fewer than half (five) assessed the significance of changes from pre- to posttest, using a comparison group. Additionally, seven evaluations included some form of follow-up to assess the program's impact over time, although results are not yet available for two. Three of these seven also included a comparison group. For those programs that included follow-up, surveys were administered at three to 17 months after students completed their abstinence-only-until-marriage program.

Because the quality of the evaluation designs varied from state to state, Advocates relied heavily on the evaluators' own analyses and words to describe each program's impact.

Summary of Results

Evaluation of these 11 programs showed few short-term benefits and no lasting, positive impact. A few programs showed mild success at improving attitudes and intentions to abstain. No program was able to demonstrate a positive impact on sexual behavior over time. A description follows of short- and long-term impacts, by indicator.

Short-Term Impacts of State Abstinence-Only Programs

In 10 programs, evaluation measured the short-term impact of the program on at least one indicator, including attitudes favoring abstinence, intentions to abstain, and/or sexual behavior. Overall, programs were most successful at improving participants' attitudes towards abstinence and were least likely to positively affect participants' sexual behaviors.

Attitudes Endorsing Abstinence—10 evaluations tested for short-term changes in attitudes.

- Three of 10 programs had no significant impact on attitudes (Maryland, Missouri, and Nebraska).
- Four of 10 showed increases in attitudes favorable to abstinence (Arizona, Florida, Oregon, and Washington).
- Three of 10 showed mixed results (California, Iowa, and Pennsylvania).**

** Mixed results indicated that attitudes changed in both desired and undesired directions, either by survey questions within one initiative, or by individual programs within an initiative.

Intentions to Abstain—Nine evaluations measured short-term changes in intentions.

- Four of nine programs showed no significant impact on participants' intentions to abstain (California, Maryland, Nebraska, and Oregon).
- Three of nine programs showed a favorable impact on intentions to abstain (Arizona, Florida, and Washington).
- Two of nine programs showed mixed results (Iowa and Pennsylvania).**

Sexual Behaviors—Six evaluations measured short-term changes in sexual behavior.

- Three of six programs had no impact on sexual behavior (California, Maryland, and Missouri).
- Two of six programs reported increases in sexual behavior from pre- to posttest (Florida and Iowa). It was unclear whether the increases were due to youth's maturation or to a program's effect, as none of these evaluations included a comparison group.
- One of the six programs showed mixed results (Pennsylvania).**

Long-Term Impacts of State Abstinence-Only Programs

Seven evaluations included some form of follow-up survey to assess the impact of the abstinence-only programs over time. Results from two of these are not yet available (Nebraska and Oregon). Of the remaining five, three were of statewide initiatives (Arizona, California, and Minnesota). Two were evaluations of programs within statewide initiatives (Missouri's *Life Walk* Program and Pennsylvania's LaSalle Program). All five evaluations included questions to assess changes in participants' attitudes and behaviors between pretest/posttest and follow-up. Four also measured changes in intentions to abstain. Three evaluations included a comparison group.

- **Attitudes Endorsing Abstinence**—Five evaluations included assessment of changes in attitudes. Four of five evaluations showed no long-term positive impact on participants' attitudes. That is, participants' attitudes towards abstinence either declined at follow-up, or there was no evidence that participating in the abstinence-only program improved teens' attitudes about abstinence relative to the comparison groups, at three to 17 months after taking the abstinence-only program (Arizona, California, Missouri, and Pennsylvania's LaSalle Program). Follow-up surveys in Minnesota showed mixed results.
- **Intentions to Abstain**—Four evaluations measured long-term intentions to abstain. Three of four evaluations showed no long-term positive impact on participants' intentions to abstain from sexual intercourse. That is, participants' intentions either declined significantly at follow-up or there was no statistically significant difference in participants' attitudes relative to controls at follow-up (Arizona, California, and Minnesota). In one of the four (Pennsylvania's LaSalle

Program), evaluation showed a positive impact at follow-up on program participants' intentions to abstain relative to comparison youth.

- **Sexual Behavior**—Five programs measured long-term impacts on sexual behavior. No evaluation demonstrated any impact on reducing teens' sexual behavior at follow-up, three to 17 months after the program ended (Arizona, California, Minnesota, Missouri, or Pennsylvania's LaSalle Program).

Comparisons of Abstinence-Only-Until-Marriage versus Comprehensive Sex Education

Two evaluations—Iowa's and the Pennsylvania's Fulton County program—compared the impact of comprehensive sex education with that of abstinence-only-until-marriage programs.

In Iowa, abstinence-only students were slightly more likely than comprehensive sex education participants to feel strongly about wanting to postpone sex but less likely to feel that their goals should not include teen pregnancy. There was little to no difference between the abstinence-only students and those in the comprehensive sex education program in understanding why they should wait to have sex. Evaluation did not include comparison of data on the sexual behavior of participants in the two types of programs.

In Fulton County, Pennsylvania, results found few to no differences between the abstinence-only and comprehensive approaches in attitudes towards sexual behavior. Evaluators found that, regardless of which program was implemented in the seventh and eighth grades, sexual attitudes, intentions, and behaviors were similar by the end of the 10th grade.

Discussion

These evaluation results—from the first five-year cycle of funding for abstinence-only-until-marriage under Section 510(b) of Title V of the Social Security Act—reflect the results of other studies. In a 1994 review of sex education programs, all the studies available at the time of school-based, abstinence-only programs [were assessed] that had received peer review and that measured attitudes, intentions, *and* behavior. [It was] found that none of the three abstinence-only programs was effective in producing a statistically significant impact on sexual behaviors in program participants relative to comparisons. In a 1997 report for the National Campaign to Prevent Teen Pregnancy, Doug Kirby reviewed evaluations from six abstinence-only programs, again finding no program that produced a statistically significant change in sexual behavior. This was again confirmed in 2000, when another review by Kirby found no abstinence-only program that produced statistically significant changes in sexual behaviors among program youth relative to comparisons. This failure of abstinence-only programs to produce behavior change was among the central concerns expressed by some authors of the evaluations included in this document. . . . It is important to note that a great deal of research contradicts the belief that changes in knowledge and attitudes alone will necessarily result in behavior change.

A few evaluators also noted the failure of abstinence-only programs to address the needs of sexually active youth. Survey data from many of the programs indicated that sexually experienced teens were enrolled in most of the abstinence-only programs studied. For example:

In Erie County, Pennsylvania, researchers found that 42 percent of the female participants were sexually active by the second year of the program.

In Clinton County, Pennsylvania, data collected from program participants in the seventh, eighth, and ninth grades showed a dramatic increase in the proportion of program females who experienced first sexual intercourse over time (six, nine, and 30 percent, respectively, by grade).

In Minnesota, 12 percent of the eighth grade program participants were sexually active at posttest.

In Arizona, 19 percent of program participants were sexually active at follow-up. Concurrently, Arizona's evaluators found that youth's intent to pursue abstinence declined significantly at follow-up, regardless of whether the student took another abstinence-only class. Eighty percent of teens reported that they were likely to become sexually active by the time they were 20 years old.

Abstinence-only programs provide these youth with no information, other than abstinence, regarding how to protect themselves from pregnancy, HIV, and other STIs.

A third, related concern of evaluators was abstinence-only programs' failure to provide positive information about contraception and condoms. Evaluators noted more than once that programs' emphasis on the failure rates of contraception, including condoms, left youth ambivalent, at best, about using them.

In Clinton County, Pennsylvania, researchers noted that, of those participants that reported experiencing first sexual intercourse during ninth grade, only about half used any form of contraception.

Arizona's evaluation team found that program participants' attitudes about birth control became less favorable from pre- to posttest. They noted that this was probably a result of the "program's focus on the failure rates of contraceptives as opposed to their availability, use and access." . . .

Conclusion

Abstinence-only programs show little evidence of sustained (long-term) impact on attitudes and intentions. Worse, they show some negative impacts on youth's willingness to use contraception, including condoms, to prevent negative sexual health outcomes related to sexual intercourse. Importantly, only in one state did any program demonstrate short-term success in delaying the initiation of sex; none of these programs demonstrates evidence of long-term success in delaying sexual initiation among youth exposed to the programs or any evidence of success in reducing other sexual risk-taking behaviors among participants.

EXPLORING THE ISSUE

Is Abstinence-Only Sex Education the Best Way to Teach About Sex?

Critical Thinking and Reflection

1. Do you believe sex education should be abstinence based or comprehensive? For elementary school students? For high school students? Defend your answer.
2. Do you think region of the country, culture, and religion should be factors in deciding what type of sex education should be taught in schools? Why or why not?
3. Do you think abstinence-only programs will help decrease or impede the teen pregnancy and sexually transmitted disease problem?
4. If you were the parent of an adolescent, what type of sex education program would you feel most comfortable with your child being exposed to, abstinence-only education or comprehensive? Why?

Is There Common Ground?

As a society, we need to be cognizant of the fact that schools are not the only place where children receive sex education. All one has to do is listen to students during lunchtime at an elementary school, middle school, or high school to hear that they are receiving information about sex from peers. The Internet and other mass media are full of information about sex as well. Also, our own behaviors that we model to our children send strong messages about sexuality. It seems that the true mission of schools is to empower our children with accurate, developmentally appropriate information about their sexuality as a way to counterbalance the sometimes erroneous messages they receive from other aspects of their lives. Which approach most effectively addresses this goal? Or, is there a middle ground that has not been presented?

Additional Resources

Advocates for Youth. Retrieved on April 6, 2011, from http://www.advocates foryouth.org/%20%09%20index.php?option=com_content&task=view&id=46&Itemid=75.

This Web site, established in 1980 as the Center for Population Options, works to help young people make informed and responsible decisions about their reproductive and sexual health, fostering a positive and realistic approach to adolescent sexual health.

Go Ask Alice! Retrieved on April 6, 2011, from http://www.goaskalice.columbia.edu/.

Go Ask Alice! is a health question-and-answer site sponsored by Columbia University's health education program. The mission of this site is to provide in-depth, factual, and nonjudgmental information to assist individuals' decision making about their physical, sexual, emotional, and spiritual health. Questions about sexuality, sexual health, and relationships are frequent. This site includes hundreds of relevant links.

Information for Health. Retrieved on April 6, 2011, from http://www.inforhealth.org/.

The INFO Project (Information and Knowledge for Optimal Health Project), based at the Johns Hopkins University Bloomberg School of Public Health's Center for Communication Programs, is focused on understanding how knowledge and information can improve the quality of reproductive health programs, practice, and policies.

WebMD Sexual Health Center. Retrieved on April 6, 2011, from http://www.webmd.com/sex/gender-identity-disorder.

This Web site provides information from a medical perspective on gender identity disorder.

ISSUE 17

Is the Internet a Safe Place for Teens to Explore?

YES: Michele Fleming and Debra Rickwood, from "Teens in Cyberspace: Do They Encounter Friend or Foe?" *Youth Studies Australia* (vol. 23, no. 3, 2004)

NO: Chang-Hoan Cho and Hongsik John Cheon, from "Children's Exposure to Negative Internet Content: Effects of Family Content," *Journal of Broadcasting and Electronic Media* (December 2005)

Learning Outcomes

After reading this issue, you should be able to:

- Summarize the main concerns associated with children/teens' Internet use.
- Identify some ways in which parents can help their child/teen avoid exposure to harmful Internet material.
- Explain the significance of the findings of Chang-Hoan Cho and Hongsik John Cheon's research.
- Decide how safe you think teens are on the Internet.

ISSUE SUMMARY

YES: Michele Fleming and Debra Rickwood, professors at the University of Canberra in Australia, contend that parents need to be vigilant about their teens surfing the Web, but that it is generally a safe place and that the prevalence of cyber predators is overstated.

NO: Chang-Hoan Cho, assistant professor at the University of Florida, and Hongsik John Cheon, assistant professor at Frostburg State University, believe that the Web can be a dangerous place for teens to explore. They conducted a study that found that children are exposed to more negative Internet content than parents expect. Factors that reduced children's exposure to negative Internet content included parental interaction and family cohesion.

Parents naturally want to protect their children from all harm. When children are young, they are under parental control and easier to protect because they are physically in parents' sight. They are dependent on parents for physical needs such as food and shelter. As children get older, they are more mobile, particularly when they learn to drive. Parents of teens are usually sleep deprived because they cannot sleep until they know their teens are home safely from a night activity with their friends. But how can parents protect their children from the dangers of the Internet? Teens can be right in front of them in the house working on the computer and still be in possible danger. They don't even have to be out of the house to be exposed to dangers on the Internet such as sexual predators.

Is this true or is it an exaggeration? Although media reports suggest that children and teens are being sexually solicited on the Internet at an alarming rate, some researchers state that the incidence of sexual predators on the Internet is grossly overstated. Media reports often quote the statistic that one in five children, aged 10 to 17, per year, are sexually solicited online. What they don't tell you is that this statistic comes from a report that defines sexual solicitation as anything from a classmate asking his girlfriend if she is a virgin to something more serious like adults asking children to meet for a sexual encounter. One is a simple question, while the other is an example of the serious problem of online predators.

Studies on Internet use and its effects report conflicting and varied results. Some studies on children's use of the Internet show that it has positive effects on academic achievement and no negative effects on social or psychological development. Other studies report children experience lasting psychological damage as a result of surfing the Web. For example, one study stated that 42 percent of Internet users aged 10 to17 had seen online pornography in the past year, with the majority saying that they did not seek it out and were very disturbed by it. Of the more than 450 million porn Web sites, 3 percent ask for proof of age and are more than willing to show scenes that are sexually explicit.

Not only is there confusion over how much real danger the Internet poses, but parents must also contend with the new language that children and teens use when surfing the Web. For example, "lol" means laughing out loud; "pos" means parents over shoulder. In order to protect and guide children in the new world of the Internet, parents must learn about hardware, software, and a new language!

Common Sense Media and Media Wise from the National Institute on Media and the Family list Internet safety by age and stage as well as rules on Internet safety. For children aged 2 to 6, they suggest keeping children away from the Internet, even the games. For ages 7 to 9, e-mailing is OK, but not instant messaging (IM) as it is too difficult to control. Web surfing can be done if a filter is installed. No chat rooms, online games, or downloading should be allowed for this age group. For ages 10 to 12, children begin exploring the Web much more at school, at home, and at their friends' homes. They insist on IMing and surfing the Web for games and need to be supervised closely.

MySpace, which is a Web site for social networking for young people, is inappropriate at this age. Children aged 13 to 16 can e-mail, IM, surf the Web, download, and play games as long as they follow the rules of Internet safety.

In the following selections, Internet safety for children and teens is debated. Michele Fleming and Debra Rickwood recognize that dangers on the Internet exist, but that children use the Web mostly to interact with friends from their existing social networks, for homework, and for entertainment. From their study of 178 families, Chang-Hoan Cho and Hongsik John Cheon found that children are exposed to more negative Internet content than most parents had previously thought.

YES

**Michele Fleming and
Debra Rickwood**

Teens in Cyberspace: Do They Encounter Friend or Foe?

Recent media reports of relationships developed "online" have fuelled parents' concerns about the safety of their children using the Internet ('Runaway schoolgirl contacts family after Internet liaison', The *Canberra Times*, 17 July 2003, p. 15). Many parents hold ambivalent views about the Internet, being aware of its positive educational value but fearful of its "influence" on their children. In particular, parents are concerned that their children might become socially isolated due to excessive Internet use, might view sexually explicit images, and might divulge sensitive information to strangers.

The effects of "excessive" use of the Internet have not yet been clearly established. Some studies have looked at "computer" addiction and some at time spent playing video games. Both these activities have been linked to negative outcomes when done to excess. Excessive video game play, even when not of a violent nature, has been linked to aggression in numerous studies. Teens who use computers to excess have been found to report psychiatric symptoms, such as anxiety, hostility and obsessive-compulsivity. However, studies on the effects of excessive use of computers have not clearly shown the direction of the relationship and the negative outcomes reported may themselves be the cause of overuse.

Many teens are logging onto the Net both at school and at home but it is not yet known how many of them are using it to excess. Different criteria for Internet "addiction" are used by different researchers, making any valid assessment of how many individuals might be classified as addicted very difficult. Nonetheless, young people who spend inordinate amounts of time online, to the detriment of other activities, might be classified as "at-risk." Griffiths, in examining the impact of electronic technology on children and adolescents, suggested that when any activity is engaged in for such large amounts of time and other activities are displaced, it is likely that educational and social relationships will suffer.

The association between Internet use and psychological well-being in adults has been studied by Robert Kraut of the Carnegie Mellon University over the past few years. Kraut and colleagues have found greater Internet use to be associated with reduced psychological well-being, and reduced social support and increased depression. In a 1998 longitudinal study, undertaken with a relatively small but diverse US sample of 169 participants, including teenagers, greater Internet use was found to be associated with less family communication, greater loneliness and greater depression. In partial support of Kraut et al.'s findings, a study of high school seniors in the USA found that level of Internet use was not related to depression but was found to be related to poorer relationships with mothers and friends. However, it has also been suggested that it is people who are already lonely who spend time on the Internet.

In contrast, some research suggests that the Internet increases social connectedness and results in many positive face-to-face relationships. The anonymity of online relationships can increase intimate self-disclosure. For those who have difficulty with face-to-face relationships, the Internet may allow them to more easily express themselves and thereby experience social connectedness. Some people seem to feel that they are more their real selves on the Internet, which in turn leads to the formation of strong online attachments. For many teens, online communication may be just another way of keeping in touch with existing friends. Instead of being on the phone after school, teens are "talking" to their friends online.

Parents are also concerned about the amount of pornography children are exposed to online. Although some young people may deliberately seek out pornographic sites, others may be subjected to it unwittingly. Parents fears are not entirely unfounded, with 25% of youth aged 10 to 17 years indicating they had been exposed to unwanted pornography in a national survey conducted in the USA.

However, the biggest concern for parents is "stranger-danger." Parents have long been concerned about stranger-danger in the real world and this has now extended to the virtual world. Parents are fearful that children might divulge information that makes them vulnerable to potential predators who might be able to trace them through information disclosed on the Internet. Parents also fear that children might form a relationship with someone unsuitable online, possibly even a paedophile. Certainly, young people are the most vulnerable section of society when it comes to sexual assault and abduction. Crime statistics for Australia show that children aged 10 to 14 years and adolescents aged 15 to 19 years are three times more likely than the general population to have been recorded as a victim of sexual assault. Adolescents are also three times more likely to be the victims of robbery and kidnapping than the general population. Thus fears about safety in the real world are based in fact. To date, there is little but growing evidence that fears about safety as a result of contacts made online are also well-founded.

How Often Are Youth Online?

Children and young people are using the Internet in ever-increasing numbers. Research done in the USA has found that teenagers are much heavier users of the Internet than are adults. In one US study of 754 teens aged 12 to 17 years, it was found that 73% used the Internet and of these 42% went online daily.

In a national survey conducted by the Australian Broadcasting Authority in 2000, 58% of Australian children aged 5 to 12 years and 86% of teens aged 13 to 18 years were reported to have Internet access either at home or at school. The latest Australian Bureau of Statistics figures, using 2001 data, found that 28% of Australian children aged 0 to 17 years had accessed the Internet from home in the previous week. Given that this figure includes very young children and babies, the likelihood is that use by teens is substantially higher than indicated by these figures. Furthermore, many young people use the Internet at school and some of this use is undoubtedly for reasons other than schoolwork.

Why Do Young People Use the Internet?

Research into reasons for young people's use of the Internet is relatively scarce. However, research with adults suggests that the Internet is used for entertainment, education, information gathering and communication. In a sample of 236 American college students with a mean age of 20 years, the main reasons for using the World Wide Web were entertainment, passing time, social information, relaxation and information. In a survey of 684 adults, the main reasons reported for using the Internet were to find information, to relieve boredom, to get to know others and for entertainment.

Recently, some studies have begun to investigate the reasons for teens' use of the Internet. An American survey conducted by America Online of 6,700 teens aged 12 to 17 years, found that 81% used their computers for email; 70% for instant messaging; 70% to play online games; 58% for homework research; and 55% for listening to and downloading music. In a study of 625 American youth aged 10 to 17 years, 71% used the Internet to get news or information about current events; 68% used their computers to send and receive emails; 56% to get information about sports, entertainment and hobbies; 54% to talk in chat rooms; 17% to get health or medical information; and 17% to shop.

Younger children's reasons for using the Internet were examined in a study of 194 Dutch children aged 8 to 13 years. Children reported using the Internet because they had an affinity with computers; in order to gather information; for entertainment; to avoid boredom; for online social interaction; and for off-line social action, in that order. The last mentioned reason "off-line social interaction" referred to children's desire to talk about the Internet with friends because their friends were also using it.

Results of the Pew Internet and American Life Project showed that teens go online for entertainment and information. Some of the things teens specifically reported going online for were to send or receive email; to use instant messaging (IM); to visit web sites about movies, television shows, music groups and sports stars; to look for news; to look for hobby information; to play and download games; to research information on items they might like to buy; and to play and download music. Teens reported that IM messaging is very important to them, with 74% of online teens using IM. One-fifth of teenagers in the study reported using IM as the main means of contacting friends.

Cyberspace: Consequences for Children and Adolescents

The overwhelming concern of parents and the public alike is that young people will form cyber-relationships with predatory strangers, which in turn may lead to them being lured into a meeting with a paedophile. A growing body of evidence suggests that both adults and teens are forming relationships online, and in some cases turning online relationships into offline ones. However, American studies report that most teens and adults are taking appropriate precautions when meeting with online "friends." The news from Japan, however, is rather more worrying, with reports of a number of sexual assaults on teens as a result of meetings arranged via online dating sites. On the positive side, American research also suggests that most young people tend to form relationships with similar age peers rather than with older people, and that many of these online relationships are initiated through existing social networks. Similarly, there appears no evidence as yet that spending time online results in social isolation; on the contrary, research to date with adolescents suggests that Internet use increases social interaction.

Psychological Well-Being and Social Connectedness

Most of the time, young people online are interacting with friends from their existing social networks. In an American study of 130 children aged 11 to 13 years, participants' IM partners were usually friends from school. However, 12% of IM partners in this study had been met online. Most of the online communication was devoted to the usual topics discussed offline, such as friends and gossip, and was motivated by a desire of companionship. Of concern, however, is the finding that those young people who felt lonely and/or anxious were more likely to have online relationships with people with whom they did not have a close affiliation. This is consistent with research which suggests that not all teens are equally likely to form new online relationships. In one US study, boys who had poor communication with their parents or were highly troubled were more likely to form close online relationships than were other boys. Similarly, girls who had high levels of conflict with their parents or were highly troubled, were more likely to form close online relationships than were other girls.

Some teens, however, have reported that use of the Internet improves their relationships with friends. Results of the Pew Internet and American Life Project, in which 754 young people aged 12 to 17 and 754 of their parents were interviewed, showed that 73% of teens were online. Of these online youths, 48% said that use of the Internet improved their relationships with friends; and 32% reported that the Internet had helped them make new friends. Girls aged 12 to 14 years were the most enthusiastic about the Internet's ability to help them make new friends online. Teens in this study reported that the Internet allowed them to be more their true self, which is in line with research with adults.

Frequent Internet users have reported engaging in more social activities than less frequent users. In a study with 927 Israeli teenagers aged 13 to 18 years from a representative sample of Israeli households, it was reported that more than a third of the respondents were frequent Internet users, although the authors classified frequent use as anything more than once per week. Only 10% of respondents reported using the Internet daily. Importantly, however, frequent users reported having fewer friends and feeling more socially isolated than did light users.

Pornography and Sexual Harassment

Parents' concerns that their children will be subjected to online pornography are valid. Young people may visit pornographic sites by choice but also they may be subjected to pornographic material unwittingly. In a national survey of American youth aged 10 to 17 years who were regular Internet users, 25% had been exposed to unwanted sexual pictures in the previous year. Of these, the majority reported no negative effect of their exposure but 25% reported distress at being exposed. More boys than girls reported exposure and older youths reported substantially more exposure than did younger children.

With a younger sample of Dutch children aged 8 to 13 years, 4% reported experiencing violence on the net, 4% reported experiencing pornography, and 1.5% reported experiencing sexual harassment. Although these figures are small, they are nonetheless of concern.

As part of the Australia Broadcasting Authority's survey of Internet use in the home, a cyber-panel of Australian families was questioned regarding exposure to offensive material on the Net. A total of 192 of the cyber-panel members were teens aged 11 to 17 years and almost half (47%) of them reported having been exposed to offensive content such as violence, pornography and nudity. The overwhelming majority of offensive content cited by these teens was pornography.

Even more disturbing than viewing unwanted pornography is being sexually solicited online. A survey of American youth found that 19% of Internet users aged 10 to 17 years had received an unwanted sexual solicitation in the previous 12 months. Thankfully, none of these solicitations resulted in any sexual contact or assault.

Safety

Young people, for the most part, spend their time online with people they already know but nonetheless many do appear to form friendships with strangers. In a large US survey of 1,501 adolescents aged 10 to 17 years who regularly used the Internet, 55% had used chat rooms, IM and other forms of online communication in the previous year, to communicate with people they did not know face-to-face. For some of these youths, the online strangers were in fact friends-of-friends. Twenty-five percent of the participants reported forming a casual online friendship, while 14% reported forming a close online friendship, 7% had a face-to-face meeting, and 2% had established an online romantic relationship. In all, 17% of young people reported establishing some form of close online relationship. The majority of participants stated that mutual interests and activities were what initially drew them together. Of the 101 young people who had face-to-face encounters, 77% were accompanied to the meeting by a friend or relative, 1% were made to feel afraid at the meeting, and none of the youths were physically or sexually assaulted at the meeting.

Reassuringly, the majority of teens in the Wolak, Mitchell and Finkelhor study who met their online friends face-to-face, were accompanied to the meeting. This caution in face-to-face encounters is consistent with research conducted with a group of 30 undergraduates who regularly used the Internet. In this study, 80% of the undergraduates had formed online friendships and 33% met their online friends face-to-face. Most of the participants reported that they were careful to protect their anonymity and took precautions before meeting face-to-face. Nonetheless, not all teens are cautious, which raises serious concerns for parents.

In contrast to the relatively small number of face-to-face encounters reported in the Wolak, Mitchell & Finkelhor study, are findings from a survey conducted in Japan and reported by Yasumasa Kioka of the Japanese National Policy Agency at a conference earlier this year. Japan adopted the latest third-generation (3G) technologies early on, thus Japanese children were some of the first to use mobile-Internet services. In 2002, Japan had 3,401 "dating sites" available from Internet-mobiles and Kioka reported that a survey completed in 2002 showed that 22% of female high school students and 18% of male high school students had used one of these dating sites. Of these, 43% of females and 28% of males had met their date face-to-face. The arrest statistics for dating sites in Japan showed that 84% of a total of 1,517 crime victims were children under the age of 18 and that the majority of dating site crimes were related to mobile-Internet use.

Fears that children and teens may be tracked on the Internet to their home addresses are also not entirely without foundation. Although many web sites have privacy policies, they do not cover the advertising banners that pop up seemingly endlessly when accessing many web sites. Young people may be lulled into a false sense of security when on the Internet and may disclose sensitive information. In research conducted in the US with 304 youth aged 10 to 17 years, one-third of younger teens or "tweens" aged 10 to 12 years reported visiting chat rooms while half of those aged 13 to 17 years reported doing so. Of those going online, 73% said they "look to see if a web site has a privacy policy before answering any questions" and 79% agreed that teenagers should get consent from their parents before they give out information online. However, many of the youngsters in this study were prepared to give out sensitive information when a free gift was offered. Interestingly, gender differences were found, with girls less prepared than boys to provide information to web sites in return for a free gift; girls were also less prepared than boys to trust web sites not to share information with others. Girls were also significantly more likely than were boys to have talked to their parents about how to deal with giving out information on the web. While this study suggests that many teens are conscious of cyber-safety, a sizeable minority are not. Lack of caution was also shown by teens surveyed in the Pew Internet and American Life Project, with 22% of online teens who used IM reporting that they had shared their password with a friend.

Although many parents report closely supervising children's Internet use, there appears to be a gap between children's reporting of parental supervision and parents' reporting, with parents saying they keep a closer eye on children's Internet use than their children report. This inconsistency might be due to teens being unaware of their parents' supervision; alternatively, parents may be over-reporting their level of supervision.

For parents who are particularly concerned that their children may be accessing inappropriate material on the Net, there are various tools which can be used to block access, such as filters, labels and safe zones. A good Internet site, which provides information about these tools and other tips on safety for both children and parents, is the Australian Broadcasting Authority Cyber-smart Kids site. . . .

Teens in Cyberspace: Finding Friend or Foe?

There appears to be strong agreement between parents and teens that the Internet is valuable tool that helps young people with their schoolwork. For many young people the Internet is also useful for entertainment, information and social communication. Although no definite figures exist for the numbers of teenagers that use the Internet to "excess," it is likely that those who are neglecting their schoolwork, their sports and their leisure activities in order to surf the Net, are in danger of becoming addicted.

It is likely that children and teens will be subject to occasional violent and pornographic images and parents need to be aware of this and discuss it with their children. Older teens are more vulnerable than younger teens to this type of exposure, probably because of the amount of time they spend on the Net and perhaps because they are more likely than younger children to explore more and varied sites. The consequences of young people's exposure to pornography are not yet known; however, research with adults suggests negative consequences. In particular, exposure to violent pornography has been found to be associated with violence against women and repeated exposure to non-violent pornography has been found to be associated with the promotion of more permissive sexual attitudes.

To date, research suggests that online relationships of some kind, whether casual or close, are formed by large numbers of teens. Reassuringly for parents, most of these relationships seem to be extensions of the young person's social circle. The early evidence from American studies suggests that cyber-safety is not a big problem as yet; however, evidence from Japan suggests otherwise. Japan is perhaps a few years ahead of most other countries in terms of ease of Internet accessibility. Nonetheless, it remains to be seen whether the problems with "dating sites" is one that is peculiar to Japanese culture, or whether the type of problem currently seen in Japan will emerge in Australia and other Western cultures in the near future.

For some children and young people, the anonymity of online relationships may be helpful as they go about practising their social communications. Teens with healthy, happy offline relationships are likely to continue to explore and expand those relationships further via online chat. Young people who are geographically remote, disabled or housebound due to illness, may find online chat an important form of communication. However, of concern, is the fact that a small minority of young people who are socially anxious or lonely may deliberately seek out relationships online.

Parents need to be aware that some children and teens will form close, intimate relationships online. Existing relationships that are extended and consolidated on the Internet, appear to be healthy ones although the jury is still out on the quality of relationships that are newly formed online. It is important that parents discuss issues of Internet safety with children and teens and try to discourage face-to-face meetings; however, if these do take place, children and even older teens should be accompanied to the meeting by a friend or family member and it should occur in a very public place. Girls appear to have taken the messages of privacy and safety to heart more than boys have. This may be due to parents talking more to their daughters about Internet safety than to their sons.

The Internet is a juggernaut which parents cannot stop. Even without home access, many teens have access to the Internet at school, at friends' houses or at Internet cafés. Rather than banning online communication, parents need to be aware of what children and adolescents are doing online by talking to them about their Internet use and showing an interest in what they are doing. Imposing some restrictions on the information that young people are allowed to disclose online and imposing restrictions on the amount of time spent online are first steps towards keeping kids safe. Even though many teens appear Net-savvy, they still need to be reminded of the potential dangers lurking online. There may be many friends in cyberspace but there are undoubtedly a number of foes.

Chang-Hoan Cho and
Hongsik John Cheon

 NO

Children's Exposure to Negative Internet Content: Effects of Family Content

The Internet has become an indispensable element of life for most people in the contemporary world, and children are not excluded. Because of the ubiquitous availability of Internet access, in schools and libraries, children are increasingly becoming involved in this new technology. As of December 2003, 23 million children in the United States ages 6 to 17 have Internet access at home, which is a threefold increase since 2000. According to a survey conducted by the Corporation for Public Broadcasting in July 2002, 78% of family households with children have Internet access at home. A survey by Yahoo and Carat showed that children ages 12 to 17 used the Internet an average of 16.7 hours per week in 2003. Given this extensive usage, the Internet has the potential to be a very powerful socialization agent.

The Internet has a double-edged sword characteristic for children: providing many opportunities for learning while exposing children to potentially negative content. The Internet not only provides significant benefits for children, such as research access, socialization, entertainment, and a communication tool with families, but it also connotes negative aspects such as violence, pornography, hate sites, isolation, predators, and commercialism. The Web sites considered detrimental include those dedicated to negative content such as pornography, violent online games, online gambling, and so forth. For example, many children can easily access pornographic content on the Internet. They can also be accidentally exposed to numerous obscene pop-up banner ads and extensive pornographic content when they type seemingly innocent key words into a search engine, for example, the name of a singer such as Britney Spears, Christina Aguilera, or Madonna. According to Finkelhor et al., 25% of the respondents ($n = 1,501$, ages 10–17) reported receiving unwanted exposure to sexual materials while online, and 19% received a sexual solicitation online.

Despite the potential negative effects on children using the Internet, more than 30% of surveyed parents had not discussed the downside of Internet use with their children, and 62% of parents of teenagers did not realize that their children had visited inappropriate Web sites. Recognizing the ever-serious negative aspects of children using the Internet and parents' possible underestimation of, or ignorance about, their children's Internet usage and its effects, this study explores the degree of children's exposure to negative Internet content and detects the possible discrepancy between what parents think their children are doing online and their children's actual activities. In doing so, this study carefully dissects the possible causes and consequences of perceived parental control over children's Internet usage. Concerned that inappropriate Internet content may jeopardize the health or safety of children, the present study is a crucial attempt that aims to address the following research inquires with regard to children's Internet usage: (a) to understand the degree to which children are exposed to negative Internet content, (b) to detect a possible discrepancy between parents' perception and children's actual exposure to negative Internet content, (c) to examine various antecedents explaining perceived parental control over children's Internet usage, and (d) to suggest various ways to decrease children's exposure to negative Internet content.

Literature Review

In fall 2002, 99% of public schools in the United States had access to the Internet and 64% of children ages 5 to 17 had Internet access at home (National Center for Education Statistics, 2002). Children ages 13 to 17 spent more time online than watching television—3.5 hours versus 3.1 hours per day, and used the Internet mostly for exploration (surfing and searching), followed by education (learning and homework), multimedia (music, video, etc.), communications (e-mail, chat, and instant messages), games, and e-commerce. The place children were most likely to use the Internet was in the home, rather than at a library or school: 20% of children ages 8 to 16 had a computer in their bedroom, of which 54% had Internet access.

Negative Effects of Using the Internet

There is an increasing concern from educators, psychologists, and parents about the negative effects of using the Internet on the physical (e.g., information fatigue syndrome), cognitive (e.g., inability to discriminate between the real and cyber world), and social development (e.g., identity confusion) of children, among which, detriment to social development (hurting children's skills and patience to conduct necessary social relations in the real world) is a paramount problem. One of the most serious concerns regarding children's social development involves the proliferation and easy accessibility of negative content on the Internet, such as pornography, violence, hate speech, gambling, sexual solicitation, and so forth. It is easy to see how these types of negative content harm children and destroy their development. Extant literature shows that children's exposure to inappropriate media content yields many negative outcomes such as increased aggression, fear, desensitization, poor school performance, prevalence of symptoms of psychological trauma, antisocial behavior, negative self-perception, low self-esteem, lack of reality, identity confusion, and more.

In particular, sexually explicit materials on the Internet can desensitize children to deviant sexual stimuli and encourage them to enact antisocial aggressive sexual behaviors. Furthermore, the anonymity of the Internet makes it easier for pedophiles to approach children through online chatting. Children who spend hours in chat rooms looking for friends or just passing time can be easily targeted and abused by unknown adult sexual offenders. Violent online games are another serious concern. It is known that violent computer games increase children's physical, verbal, relational, and antisocial aggressions. These negative effects of violent games on children are even more serious regarding the Internet because access to such violent games has become easier for unsupervised children due to free or fee-based online games. Online gambling has also been cited as a serious Internet problem affecting children. It can seriously disrupt children's social and psychological development, for example, addiction, being unable to repay debts, missing school, and so forth.

However, little is known about children's actual amount of exposure to such inappropriate content and activities on the Internet. Extant literature shows that a discrepancy exists between the reports of parents and children on children's media usage; for example, parents tend to underestimate time spent on television viewing and the amount of violence to which children are exposed. This discrepancy leads parents to underrate the impact of media messages on their children and to not exert much control over their children's media use. Surprisingly, 38% of surveyed children ages 8 to 18 said that their parents do not enforce any rules on watching television, 95% of older children watch television without their parents, and 81% of children ages 2 to 7 watch television unsupervised. This may be true for children's Internet usage, but we know little about the possible discrepancy between parental estimates and children's actual Internet usage. In this vein, the present study tries to detect the degree to which children are exposed to these sources of negative content and whether parents overestimate or underestimate their children's exposure to such content. In doing so, this study strives to examine how children's exposure to such negative Internet content relates to the social context of Internet usage, that is, the role of family communication and relationship on children's exposure to such content.

Social Context of Children's Internet Use

People use media within a social realm, and children are no exception. Social context of media usage, especially parental influence, is crucial in children's social development. However, many social aspects of children's Internet usage are still unknown. Therefore, this study focuses on the social context of children's Internet use, especially relative to family environment such as parental guidance, influence, and relationship with children.

Children live within a family boundary; therefore, parental influence on children's media usage and effect is very important. Extant research shows that family communication exerts the greatest influence on children's socialization and development. Stemming from political socialization research, family communication patterns have been widely applied to various socialization contexts such as consumption, political process, media usage, and so forth. In particular, in mass media research, it was found that family communication patterns mediate the extent and type of children's mass media use and effects, for example, watching public affairs television programs, interest in and knowledge about politics, imitating their parents' television usage, interpreting televised violence, attitude towards nontraditional sex roles, child consumer learning, and so forth.

More specifically, concerning children's Internet usage, Wartella et al. found that parental attitude and guidance significantly influence children's judgment of quality Internet materials. Recognizing the importance of family context on children's Internet usage, the present study tries to examine the role of family context (parent–child communication, relationship, and activity) on children's exposure to Internet content and parents' control over children's Internet use. In short, the research contributes to this area in the following three aspects: (a) understanding children's actual Internet usage in terms of content, not by Web sites or general activities; (b) examining the role of family environment on children's negative Internet exposure; and (c) providing a theoretical framework to explain children's exposure to negative Internet content and parents' perceived control over their children's Internet usage. . . .

Discussion

This study was an exploratory study to understand children's exposure to negative Internet content. The objective was to provide insight into family context factors that influence children's exposure to negative Internet content and to test their proposed interrelationships. In pursuing that goal, a theoretical model of children's negative Internet exposure was synthesized from the theoretical traditions of a representative body of diverse referent disciplines. Possible contributions of this study are threefold. First, it is the first attempt toward understanding children's negative Internet exposure in terms of content, rather than by Web sites or general activities. Second, this study builds a theoretical model explaining children's exposure to negative Internet content. Third, the study identifies the importance of family environment on children's negative Internet exposure and suggests two important family context variables that reduce children's exposure to negative content.

This study found that parents generally underestimate their children's exposure to negative Internet content. This finding suggests that children are more exposed to negative Internet content than what parents expect. It implies that the effect of negative Internet content on children can be more serious than what most parents estimate. Moreover, among various demographic variables such as family income, parents' education level, and age and gender of children, only the gender of children is related to children's exposure to negative content (male children are exposed to negative content more than female children). This finding suggests that demographic variables do little to explain children's negative Internet exposure, which amplifies the importance of identifying other significant factors that explain children's Internet exposure. This study proposed family relationship, interaction, and control as important antecedents of children's exposure to negative Internet content and built a theoretical model on the effect of family context on children's negative exposure.

The acceptable fit of the final model generally supports the stated hypotheses: Parents' perceived control is explained by shared Web activity and family cohesion, and perceived control results in more appropriate use of the Internet by their children (less exposure to negative Internet content). . . . There was a significant effect of family cohesion/intimacy on parents' perceived control over children's Internet usage. The result suggests that parents who perceive high family cohesion/intimacy tend to have high perceived control over their children's Internet usage. This finding implies that parents need to maintain intimate emotional bonding with their children to have better understanding of, and control over, their children's behaviors (negative Internet exposure). The result is consistent with previous studies on the role of family cohesion on the parent–child relationship, and this study substantiates the importance of family cohesion in the context of children's negative Internet exposure.

. . . Findings demonstrate a significant effect of shared Web activities on parents' perceived control over children's Internet usage. The result implies that parents who spend more time online with their children are more likely to have high perceived control over their children's Internet usage. The result is consistent with previous studies on the role of shared family activities on parent–child mutual understanding and children's media usage and learning. This study further confirms the importance of shared family activities in the context of children's negative Internet exposure. Although not initially hypothesized, a new causal relationship (family cohesion → shared Web activity) was discovered. This relationship seems conceptually sound because high emotional bonding among parents and children may lead to more shared activities and interactions between them. Actually, previous studies have demonstrated the positive relationship between family bonding and family interaction.

Unexpectedly, however, the effect of parents' Internet skill on perceived control over children's Internet usage was not confirmed. The hypothesized relationship was derived from "flow" research (more skill, higher cognitive control), but the result failed to show the importance of parents' Internet skill on the perceived control over their children's Internet usage. The finding suggests that parents' Internet knowledge and skill do not necessarily give high competency and control to parents; instead, emotional bonding and shared Web activities contribute to increase parents' perceived control over children's Internet usage. In terms of relative importance, shared Web activity exhibited the strongest predicting power of parents' perceived control ($\gamma = .43$), followed by family cohesion ($\gamma = .39$). The result suggests that the most important contributor of parents' perceived control over children's Internet usage is shared Web activities between parents and children. In addition, parents' perceived control led to decreased children's exposure to negative Internet content. This suggests that parents' perceived control through shared Web activities and family cohesion actually reduces children's exposure to negative Internet content.

The findings of the present research provide substantial implications for child education in school and at home. This study suggests possible home education strategies to parents, for example, locating the computer in a common area and having regular shared Internet sessions, encouraging children to evaluate Web sites and Internet ads and commenting on and explaining the subjects, teaching quality Web browsing and clicking choices, building and maintaining family love, affirmation and intimate relationship with children, and so forth. Parental oversight and interaction through these home education strategies can help reduce the temptation for children to use the computer to explore inappropriate content. The results of the study also can help educational organizations and governmental agencies develop various workshops or educational programs for children and parents to teach quality Internet use and importance of family context in children's negative Internet exposure. The study also provides implications for government regulations regarding Web sites that are potentially negative to children, for example, the need for developing a universal rating system for inappropriate Internet content (such as early childhood, everyone, teen, mature, and adults only) and requiring the Web sites to post the rating to better inform children and parents about the content of the Web sites before they observe the content.

Limitations and Future Research

This study has several noted limitations. The first concern relates to sampling issues. First, the sample was relatively more upscale in terms of reported family income and parent education level than reflected in the sample school's general student population. Second, the sample size of 178 was relatively small and was not a national sample. Third, the sample was limited to children ages 11 to 16. Therefore, it would be valuable to replicate the present study with a larger and more representative national sample including younger, more vulnerable children. Another concern is that the study employed self-reported measurement of children's Internet exposure without any actual observation of the children's behavior. Even though this study tried to address social desirability effects by assuring the anonymity of participants and employing accidental exposure, as well as intentional exposure, there is still a chance that social desirability may have factored into the responses. Hence, it would be fruitful to conduct an experiment that directly measures actual children's Internet exposure (e.g., log file analysis, surveillance software, etc.) by controlling social desirability effects. Similarly, for the measure of parents' control, it might be more valid to assess actual behavioral control, instead of perceived control, for example, how often parents intervene, monitor, filter, and/or supervise. In addition, the list of inappropriate Internet content could have been more exhaustive; for example, hate Web sites were not included. Hence, it would be useful to include a more exhaustive list of inappropriate content for future research. Last, Family communications patterns inventory could be another important indicator of parents' perceived control of their children's use of the Internet. Therefore, the relationship would be worthwhile for future study.

In conclusion, this study has provided a theoretical framework for understanding the role of family environment on children's negative Internet exposure, such as family cohesion, shared Web activity, and parents' perceived control. The proposed model is an initial step in understanding the relationship between family context and children's exposure to negative Internet content. Theoretical approaches to understanding children's Internet exposure have rarely been conducted in previous literature, and this study was undertaken to guide future empirical research and theoretical work. For example, the focus was on the family environment from the parents' perspective. It would be worthwhile to examine children's perspectives of family context, such as the role of children's Internet skill, children's perceived intimacy with their parents, children's perceived shared Web activities with their parents, and children's perceived control over Internet content. Second, this study only examined the role of family environment on children's negative Internet exposure. It should be noted that other social contexts might also be crucial in children's media usage. For example, children interact with other peer students outside family boundaries in school or other places. Children's exposure to negative content may be influenced by their interactions with other peer children. In addition, education in school on quality Internet usage may also significantly reduce children's negative Internet exposure. Therefore, as future research, it would be fruitful to examine the effects of peer interaction and school education on children's exposure to negative Internet content.

EXPLORING THE ISSUE

Is the Internet a Safe Place for Teens to Explore?

Critical Thinking and Reflection

1. What are some of the concerns with children and teens being on the Internet that were mentioned in both articles?
2. What did the authors identify as some ways in which parents can help decrease their child/teen's exposure to negative Internet material? Can you think of any other ways parents can help ensure their teen's safety?
3. Cho and Cheon conducted a study examining how parental guidance, influence, and relationship with their children affect children's Internet use. What were their findings and how are they significant to families?
4. The YES article argues that although there are dangers on the Internet, with proper monitoring and teaching from parents, teens can be safe while utilizing this resource. The NO article points out that parents many times underestimate the dangers that their children/teens are exposed to, although their study points out that high parental involvement tends to decrease this as well. What is your opinion of teens' safety and the Internet?

Is There Common Ground?

The articles presented in this issue cited information as early as 1998; 13 years ago. What technologies have been developed with Internet browsers and anti-virus protection to help combat inappropriate pop-up material that might be viewed by children?

Another Internet problem that has become prevalent since these articles were published, and was not addressed, is Internet bullying (cyberbullying) among children and teens. What are some of the negative consequences that can result from this problem and what ideas do you have for helping parents prevent this from occurring?

In Cho and Cheon's study, they found that parents' knowledge and skill with regard to the Internet was not directly related to perceived control over their child's Internet use. However, does this mean that parents do not need to have general knowledge of their computer and the Internet to ensure their child's safety? How can parent's level of knowledge affect their ability to monitor their child's Internet use?

Additional Resources

National Center for Missing and Exploited Children. (2010). Net Smartz Workshop. Retrieved on April 29, 2011, from http://www.netsmartz.org/Teens.

This Web site provides information about remaining safe online and also has videos of teens telling their own stories of becoming victims of online predators and other situations.

Teens Health. (2011). Internet Safety: Safe Surfing Tips for Teens. Retrieved on April 29, 2011, from http://kidshealth.org/teen/safety/safebasics/internet_safety.html.

This Web site provides information for teens to help them identify information that should always be kept private as well as how to deal with encountering uncomfortable situations in chat rooms or handling cyberbullying.

Washington State Office of the Attorney General. (2008). Internet Safety. Retrieved on April 29, 2011, from http://www.atg.wa.gov/InternetSafety/Teens.aspx.

This site provides information and tips on how to remain safe on the Internet and social networking sites. It provides some scenarios and points out common mistakes that teens make while using the Internet that can put them at risk.

Contributors to This Volume

EDITORS

ROBERT L. DELCAMPO, Ph.D., is a professor of family science at New Mexico State University in Las Cruces, New Mexico. He is a licensed marriage and family therapist, clinical member, and approved supervisor of the American Association for Marriage and Family Therapy. He also holds memberships in the National Council on Family Relations and the American Psychotherapy Association and is a former president of the New Mexico Association for Marriage and Family Therapy. He received a B.S. from the State University of New York, an M.S. from Virginia Tech, and a Ph.D. in family relations and child development from Florida State University. He co-edits *Taking Sides: Clashing Views in Childhood and Society*, which is in its ninth edition. His work has also appeared in such journals as *Family Relations* and *Contemporary Family Therapy*.

DIANA S. DELCAMPO, Ph.D., is a professor and the child development and family life specialist with the New Mexico Cooperative Extension Service at New Mexico State University in Las Cruces, New Mexico. She is a member of the National Council on Family Relations and the National Extension Human Sciences Network. She received a B.S. from Concord College in West Virginia, an M.S. from Virginia Tech, and a Ph.D. in curriculum and instruction from the University of Michigan. She presently develops educational programs in child and family development, supervises the New Mexico CYFAR grant project (Just Be It! Healthy & Fit, www.nmcyfar .org) and coordinates parenting content for http://www.babysfirstwish.org and http://www.eXtension.org/parenting. She co-edits *Taking Sides: Clashing Views in Childhood and Society*, which is in its ninth edition. She also has published educational guides, chapters in several books, symposium proceedings, and articles in various journals.

KOURTNEY T. VAILLANCOURT, Ph.D., is an assistant professor of family science at New Mexico State University in Las Cruces, New Mexico. She is a licensed marriage and family therapist and drug and alcohol abuse counselor, clinical member, and approved supervisor of the American Association for Marriage and Family Therapy. She also holds memberships in the National Council on Family Relations and the International Family Therapy Association. She received a B.S. from New Mexico State University, an M.S. from New Mexico State University, and a Ph.D. in family studies from Virginia Tech. She co-edits *Taking Sides: Clashing Views in Childhood and Society*, which is in its ninth edition.

AUTHORS

CONSTANCE AHRONS is co-chair of the Council on Contemporary Families. She is a therapist and author of three books. She is Professor Emerita from the Department of Sociology and former director of the Marriage and Family Therapy Doctoral Training Program at the University of Southern California in Los Angeles.

ELIZABETH BARTHOLET is the Morris Wasserstein Public Interest Professor of Law and faculty director of the Child Advocacy Program at the Harvard Law School.

DIANA BAUMRIND is a researcher at the Institute of Human Development, University of California at Berkley and is known nationally for her publications and research on parenting and spanking.

RACHEL L. BERGERON is an assistant clinical professor of psychiatry at Yale University, School of Medicine.

T. BERRY BRAZELTON is founder of the Child Development Unit at Children's Hospital Boston and has been a practicing pediatrician for 45 years. He has authored many books on children and families.

JEANNE BROOKS-GUNN is professor of child development and education at Teacher's College, Columbia University, and the author of numerous publications. Her specialty is policy-oriented research focusing on family and community influences on child and youth development.

NATASHA J. CABRERA, Ph.D., is an associate professor of human development at the University of Maryland. She directs the Family Involvement Laboratory at the University of Maryland. Her research interests include parent–child relationships, children's social and emotional development in different types of families and cultural/ethnic groups, school readiness, fatherhood, predictors of adaptive and maladaptive parenting, and translation of research into practice and policy.

PAUL CAMERON is the publisher of the Family Research Report, Colorado Springs, Colorado, which examines data on families, sexual social policy, drug addiction, and homosexuality.

MARK A. CARROZZA is the director of the Institute of Health Policy and Health Services Research at the University of Cincinnati. The Institute addresses local, state, and national health care issues from an interdisciplinary perspective.

CENTER FOR SCIENCE IN THE PUBLIC INTEREST is a consumer advocacy organization that conducts research in order to represent citizens' interests and provides information to consumers about health.

HONGSIK JOHN CHEON is an assistant professor in the department of marketing and finance, College of Business, at Frostburg State University. His research interests include interactive marketing, international marketing, and consumer information processing.

CHANG-HOAN CHO is an assistant professor of advertising, College of Journalism and Communications, University of Florida. His research interests include Internet advertising, new media technology, product placement, interactive television, multicultural advertising, and international advertising.

STEPHANIE COONTZ is co-chair of the Council on Contemporary Families and teaches history and family studies at Evergreen State College in Olympia, Washington. She has written several books, including *The Way We Never Were: American Families and the Nostalgia Trap* (Basic Books, 1992).

PHILIP A. COWAN is a researcher at the Institute of Human Development, University of California at Berkley.

NICKI R. CRICK is the director of the Institute of Child Development at the University of Minnesota. She is also head of the Crick Social Development Lab, which is currently focused on the study of relational aggression.

FRANCIS T. CULLEN is the Distinguished Research Professor of Criminal Justice at the University of Cincinnati and has interests in criminology and white collar crime. He has written four books in the area of crime and theory.

CYNTHIA DAILARD was a senior public policy associate for the Alan Guttmacher Institute, a nonprofit research and advocacy group on women's sexual and reproductive health issues. She wrote numerous articles and spoke prolifically on matters such as family planning and adolescent sexual behavior. She passed away on December 24, 2006, at the age of 38.

PEGGY DREXLER, is an assistant professor of psychology in psychiatry at Weill Medical College of Cornell University.

KYLA DUNN is a former biotech researcher and is now a reporter for PBS and CBS.

LEONARD D. ERON is a researcher for the Research Center for Group Dynamics, Institute for Social Research at the University of Michigan.

MICHELE FLEMING is a lecturer in the Center for Applied Psychology at the University of Canberra, Australia. Her current research focuses on the effects of new media, such as video games and the Internet, on children's well-being.

NANCY FOLBRE is co-chair of the National Network on the Family and the Economy and is professor of economics at the University of Massachusetts. Her interests include the interface between economics and feminist theory. She has written numerous books and papers.

JIB FOWLES is a professor of communication at the University of Houston–Clear Lake. He is the author of *The Case for Television Violence* (Sage Publications, 1999).

TASHA C. GEIGER is a clinical instructor in the department of pediatrics at the University of Rochester medical school. Dr. Geiger's specialty is developmental disabilities with a concentration on Autism Spectrum Disorders.

ELIZABETH THOMPSON GERSHOFF is a researcher with the National Center for Children in Poverty, Columbia University, Mailman School of Public Health.

STANLEY I. GREENSPAN is clinical professor of psychiatry and pediatrics at George Washington University Medical School.

EZRA E. H. GRIFFITH is deputy chair of clinical affairs and a professor of psychiatry and African American Studies at Yale University, School of Medicine.

LINDEN GROSS is a former special features editor for the *Los Angeles Times* and a ghostwriter for several books.

WEN-JUI HAN is assistant professor of social work at the Columbia University School of Social Work. Her professional interests include effects of maternal employment and impact of welfare reform.

DEBRA HAUSER is Executive Vice President for Advocates for Youth and previously served as Director of Community Health Services for the City of Atlantic City where she designed, implemented, and evaluated sexuality education, health promotion, teen pregnancy prevention, and teen parenting programs for an urban population.

THE HENRY J. KAISER FAMILY FOUNDATION is a nonprofit, private operating foundation that focuses on providing unbiased information on major health care issues.

WADE F. HORN is assistant secretary for children and families in the department of health and human services. He has been a clinical psychologist, president of the National Fatherhood Initiative, and a columnist for the *Washington Times*.

L. ROWELL HUESMANN is a researcher for the Research Center for Group Dynamics, Institute for Social Research at the University of Michigan.

ARI KAUKIAINEN is a professor of psychology at the University of Turku, Finland. He also works with Kiva School, a project aimed at reducing school bullying.

ROBERT E. LARZELERE is a researcher with the department of psychology's Munroe-Myer Institute, Nebraska Medical Center in Omaha, Nebraska.

BRIDGET E. MAHER is a policy analyst at the Center for Marriage and Family Studies at Family Research Council. She has authored several Family Research Council publications including two editions of *The Family Portrait*, a comprehensive book of data, research, and polling on the family.

ELIZABETH MARQUARDT is the director of the Center for Marriage and Families and authored *Between Two Worlds: The Inner Lives of Children of Divorce* (Crown, 2005).

SHANNAN MARTIN is a research assistant in welfare policy at the Heritage Foundation.

JESSICA MOISE-TITUS is a researcher for the Research Center for Group Dynamics, Institute for Social Research at the University of Michigan.

NATIONAL ADOPTION INFORMATION CLEARINGHOUSE provides accurate information related to adoption and is a federal service of the Children's Bureau, Administration for Children Youth and Families, U.S. Department of Health and Human Services.

MELISSA G. PARDUE is a former policy analyst for the Heritage Foundation.

GREG PARKS is an intern program specialist in the Research and Program Development Division at the Office of Juvenile Justice and Delinquency Prevention, which is part of the United States Department of Justice.

CHERYL-LYNN PODOLSKI is a researcher for the Research Center for Group Dynamics, Institute for Social Research at the University of Michigan.

RONI RABIN is a columnist for *The New York Times* who writes extensively on women's health issues.

ROBERT E. RECTOR is a senior research fellow for the Heritage Foundation. He is an authority on poverty, marriage, and the U.S. welfare system.

ROB REICH is an assistant professor of political science and ethics in society at Stanford University and senior research associate for the Aspen Institute Program on Education in a Changing Society.

DEBRA RICKWOOD is an associate professor in psychology at the University of Canberra, Australia. Her research interests include adolescent help-seeking behavior and the use of new media with regard to enhancing the well-being of young people in Australia.

CHRISTINE ROSSELL is a professor of political science at Boston University. She holds the Maxwell Chair in United States Citizenship and is the author of five books and many other scholarly articles and reports in the areas of school desegregation and bilingual education policy.

CHRISTINA SALMIVALLI is a professor of applied psychology at the University of Turku, Finland. She studies peer relations in childhood, bullying and victimization, and social cognition and adjustment.

DIANE SCHETKY is a forensic child and adolescent psychiatrist and clinical professor of psychiatry at the Maine Medical Center.

JACQULINE D. SHANNON, Ph.D., is assistant professor of early childhood education at Brooklyn College, CUNY. She is a member of the National Early Head Start Research consortium. Prior to joining Brooklyn College, she was a research scientist at NYU and postdoctoral research fellow with NICHD. Her research interests include parenting (with a special focus on fathers) and young children's cognitive and socioemotional development within families living in poverty, using mixed methods.

SEXUALITY INFORMATION AND EDUCATION COUNCIL OF THE UNITED STATES (SIECUS) is a national nonprofit organization in New York that promotes comprehensive education about sexuality and advocates individuals' rights to make responsible choices about sexual behavior.

CATHERINE TAMIS-LeMONDA is a professor of applied psychology at New York University. Her research is focused on the cultural and social contexts of language and cognitive and social development in infants' first years of life. She is the principal investigator (for NYU as a local site) on the Father Involvement in the Lives of Low Income Childrens Project.

THOMAS M. VANDER VEN is assistant professor in the department of sociology and anthropology at Ohio University in Athens, Ohio. His areas of specialization are crime and delinquency as well as linkages between work, family, and crime.

JANE WALDFOGEL is associate professor of social work and public affairs at Columbia School of Social Work. Her professional interests include social policy impact on child and family well-being as well as child protective services and child welfare policy.

THOMAS W. WASHBURNE, is the Director of the National Center for Home Education. He directs the Home School Legal Defense Association's federal policy staff and its legislative activities in Washington, DC.

ROBERT A. WEINBERG is a member of the Whitehead Institute for Biomedical Research and is a biology professor at MIT.

JOHN PAUL WRIGHT is an instructor in the division of criminal justice at the University of Cincinnati.

JILL WU received her master's degree in applied linguistics from the University of Colorado, Denver. She has taught in several different styles of bilingual education programs throughout the United States.

MELANIE J. ZIMMER-GEMBECK is an associate professor of applied psychology Griffith University–Gold Coast branch.